ON EXODUS

George V. Pixley

ON EXODUS
A LIBERATION PERSPECTIVE

Translated from the Spanish by
Robert R. Barr

ORBIS BOOKS

Maryknoll, New York 10545

The Catholic Foreign Mission Society of America (Maryknoll) recruits and trains people for overseas missionary service. Through Orbis Books Maryknoll aims to foster the international dialogue that is essential to mission. The books published, however, reflect the opinions of their authors and are not meant to represent the official position of the society.

Originally published as *Exodo, una lectura evangélica y popular,* copyright © 1983 by Casa Unida de Publicaciones, S. A.
This translation copyright © 1987 by Orbis Books, Maryknoll, NY 10545
All rights reserved
Manufactured in the United States of America

Biblical quotes, unless otherwise indicated, are taken from *The Jerusalem Bible,* copyright © 1966 by Darton, Longman & Todd, Ltd. and Doubleday & Company, Inc. Reprinted by permission of the publisher.

Manuscript editor: William E. Jerman

Library of Congress Cataloging-in-Publication Data
Pixley, Jorge V.
On Exodus: a liberation perspective.

  Translation of: Exodo, una lectura evangélica y popular.
  Bibliography: p.
  1. Bible. O.T. Exodus—Commentaries. I. Title.
BS1245.3.P5913   1987   222'.12077   87–7835
ISBN 0-88344-560-3
ISBN 0-88344-559-X (pbk.)

**DEDICATED TO THE HEROIC STRUGGLE
OF THE SALVADORAN PEOPLE**

Contents

Introduction

All through our long history, we Christians have been aware, in reading the Bible, that it treats of many themes. And so we searched for the fundamental element in the many and varied writings that make up the Bible. In the last fifty years we have gradually come to be convinced that it is the exodus—the event and its written account—that forms the basis of the Old Testament.

This conviction arose first in the great theological centers and universities of Europe, as part of the massive reaction against the idealism of the liberalism that dominated theological faculties during the nineteenth century and the early part of the twentieth. A liberal exegesis had found the most valuable part of the Old Testament in the prophets and their preaching of justice. It was they, we heard, who were the discoverers of the great ethical values of humanity.

By contrast, the exegetical movement that began to flourish before World War II, and reached its zenith after the war, acknowledged that the preaching of the prophets was not the work of ethical geniuses, but of men and women who, moved by God, were sensitive to divine inspiration because they were part of a people that knew God as a liberator of the poor from the time of the exodus from Egypt. The prophets' astonishing ethics, then, had its material basis in the original experience of the people of Israel and in the account of the exodus, which, recast and updated, was passed on from generation to generation.

This discovery of the exodus as the basis of the Old Testament, originally made in academic circles in the First World, has subsequently been repeated in biblical reading at the popular level in the dependent countries of the Third World, especially in Latin America. As oppressed urban and rural Christians have gradually come to appropriate the sacred books of our faith in the absence of a ubiquitous and dominating tutelage of priests and ministers trained in more or less traditional theological centers, these ordinary persons, too, in their nonscientific reading, have accorded the exodus a privileged place. They have done so because it is here that they have discovered that the true God of their faith is the God who accompanies them in their struggle for liberation from the modern tyrants who oppress and repress them as the pharaoh did the Hebrews.

My commentary has been written from a point of confluence of these two currents. For scientific reasons, as well as by reason of my own experience in popular liberation struggles, I take it as a fact that the exodus is the basic account of the Old Testament: the liberation of which it tells is the foundational fact of the people of God who will be the subject of all the books of the Bible. For Christians, it is indispensable to be able to read the book of Exodus. If we would understand why the proclamation of the kingdom of God in the New Testament is called the "gospel," or "Good news," we need to know the God whom Jesus proclaimed to be his Father, and whom he and his people knew as "the God who brought us out of Egypt, out of the house of slavery."

I have intended my commentary to be a reading of the book of Exodus that will be *evangelical* and *popular*. Both of these terms are ambiguous and require a preliminary explanation, although the fullest explanation and hence justification of them will necessarily have to await the actual commentary.

In the first place, I wanted this reading to be *evangelical,* in the current usage of this word in the "evangelical," or non-Catholic, churches of Latin America. These churches, deriving in different ways from the Protestant Reformation in Europe in the sixteenth century, believe that it is in the Bible that the highest authority for their faith is to be found, and reject any church authority or scientific authority as a necessary mediation for its appropriation. Not that they necessarily reject church structures or scientific research. But they contend that these mediations, useful as they may be, are not essential.

But in the more important sense of the term, I intended this commentary to be "evangelical" because I believe that, well beyond our various ecclesiastical traditions, God has good news for everyone. And so this gospel—*godspel* (*gōd* good + *spell* [tale])—will be accessible wherever the text of Exodus is read by anyone sensitive to what God wants to do today in the liberation of oppressed individuals and peoples. In this second sense, my *evangelical* reading overflows the boundaries of non-Catholic churches and seeks to be of service to a much broader readership.

I also intended a reading that would be popular. Here I am referring to a sensitivity arising from contact with the struggles of peoples against the oligarchies and dictatorships that have dominated them, and the great transnational enterprises that have been, and continue to be, allied with the dominators, in almost all Latin American countries. I believe that there is an affinity between the struggle of the Hebrew people against the forced labor and genocide imposed by the Egyptian state, and the current struggles of the popular classes in such places as Central America. The exodus belongs to the people of God, not to the hierarchies of the churches or to the academicians of the universities. I hope that my commentary will contribute something to the work of restoring the book of Exodus to the people, whose book it rightfully is. But this commentary has not been written, in the first instance, for persons with little educational background; it is not "popular" in the sense of being a "popularization." I have attempted to take advantage of the scientific discovery of what is fundamental in the book of Exodus and place it at the disposition of Latin American peoples. Thus, just as this commentary owes so much to popular struggles against economic and political domination, it likewise owes a great deal to scientific scholarship. But it is not a scientific commentary proposing theoretical novelties for the consideration of biblical experts. It does owe much to biblical science, and some indications of my debt appear in the annotated bibliography—indications that will be of special usefulness to readers with an academic background in the reading of the Bible.

The intention of my commentary is to harness its twofold source—biblical science and the experiences of Christian believers who are struggling for their liberation—in order the better to read the text of Exodus. The principal addressee of this commentary will be the person who feels an identification with the oppressed in their urgent longing for liberation. To this minister or priest, religion teacher, theology student, or pastoral minister, I seek to offer a scientifically reliable tool for their pastoral work.

DIVISIONS AND SUBDIVISIONS OF THE TEXT

Any reading of any text must attend to the structure of that text. To appreciate the parts of a book one must be able to situate them within the whole book and recognize their interrelationship. In the case of the book of Exodus, our bibles present it as a part of a larger work—the Pentateuch, the five books of Moses, of which Exodus is the second. Thus Exodus is not an independent book, but part of a larger account of the formation of the people of Israel, and of the laws associated with Mount Sinai that served this people as social legislation. Our reading of the book of Exodus will involve some reference to Genesis, which precedes it, and to other books that follow it. But this will not present major problems.

More difficult is the internal division of the book of Exodus. In our bibles, it is divided into forty chapters, sequentially numbered, with each chapter sub-divided into verses. This is the uniform system by which the biblical text has been transmitted from many centuries, and it permits rapid reference to any point in any book. This system of division entails a defect, however. The forty sections to which it reduces the text form a series that fails to indicate the relationships obtaining among its various parts, beyond those of sequence only. For this reason I have used another system—one more in conformity with my analysis of the overall structure of the book. Exodus consists of four blocks of text, to which the four parts of this commentary correspond: part 1 (Exod. 1:2–2:22), part 2 (2:23–13:16), part 3 (13:17–18:27), part 4 (19:1–40:38). The text of part 4 is further subdivided into 4A, 4B, and 4C, explained in the Introduction to part 4, "Critico-Literary Analysis of Exodus 19–40" (see p. 121). Each major block of text is divided into a number of subdivisions indicated by a two-digit number (e.g., 1.2, 2.0, 4B.2). These in turn are sometimes further subdivided into sections indicated by a three-digit number (e.g., 1.2.4, 2.4.10). And some of these sections are further subdivided into sections given a three-digit number followed by a lowercase letter (e.g., 2.5.2a, 4C1.3j).

In order to make good use of this numbering system, it will be important for readers to refer frequently to the detailed table of contents in order to keep abreast of the location of the unit under study with respect to other units of the book of Exodus. There will be some places, all of them in the fourth part of this book, where my commentary will depart from the customary order of the text in our bibles. This I have done only when it facilitates an understanding of the text. Here again, reference to the table of contents, together with attention to the traditional chapter-and-verse numbering in parentheses (retained because of its great utility for rapid reference), will keep readers from "losing their place." Once readers have become familiar with this system, it will help them grasp the structure of the book of Exodus.

APPENDIXES

My commentary is intended to explain the text of Exodus as such—that is, as a literary whole. However, we shall come upon passages where the text cannot be understood by itself: reference to matters outside the text is demanded. And so, in order not to interfere with the running commentary, which refers directly to the text of Exodus, I have inserted appendixes, some longer than others, independent of the commentary but useful for its understanding. These appendixes are to be found at the end of the four parts of this book. There are thirteen of them in all.

The appendixes are of diverse types. Some treat of matters of history or geography mentioned in the text of Exodus: "Pithom and Rameses," "The Levites," "The Amalekites," and so on. Appendix 5 ("The Divine Name 'YaHWeH' ") deals with an important philological problem. Appendix 8 ("In What Sense Did Yahweh Bring Israel out of Egypt?") discusses a philosophical and theological theme. Other appendixes treat of matters of literary composition ("Formal Analysis and Prehistory of the Decalogue," and the like). All these appendixes can be read independently of the commentary.

CRITICO-LITERARY ANALYSIS

There is a broad consensus among exegetes today that the text of the Pentateuch is the result of an amalgamation of three major narrative traditions—the Yahwist (J), the Elohist (E), and the sacerdotal or priestly (P)— together with a legal unit (Deuteronomy). Thus the Pentateuch is not the work of a single author or school of authors. Originally there were three more or less independent versions of the principal event narrated in the Pentateuch—the exploits of Abraham, Isaac, and Jacob; the exodus; the journey through the desert; the revelation on Mount Sinai—which were then spliced into a single text by anonymous redactors of the postexilic period. My commentary accepts this consensus, and generally follows the form of this consensus set down by Martin Noth in his *A History of Pentateuchal Traditions* (see the Bibliography for full bibliographical data, here and for all other references in the text).

I do not always, however, point out where one textual tradition leaves off and another begins. The main reason for this is that I am commenting on the text of the book of Exodus as we have it today, I am not writing its prehistory. The book of Exodus in its final form has an integrity of its own, and I intend to respect that integrity. I shall reach back into the history of the merging of sources only when this history is required for an understanding of the text itself. It will sometimes be necessary, especially in the long section on the revelation on Mount Sinai, in chapters 19 through 40, where the sacerdotal version has a very special notion of this revelation not shared by the other sources. In the sacerdotal version, what Yahweh revealed on Sinai was the model for the tabernacle and other implements of worship. The other sources center the revelation on the laws Yahweh gave for the governance of the social life of the people of Israel. The Sinaitic material of the sacerdotal source forms a particular block that calls for explanation, and requires critico-literary analysis. There will be other moments, as well, where an analysis of composition will be necessary, and where it will not be a betrayal of my basically literary focus to enter into the question of sources. The task of a commentator is to offer an aid to the reading of a text in its current form, and this aid should provide for the recognition of whether the current form of a passage is due to a merging of sources that do not interlock perfectly. When the result of a merger of sources is an even, clear text, a commentary need not attempt to track down the literary sources, even when a plurality of sources is probable. But when the end result is a text that is not perfectly integrated, the reader will need to look into the history of its composition.

The second problem posed by recourse to critico-literary consensus is that the three sources of the Pentateuch appear with greater clarity in Genesis than they do in Exodus. It was thanks to an analysis of the accounts of the creation, the flood, Abraham, and Jacob, that the contemporary general theory of the three traditions appeared, after a great deal of study. To the vast majority of open-minded readers, it is clear that there are three continuous traditions running through the book of Genesis—the Yahwist, the Elohist, and the sacerdotal—and the characteristics of each are recognizable. In Exodus, however, the recovery of the three great sources discovered in Genesis is difficult. The Sinai text clearly reflects textual conflation, and it is not difficult to recognize the sacerdotal source. But it is not so evident what parts of the remaining material belong to the Yahwist and the Elohist traditions. Any attempt at analysis has "something left over"—material belonging to neither of the two, and seemingly having nothing in common with any of the familiar narrative sources in Genesis, nor having anything to do with the flight from Egypt as recounted in Exodus 1–13.

It is not the purpose of a commentary to attempt to resolve these problems: my purpose is to facilitate the reading of the text of the book of Exodus as we have it today. Hence I shall touch on these points not to resolve problems of composition, but only to explain the text as we have it today. The reader desirous of a more complete framework of critico-literary analysis will have to consult other works. (A commentary that treats critico-literary matters exhaustively—and others too cursorily—is the one by Martin Noth, *Exodus: A Commentary.*)

THE SOCIO-POLITICAL CONTEXT
OF THE PRODUCTION OF THE TEXT

The account of a struggle with a pharaoh, a flight from Egypt, and the beginning of a journey through the wilderness to a land where milk and honey flowed, refers to historical events—and not just any event, but the founding event of the people of Israel. The reason why this account was kept alive was that it stated, for each succeeding generation in Israel, who Israel was as a people, who its God was, and how Israel differed from neighboring peoples. The events narrated in this account occurred toward the end of the thirteenth century B.C. But the book of Exodus reached its current form during the fifth century, or perhaps the fourth, B.C. For eight centuries, then, the account was passed down from generation to generation, with modifications corresponding to the interests of the people at different moments of its existence. Thus the account was produced on the basis of the thirteenth-century events it narrates, but it was reproduced in each generation for eight centuries. The bulk of this work of reproduction is beyond recovery in the twentieth century A.D., nor is it of great importance for the reading of the book of Exodus.

Within this broad process of the reproduction of the account of the exodus, we can recognize different "moments" that are important for the reading of the book of Exodus itself, because they have left traces in the internal tensions of the account as we have it today. For clarity and simplicity, in this commentary I shall distinguish only four "moments" or levels in the text, corresponding to the reproduction of the account in four different socio-political contexts.

1. The first level is that of the original production of the account by the group of persons who actually experienced the liberation from Egypt. This level of the text is so covered over by subsequent layers that it can no longer be identified in the text as we have it today. But it is of some importance not to lose sight of it altogether, precisely because it is the first account of the exodus. In this commentary, I propose the hypothesis that the group that was the actual subject of the exodus was a heterogeneous group of peasants in Egypt, accompanied by a nucleus of immigrants from regions to the east. Owing to the importance of the Levite Moses in the movement, this heterogeneous group came to be known as "the Levites." In the hypothetical original account of the exodus, its subject was this group of Levites, guided by Moses in a movement of insurrection against the Egyptian pharaoh, ending in flight from Egypt for the wilderness of Sinai, and subsequently for the land of Canaan.

2. A second level of the account is characterized by its reproduction at the hands of the tribes known as "Israel" in the land of Canaan. In the course of the fourteenth to the eleventh centuries B.C., Canaan witnessed a series of peasant uprisings against the lords of the cities who demanded tribute of them. The tribes that were the protagonists of the various uprisings in different regions of the country had taken refuge mainly in the hill country—the less populous parts of the land—and had formed alliances there for their mutual

defense. At sometime or other, one of these alliances of peasant tribes took the name "Israel."

When the Levites arrived in Canaan, they were received into the "Israel" alliance. The account of their original liberation experience was then read as the experience of a struggle against exploitation at the hands of an illegitimate royal apparatus. The experience of the original exodus was thus read as the reflection of this later experience of the new alliance in its struggle with the kings of the cities of Canaan, who demanded submission and tribute. In Yahweh, the God of the exodus, the tribes of the "Israel" alliance recognized the God who could sustain them in their struggles with the Canaanites. (I have presented this view of the origins of Israel in my work *God's Kingdom*. The reader may likewise consult John L. McKenzie, *The World of Judges*. The most exhaustive argumentation in favor of this interpretation of the facts is that of Norman K. Gottwald, *The Tribes of Yahweh*.)

Thus it came about that, in this socio-political context, the subject of the exodus was read as "Israel" by the descendants of the patriarchs of the tribes of "Israel"; and the exodus was read as a social revolution against the institution of monarchy. This second level, as well, is largely obliterated in the text of Exodus as we have it today. But it is decisive for the development of the accounts of oppression there—for understanding the figure of the monarch of Egypt as a genocidal tyrant unwilling to negotiate except under pressure—and for evaluating the laws that envisaged a just and egalitarian society.

3. The moment came when Israel itself, under pressure from the Philistines—a militaristic people who had invaded Canaan—established a monarchy and organized a professional army of its own. The existence of an Israelite monarchy necessitated an ideological indoctrination that would sustain the new national consensus, and counteract revolutionary or anti-monarchical tendencies. As part of this effort, the indispensable account of the exodus was reproduced, to make the exodus a national liberation struggle—no longer a class struggle. The exodus event is read on this level as a struggle between two peoples: Israel and Egypt. Moses is the leader of all Israel, and the pharaoh that of Egypt.

This is the level on which we must see the Yahwist source that has been isolated by the work of literary criticism. The Yahwist tradition took its general lines during the period of the unified monarchy, with its capital in Jerusalem (which does not necessarily mean that this monarchy had attained a fixed form by that time). (The most complete analysis of the Yahwist tradition I know is by Peter F. Ellis, *The Yahwist, the Bible's First Theologian*. For the Yahwist theology, see H. W. Wolff, "The Kerygma of the Yahwist"; Lothar Ruppert, "El yahvista: pregonero de la historia de la salvación.")

It is also at this level that we come upon the production of the Elohist version of the exodus account—the version that, in the book of Genesis, gives evidence of being of northerly, prophetic origin: it is critical of absolute monarchy and staunchly defends an Israelite national identity. (The most complete analysis of the Elohist is unquestionably that of W. Jenks, *The Elohist and North Israelite*

Traditions.) Very often in the book of Exodus it is impossible to separate the material coming from these two sources, precisely because, in essentials, they represent a common vision, emphasizing national identity. In this commentary it will not be necessary or important to distinguish between these two sources: they both derive from a similar socio-political context.

4. The fourth level of the exodus account as we have it today is the one that makes the liberation event an act of Yahweh, to demonstrate Yahweh's indisputable divinity. It sets in relief the event of Mount Sinai, when the worship to be paid to Yahweh was revealed. This is now the period of Jewish life under the Persian empire, in the fifth century B.C. The Jewish community no longer enjoyed national independence. Its identity had become purely religious. The story of the exodus is converted into the story of the foundation of the religious community of those who recognize the exclusive divinity of Yahweh and submitted to Yahweh's precepts. A critico-literary analysis enables us to identify with sufficient clarity the literary development of this moment or level as the ideological work of the priestly class.

These four levels of composition of the exodus account by no means exhaust the socio-political contexts that have left their mark on the text of the book of Exodus. But they do enable us to distinguish the most important ideological motifs that have shaped the account. In order to understand the text, it will be necessary to refer from time to time to one or another of these four levels of development, each corresponding to its own socio-political context.*

---

*In the original Spanish edition of this work, the Introduction ends with an explanation of why the author chose to give his own Spanish translation of the Hebrew (Massoretic) text of Exodus, rather than use one of the published Spanish versions available. The English translation of this work uses the text of the *Jerusalem Bible* for all Bible quotations, departing from it (with explanation) only when it fails to make the author's point. In the Bible passages preceding each segment of commentary, the author's preferred readings are printed within square brackets. The spelling of proper names, personal and geographical, is also that of the *Jerusalem Bible.*—ED.

Part One

Oppression: Project of Death (Exod. 1:1–2:22)

1.1 THE SONS OF ISRAEL
(EXOD. 1:1–7)

These are the names of the sons of Israel who went with Jacob to Egypt, each with his family: Reuben, Simeon, Levi and Judah, Issachar, Zebulun and Benjamin, Dan and Naphtali, Gad and Asher. In all, the descendants of Jacob numbered seventy persons. Joseph was in Egypt already. Then Joseph died, and his brothers, and all that generation. But the sons of Israel were fruitful and grew in numbers greatly; they increased and grew so immensely powerful that they filled the land.

In this introduction to the book of Exodus, the most important character in the book comes on the scene: the "sons of Israel," the offspring of Israel (Jacob) and their families. Simultaneously, the narrative that begins here is joined to the foregoing narrative of Jacob and Joseph (Gen. 27–50). The reader is informed that the story does not begin *ab ovo*: matters treated in the stories of the patriarchs are taken for granted here.

Specific reference is made to the history of Jacob's emigration from Canaan to Egypt (Gen. 46). Before leaving for Egypt, Israel—Jacob—offered a sacrifice to the "God of his father Isaac," and God spoke to him in a vision: "I am here," he said. "I am God, the God of your father. Do not be afraid of going down to Egypt, for I will make you a great nation there. I myself will go down to Egypt with you. I myself will bring you back again" (Gen. 46:3–4). The transition of the family of the sons and daughters of Israel to the nation of the Israelites is connected in the text of Genesis with the emigration to Egypt and sojourn there. In Genesis 46:27, seventy is also the number of the members of Jacob's household who went down to Egypt. Our text proclaims the change, the development, foretold in the earlier text: with the death of Joseph and his generation, the family history is over and the story of a people begins, just as God had promised Jacob.

The list of the twelve sons of Jacob coincides with the list of the twelve tribes forming the premonarchial Israelite alliance in official history. This list appears in two forms in the biblical texts. Our list here is the same as in Genesis 29-30, 35:23-46, 46:8-27, 49, and Deuteronomy 33, although the order varies a bit. The other form of the list—appearing in Numbers 1 and 26—omits Levi, and replaces Joseph with his two sons, Ephraim and Manasseh. The list with Ephraim and Manasseh better reflects the historical reality of the tribes (see §2.3, below, Appendix 7), but Levi will play an important role in the exodus as the ancestor of Moses and Aaron. And of course here in the introduction to the book of Exodus we do not have a list of the *tribes* of Israel, but of the *sons* of Israel (Jacob), who are in the process of being transformed into corporate Israel, a copious and mighty people.

1.2 CONFLICT OF DEATH AND LIFE (EXOD. 1:8-2:22)

1.2.1 Exploitation to Prevent a Liberation Struggle (Exod. 1:8-14)

Then there came to power in Egypt a new king who knew nothing of Joseph. "Look," he said to his subjects, "these people, the sons of Israel, have become so numerous and strong that they are a threat to us. We must be prudent and take steps against their increasing any further, or if war should break out, they might add to the number of our enemies. They might take arms against us and so escape out of the country." Accordingly they put slave drivers over the Israelites to wear them down under heavy loads. In this way they built the store cities of Pithom and Rameses for Pharaoh. But the more they were crushed, the more they increased and spread, and men came to dread the sons of Israel. The Egyptians forced the sons of Israel into slavery, and made their lives unbearable with hard labor, work with clay and with brick, all kinds of work in the fields; they forced on them every kind of labor.

For the first time, the idea dawns that the Israelites might be able to "escape out of the country," and it is the king of Egypt who first sees the revolutionary potential in this family that has grown so large that it has become a people. The king who has had this foresight, and who mounted the death project, does not become a significant character in the story of the exodus: he dies before the liberation movement foreseen by him can be unleashed. But his successor continues his policy, so that together these two kings can be considered to constitute the second character in the story.

"These people . . . have become so numerous and strong that they are a threat to us." On level three of the narrative, the conflict is between two nations, Egypt and Israel, and at this level it is inconceivable that the people of Israel could have been more numerous than the people of Egypt. But if it is a *class* conflict with which we are dealing, it is perfectly understandable that the "us" refers to the king and the dominant class, and that the ones they must confront are more numerous and potentially stronger. On level two, that of the struggle of the rural poor against the Canaanite kings, what we have is precisely a class struggle. It is more difficult to discern the reality of level one, that of the historical group of Levites who left Egypt with Moses, but it is probable that it too, at least in part, was a class struggle—the apparatus of the Egyptian state against the masses of farmers and laborers.

The war foreseen by the king as a menace is not a war for the destruction of the "us" in our text, but a war of liberation, a war to "escape out of the country." This is intolerable in the eyes of the king and his associates, and they decide to take the necessary measures.

The mention of store cities (v. 11) refers us once again to the history of Joseph in the book of Genesis. In Genesis 41:33–36 we have Joseph's advice to the king concerning storage of grain during the years of abundant harvest, in order to have the means to endure the seven years of drought of which the king has been warned in his dream. Thus, one of the functions of the Egyptian state was to provide storage for the people to be able to live. But, ironically, the construction of the storage in question here was also used by this king to control the Israelites.

The irony does not end here. According to Genesis 47:13–26, it was Joseph who was the architect of the social structures of Egypt—the structures the new king uses to grind the people down with heavy burdens. Here I ask readers to take up their Bible and carefully read the passage in Genesis just mentioned. What could be clearer? In exchange for foodstuffs in times of drought, the Egyptians handed over to the king—that is, to the state—their right to their herds, their lands, and their very bodies. And they felt this to be a very fine arrangement: "You have saved our lives. If we may enjoy my lord's favor, we will be Pharaoh's serfs" (Gen. 47:25). According to this text, then, servitude in Egypt was generalized and by no means limited to immigrants.

The social system described in Genesis, and de facto prevailing in Egypt, was the one that social scientists call the Asian mode of production. The rural poor were not slaves in the sense of being the private property of the rich, to be bought and sold at will, it is true. But they all owed their labor to the state when the state demanded it. Technically the state was proprietor of all lands, and collected a part of the harvests as tribute, or land rent. Nevertheless, the farmers continued to live on these lands, and left them only when the king had need of them for a state undertaking, such as the construction of pyramids or the reinforcement of a dyke. When the king was capable of respecting the rhythms of farm labor, he demanded direct labor for the state only in times of relative leisure, and the system functioned well, even though all persons were legally the king's slaves.

The Asian mode of production provided for a stable, semiautonomous village life, and villages often had their own governments and their own administration of the lands that were legally the king's. According to Genesis 47:27, Israel had certain lands at its disposition in Egypt—the lands of Goshen. It would not appear that the construction labor with which the new king oppressed the Israelites entailed the loss of these lands, and they were mentioned again in Exodus 9:26.

There is nothing new, then, in the servitude suffered by the Israelites. Their very ancestor, Joseph, took part, according to their traditions, in the establishment of a system of generalized servitude. And this servitude in no way differentiated immigrants from the native-born. Everyone was liable to be requisitioned for the works of the king from time to time. To understand the Exodus text correctly, we shall have to read carefully what it is telling us here, taking it together with the story of Joseph. With this reading as our basis, we shall have to separate the structural elements of this oppression from its conjunctural elements—its incidental, "adventitious," merely contingent, merely historical, elements.

Structurally, Egypt was a class society. The king and his functionaries lived from the tribute of the farm villages—a tribute paid in grain, beasts, and labor. The importance of this fact is very great for level two of the narrative, inasmuch as Canaanite society was also structured according to the Asian mode of production, and the rebellion of the tribes was occasioned precisely by the tribute demanded by the Canaanite kings. Accordingly, the tribes of Israel understood the story of the exodus as the story of a revolutionary movement. What had been overthrown in Egypt was the generalized slavery of the Asian mode of production. A new, classless society had been set up, established by Yahweh in the justice of the laws of Mount Sinai. If we fail to grasp the structural change implied by the exodus event, to speak of it as a revolution will only be demagogy. But if we analyze the overthrow of the structures of the Asian mode of production, and the establishment of a society on other bases— the bases of a primitive communism—then it will be precise and correct to designate this phenomenon as revolution.

Obviously, our text speaks to us of a conjunctural situation, as well, with the appearance on the scene of a new king who has not known Joseph. Class structures have enabled the people to survive a raging famine, but now a different situation presents itself: the dominant class has become aware of the danger of an armed movement ("war . . . our enemies"), and has responded in an altogether predictable fashion, tightening the screws placed in their hands by the system. By subjecting the Israelites to hard labor, the king hopes to cut off the possibility of action against the system that could end in the departure of some of his laborers. He embitters their life, then, with forced labor.

1.2.2 Genocide: On with the Death Project (Exod. 1:15–22)

The king of Egypt then spoke to the Hebrew midwives, one of whom was named Shiphrah, and the other Puah. "When you midwives attend Hebrew women," he said, "watch the two stones carefully. If it is a boy, kill him; if a girl, let her live." But the midwives were God-fearing: they disobeyed the command of the king of Egypt and let the boys live. So the king of Egypt summoned the midwives. "Why," he asked them, "have you done this and spared the boys?" "The Hebrew women are not like Egyptian women," they answered Pharaoh, "they are hardy, and they give birth before the midwife reaches them." God was kind to the midwives. The people went on increasing and grew very powerful; since the midwives reverenced God he granted them descendants.

Pharaoh then gave his subjects this command: "Throw all the boys born to the Hebrews into the river, but let all the girls live."

The king of Egypt is defined for us as someone who is prepared to go to the last extremes to prevent the escape of his laborers. Severe exploitation has failed to prevent the increase of the Israelite population, and genocide is in order. The king's intent is to keep the people from growing strong, joining his enemies, and then leaving the country. He would rather kill them than allow them to leave the region where he can utilize their labor. But he would rather not eliminate them altogether, for the Israelite fields, which are his now, would then remain uncultivated. To seek to reduce the population by the death of the male infants is a genocidal measure calculated on principles of demographic control. Once caught up in a project of exploitation based on a class system, the pharaoh is the ally of death whether he likes it or not.

The midwives refuse to cooperate with the plan. They come to the pharaoh and point out that Hebrew women are "hardy"—or, in the very suggestive Hebrew idiom, they "have life." And the conflict between the pharaoh and the Israelites begins to take shape as a conflict between death and life.

It is in this incident that "God" appears for the first time, albeit in a most modest role—the midwives are "God-fearing," and God grants them descendants. But "God" is not yet specifically Yahweh, the God of Israel's forebears. The midwives, by their respect for life, demonstrate a reverence for a vague divinity; and the midwives' gift of descendants—their reward—demonstrates that God is on their side—the side of life.

This passage repeatedly uses the word "Hebrew." This word occurs only thirty-three times in the Hebrew Bible, and eleven of those occurrences are in these first chapters of the book of Exodus. The same term is found in various languages and dialects, places, and times in the ancient Near East. It has no ethnic connotation in preexilic times. It is only used to designate groups that, for one reason or another, were "outside the laws" of a given society. They could be mercenaries, they could be insurgents, or they could be simply itinerant traders or shepherds. In our text, "Hebrew" is a synonym for "Israelite"—although its use in this precise context appears to be an echo of level one or two of the account, when the subject of the oppression was a class, not a national group.

The king's attempt to use the Hebrew women's midwives in their partial extermination has failed. And so he gives "his subjects," his minions, the command to carry the male Hebrew infants to the river. What "subjects"?— the expression is unclear. On level three, it would mean the Egyptian nation, with all its classes. On level one or two, we would have to understand the state bureaucracy, which depended directly on the state for its sustenance. But further on, the narrative will be more precise in dividing the Egyptians into three elements: the king, his servants, and his people. Up to this point, only the personage of the king has been singled out, although there has been mention as well of his slave drivers and his people, without further specification.

1.2.3 In the Abode of Death, Signs of Life (Exod. 2:1–10)

There was a man of the tribe of Levi who had taken a woman of Levi as his wife. She conceived and gave birth to a son and, seeing what a fine child he was, she kept him hidden for three months. When she could hide him no longer, she got a papyrus basket for him; coating it with bitumen and pitch, she put the child inside and laid it among the reeds at the river's edge. His sister stood some distance away to see what would happen to him.

Now Pharaoh's daughter went down to bathe in the river, and the girls attending her were walking along by the riverside. Among the reeds she noticed the basket, and she sent her maid to fetch it. She opened it and looked, and saw a baby boy, crying; and she was sorry for him. "This is a child of one of the Hebrews," she said. Then the child's sister said to Pharaoh's daughter, "Shall I go and find you a nurse among the Hebrew women to suckle the child for you?" "Yes, go," Pharaoh's daughter said to her; and the girl went off to find the baby's own mother. To her the daughter of Pharaoh said, "Take this child away and suckle it for me. I will see you are paid." So the woman took the child and suckled it. When the child grew up, she brought him to Pharaoh's daughter who treated him like a son; she named him Moses because, she said, "I drew him out of the water."

The present passage is a continuation of the narrative of the midwives, who manifest, in the land of Egypt—which the pharaoh's actions have made a place of death—a will to serve the ends of life for "fear of God." And now here, in the continuation, it devolves upon the daughter of the criminal pharaoh to be the agent of the preservation of life. She acts as this agent even though she is aware that the infant she has discovered in the river is a child of the Hebrews. This is not the first time that oppressors have been encumbered with compassion in their own houses—nor will it be the last. And whenever it is found there it interferes with the implementation of death-dealing plans. Neither God nor fear of God enter into the picture, but the compassion of the pharaoh's daughter now yields the same life-giving result as has the fear of God in the midwives.

The general form of this story of a child in the ancient Near East who is exposed to death, then rescued, and who grows up to be king, is familiar from the story of Sargon, king of Akkad, in the third millennium B.C. Later it appears in Greece in the story of Oedipus. So we already have a hint here that this Levite child is destined to play an important role in the rescue of his people.

This child is indeed the son of "a man of the tribe of Levi." In Exodus 1:1–7, Levi appears as the third of Jacob's sons. Despite the inclusion of the Tribe of Levi in so many lists of tribes, it never actually became an Israelite tribe like the others (see Appendixes 6 and 7). But further on (Exod. 32:25–29) it will be mentioned how the Levites consecrated themselves to the service of God. Thus they formed a priestly caste among the Israelites in the land of Canaan. According to our text, Moses was of a Levitical family. In Exodus 6:20, it will be explained that his father was Amram, Levi's grandson, and his mother Jochebed, Levi's daughter. According to the law as stated in Leviticus 18:12, sexual relations between a man and his father's sisters were illicit, and it comes as no surprise to us here that Moses is sprung from just such a relationship. As in the case of Isaac and Rebecca (Gen. 24), our text would have it that the price of Moses' ethnic purity was incest.

The name given the child by the pharaoh's daughter is Moses—in Hebrew *Mosheh.* If this were a Hebrew word, it would be an active participle, meaning "extracting"—hence the etymology in the text. But it is more likely that the name is actually Egyptian, *mešu,* a particle appearing in the names of Egyptian kings Ahmose and Thutmose. The liberator's name, then, would seem to confirm the tradition that he was sprung from the dominant Egyptian class itself. The account of his rescue from the waters would have the function of harmonizing the tradition of his Egyptian origin with the importance of asserting his authentic Levite lineage.

But the basic interest of the text in its finished form is to show that, at the very heart of the den of death that was the royal palace, were to be found allies of life—that there was a compassionate woman there, who cooperated with a valiant mother to save a baby's life.

1.2.4 Someone to Defend the Right to Life (Exod. 2:11–22)

Moses, a man by now, set out at this time to visit his countrymen, and he saw what a hard life they were having; and he saw an Egyptian strike a Hebrew, one of his countrymen. Looking around he could see no one in sight, so he killed the Egyptian and hid him in the sand. On the following day he came back, and there were two Hebrews, fighting. He said to the man who was in the wrong, "What do you mean by hitting your fellow countryman?" "And who appointed you," the man retorted, "to be prince over us, and judge? Do you intend to kill me as you killed the Egyptian?" Moses was frightened. "Clearly that business has come to light," he thought. When Pharaoh heard of the matter he would have killed Moses, but Moses fled from Pharaoh and made for the land of Midian. And he sat down beside a well.

Now the priest of Midian had seven daughters. They came to draw water and fill the troughs to water their father's sheep. Shepherds came and drove them away, but Moses came to their defense and watered their sheep for them. When they returned to their father Reuel, he said to them, "You are back early today!" "An Egyptian protected us from the shepherds"; they said, "yes, and he drew water for us and watered the flock." "And where is he?" he asked his daughters. "Why did you leave the man there? Ask him to eat with us." So Moses settled with this man, who gave him his daughter Zipporah in marriage. She gave birth to a son, and he named him Gershom because, he said, "I am a stranger in a foreign land."

This account continues the theme of oppression that leads to a politics of death—an oppression that has to wrestle with the will to live demonstrated not only by the oppressed themselves, but by others also, who come in contact with them. The pharaoh has launched his not merely exploitive, but murderous, policy out of fear that the Hebrews might come to know their own strength, unite with his enemies (literally, "those who hate us"—enemies of Egypt, personal enemies of the king, or enemies of the state) and fight him. But his genocidal commands have aroused passive resistance among the midwives attending the Hebrew women, and active resistance in the pharaoh's own family when his daughter adopts a Hebrew boy to deliver him from death. Now, in the present text, the young Hebrew, reared in the palace, makes an option of commitment to the cause of the oppressed. And the king's fears that the Hebrews might make war upon him are realized.

Moses turns to "his countrymen"—literally, "his brothers." In this expression we have the product of level three, where the conflict is conceptualized in nationalistic terms. But Moses' countrymen are not called "Israelites" here. They are called "Hebrews"—connoting the class struggle of level two of the exodus account. On level two, Moses' action is class betrayal: it is the action of a person sprung from the dominant class who casts his lot with the dominated (although his action is not yet revolutionary, but only defensive).

Moses' killing the Egyptian is presented in our text as a simple case of capital punishment. Moses' "countrymen" were at hard labor under oppressors. We know that the intent of this excessive labor was to reduce the number and strength of the Hebrews. The verb used for the Egyptian's action against the Hebrew, as well as for Moses' action against the Egyptian, is *rayach*—translated here as "kill," and used a great deal in the context of war. But there is a significant switch of verbs in the protest of the Hebrew the following day: "Do you intend to kill me . . . ?" (*lehorgeni*—literally, "murder"). A contrast is made between "hitting" (which *could* cause death) and "murdering." And then the pharaoh, upon hearing of Moses' action, seeks to "kill" him—*leharog*, "murder," once more, even though, inasmuch as the pharaoh is the one in authority, the killing in this case would have been an "execution," juridically speaking.

The action of the young Moses is in continuity with the actions of the midwives and of the pharaoh's daughter. We are confronted with a series of life-preserving actions, as over against the lethal intent of the king. We note that neither for the pharaoh's daughter nor for Moses is there any question of religious motivation. God does not come into these stories. The pharaoh's daughter is an Egyptian, but she defends life. By contrast the guilty Hebrew, although he is himself oppressed, fails to respect his neighbor's life. It has already been forecast, in the account of the midwives, that God will be on the side of those who defend life. But God is still a distant, misty figure. Thus far, it is only the midwives, the pharaoh's daughter, and Moses who defend life.

Moses' flight "for the land of Midian" establishes a "geographical alternative" to the land of Egypt. The whole account of the exodus will move back and forth between Egypt and the wilderness. According to the geography of the account, the "land of Midian" is part of the wilderness. It is there, in the wilderness, that space is found for freedom and life—a curious thing, really, inasmuch as, in the general consciousness of ancient peoples, the wilderness, the desert, is precisely the place where one cannot live (see Deut. 8:15–16). Egypt—great, fertile land of the river Nile—has been converted, in this account, in virtue of its oppressive national state, into a place where one cannot live.

At the spring or well, Moses once more shows his love for justice and life by defending the seven women against the shepherds. The priest of Midian takes him into his house and gives him one of his daughters to be his wife. Here we face several historical problems: the land of Midian; Reuel, priest of Midian; and Gershom, the son of Moses. For these matters see Appendixes 2, 3, and 4.

With this, the introductory section of the book of Exodus comes to a close. Three characters have been introduced: (1) *Israel*—whose makeup involves a serious ambiguity, in terms of the three levels of the account; (2) the *king of Egypt,* dealer of death with his desire to oppress the Hebrew-Israelites (this king dies very soon, but his successor's policy is so nearly identical that the two play the role of the same character, in effect), and (3) *Moses,* a member of the Egyptian elite, who nevertheless identifies with the exploited laborers, and who also demonstrates his love for life—especially the life of the very weakest—in the land of Midian.

APPENDIX 1:
PITHOM AND RAMESES

The construction of great cities, with their temples, their sumptuous palaces, and their warehouses, was accomplished in tributary societies—societies with an Asian mode of production—by means of the forced labor of peasants. With variants, this was how the cities of Mesopotamia, Egypt, and pre-Hispanic Mexico, and Mohenjo-Daro in India were built. The success of this practice depended on leaving primitive village structures intact, and not interfering with natural ties of blood and marriage that shaped each village unit. The villages maintained their traditions, replicated their own labor force, and produced the surplus that supported the apparatus of state. They also supplied labor for construction.

The mention in our text of the city of Rameses makes it possible to situate all these events in the thirteenth century B.C., during the expansionist reign of Rameses II. After several centuries of retrenchment consequent upon the invasion of the Hyksos, Egypt was now enjoying a period of expansion, principally in the direction of Syria and Palestine. Various groups from these regions had arrived in Egypt from time to time and settled there. Egyptian texts mention the *'apiru* (see Gottwald, 394–409), or rebel groups from different kingdoms who enlisted as mercenaries, and the *Shosu* (Gottwald, 456–59), who were nomadic groups, also militarized, who had established contact for the purpose of military service. *'Apiru* is a sociological, not an ethnic, term; they came from different regions. The *Shosu* had their geographical center in the arid zone to the south of the land known in the Bible as the land of Edom.

In a period like that of Rameses II, when large construction projects were being undertaken, these groups of foreigners settling in the eastern parts of the kingdom would have been the first to feel the burden of tribute to be paid in the form of labor. It is among these groups that we must look for the proto-Israelites who were the central figures of the events giving rise to the story of the exodus.

If we compare Genesis 46:34, where the pharaoh gives Jacob's family the land of Goshen, and Genesis 47:11, where the same land is called the region of Rameses, we shall find it easy to conclude that it was the population of the villages in the vicinity of construction projects who would have had to bear the brunt of the toil. According to Exodus 12:37 and Numbers 33:3, 5, it was from Rameses that the people fled in the exodus, which of course would lend plausibility to the hypothesis that it was the forced labor of construction projects that sparked the rebellion.

Pithom and Rameses have not been definitively identified by Egyptologists. "Pithom" is a Hebraic form of *PR TM,* or "House of Atum," a name suggesting a city of many temples. "Rameses" would be *PR Rameses,* or "house of Rameses," a city, known from Egyptian inscriptions, where Rameses II established his residence.

For the location of these cities, we should doubtless look to the eastern delta, the region of the land of Egypt facing Palestine, where we find places that were militarily secure, and close to fertile land (like the land of Goshen, or "of Rameses"). Egyptologist E. P. Uphill comes to the conclusion that these places were most probably Heliopolis and Qantir. Both were very large cities, of the dimensions of a Babylon, and both flourished in the thirteenth century. In Qantir, there is evidence of immense centers for the manufacture of ornamental brick. Qantir was sacked by the kings of the next century for construction materials to be used for cities such as Bubastis, which was also in the Nile delta (Uphill, "Pithom and Rameses").

Finally, it is altogether likely that proto-Israelites, "people of various sorts" (Exod. 12:38), an Asian and Egyptian "rabble" (Num. 11:4), had been obliged to fill excessive quotas of construction work, and that this provoked both their rebellion and their departure for the uncertainties of the desert. It is no longer possible today to reconstruct the historical event of the flight, or even to determine precisely who it was who fled. But the circumstances provoking the departure are entirely comprehensible in thirteenth-century Egypt. The narrative of the book of Exodus, the product of a number of successive Israelite centuries, posits as its subject the families of the twelve sons of Jacob (Israel), now transformed into a nation. But the patriarchs Abraham, Isaac, and Jacob are remembered in the traditions of other proto-Israelite groups than those figuring in the exodus—groups already established in Canaan. The story of Joseph, as we find it in the Pentateuch narrative today, was created by splicing the patriarchal traditions of the proto-Israelites of Canaan with the narrative of the exodus of the proto-Israelites of Egypt.

The objective of a commentary is to understand the text, more than the history that gave rise to it. In our text, it is the whole of Israel that is oppressed and subsequently liberated.

APPENDIX 2:
THE LAND OF MIDIAN

The geography depicted in Exodus is developed between two counterposed entities: Egypt and the wilderness. On the horizon, but far from the actual geography of the account, shimmers the "land where milk and honey flow," objective of the flight from Egypt. But the successful attainment of this objective falls outside the scope of Exodus, which finishes "up in the air," so to speak, as far as getting to the promised land is concerned.

In the geography of the wilderness, our account singles out certain points, such as Horeb, "the mountain of God" (3:1), Massah and Merivab (17:7). It would appear that the "land of Midian" was beyond the wilderness, or perhaps a remote part of the wilderness. Its function in our narrative is to serve as a base for the priest of Midian and as a place of refuge for Moses. Moses will have known the wilderness since the days of his exile in the land of Midian, and this knowledge will be of service to him as he guides the Israelites in wilderness after their flight from Egypt.

But the account of Exodus has been reworked a great deal, by successive generations of Israelites with different class interests. Their geography does not necessarily correspond to that of cartographers. And Midian, besides being a geographical area, is a political entity entering into the history of Israel at various points.

In one incident in the premonarchic history of Israel, Midian intervenes as an enemy of the tribe of Manasseh, crossing the Jordan on camels to plunder the Israelites' harvest (Judg. 6:1–6). They are of the number of the "sons of the East" (Judg. 6:3, 8:10). When Gideon has routed them, he pursues them and their allies through the heights of Transjordan, "up the nomads' way, eastward of Nobah and Jogbehah" (Judg. 8:11). To come to this place, Gideon and his army pass Succoth and Penuel, reaching the headwaters of the river Jabbok. The Midianites, then, lived between the wilderness and the farming region, and are the first people to appear in Palestine with domesticated camels. The time of this conflict is about 1100 B.C.

In the narratives of Israel's first conflicts with Moab, Midian appears as an ally of the latter: Numbers 22–24 (Balaam), and Numbers 25 (the Baal of Peor). In the introduction to the Balaam cycle, the Moabites, afraid, propose a defense plan, as well as the engagement of the prophet Balaam, and the two nations undertake this project jointly (Num. 22:3–4, 7). From this incident, and from the broad geographical distribution of the Midianites, some authors advance the hypothesis that Midian had established a small empire, based on trade and military superiority (see Eissfeldt, "Protektorat"; Gottwald, pp. 431–33, 573–74). The Midianite hegemony, in this hypothesis, would have extended to the peoples of Transjordan: the Ammonites, the Amalekites, the Moabites, and the Edomites.

Numbers 25:6–18 tells of the bloody end of Israel's fellowship with Midian in a sanctuary of Transjordan. A pestilence was arrested when the priest Phinehas killed an Israelite male in the act of celebrating a rite with a Midianite woman. The redactors have joined this account with that of the religious conflict with Moab in the plain of the Baal of Peor. If there is a historical basis for this account, it would indicate still another coalition of Moab with Midian (see Mendenhall, *Generation,* chap. 4, pp. 105–21).

Finally, Numbers 31 recounts a battle between the forces of Israel, commanded by

Moses, and the forces of the Midianites. This text mentions, without explanation, the appearance of the five kings of Midian.

Thus, in the history of Israel the Midianite nation enters the picture as an enemy people, exercising control over a vast zone of Transjordania. It is a region where there were Israelite elements as well: the tribes of Gad, Reuben, and Manasseh. It is the region from which the Israelites routed the "Amorite" kings Og and Sihon (Num. 21:21-35; Deut. 1:4, 3:1-11). It is the region where the kingdoms of Ammon, Moab, and Edom lasted for centuries, sometimes under the Israelite yoke, sometimes independent. We must suppose that Transjordan was a bone of contention between the classist society of Midian and the egalitarian society of Israel. The might of the Israelite rural population in this region was insufficient to drive out—once and for all—kings who had the military support of the Midianites.

The Exodus account, however, evinces no influence by this conflictual history. Midian appears rather as a place of refuge for Moses; its priest appears as the ally and counselor of the Israelites. This anomaly is probably to be explained by the existence of a subgroup of Midianites, the Kenites, with whom Israel maintained a mutual defense pact (see Appendix 3).

APPENDIX 3:
REUEL, PRIEST OF MIDIAN, MOSES' FATHER-IN-LAW

Moses' Midianite father-in-law is given two names in Exodus—Reuel and Jethro. (In another tradition he seems to have a third name: "Hobab, the father-in-law of Moses" [Judg. 4:11].) It is likely that Reuel was the name transmitted in Jerusalem (in Yahwist traditions), and Jethro the one that came from northern groups (Elohist traditions). (W. F. Albright seeks to resolve the enigma with a textual emendation—not a very convincing one—in his "Jethro, Hobab, and Reuel in Early Hebrew Tradition.")

Reuel appears in the Greek Bible as the descendant of Abraham by the latter's second wife Keturah—Reuel being the son of Dedan (Gen. 25:1-3, LXX). This suggests that Reuel was of a clan related to the Midianites: Midian appears in Genesis 25:2 as the son of Abraham and Keturah, so that he would be Reuel's uncle.

But in order to grasp the historical significance of Israel's positive relationship with Midian in Exodus, we may avail ourselves of a more important datum, found in Judges 1:16: that Moses' father-in-law was a Kenite, an inhabitant of the Negeb in the heights of Arad to the south of Judah. Israel maintained good relations with the Kenites during the first centuries of its existence. If both traditions are correct—that Moses' father-in-law was a Midianite (see also Num. 10:29) and that he was a Kenite—this would solve the problem of how Midian could be the enemy in so many other traditions and yet be Moses' friend and protector in Exodus. In this case, the Kenites (whose heroic eponym is Cain—obvious in Hebrew, though not in Spanish or English) would be a clan of the Midianites with whom Israel maintained good relations. These relations may have been formalized in a mutual defense pact (see Fensham, "Treaty"; Cody, "Exodus").

The evidence for a positive relationship between the Israelites and the Kenites is quite persuasive. The Kenites settled down with Judah, in Arad and the neighboring cities of the Negeb of Judah (Judg. 1:16, 1 Sam. 30:29). David had them as allies at a difficult moment: when he was setting up a political base in order to gain the throne (1 Sam. 30:26-31). When King Saul made war on the Amalekites, he warned the Kenites who lived in Amalekite cities to leave and thereby escape the sufferings of war (1 Sam. 15:6). Jael, wife of Heber the Kenite, who in turn was "of the sons of Hobab, the father-in-law of Moses" (Judg. 4:11), killed Sisera, enemy of Israel, in her tent (Judg. 4:17–22).

Another element to consider, in order to situate the Kenites correctly, is their probable characterization as "hebrews"—artisans who worked with metals. The noun *ķeni* in several Semitic languages means "smith," and the Israelite tradition states that Cain was the "ancestor of all metalworkers" (Gen. 4:22). Gottwald explains the presence of Kenites in the Negeb to the south and in Jezreel to the north by hypothesizing that they constituted an ironworkers' guild (*Tribes,* 577–79). The genealogy of 1 Chronicles 2:55 links the Kenites of Hammath (in the extreme north) with Rechab, the ancestor of the wandering Rechabites, who appear in Samaria at the time of Elisha (2 Kings 10:15–16), and in Jerusalem at the time of Jeremiah (Jer. 35). This lack of geographic localization would be explained if the Kenites formed a guild, who lived here and there, wherever they could practice their profession.

To sum up: the most plausible explanation is the one linking Moses' father-in-law with the Kenites, and these with the metalworking profession. Their relationship with Israel would, then, be a symbiotic one, and would recall bonds of blood relationships, real or fictitious, with the Midianites.

APPENDIX 4:
GERSHOM, MOSES' SON

Exodus 2:22 offers a popular etymology for the name "Gershom," taking it as derived from *ger sham,* or "stranger there." *Ger* in Hebrew means a person who resides in a place without being integrated into its society or holding real property. The *ger* is to be distinguished from the *nokri,* who speaks a foreign language and lives outside his native country, and is therefore a "foreigner" in the strict sense.

This popular etymology is no more than a secondary element in our account, however, and is of no historical importance. (On the significance of this type of genealogy and its place in biblical literature, see B. O. Long, *The Problem of Etiological Narrative in the Old Testament.*)

More important is the existence of a priestly group known as Gershomites—mentioned in Judges 18:30—who were priests of the tribe of Dan. The Massoretic text tells us that they were descended from "Jonathan son of Gershom, son of Moses." This was emended to read "Manasseh" for "Moses" even before the text came into the hands of its Greek translators.

This history of the various priestly families in Israel has not been adequately clarified. (On the complicated problems of the priestly families in Israel, the following works may be consulted: Cross, *Canaanite Myth and Hebrew Epic,* chap. 8, pp. 195–215; Cody, *A History of Old Testament Priesthood.*) In postexilic traditions and texts, the only legitimate priests were those of the family of Aaron. Thus these traditions and texts give us to understand that an ancient priestly family joined its lineage to that of Moses, and their ancestor Gershom appears in Exodus as a son of Moses.

According to the official versions of the last stage of the composition of the Pentateuch, and according to the Chronicler, Levi had three sons—Gershom, Kohath, and Merari—and all Levites are their descendants. Levi's son Gershom is not the same Gershom as the one who was Moses' son, but it is impossible to explain what relationship among the priestly families underlies these genealogies. The only thing clear is that, before the Babylonian exile, there were priestly families who did not claim to be descended from Aaron, but from Moses, and that they influenced the text of Exodus.

Part Two

Liberation: Project of Life
(Exod. 2:23–13:16)

2.0 GOD HEARS THE CRY OF THE SLAVES (EXOD. 2:23–25)

During this long period the king of Egypt died. The sons of Israel, groaning in their slavery, cried out for help and from the depths of their slavery their cry came up to God. God heard their groaning and he called to mind his covenant with Abraham, Isaac and Jacob. God looked down upon the sons of Israel, and he knew . . . .

With this brief passage, our story changes direction. Up to this point, the dominant note has been oppression. The struggle for survival has been defensive, and one with little prospect of success. With this new passage, a new character comes onto the scene, who will make the difference in the nature of the struggle: the God who hears the cry of the Israelites, and becomes aware of their oppression.

The death of the king of Egypt, who had intensified the oppression of the Hebrew-Israelites with the intent of reducing the strength of the people, has changed nothing. The account records for us neither the name of the king who initiated the new oppression, nor that of his successor, who will lose the battle to hold the workers. It is not interested in defining these two personalities in order to differentiate them. Together they form a single *dramatis persona*, and the death of the king who initiated the new oppression will serve the solitary purpose of permitting the return of the character who killed the Egyptian, Moses.

The allusion to a pact with Abraham, Isaac, and Jacob sends the reader back once more to the narratives of the book of Genesis. Here we are on level three of our present account. Abraham, Isaac, and Jacob were the ancestors of their respective groups in the coalition of Israel, and their joint presentation here in the context of a pact is the consequence of a more or less broad process of fusion of popular traditions consequent upon the political unification of the nation.

14

The mention of God's treaty with Abraham sends us back to Genesis 15 (a product of the combined Yahwist and Elohist traditions) and 17 (the sacerdotal tradition). According to these texts, God struck a bargain with Abraham, promising to make his offspring a populous nation, and to give him the land of Canaan. Abraham himself is a personage linked with Hebron and Beersheba, both to the south of Canaan. Hebron was a principal city of the tribe of Judah, which in turn was one of the last tribes to be incorporated into Israel, but which, with the rise of the Davidic monarchy, came to be one of the leading tribes. (For the primitive history of Israel, see Roland de Vaux, "The Settlement of the Israelites in Southern Palestine and the Origins of the Tribe of Judah"; idem, *The Early History of Israel.*)

The patriarch Jacob had his geographical center in Bethel, in the territory of the tribe of Ephraim, one of the principal tribes in the period of Israelite consolidation. After the division of Israel toward the end of the tenth century B.C., in the time of Jeroboam I, Judah came to be an independent kingdom in the south, and Ephraim became the new center of Israel. The tradition of God's pact with Jacob (Gen. 28) is probably influenced by the Judaite tradition of the pact with Abraham. In the unification of Israel—which did not crystalize until the time of David, and which lasted only two generations—Jacob, Ephraim's patriarch, becomes Abraham's grandson, and Isaac takes his place between them as Abraham's son, Jacob's father.

The passage I am commenting on presupposes the account of the book of Genesis as we have it today, with the unification of Israel an accomplished fact, and the pact with Abraham a pact with all the patriarchs of Israel. Let us remember that this paragraph is introducing, for the first time, the God who will liberate the Hebrew-Israelites. The allusion to the pact with Abraham serves to establish the identity of the God of the exodus and the God of Judah and of the other proto-Israelite tribes that lived in Canaan at the time of the exodus.

God comes on the scene because of the cry of the oppressed slaves. This cry comes in for a great deal of emphasis: this short passage uses four different words for it. The incident of the midwives had spoken, in general terms, of the fear of God, and of how God gave the midwives families. But that God had no personality as yet. You could just as well have replaced "God" with a vague expression like "heaven." By contrast, here God actually hears the cry of the oppressed and takes their side—which, very quickly now, will mean confrontation with the oppressor. God behaves as Moses behaved in the presence of the — Egyptian who had killed the Hebrew—only, God is responding to a collective situation, not just to an individual case.

The last word, "[God] knew . . . ," is not altogether clear in its meaning in Hebrew. What we have in our English is an "absolute" construction. However, in Hebrew as in English, "to know" is a transitive verb, and calls for a direct object. We have a similar case in Genesis 18:21, where the omission of an object of knowing is probably an oversight. The sense is that of "becoming aware" of something, of "being considered as informed," perhaps of "feeling compassion." At all events, God appears here as an interested party—interested in reorientating the intolerable situation of the slaves.

2.1 GOD'S RESPONSE: MOSES IS SENT ON A MISSION OF LIBERATION (EXOD. 3:1–4:31)

The prerequisite sine qua non for any revolutionary movement is awareness that a given situation is intolerable—and not because of any accidental merger of contingencies, but in its very structure. In the exodus, the problem was not only that Rameses had launched a construction project that called for hard labor on the part of the Hebrews, but that the system itself permitted the king to use their manual labor whenever he was so inclined. In our text, the cry of the people expresses only a stage of "preawareness." It is only God who is seen to be completely aware, and it is God who takes the initiative in getting the liberation process under way.

The second step in any revolution, once there is sufficient awareness of the need for structural change, is organization. God launches the organization of the oppressed in our text by selecting Moses as the leader. Moses, who had shown he was suited to this role in making his option for the oppressed, killing the Egyptian and protecting the women at the spring, must now approach the elders of the Hebrews to take action.

In the section on the liberation process (Exod. 2:23–13:16), the passage from 3:1 to 4:31 deals with this organization under the divinely appointed leader. (For the question of the divine initiative in this revolution, see Appendix 8.)

2.1.1 God's Self-revelation to Moses (Exod. 3:1–6)

Moses was looking after the flock of Jethro, his father-in-law, priest of Midian. He led his flock to the far side of the wilderness and came to Horeb, the mountain of God. There the angel of Yahweh appeared to him in the shape of a flame of fire, coming from the middle of a bush. Moses looked; there was the bush blazing but it was not being burned up. "I must go and look at this strange sight," Moses said, "and see why the bush is not burned." Now Yahweh saw him go forward to look, and God called to him from the middle of the bush. "Moses, Moses!" he said. "Here I am," he answered. "Come no nearer," he said. "Take off your shoes, for the place on which you stand is holy ground. I am the God of your father," he said, "the God of Abraham, the God of Isaac and the God of Jacob." At this Moses covered his face, afraid to look at God.

The definite articles—"the" mountain of God, and (in the Hebrew original) "the" bush—indicate that the text presupposes that its readers already know the place of the event here narrated. Perhaps it was a place of pilgrimage in the classic times of Israel.

There are various indications in this passage that its present form is the result of a combination of the Yahwist and Elohist traditions: the alternation of "Yahweh" with "God," the name Jethro for Moses' father-in-law (after having called him Reuel in the narrative of Moses' flight to Midian), Horeb as the name of God's mountain (not Sinai, as elsewhere). In order to read the text, however, it is not necessary to separate these traditions, which have come to their final form on level three of the composition of Exodus.

The narrative follows the usual outline for prophetic calls—a structure that may be observed in the call of Gideon (Judg. 6:11–17), of Jeremiah (Jer. 1:4–10), of Isaiah (Isa. 6:1–13), and so forth (Habel, "Form and Significance"). This structure contains five elements, in a fixed order:

1. God comes on the scene.
2. God calls the prophet to perform a task.
3. The prophet resists.
4. The call is repeated.
5. A sign is foretold.

In the case of the call of Moses, this outline is filled in and artistically developed, especially in steps 3 and 4. The presentation of the call of the liberator here in the traditional schema of the call of a prophet is a tribute to the importance of the prophets in the life of Israel. It was they who kept alive in the hearts of their hearers the memory of the egalitarian practices that Yahweh demanded of Israel, during the years when the kings were establishing a class society on the very model rejected by the Mosaic group of proto-Israelites in Egypt and by the proto-Israelite tribes in Canaan. Here, in the account of his call, Moses is presented as a prophet, not a king, in spite of the fact that level three took shape precisely in the period in which Israel was a monarchy, and was adapting its revolutionary traditions to a situation that had ceased to be revolutionary.

The first element in the paradigm of a prophetic call is presented: God appears on the scene—"the God of your father, the God of Abraham, the God of Isaac, and the God of Jacob." I have commented on this formula in § 2.1.1, above. As addressed to Moses—rescued by the daughter of a pharaoh, and received in Midian as a fugitive Egyptian—it has special meaning. Abraham, Isaac, and Jacob are the forebears of the oppressed peasantry. Since infancy, Moses has lived as an Egyptian prince, although the text supposes that he knows his natural kinship with a peasant family. Publicly, he is an Egyptian aristocrat. But with his violent dispensation of justice against the Egyptian who had killed a Hebrew, Moses sacrificed his position, and now lives in exile, like a nobleman fallen on hard times. God then makes a self-presentation to him, not after the fashion of a familiar divinity of the temples of the Egyptian nobility, but as one who has taken sides with the oppressed. Learning that God is on the side of the oppressed is always a shock for an oppressor, and in the majority of instances the experience is denied outright, with the indignation that only guilt can orchestrate. Nothing in the text marks Moses as a religious person. He has been just, yes, but not out of religious motives. Here, for the first time, he comes to know God—and learns that God is with the Hebrews. This knowledge, taken seriously, will demand a conscious disengagement from his aristocratic class. Of course, he has for all practical purposes broken with his court ambience already. But now that he knows God, he will have to identify with the class in whose oppression he has participated, if he is to act consistently with his new knowledge about God.

2.1.2 God Calls and Sends Forth a Prophet (Exod. 3:7-10)

And Yahweh said, "I have seen the miserable state of my people in Egypt. I have heard their appeal to be free of their slave drivers. Yes, I am well aware of their sufferings. I mean to deliver them out of the hands of the Egyptians and bring them up out of that land to a land rich and broad, a land where milk and honey flow, the home of the Canaanites, the Hittites, the Amorites, the Perizzites, the Hivites and the Jebusites. And now the cry of the sons of Israel has come to me, and I have witnessed the way in which the Egyptians oppress them, so come, I send you to Pharaoh to bring the sons of Israel, my people, out of Egypt."

In the classic structure of the prophet's call, this passage corresponds to step two: mission. Exodus takes this occasion to lay before its readers the ultimate objective of the movement here being initiated by God: a land "where milk and honey flow." This expression—like "kingdom of God" in Jesus' preaching—seeks to place before our eyes, in historical terms, the ultimate, metahistorical goal of all our historical efforts. Our text uses this image to point to social salvation—the final, definitive goal of our endless efforts.

In God's self-introduction to Moses, God had indicated to him that he would have to solidarize with the oppressed as a group, because that was where God was. And now God confronts Moses with the ultimate goal of a basic social movement. It will not be enough to seek reforms, or claim damages, or otherwise soften the oppression in Egypt and make it bearable. No, the divine goal, and hence the goal of God's prophet, is a new land, a land flowing with milk and honey.

The book of Exodus nowhere indicates that Israel ever attained the promised land. In fact, nowhere in the Pentateuch do we read of its attainment of such a goal. Not even the conquest of Canaan, narrated in the books of Joshua and Judges, amounts to attainment of definitive possession of the land. Possession of the land of promise is a utopian goal, calculated to orientate Israel's efforts. The introduction of this goal at the beginning of the liberation account serves to orientate the subsequent action. The first stage—the liberation properly so called, the "delivery from the hands of the Egyptians"—is not enough. The account devotes a great deal of time to this first stage, but it is only the first stage, and another one follows: "bringing them up out of that land to a land rich and broad, a land where milk and honey flow" (on this aspect of the exodus, see J. N. M. Wijngaards, "HOSI' and HE' ELAH"). Those who lose sight of the goal during their journey will think that life in Egypt was better—there was always enough to eat at least, whereas here in the wilderness, still only on the road to the land where milk and honey flow, life is so precarious. The prophet will have to know, right from the start, what the terminus of that road will be.

But the land where milk and honey flow is not a fantasy goal. It is also the land of the Canaanites, the Hittites, the Amorites, the Perizzites, the Hivites, and the Jebusites. The goal of the revolution has something transcendent about it, never to be fully attained—otherwise the revolution would cease to be a movement—but it is not metahistorical, it is not outside history—otherwise the revolution would lose its bearing, its course. There is a de facto territory, the raw material of the vision of a land where milk and honey flow. The list of the peoples currently occupying it reflects, especially by its inclusion of the Jebusites, the historicity of the reigns of David and Solomon. The Jebusites were the inhabitants of Jerusalem, a city that was not incorporated into Israel until its conquest by David. Thus the goal of the movement of the exodus is conceived in terms of the kingdom that had been built up in the time of David, even though the vision transcends any concrete expression of the attainable.

Today we can liken the land where milk and honey flow to the utopic goal of the kingdom of God, with the land of Canaan as its necessary mediation, socialism. To speak of the utopia without its concrete historical mediation would be merely to dream an empty dream; and to speak of the mediation as if it were the utopia would be to impose a straitjacket on the revolution in order to render it manipulable.

2.1.3 The Prophet Objects (Exod. 3:11-12)

Moses said to God, "Who am I to go to Pharaoh and bring the sons of Israel out of Egypt?" "I shall be with you," was the answer, "and this is the sign by which you shall know that it is I who have sent you . . . After you have led the people out of Egypt, you are to offer worship to God on this mountain."

The prophet's objection is very much like Gideon's when he was confronted with a similar divine mission: "Forgive me, my lord, but how can I deliver Israel? My clan, you must know, is the weakest in Manasseh and I am the least important in mȳ family" (Judg. 6:15).

Moses' objection is understandable. He has shared neither the Hebrews' sufferings nor their forced labor: first he had lived in the palace of the daughter of the pharaoh, and then he had lived far from Egypt, in the land of Midian.

The answer is that Moses will not be going alone. God will be with him. Yahweh, who will come to be one of the principal characters in the account, knows that a great deal is being asked of Moses. Further, Moses has not yet had the least evidence that Yahweh has heard the cry of the people. The case is once more analogous to that of Gideon, who cannot believe that God is present in Israel in moments of national peril. God offers Gideon, as a sign of divine presence, the wonder of the fleece that is dry after the heavy dewfall. But what will be the sign for Moses? Some have thought that, in some ancient version of the account, the sign was the burning bush that was not consumed—that that would have been the wonder calculated to bolster Moses' faith. But in the final form of the account this sign does not seem to have had much effect. When Moses has brought the people up from Egypt (for Yahweh has indeed signified, in the previous verse, the intention to deliver, to liberate, the people), then he will be able to bring the people to this mountain to worship God. Thus, it would appear, Moses has to base his confidence on a hope that as yet has no material support.

The alternation of the subject who is to perform the liberation—God/Moses—introduces a basic theme of Exodus. Repeatedly, God and Moses are both asserted to have liberated Israel. According to our text, the initiative for the liberation will have come from God; but for its execution, the leadership of Moses will be indispensable. The fact that the exodus is an act of divine salvation does not militate against its being a human revolution as well, with all the political management a revolution requires. To forget this is to separate the exodus, when God went into action for the salvation of a people, from human reality, which demands that we organize, with effective management, to make revolution a success.

2.1.4 A Second Objection (Exod. 3:13–15)

Then Moses said to God, "I am to go, then, to the sons of Israel and say to them, 'The God of your fathers has sent me to you.' But if they ask me what his name is, what am I to tell them?" And God said to Moses, "I Am who I Am. This," he added, "is what you must say to the sons of Israel: 'I Am has sent me to you.' " And God also said to Moses, "You are to say to the sons of Israel: 'Yahweh, the God of your fathers, the God of Abraham, the God of Isaac, and the God of Jacob, has sent me to you.' This is my name for all time; by this name I shall be invoked for all generations to come."

Moses raises a second objection to the mission that God has entrusted to him. It springs from realism: Moses has not lived with the oppressed people in Egypt. He is publicly known as the son of a pharaoh's daughter, who has lived in the royal palace, and has been absent from the country for a long time, living as an exiled Egyptian in Midian. It is natural that he should ask whether the Israelites will accept him as a prophet of God.

God's response takes the question in greater depth than it might seem at first blush. True, God does give Moses an answer that he can give the Israelites: "Yahweh, the God of your fathers, the God of Abraham, the God of Isaac, and the God of Jacob, has sent me to you." With these words, Moses will be informing the Israelites of two things: that he knows the names of the patriarchs of Israel, and that he knows the name of their God. And it will be more likely that they will accept him as God's envoy. But at the same time Moses is also given an indication of the meaning of God's name. Thereby God demonstrates that Moses' question has been taken as an expression of the real reason for his insecurity. Before going to Egypt on his mission, Moses must believe that it is possible to liberate the Hebrews. Thus, God is "I Am who I am," and Moses "must say to the sons of Israel: 'I Am has sent me to you.' "

One way of exploring the meaning of words in everyday use is to explore their origins, their etymologies. This is what our text does at this point, with the name that God had in Israel: *YHWH,* Yahweh. In what God says to Moses, the divine name is explained in terms of the common word *HYH (hayāh),* "to be." I leave for Appendix 5 discussion of the scientific explanation of the etymology of this divine name. Of interest here is the meaning it has in the mouth of God, as *dramatis persona,* who uses it to strengthen Moses' faith that his mission has genuine possibilities of success.

The construction *yahweh-'isher-yihweh* admits of only two interpretations of its syntax. It is possible to take it as evasive: "I am who I am; period." This interpretation has been defended by many exegetes, as perhaps best represented by M. Dubarle ("La sigification du nom de Iahwéh"). Citing syntactically analogous expressions whose purpose is to evade a direct response (1 Sam. 23:13, 2 Sam. 15:20, 2 Kings 8:1, Exod. 4:13), Dubarle interprets the divine response to Moses as evasive. God tells Moses in effect that there is no reason to reveal the divine name to anyone. The problem with this reading, however syntactically defensible it may be, is that it does not fit the context. Moses has not expressed curiosity about God's name. He has posed a problem that he will have when he reaches the Israelites. An evasive response does not seem called for.

The other possibility is to read the text as an assertion based on the etymology of *HYH:* "I am the one who is." The principle of Hebrew grammar that supports this reading is amply documented by E. Schild ("On Exodus iii, 14—'I Am That I Am' "). Hebrew, unlike European languages, requires that pronouns and verbs of a dependent clause agree with the pronoun subject of the principal clause governing it, and not with the noun of the predicate. We have a parallel in Genesis 15:7, where the Hebrew says literally: "I am Yahweh, who have brought you out of Ur . . . —which we naturally would translate " . . . who has brought you out of Ur. . . ." Compare Daniel 1:15 and 1 Chronicles 21:17. In other words, Yahweh's words to Moses should not be translated, "I am who I am, " but rather "I am [the one] who is." By saying "I am who is," God is responding to an unexpressed doubt on Moses' part. God is assuring him that God is the one who (genuinely) is. Moses is to understand that God, the God of the oppressed, is a reality, and this will give him courage to set out on his mission.

The implications of the assertion "I am who I am" were translated into Greek by the expression *ho ōn*—the existing one. Jewish and Christian philosophers have extracted here an assertion that the divine essence includes its existence, that God is self-subsistent, not existent by the creation of another, that God exists necessarily, not contingently as other beings do. All of this goes beyond what our text says, but it continues in its line, and does not represent—contrary to what some modern interpreters have held—an illegitimate hellenization of the Hebrew expression.

God is responding to two questions in one: (1) Moses' implicit doubt: Who is this God? and (2) Moses' problem as to what tactics to use to convince the Hebrew-Israelites that it is the God of their own ancestors who has dispatched him on his mission of liberation. But even this division of God's answer does not do justice to what is in effect three responses on God's part: (1) I am the One who is; (2) you shall say, "I Am has sent me to you"; and (3) you shall say, "Yahweh, the God of your ancestors, has sent me to you."

This is a good example of the profit that can be drawn from the prodigious scholarship that has been invested in recovering the three literary sources of the Pentateuch. Here, one can see that the Yahwist and the Elohist accounts have been combined. According to the Elohist version of the Exodus, God revealed the divine name Yahweh at this moment not only to Moses, but to all humankind. In the Elohist version of the stories of the patriarchs, Abraham, Isaac, and Jacob did not yet know Yahweh's name, but worshiped God under the generic name used by the gentiles, the "nations" around them (see Appendix 5). I shall make no attempt, however, to separate the Yahwist and Elohist elements of our text: for our purpose the only important thing is to understand why the text contains certain redundancies.

2.1.5 The Liberation Strategy (Exod. 3:16–22)

"Go and gather the elders of Israel together and tell them, 'Yahweh, the God of your fathers, has appeared to me—the God of Abraham, of Isaac and of Jacob; and he has said to me: I have visited you and seen all that the Egyptians are doing to you. And so I have resolved to bring you up out of Egypt where you are oppressed, into the land of the Canaanites, the Hittites, the Amorites, the Perizzites, the Hivites and the Jebusites, to a land where milk and honey flow.' They will listen to your words, and with the elders of Israel you are to go to the king of Egypt and say to him, 'Yahweh, the God of the Hebrews, has come to meet us. Give us leave, then, to make a three days' journey into the wilderness to offer sacrifice to Yahweh our God.' For myself, knowing that the king of Egypt will not let you go unless he is forced by a mighty hand, I shall show my power and strike Egypt with all the wonders I am going to work there. After this he will let you go.

"I will give this people such prestige in the eyes of the Egyptians that when you go, you will not go empty-handed. Every woman will ask her neighbor and the woman who is staying in her house for silver ornaments and gold. With these you will adorn your sons and daughters; you will plunder the Egyptians."

Yahweh, God of the Hebrews' ancestors, presents the prophet Moses with this plan of action, whose purpose is to accomplish the flight from Egypt, and later the entry into the land where milk and honey flow. Within the account taken as a whole, this passage performs the function of preparing the reader for the action to come, and of offering a chronology of the liberation process.

The first step is to gather the elders, the natural leaders of the people, and explain to them the support that Yahweh, the God of their forebears, will give them to deliver them from slavery, so as to mobilize them for an emigration to the land where milk and honey flow. The leader who has had the vision of the liberation will need to incorporate into the project the leaders recognized by the people. Nothing will be attained without this minimal organization. Not even God can have a revolution without a people, or without the leaders, good or bad, recognized by the people. In this case forced labor and the genocidal intentions of the king of Egypt create a favorable climate for the acceptance both of the plan by the leaders, and of the leaders by the people.

The second step is to initiate a process of demands addressed to the king. Moses and the elders will seek a three-day leave—for a trip to the mountain where God had appeared, a pilgrimage to celebrate the manifestation of God. This will be a cunning petition, of course, because the leaders' intent is to leave Egypt for good, and head for the land where milk and honey flow. Yahweh's plan renounces reformist measures from the start. It posits the necessity of a radical change. But Yahweh knows full well that the pharaoh is not about to fall into this obvious trap. So—we might wonder—why make the request? Probably the reason is to convince reformists that means of making life tolerable are impossible within the prevailing tributary system, and the only way out is a revolutionary one. Yahweh and Moses know this, but they must also convince the elders and the people.

The third step is to apply force as a means to oblige the pharaoh to permit them to leave his land. Yahweh will use a "mighty hand" and "wonders" to pressure the king, even though knowing beforehand that the latter will not accede to mere petitions.

The fourth step is the plunder of the Egyptians. It will not be enough that the king, under pressure of God's "wonders," give his permission for the Israelites' departure. They must leave with the wealth of Egypt. The phrase, "prestige in the eyes of the Egyptians," gives a special twist to the motivation of the Egyptian women who will lend their jewelry and raiment to their neighbor Israelites. Probably we should understand here a combination of religious reverence and fear of the terrorist methods of God and the Hebrews, who besides striking the king, will have afflicted the lives of the Egyptians as well. Be this as it may, the Egyptians will fall into the trap and give the Israelites their "silver ornaments and gold," and thus Israel will plunder the country.

And so we have the outline of the strategy to bring ruin on the oppressor, and to flee a country where this people can never be anything but an enslaved people.

2.1.6 A Third Objection (Exod. 4:1-9)

Then Moses answered, "What if they will not believe me or listen to my words and say to me, 'Yahweh has not appeared to you?' " Yahweh asked him, "What is that in your hand?" "A staff," Moses said. "Throw it on the ground," said Yahweh; so Moses threw his staff on the ground— it turned into a serpent and he drew back from it. "Put your hand out and catch it by the tail," Yahweh said to him. And he put out his hand and caught it, and in his hand the serpent turned into a staff . . . "so that they may believe that Yahweh, the God of their fathers, the God of Abraham, the God of Isaac and the God of Jacob, has really appeared to you."

Again Yahweh spoke to Moses, "Put your hand into your bosom." He put his hand into his bosom and when he drew it out, his hand was covered with leprosy, white as snow. "Put your hand back into your bosom." He put his hand into his bosom and when he drew it out, there it was restored, just like the rest of his flesh. "Even so: should they not believe you nor be convinced by this first sign, the second will convince them; but if they should believe neither of these two signs and not listen to your words, you must take water from the river and pour it on the ground, and the water you have drawn from the river will turn to blood on the ground."

The plan of action sketched in §2.1.5 presupposes that the people will believe Moses, and will be ready to confront the tyrant. But now Moses begins to doubt again. He doubts that his knowledge of the names of the Israelite patriarchs, and the secret name of their God, will be sufficient to persuade the Israelites to follow him. The problem is real, and is not limited to the particular circumstances of this account. Any revolutionary movement has need of a phase of organization for insurrection, and has need of the people's confidence in its leaders. This confidence, in turn, requires that the people believe that victory is possible, and that its leaders are capable of correctly formulating its aspirations. Inasmuch as this is a revolution where, at least on the levels of the account that are accessible to us, God plays a central role, this confidence in the real opportunities for triumph for the uprising can be expressed in terms of Moses' authentic call as Yahweh's prophet. The signs that Yahweh gives Moses are "minor miracles," whose sole function is to lend authority to his words. Unlike the sign discussed in §2.1.3, these do appear apt for strengthening faith.

In the subsequent account, Moses uses these signs not only to convince the people, but also to gain authority for his demands upon the king. The signs are taken as powers permanently residing in Moses, and he may use them for whatever ends he may deem necessary.

2.1.7 A Fourth Objection (Exod. 4:10–12)

Moses said to Yahweh, "But, my Lord, never in my life have I been a man of eloquence, either before or since you have spoken to your servant. I am a slow speaker and not able to speak well." "Who gave man his mouth?" Yahweh answered him. "Who makes him dumb or deaf, gives him sight or leaves him blind? Is it not I, Yahweh? Now go, I shall help you to speak and tell you what to say."

The reader may well surmise that Moses, brought up in the royal palace, has sufficient education to speak to the pharaoh, and certainly to the Hebrews. In subsequent passages he often has something to say, in diverse kinds of situations, and never gives the impression of being unable to speak clearly and with authority. With this fourth objection, then, it is evident that real problems are not at issue, and the reader knows that Moses' objection reflects his personal fears. It does not diminish the stature of the prophet of liberation. It is only that the prospects of the struggle are such that one would not throw oneself into it without considering the consequences.

The series of rhetorical questions by Moses in alternation with responses by Yahweh is a well-developed poetic technique found elsewhere in the Old Testament. The subject matter of these questions recalls Psalm 94:9, as well as, less directly, Isaiah 40:12, 21, Isaiah 28:23–26, and Job 38:25–27. The ideological work of generations of Israelite masters of religion is visible in this passage, proclaiming the capacities of God (and by implication, the incapacities of human nature). No transformation has fallen magically from the sky. Not for a moment do we believe that the social revolution—which to the Hebrews meant flight from Egypt, where they were exploited peasants, to build a classless society in a new land—could have been realized without a great deal of effort, organization, and struggle.

It is the concern of a dominant class, monarchical or priestly, to deck itself out in the aura of divinity, and thus suggest a vivid contrast between the majesty of heaven and the impotence and dependency of earth. This is the work of an ideology, in the pejorative sense of camouflage and mystification. All responsibility for the revolution is credited to heaven. To be sure, in recognizing its dissimulating function, I do not deny that this type of rhetoric has a certain religious force—without which, precisely, it would not be efficacious ideology.

2.1.8 The Final Objection (Exod. 4:13–17)

"If it please you, my Lord," Moses replied, "send anyone you will!" At this, the anger of Yahweh blazed out against Moses, and he said to him, "There is your brother Aaron the Levite, is there not? I know that he is a good speaker. Here he comes to meet you. When he sees you, his heart will be full of joy. You will speak to him and tell him what message to

give. I shall help you to speak, and him too, and instruct you what to do. He himself is to speak to the people in your place; he will be your mouthpiece, and you will be as the god inspiring him. And take this staff into your hand; with this you will perform the signs."

Without being able to offer further objections, the prophet nevertheless indicates his indisposition to undertake the task. "Send anyone you will!" he says. For the first time in the account, Yahweh becomes angry.

The wrath of God plays a very important role in the Bible. A false, and dissimulating, notion of love has seen an incompatibility between anger and love. Would this spring from a middle-class confidence in legality—the petit bourgeois trusts that the wrongs of this world can be resolved through the application of laws? If the laws are "not quite perfect," the solution, we are told, is not to become angry and take the law into one's own hands, but to transform the law, using mechanisms constitutionally sanctioned for this purpose.

Perhaps it is for this reason that so many theologians have sought to erase God's real anger from the Bible. But, according to the prophets, Yahweh is genuinely displeased with persons who dare cloak their exploitation with their religion (Amos 5:21–24, Isa. 1:10–17, Jer. 7:1–15). In the Psalms, Yahweh is a God who takes wrathful vengeance on the oppressor (Pss. 58, 82, 94, 98). And in the old popular histories, God becomes infuriated with those who resist the liberating advance of the forces of Israel, and mercilessly goes about the extermination of the Canaanite kings who oppress the tribes of Israel (see Josh., Judg.).

It is important to be clear on this point. We must not, in the name of our religion, deprive the oppressed of the right to become angry with those who deprive them of their right to life. The Chilean experience of the ill-starred popular undertaking of the Popular Unity government (1970–73) is instructive in this regard. The cardinal of Santiago maintained that the imposition of justice by force would be an exercise of violence—meaning that exploiters ought to be convinced of the need for *conceding* justice. The government, in its reverence for the constitutionalist stance of the bourgeoisie, stubbornly held to strict legality, refusing to undertake reforms that were not supported by a parliamentary majority. But when it was seen that the number in favor of thoroughgoing reform was increasing, the bourgeoisie abandoned its legal posture and had recourse to violence and massacre, precisely to prevent justice. And so the straightforward language of the Bible about the wrath of God should put us on our guard against the hypocrisy of those who so brazenly disguise the defense of their own interests with religion, or with "law and order." (An excellent analysis of the role of religion in the Chilean experience is that of Franz Josef Hinkelammert, *Ideología de sometimiento: La Iglesia Católica chilena frente al golpe: 1973-74.*) If Yahweh can become angry with resistance to liberation plans, who can deny the same right to those who suffer oppression?

But in spite of this anger, God grants Moses not a replacement but a lieutenant. Here, for the first time, Aaron appears, identified as a Levite. According to what we have seen in § 1.2.3, Moses was a Levite, and it might appear superfluous to identify his brother as one. In Exodus passages Aaron will frequently appear at Moses' side. Nevertheless, at no moment will he play the important role of "mouthpiece" for Yahweh and Moses that is stated here. The priestly revision of the account of the manifestations of Yahweh in the Sinai will make Aaron the patriarch of the priesthood—even though he does not play this role in the liberation account.

From the very first literary stratum, Aaron is present, but he is no more than Moses' companion. The key to an understanding of Aaron is precisely his presentation as a Levite. Moses, according to the account, is a Levite, but he is not publicly known as one. Aaron, on the other hand, has lived among the Levites, and no one doubts his identity as one himself. In accompanying Moses, Aaron the Levite confirms his solidarity with the Levite people whom he means to lead to its liberation. Surely, therefore, Aaron is not introduced in reaction to the objection that Moses was not eloquent. His real role is not to speak, but to legitimate the liberator, who has no clear credentials, inasmuch as he has not participated in the suffering of the oppressed.

We may wonder why the account places so much emphasis on Moses' opposition to his mission, voicing his objections, in various forms, five times. First, of course, we must recognize that we are dealing with a familiar pattern—the prophet's resistance to his call. The emphasis on these objections, as in the case of Amos, Jeremiah, and other prophets, seems to have the purpose of underscoring the authority of the prophet, who does not speak on his own behalf, then, but in virtue of a mission he has received from God. Naturally there were those who doubted the divine patronage of prophecies as unwelcome as those of Amos or Jeremiah, and these prophets had to insist that they did not speak on their own behalf.

In the case of the Exodus narratives, however, the case is not exactly the same. Narrators and audience, as well as those who will read the account, know that Moses had an authentic divine mission. The real reason for these five objections, finally bringing down Yahweh's wrath, is to place the initiative for the revolutionary action in heaven, not on earth. That is, on level three, the promonarchical ideologues wish to inculcate that it was not popular organization, but divine initiatives, that guaranteed the success of the revolution. The people must learn to depend on God (and on God's representatives—the kings and priests).

Be all this as it may, we are struck by the force with which the account presents Yahweh to us as a God who is determined to carry out a plan of liberation in response to the cry of these slaves, a God who will not permit anyone or anything to prevent revolutionary salvation.

2.1.9 Moses Departs for Egypt (Exod. 4:18–23)

Moses went away and returned to his father-in-law Jethro, and said to him, "Give me leave to go back to my relatives in Egypt to see if they are still alive." And Jethro said to Moses, "Go in peace."

> *Yahweh said to Moses in Midian, "Go, return to Egypt, for all those who wanted to kill you are dead." So Moses took his wife and his son and, putting them on a donkey, started back for the land of Egypt; and Moses took in his hand the staff of God. Yahweh said to Moses, "Now that you are going back to Egypt, be prepared to perform before Pharaoh all the marvels that I have given you power to do. I myself will harden his heart, and he will not let the people go. Then you will say to Pharaoh, 'This is what Yahweh says: Israel is my first-born son. I ordered you to let my son go to offer me worship. You refuse to let him go. So be it! I shall put your first-born to death.' "*

There is in this passage a double movement that we must not let go unnoticed. First, Moses takes the initiative in departing for Egypt in order to learn the fate of his "relatives," the oppressed Hebrews. Then, at once, the same event is related with the initiative coming from God, who informs Moses that he can now return from his exile. This double viewpoint pervades the whole account. Yahweh goes down to liberate the people from oppression (Exod. 3:8), and also sends Moses to lead Israel out of Egypt (3:10). The Israelites, at the foot of Mount Sinai, speak of Moses as "the man who brought us up from Egypt" (32:1), and then profess that it is "God . . . who brought [us] out of the land of Egypt" (32:4). This duality is intrinsic to any religious view of the revolutionary movement: it would be incorrect to say that it was simply on Moses' initiative that he undertook his task as a revolutionary, and equally incorrect to say that it was God who did everything. Both expressions are partial truths, and mutually complementary.

The passage under consideration here sends us back to the first part of the book of Exodus, where we learn that the king of Egypt was seeking to kill the people. Moses has intervened to put a stop to this genocide. Now he wishes to know whether the king has failed of his intent. God assures him that the situation is such that he can return without fear for his personal safety.

The message for the pharaoh—"Israel is my first-born son. . . . You refuse to let him go. So be it! I shall put your first-born son to death"—links this initiation of the revolutionary activity with the death of the first-born of the pharaoh in Exodus 12:29–32, passing over all the intermediate action. The prodigies and plagues with which the pharaoh and Egypt are assaulted are presented here as the result of divine "hardening of the heart" of the pharaoh—in contrast with the programmatic text of §2.1.5 (Exod. 3:16–22), where the plagues are seen to have the purpose of bending the king's will and forcing him to discharge his laborers. This twofold vision of the blows dealt the tyrant run all through the account.

Yahweh gives Moses (and the reader) to know that it will be necessary to kill in order to find a place to live without the threat of extermination implicit in the Egyptian class system, where life depends on the whim of the reigning monarch and where an unjust king can slaughter the people. Moses, without knowing anything of Yahweh as yet, already intued this when he killed the Egyptian who had been mistreating the Hebrew laborer (§1.2.4).

2.1.10 Yahweh Assaults Moses (Exod. 4:24–26)

On the journey, when Moses had halted for the night, Yahweh came to meet him and tried to kill him. At once Zipporah, taking up a flint, cut off her son's foreskin and with it she touched the genitals of Moses. "Truly, you are a bridegroom of blood to me!" she said. And Yahweh let him live. It was then that she said, "bridegroom of blood," on account of the circumcision.

This enigmatic passage has never been adequately explained. But it is reminiscent of God's attack on Jacob in Peniel (Gen. 32:22–32). There, God's struggle with Jacob ends with a blessing for the latter. The parallel is not exact, but it does show that it was not inconceivable in Israel that God should have a "demonic side." We likewise think of God's command to Abraham that he sacrifice his son Isaac (Gen. 22).

Details of the account are unclear because personal pronouns in the text are ambiguous. Does God attack Moses or Moses' son? Whose genitals—or feet, as the Hebrew says—does Zipporah touch? If it was the child who was attacked, the text would have the sense of retribution against Moses for not having circumcised his son, who is saved only by Zipporah's prompt circumcision. (See Hans Kosmala, "The Bloody Bridegroom." Kosmala proposes that the account is a Midianite justification for infant circumcision.) But this leaves unexplained the expression "bridegroom of blood," which is repeated for emphasis.

The Greek Bible (the Septuagint) differs considerably from the Massoretic (Hebrew) text here. In the Septuagint, it is an angel of the Lord who attacks. Instead of touching the genitals (in the Hebrew, the "feet") with the bloody foreskin, she falls at the angel's "feet" and declares that she has accomplished the rite: "The blood of my son's circumcision has been spilled." This is a more coherent account than that of the Hebrew, but one suspects that the translators may have taken liberties, to make some sense out of the text.

We do not know whether it was Moses' life or his son's that was in danger, then. Nor do we know whether the "bridegroom of blood" was Moses or Yahweh. But at least this little account serves notice of Yahweh's fearsome nature, coming as it does hard upon the threat against the pharaoh's firstborn. Yahweh is not always specific. Yahweh can kill.

2.1.11 Conclusion of the Preparations: The Elders Accept Yahweh's Prophet (Exod. 4:27–31)

Yahweh said to Aaron, "Go into the wilderness to meet Moses." And so he went, and met him at the mountain of God; and he kissed him. Moses then told Aaron all that Yahweh had said when he set him his task and all the signs he had ordered him to perform. Moses and Aaron then went and gathered all the elders of the sons of Israel together, and Aaron told all that Yahweh had said to Moses, and in the sight of the people he performed the signs. The people were convinced, and they rejoiced that Yahweh had visited the sons of Israel and seen their misery, and they bowed down and worshiped.

The meeting with Aaron is the fulfillment of what Yahweh announced in answer to Moses' final protest (§2.1.8). Moses and Aaron meet on God's mountain, a frequent place of encounter at various points of our narrative.

Aaron's participation in this reunion with the "elders" of the Israelites is perfectly correct as a political tactic. Aaron has lived the oppression and is recognized as a Levite, whereas Moses, who will be the supreme chief of the revolution, is an exile at this moment, lacking a clear bond with the Hebrews. At the same time, Aaron's presence has the disadvantage of detracting from the effect of Moses' knowledge of the names of Israel's patriarchs and God.

As Yahweh has foreseen in formulating the strategy for the revolution (§2.1.5), the leaders of the Israelites accept the plan with alacrity. The fact that Moses and Aaron had no difficulty in reaching them indicates that they lived in an area of their own, the land of Goshen, and that they were not slaves of the state in the strict sense, but peasants who worked at obligatory tasks for the state without abandoning their fields.

2.2 FAILURE OF LEGAL RECOURSE (EXOD. 5:1–6:9)

Having gained the agreement of the Israelite community leaders to set out on the road for liberation, Moses and Aaron proceed to the second step of the strategy sketched out by Yahweh (§2.1.5). This consists in going directly to the pharaoh, informing him of Yahweh's revelation on the mountain in the desert, and obtaining sufficient "time off" to make a three-day journey to celebrate the festival of Yahweh. Once permission has been obtained for the trip to the desert, the intention would be not to return, because Moses is convinced that Egypt is a land of death for the Israelite laborers. But the plan is not expected to succeed at this stage. Yahweh has warned that the pharaoh will refuse permission.

The use of the legal recourse provided for by the system—seeking a holiday for a religious pilgrimage—is a necessary step in the liberation process. This is because, among any oppressed group of persons, there are always many who do not think it necessary to bear the sacrifices and run the risks of a revolution, or who think that the evils they have to suffer can be healed with the resources offered by the system, or in any case by the reform of the system. To form a revolutionary consciousness, it is important to show the intrinsic limits of the prevailing system, when it comes to satisfying the vital needs of the working class, in a society composed of peasants subject to forced labor for the state.

In this public process of a demand for concessions, the revolutionary movement is at great disadvantage vis-à-vis the dominant class—in this case, the pharaoh and his state bureaucracy. The pharaoh has the means to make the working conditions and life of his subjects better or worse. He will use these means to nip this revolution in the bud, disparaging its leaders as dreamers who are only creating trouble for the people.

2.2.1 Petition for a Pilgrimage (Exod. 5:1-5)

After this, Moses and Aaron went to Pharaoh and said to him, "This is what Yahweh, the God of Israel, has said, 'Let my people go, so that they may keep a feast in the wilderness in honor of me.' " "Who is Yahweh," Pharaoh replied, "that I should listen to him and let Israel go? I know nothing of Yahweh, and I will not let Israel go." "The God of the Hebrews has come to meet us," they replied. "Give us leave to make a three days' journey into the wilderness to offer sacrifice to Yahweh our God, or he will come down on us with a plague or with the sword." The king of Egypt said to them, "Moses and Aaron, what do you mean by taking the people away from their work? Get back to your laboring." And Pharaoh said, "Now that these common folk have grown to such numbers, do you want to stop them laboring?"

Although there is no reason why the pharaoh should have any knowledge of Yahweh, the God of the "Hebrews" (a meaningful use here, by reason of the connotation of rebellion in its etymology), the pharaoh's reply sounds insolent, as he refuses to take seriously the God of the weak.

Moses and Aaron, who will emerge as authentic revolutionaries, in the uprising as well as in the transition to a new society, exercise fine self-control on this occasion. To the insolence of the powerful one they simply reply by repeating their request, bolstering it this time by citing calamities that could come about if God's revelation were to remain without response.

The pharaoh's second reply is one of the classic responses of an oppressor. He accuses these leaders, Moses and Aaron, of putting strange ideas in the Israelites' heads, and so distracting them from their customary tasks. The laborers are numerous, and the pilgrimage to the desert would mean the loss of many hours of work.

Our attention is arrested by the expression "common folk" (in the original, "people of the land"). In the time of the kingdom of Judah, this expression will denote the free segment of the national population, the persons of the social category who support David's dynasty (2 Kings 11:18, 21:24). Perhaps because they did not think it could be correct to have such a designation for a slave people, the Septuagint translators rendered simply, "I have a numerous people here." The ancient Hebrew text of the Samaritan Pentateuch says: "They are more numerous than the people of the country," which would preserve the more usual sense of the expression "people of the land," or "people of the country," and resume the theme of §1.2. Brevard Childs suggests that the

Samaritan reading is the oldest (*Exodus,* 93). But it is also possible that this is a remnant of level one of the account, which records that the Hebrews were not all foreigners in Egypt, but a mixed multitude of peasantry. On levels one and two, we must remember that Israelite unity was an acquisition of the revolution, and not a previously prevailing condition.

2.2.2 The Pharaoh's Response: Intensification of Exploitation (Exod. 5:6–14)

That same day, Pharaoh gave this command to the people's slave drivers and to the overseers. "Up to the present, you have provided these people with straw for brickmaking. Do so no longer; let them go and gather straw for themselves. All the same, you are to get from them the same number of bricks as before, not reducing it at all. They are lazy, and that is why their cry is, 'Let us go and offer sacrifice to our God.' Make these men work harder than ever, so that they do not have time to stop and listen to glib speeches."

The people's slave drivers went out with the overseers to speak to the people. "Pharaoh has given orders," they said: " 'I will not provide you with straw. Go out and collect straw for yourselves wherever you can find it. But your output is not to be any less.' " So the people scattered all over the land of Egypt to gather stubble for making chopped straw. The slave drivers harassed them. "Every day you must complete your daily quota," they said, "just as you did when straw was provided for you." And the foremen who had been appointed for the sons of Israel by Pharaoh's slave drivers were flogged, and they were asked, "Why have you not produced your full amount of bricks as before, either yesterday or today?"

The pharaoh's reaction to the workers' demands follows an oft repeated pattern in history. First, he seeks to disparage the leaders who have attempted to organize the workers. Secondly, he uses his control over working conditions to "teach the workers a lesson": teach them that the consequence of seeking relief will be heavier labor. The workers must be brought to see that their lot depends on the good will of the pharaoh, and that his good will is compromised when he is forced to deal with petitions and demands. Thirdly, for getting the most burdensome tasks done, he selects gang leaders from among the workers themselves, thus dividing the people.

The pharaoh has all the astuteness of the experienced oppressor. Because he has it in his power to realize his desires (up to a certain point), he will describe the ominous words of Moses and Aaron as "glib speeches"—in the original, "lying words." The workers will see: the fruit of promises of liberation will be more oppression! Similarly, in Latin America we are familiar with the rhetoric of those who accuse the defenders of the workers as being dreamers, victims of delusion, whereas they themselves, the ones who hold power, know what reality is. They have the power to realize the possible, and need not dream the impossible.

Particularly despicable is the tactic of selecting foremen from among the workers themselves. This provides the others with walking examples of their "opportunity to improve their standard of living" by accepting the system of exploitation, and participating in it, according to the oppressor's rules. In exchange for supervising the work that promotes the pharaoh's interests, these Hebrews who have sold out to the system are rewarded with positions in which they will not have to perform the most repugnant tasks themselves.

The slave drivers are functionaries of the state. They are the lowest rung on the bureaucratic ladder, but are acutely aware of their superiority over the foremen. They are the channels of orders from above, and they will hold the foremen responsible for any failure in meeting work quotas. Thus in a few deft strokes of the pen, we are presented with the functioning of a whole system of oppression, with its basic division between oppressors (the pharaoh and his officials, including the slave drivers) and oppressed (foremen and workers).

Both social classes have multiple subdivisions, and the whole system is manipulated from the top of the social pyramid so as to guarantee that the few benefit from the labor of the many. The privileges accorded to foremen function as a kind of bribe, and buy loyalty to the pharaoh, entailing as they do the threat of the loss of privileges and reduction to the condition of workers, along with the promise of improvement of their benefits if they manage to maintain and perfect the exploitation of the work force of the masses.

2.2.3 The Foremen's Dilemma (Exod. 5:15–21)

The foremen for the sons of Israel went to Pharaoh and complained. "Why do you treat your servants so?" they said. "No straw is provided for your servants and still the cry is, 'Make bricks!' And now your servants have been flogged! . . ." "You are lazy, lazy," he answered, "that is why you say, 'Let us go and offer sacrifice to Yahweh.' Get back to your work at once. You shall not get any straw, but you must deliver the number of bricks due from you."

The foremen for the sons of Israel saw themselves in a very difficult position when told there was to be no reduction in the daily number of bricks. As they left Pharaoh's presence they met Moses and Aaron who were waiting for them. "May Yahweh see your work and punish you as you deserve!" they said to them. "You have made us hated by Pharaoh and his court; you have put a sword into their hand to kill us."

The tactic of intensifying the exploitation produces its bitter fruit. The position of the foremen becomes intolerable. They will be held accountable if the workers are unable to fill the impossible quotas the pharaoh has imposed on them. But the pharaoh feels secure in his position, and does not yield an inch. The pharaoh thinks—rightly—that the foremen will exert pressure on the workers to withdraw their support from Moses and Aaron with their liberation plan. Then, once Moses' popular support has been eliminated, the pharaoh can normalize working conditions and his gesture will be taken as evidence of his mercy. And the slaves will learn that their well-being depends exclusively on the pharaoh's good will.

Naturally, the foremen are right when they say that the blame for not meeting the work goals lies with those who set the quotas, and not with themselves, who have been unable to get the workers to meet the goals. They do not dare to point the guilty finger at the ultimate guilty party—the pharaoh himself. Or perhaps they have convinced themselves that it *is* the bureaucrats who are guilty, rather than the monarch. In any case, the pharaoh knows what he is doing. His interests are best served by projecting an alternative scenario, in which the guilty ones are Moses and Aaron for wanting to reach out to an illusion, a dream that the pharaoh has declared to be unrealizable: freedom. And so the pharaoh is not disposed to pay attention to the reasoning of the foremen.

The situation of Moses and Aaron is a sad one. Knowing that there is scant likelihood that the pharaoh will grant what the foremen want, they await them outside the palace at the close of the interview. As the pharaoh has foreseen, the foremen throw the blame for the worsening of their oppression on Moses and Aaron for having provoked the pharaoh's wrath. The foremen, although they agreed to the plan to ask for a three-day leave, are deeply involved in a contest where the pharaoh makes the rules and the welfare of the workers depends on the good will of a tyrant. According to those rules, Moses and Aaron have provoked the pharaoh's anger, and are to blame for the new misfortune. With the foremen's indictment of Moses, the pharaoh has achieved his end of dividing the workers, and sundering the unity that has been achieved by the prophet of Yahweh.

2.2.4 The People's Discouragement (Exod. 5:22–6:9)

Once more Moses turned to Yahweh. "Lord," he said to him, "why do you treat this people so harshly? Why did you send me here? Ever since I came to Pharaoh and spoke to him in your name, he has ill treated this nation, and you have done nothing to deliver your people." Then Yahweh said to Moses, "You will see now how I shall punish Pharaoh. He will be forced to let them go; yes, he will be forced to send them out of his land."

God spoke to Moses and said to him, "I am Yahweh. To Abraham and Isaac and Jacob I appeared as El Shaddai; I did not make myself known to them by my name Yahweh. Also, I made my covenant with them to give them the land of Canaan, the land they lived in as strangers. And I have heard the groaning of the sons of Israel, enslaved by the Egyptians, and have remembered by covenant. Say this, then, to the sons of Israel, 'I am Yahweh. I will free you of the burdens which the Egyptians lay on you. I will release you from slavery to them, and with my arm out-stretched and my strokes of power I will deliver you. I will adopt you as

my own people, and I will be your God. Then you shall know that it is I,
Yahweh your God, who have freed you from the Egyptians' burdens.'
Then I will bring you to the land I swore that I would give to Abraham,
and Isaac, and Jacob, and will give it to you for your own; I, Yahweh, will
do this!" Moses told this to the sons of Israel, but they would not listen to
him, so crushed was their spirit and so cruel their slavery.

Moses now takes the accusations made against himself by the foremen and
directs them to Yahweh. And he reminds Yahweh of the promise to work
"wonders" to deliver the Israelites from Egypt. But Moses knew beforehand
that the pharaoh would not agree to the departure of the workers for the desert.
Yahweh tells Moses that the liberation plan is still in effect. Measures of force
will be applied, such that the king will finally expel the Israelites.

The immediate problem is that of maintaining unity and the spirit of struggle
in the hearts of the people. To this end, God gives Moses a solemn prophetic
message to transmit to the people. The function of this short but dramatic
discourse is to raise the Israelites' spirits, so that they will continue in quest of
their liberation. Nevertheless, despite Moses' eloquence, they are more im-
pressed by the hard labor imposed by the pharaoh than by the words of
Yahweh's prophet, and "they would not listen to him, so crushed was their
spirit and so cruel their slavery."

This discourse is a text of the sacerdotal redaction. We have not seen the
sacerdotal redaction since §2.0, which was concerned with the "cry of the
people." Thus the priests who composed this revision eliminated the call of
Moses in Midian and replaced it with this discourse in Egypt. In reading the
Pentateuch it is important to keep in mind the sacerdotal theory that it was the
patriarchs who first received from God the promise of the land, although they
did not know God by the name "Yahweh." This revelation was reserved for the
time of the exodus. It is also significant that it is explicitly the land of Canaan
that is spoken of here as the goal of the exodus, and not merely a "land where
milk and honey flow" (as in §2.1.2). Here the account is brought in line with a
more "realistic" goal and a less utopian spirit.

2.3 CONFIRMATION OF MOSES' MISSION AND OF AARON'S DEPUTIZATION (EXOD. 6:10-7:7)

This section belongs entirely to the sacerdotal redaction of Exodus, and
gives its own version of topics that have already been developed in the
Yahwist and Elohist material—Moses' objection and the consequent assignment of Aaron (see §2.1.7-8), and the strategy for liberation (§2.1.4). The
narration is interrupted by a genealogy (Exod. 6:14-25) whose emphasis on
Aaron clearly reflects its origin with Aaronite priests. It gives the impression
of being a sacerdotal text inserted within the other sacerdotal material. In the
book of Exodus as we have it today, this section follows the failure of the
petition presented to the pharaoh.

At this moment of discouragement, Yahweh addresses Moses once again, commissions him anew, and repeats the assignment of his brother Aaron as his lieutenant.

2.3.1 Yahweh Addresses Moses and Aaron (Exod. 6:10–13)

Yahweh then said to Moses, "Go to Pharaoh, king of Egypt, and tell him to let the sons of Israel leave his land." But Moses answered to Yahweh's face: "Look," said he, "since the sons of Israel have not listened to me, why should Pharaoh listen to me, a man slow of speech?" Yahweh spoke to Moses and Aaron and ordered them both to go to Pharaoh, king of Egypt, and to bring the sons of Israel out of the land of Egypt.

Moses' protest that he is "slow of speech" is essentially the same objection raised in §2.1.7. There is, however, a novel twist this time: in light of the people's discouragement at the redoubled oppression, Moses will now have an objective problem when it comes to presenting himself to the pharaoh. And it has nothing to do with his ability to speak. It is a political problem. If the pharaoh knows of Moses' lack of support among the people he represents, he will not be taken seriously, however eloquent he may be. The text has no evident response to this problem. No tyrant has ever paid attention to a leader of an exploited people who has not been able to count on the political support of the people, no matter how many acts of terrorism he or she has perpetrated.

In the Yahwist version of the plagues (§2.4), the Hebrew people practically disappears from the scene, until—with the pharaoh defeated by Yahweh, Moses, and Aaron—freedom is granted it as a gift. Here too, in the editing or development of §2.3.1, there is reason to suspect that the part of the people in the process of confrontation with the pharaoh has been omitted.

There are reasons for this omission, on levels three and four alike. On level three, the Yahwist version reflects the interests of David and his dynasty, who considered themselves kings chosen by Yahweh. This royal perspective is evident in Psalm 18 as well, where a victory of Israel is presented as a victory of David. In the same way, Psalm 89 presents Yahweh's pact as a pact with David, not with the people of Israel. Psalm 2 speaks of the king as Son of God, a title that in Exodus applies to the people (§2.1.9). Thus in the official Jerusalem theology, the king has replaced the people, just as in the Yahwist version of the plagues Moses has replaced the people.

The northern, Elohist, version (also on level three) does not seem to have suffered this displacement of the people and its elders from the account, if indeed the Elohist version had no account of the plagues, as seems probable. Following what I have indicated in §2.1.9, the Elohist text moved directly from the pharaoh's refusal to grant a leave for the celebration of the feast of Yahweh, to the striking of the firstborn of the pharaoh.

The sacerdotal version—level four of the account, from exilic and postexilic times—shows great preoccupation with legitimating, from the text of Exodus, the priests' monopoly over the governance of the people. It extols Yahweh's role in its version of the plagues.

For the Yahwist as well as for the sacerdotal version, then, the account of the plagues serves to fill the vacuum left by the obliteration of the popular struggles against the Egyptian tyrant. In their place is left a struggle between Yahweh and the pharaoh, in which Yahweh is represented by Moses and Aaron.

Table 1

Genealogy of Moses and Aaron

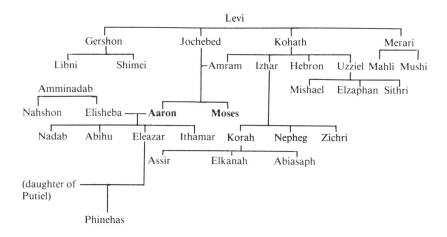

2.3.2 The Genealogy of Moses and Aaron (Exod. 6:14–27)

These are the heads of their families:

The sons of Reuben, Israel's first-born: Hanoch, Pallu, Hezron and Carmi: these are the clans of Reuben.

The sons of Simeon: Jemuel, Jamin, Ohad, Jachin, Zohar, and Shaul, son of the Canaanite woman: these are the clans of Simeon.

These are the names of the sons of Levi with their descendants: Gershon, Kohath and Merari. Levi lived for a hundred and thirty-seven years. The sons of Gershon: Libni and Shimei and their clans.

The sons of Kohath: Amram, Izhar, Hebron and Uzziel. Kohath lived for a hundred and thirty-three years.

The sons of Merari: Mahli and Mushi. These are the clans of Levi with their descendants.

Amram married Jochebed, his aunt, who bore him Aaron and Moses. Amram lived for a hundred and thirty-seven years.

The sons of Izhar were: Korah, Nepheg and Zichri.

And the sons of Uzziel: Mishael, Elzaphan, and Sithri.

*Aaron married Elisheba, daughter of Amminadab and sister of Nah-
shon, and she bore him Nadab, Abihu, Eleazar and Ithamar.*

*The sons of Korah: Assir, Elkanah and Abiasaph. These are the clans
of the Korahites.*

*Eleazar, son of Aaron, married one of Putiel's daughters who bore him
Phinehas.*

These are the heads of families of the Levites according to their clans.

*It was to this same Aaron and Moses that Yahweh had said, "Bring the
sons of Israel out of the land of Egypt in battle order." It was they who
spoke with Pharaoh, king of Egypt, about bringing the sons of Israel out
of Egypt. It was the same Moses and Aaron.*

The order followed is the traditional order of the tribes of Israel, with Reuben
first, then Simeon, then Levi—the same order as given in §1.1. The information about the clans of Reuben and Simeon is identical with the ancient list of
Numbers 26, and agrees with the list in Genesis 46:8–10 as well.

Only in the case of Levi does the list go beyond the second generation (see Table
1). The children of Levi's children are listed, and his grandson Amram has two
children listed by name: Moses and Aaron. The tabulation also shows an interest
in the descendency of Korah, the family of the cantors in the postexilic temple.
Korah holds no major interest for the book of Exodus, and the emphasis on his
lineage suggests that the list was originally created for another purpose than that
of locating Moses and Aaron as members of the tribe of Levi.

2.3.3 Moses' Call Resumed (Exod. 6:28–7:7)

*On the day when Yahweh spoke to Moses in the land of Egypt, he said
this to him, "I am Yahweh. Tell Pharaoh, king of Egypt, all that I say to
you." But Moses said to Yahweh's face, "I am slow of speech, why should
Pharaoh listen to me?"*

*Yahweh said to Moses, "See, I make you as a god for Pharaoh, and
Aaron your brother is to be your prophet. You yourself must tell him all I
command you, and Aaron your brother will tell Pharaoh to let the sons
of Israel leave his land. I myself will make Pharaoh's heart stubborn, and
perform many a sign and wonder in the land of Egypt. Pharaoh will not
listen to you, and so I will lay my hand on Egypt and with strokes of
power lead out my armies, my people, the sons of Israel, from the land of
Egypt. And all the Egyptians shall come to know that I am Yahweh when
I stretch out my hand against Egypt and bring out the sons of Israel from
their midst." Moses and Aaron obeyed; they did what Yahweh commanded them. Moses was eighty years old, and Aaron eighty-three at the
time of their audience with Pharaoh.*

Here we resume the account that was interrupted by the genealogy of Moses
and Aaron. A theme is introduced, as well, that will be decisive for the

sacerdotal version of the exodus: Yahweh hardens the heart (the will) of the pharaoh, with the purpose of multiplying signs and wonders and thereby showing who Yahweh is. This text outlines the strategic liberation plan, and is the sacerdotal parallel to the text that we have already seen in §2.1.5 (Exod. 3:16-22). According to this strategy, it is more important to demonstrate the unsurpassable greatness of Yahweh than it is to proceed forthwith to the liberation of Israel. Politics has become secondary to religion. On this level of the account, we find a certain justification for the point of view that accuses the theology of liberation of "politicizing" the Exodus account. (For a scientific, critical view of the theology of liberation, see Jorge Mejía, "La liberación: Aspectos bíblicos—evaluación crítica.") It is obvious that the sacerdotal revision is an "interested" rereading of Exodus. It is the ideological product of a class that seeks to have the people place religion at the center of its life.

2.4 MEASURES OF FORCE (EXOD. 7:8-11:10)

At this point in the account, a series of "plagues," or "signs and wonders," begins. The victim is the pharaoh. But these "wonders" seem to obstruct the advance of the liberation process, inasmuch as there are many of them, and they in no way improve the situation of the enslaved. In terms of the strict requirements of the text of Exodus, it could just as well move directly from the failure of the representation to the pharaoh, in §2.2, to the smiting of the firstborn of the Egyptians, and the subsequent departure of Israel from Egypt, in §2.5. Still, it is evident that the plagues were something that the Israelite imagination very much enjoyed, and they played an important role in the hymnodic celebration of the exodus (see Pss. 78 and 105). With the plagues, Yahweh enters into a contest with the pharaoh, and demonstrates the superiority of the God of the slaves over the god of the most powerful nation on earth.

As a help to us in our reading of this section, it will be in order to review briefly the three programmatic texts that we have already seen: §§2.1.5, 2.1.9, and 2.3. The first of these texts is very clear. Yahweh appears to Moses on the mountain in the wasteland, and lays before him the plan he was to follow to gain the liberation of the people. Part of this plan envisaged the king's rejection of the petition for a holiday to celebrate Yahweh's festival. After this rejection, Yahweh would work "wonders" to force the pharaoh and his allies to "let the Hebrews go." We see a clear allusion to the plagues here. They are perceived as forceful means to attain the objective of the exodus. This interpretation of the plagues (§2.1.5) is the Yahwist version.

Programmatic text §2.3 follows upon the account of the pharaoh's refusal. This text, as we have seen, originates with the sacerdotal tradition. Here it will be Yahweh who will harden the pharaoh's heart so that he will pay no heed to the wonders, and thus God will have the opportunity to effectuate the "I shall perform many a sign and wonder in the land of Egypt." This is an inversion of the Yahwist account of the story. Instead of the series of plagues having become necessary by reason of the king's hardness of heart, it is the hardness of heart that has the purpose of permitting Yahweh to multiply wonders. The plagues and wonders have a function independent of the exodus itself: to proclaim Yahweh, to let the Egyptians know that "I am Yahweh." This interpretation of the plagues too, then, is couched in its own literary form.

The third programmatic text, §2.1.9, contains Yahweh's instructions to Moses, who now makes ready to return from Midian to Egypt. Here we have a reference to the wonders that Yahweh has placed in Moses' hands. These "wonders" seem to be the signs of the staff that becomes a serpent, the hand that becomes leprous, and the water that changes to blood. When first introduced, these signs were intended to convince the Israelites that it was Yahweh who had sent Moses (§2.1.6). But here in §2.1.9, Yahweh broadens the use of the signs, prescribing that they be worked in the presence of the pharaoh in support of the Hebrews' petition for permission to leave Egypt. But Yahweh foresees that the signs will have no effect. It will be necessary to slay the pharaoh's firstborn son before he will permit the Israelites to depart. In view of the fact that this text does not envisage a series of plagues, but moves directly to the account of Yahweh's intent to slay the pharaoh's firstborn, it is possible that we are here dealing with the Elohist version of the liberation plan, and that it does not include an account of the plagues. Martin Noth, however, who finds no Elohist material in the accounts of the plagues, attributes this passage to the Yahwist tradition (*History,* 30: the list of Yahwist passages, and note 103). Georg Fohrer finds four Elohist plagues and attributes this text to that tradition (*Überlieferung,* 41 and the table on p. 124). This divergence of opinion indicates that literary analysis has not resolved all the problems that our text presents. However, it seems to me that the liberation plan in this text does not include the plagues, and at all events it fits in very well with an Elohist view of the exodus.

Just as there are two interpretations of the plagues—as we have seen in §§ 2.1.5 and 2.3.2—the actual accounts of the plagues, as well, take two forms. The Yahwist form develops as follows. (1) Yahweh entrusts Moses with a message for the pharaoh. The message is in two parts: it consists of a request that the pharaoh let the people go, and a threat of evil to come upon him in case he should refuse. (2) A description of the plague brought into effect. (3) The pharaoh's reaction. This reaction in some instances will be a concession, which will be withdrawn once the pressure of the plague abates.

The sacerdotal form can be outlined as follows: (1) Yahweh's command to Moses that Aaron extend his staff and thereby unleash the plague. (2) The execution of this command. In some cases, the magicians of Egypt duplicate the wonder, or seek unsuccessfully to do so. (3) The wonder has no effect on the pharaoh, whose heart—as we are told—has been hardened by Yahweh.

Some exegetes, in view of the common variants between the two accounts of the plagues of hail, locust, and darkness, suggest that we are dealing with a third form in these cases, and that this part of the account is Elohist. If so, this third form lacks clarity.

The accounts of the plagues are used by the redactors to develop various themes. One of these is the *rivalry* between Yahweh and the pharaoh. The pharaoh's magicians manage to duplicate Yahweh's wonders repeatedly, but at last have to confess their inability to continue the contest. This theme is subordinated to that of the profusion of the wonders, which is sacerdotal in origin.

Another important theme is that of *negotiation*—between Moses and the pharaoh to allow the Hebrews to leave Egypt in order to celebrate Yahweh's festival. Moses and the pharaoh emerge as powerful opposing personalities in these negotiations. This theme is part of the Yahwist interpretation of the plagues. The hardness of the pharaoh's heart prevails each time Moses eases the pressure on the king and his country—but his hardness of heart necessitates another plague, until the king at last grants permission for the Hebrews to depart.

Yahweh's differentiating between the Egyptians and the Israelites, with only the former suffering from the plagues, is related to the negotiation theme: it undermines the political support of the king's own followers. It is also connected with the sacerdotal theme that the monarch must learn that Yahweh is God.

It is obvious that the stories of the plagues were cherished by those who handed down the account of the exodus. The abundance of repetition and the length of the narrative are evidence of the eagerness with which it was transmitted. At the same time, however, this repetition and lengthiness compound the problem of the context of this transmission.

Johannes Pederson, in 1934, argued that the whole story of the exodus was composed as part of the annual Passover celebration ("Passahfest und Passahlegende"). The Israelites in Canaan, we are told, when they slaughtered the Passover lamb, recalled how Yahweh had scourged Egypt with the plagues, and had protected themselves by means of the blood of the lamb. Pederson's argument is important, because it reminds us that oral histories were transmitted only if they fulfilled a function in the life of a people. But the link between the plagues and the Passover is weak, as Eckart Otto has more recently demonstrated ("Erwägungen zum überlieferungsgeschichtlichen Ursprung und 'Sitz im Leben' des jahwistischen Plagenzyklus"). There are too many inconsistencies between the account and the celebration for it to be credible that the account took shape in the context of a festival.

Martin Buber thinks that the text on the plagues shows evidence of being a text produced in prophetic circles, highlighting the mission of the prophet to confront kings in the name of Yahweh and justice. According to Buber, this account is part of a whole group of stories of confrontations between famous kings and prophets, such as David and Nathan, Ahab and Elijah, Jeroboam II and Amos, Ahaz and Isaiah, Zedekiah and Jeremiah (Buber, *Moses,* 60–68). This conflict is one of the biblical expressions of a bitter class struggle in the history of Israel. On the one side was the state, whose supreme representative was the king. The state was maintained by tribute—taxes—collected from workers, most of whom were peasants. On the other side were the prophets, who spoke in the name of Yahweh, the God who had led the triumphal march of the slaves from Egypt and who now supported the peasants. Buber, in the account of the plagues, points to Moses' oft-repeated use of the prophetic formula, "This is the message of Yahweh. . . ."

There are important points of similarity between the account of the plagues and the prophetic histories, as well, among them those indicated by Buber. I propose the following solution. The social context of these accounts is indeed the need to maintain the morale of the Israelites in their recurrent struggles with Canaanite kings, who sought to subjugate them. With Mendenhall, Gottwald, and others, I hold that Israel was formed through a process of amalgamation of various peasant tribes in their uprisings against their urban exploiters (Mendenhall, "The Hebrew Conquest of Palestine;" idem, *Tenth Generation;* Gottwald, *Tribes of Yahweh*). The story of the exodus of the Levites from Egypt under the leadership of Moses and Yahweh served as an abiding inspiration for this peasant revolt. This ongoing struggle provided a favorable context for an enthusiastic account of the victory of Moses and Yahweh against the archenemy of the working sector of the population. Yahweh's contest with the king, and the long series of devastating plagues, would have been related in informal gatherings of the people, with amplification in the form of savory details regarding Yahweh's might and Moses' craft.

Evidently, all this raises questions about the *historical value* of these accounts: whether certain events in Egypt in fact occasioned the composition of these accounts. Here, let us first of all observe that the form of the accounts lacks verisimilitude. The representative of a group of subjects under hard labor would not easily have personal access to the king. Furthermore, in a state as efficient as the Egyptian, it is improbable that a leader as provocative as Moses would have been able to survive the acts of sabotage and terrorism that are narrated here. Yet it is only after the tenth plague, the darkness, that the king threatens Moses' life (Exod. 10:28). Given Moses' slight political support (see §§2.2.3 and 2.2.4), his physical elimination would have solved a goodly number of problems for the king, and this is what we would expect of a tyrant.

At the same time, as Greta Hort has so forcefully shown ("The Plagues of Egypt"), the actual content of the plagues reflects events that could well have occurred in Egypt. When there is heavy rainfall in the high country at the sources of the Nile, its waters become insalubrious, and have a red tint. The plague of frogs might well be a natural consequence of this contamination of the waters of the Nile. Livestock epidemics are frequent in any society without adequate veterinary medicine. And the plague of locusts is a phenomenon that still occurs in that region.

We may well imagine, then, that some of the plagues described in the book of Exodus did coincide with the Hebrews' struggle for liberation, and were considered, by Levite people and court alike, to be evidence of the intervention of Yahweh. It will never be possible to reconstruct the facts that made the exodus possible, but it appears likely that there were extraordinary phenomena that prepared the terrain. And in these phenomena Israel saw the hand of God in its liberation.

2.4.1 First Wonder: Serpents (Exod. 7:8–13)

Yahweh said to Moses and Aaron, "If Pharaoh says to you, 'Produce some marvel,' you must say to Aaron, 'Take your staff and throw it down in front of Pharaoh, and let it turn into a serpent.' " To Pharaoh, then, Moses and Aaron duly went, and they did as Yahweh commanded. Aaron threw down his staff in front of Pharaoh and his court, and it turned into a serpent. Then Pharaoh in his turn called for the sages and the sorcerers, and with their witchcraft the magicians of Egypt did the same. Each threw his staff down and these turned into serpents. But Aaron's staff swallowed up the staffs of the magicians. Yet Pharaoh's heart was stubborn and, as Yahweh had foretold, he would not listen to Moses and Aaron.

In its material content, what Yahweh commands here is not the unleashing of a plague upon the pharaoh, but the working of a wonder to show him that Moses and Aaron speak with authority. In its structure, this text belongs to the sacerdotal series: we have, first, Yahweh's command to Moses for Aaron with his staff, then the execution of the order, and finally the hardening of the pharaoh's heart. This last, of course, not only is not an obstacle to Yahweh's plans, but serves to provide the occasion for a multiplication of wonders.

The pharaoh has a surprise in store for Moses and Aaron. His magicians step forth at his call and seek to duplicate the wonder with their witchcraft. And they succeed! This is the first appearance of the theme of *rivalry*. The ultimate victory of Moses and Aaron in this context can be foreseen, of course, when Aaron's staff devours the staffs of the Egyptian magicians.

2.4.2 Second Wonder: Water Turned to Blood (Exod. 7:14–25)

2.4.2a YAHWEH'S MESSAGE (EXOD. 7:14–18)

Then Yahweh said to Moses, "Pharaoh is adamant. He refuses to let the people go. In the morning go to him as he makes his way to the water and wait for him by the bank of the river. In your hand take the staff that turned into a serpent. Say to him, 'Yahweh, the God of the Hebrews, has sent me to say: Let my people go to offer me worship in the wilderness. Now, so far you have not listened. Here is Yahweh's message: That I am Yahweh you shall learn by this: with the staff that is in my hand I will strike the water of the river and it shall be changed into blood. The fish in the river will die, and the river will smell so foul that the Egyptians will not want to drink the water of it.' "

This second wonder begins in the Yahwist form, with instructions to go before the king and demand the release of the Hebrews, with the threat of a plague in case of resistance on the part of the king. The wording of the threat of the plague, however, is in the sacerdotal form, as we may see from the sacerdotal plan of §2.3: that the pharaoh may know that "I am Yahweh."

Researchers and geographers have pointed out that, in the season when the rains commence in the region of the upper sources of the Nile, a noticeable change in the color of the Nile waters occurs, due to the earth swept along by the river. In years of especially heavy flooding, the effect is remarkable, and could be the natural basis for the story of this plague (Hort, "Plagues").

2.4.2b WATER BECOMES BLOOD (EXOD. 7:19–21)

Yahweh said to Moses, "Say this to Aaron, 'Take your staff and stretch out your hand over the waters of Egypt, over their rivers and their canals, their marshland, and all their reservoirs, and let them turn to blood throughout the land of Egypt, even down to the contents of every tub or jar.' " Moses and Aaron did as Yahweh commanded. He raised his staff and in the sight of Pharaoh and his court he struck the waters of the river, and all the water in the river changed to blood. The fish in the river died, and the river smelled so foul that the Egyptians found it impossible to drink its water. Throughout the land of Egypt there was blood.

This second instruction of Yahweh's to Moses follows the sacerdotal schema. Yahweh directs Moses to give Aaron orders to execute the wonder without warning the pharaoh of what is about to happen and without directing any petition to him.

The text betrays its composite nature in its ambiguity with respect to how much water became blood—that of the Nile only, or that of the whole country.

2.4.2c THE WONDER DUPLICATED (EXOD. 7:22–25)

But the magicians of Egypt used their witchcraft to do the same, so that Pharaoh's heart was stubborn and, as Yahweh had foretold, he would not listen to Moses and Aaron. Pharaoh turned away and went back into his palace, taking no notice even of this. Meanwhile, all the Egyptians dug holes along the banks of the river in search of drinking water; they found the water of the river impossible to drink. After Yahweh had struck the river, seven days passed.

The *contest* motif appears a second time. This time too the magicians manage to duplicate the wonder, although one might wonder where they have found the water to change into blood. But in any case the pharaoh can go home in peace, and not have to worry about the Hebrew "magicians."

One might think that the contamination of the sources of water would constitute a calamity of great magnitude. The account does not present it as such. The pharaoh, doubtless, can drink his wine, and the people will perhaps find water by poking in the mud along the river bank. Be this as it may, for the Yahwist the target of these blows is the pharaoh, not the people, and the contamination of the waters does not really affect the king, only the people, and so the plague remains ineffective. For the priest-redactors, what is important is not the power of the blows to affect the pharaoh, but the nature of the wonders. And yet these wonders are not matchless. The Egyptian magicians can do the same thing.

2.4.3 Third Wonder: Frogs (Exod. 7:26–8:11)

2.4.3a YAHWEH'S MESSAGE (EXOD. 7:26–29)

Then Yahweh said to Moses, "Go to Pharaoh and say to him, 'This is Yahweh's message: Let my people go to offer me worship. If you refuse to let them go, know that I will plague the whole of your country with frogs. The river will swarm with them; they will make their way into your palace, into your bedroom, onto your bed, into the houses of your courtiers and of your subjects, into your ovens, into your kneading bowls. The frogs will even climb all over you, over your courtiers, and over all your subjects.' "

It might be thought that the multiplication of the frogs would not be as threatening as the contamination of the water. But the foregoing account did not treat the bloody water as a plague, and allowed the pharaoh to return home unconcerned.

Here, for the first time, we come upon the verb "to strike"—*măgaph*. (The English word "plague" is derived from the Greek *plēgē*, likewise meaning "blow" or "misfortune.") Perhaps this wonder is a more serious blow than the one preceding it because the frogs actually approach the king's bed. They "hit home," we might say.

This introduction to the plague of the frogs follows the Yahwist schema: Yahweh sends Moses to the king with the demand that he permit the departure of the Hebrews, with a threat in case he does not comply.

2.4.3b THE WONDER DUPLICATED (EXOD. 8:1–3)

Yahweh said to Moses, "Say this to Aaron, 'Stretch out your hand, with your staff, over the rivers, the canals, the marshland, and make frogs swarm all over the land of Egypt.' " So Aaron stretched out his hand over the waters of Egypt, and the frogs came up and covered the land of Egypt. But the magicians did the same with their witchcraft, and made frogs swarm all over the land of Egypt.

This appears to be a new introduction to the same plague, following the sacerdotal schema, in which the king is not advised of the plague that is about to come upon him. As in the case of the two previous wonders, there is a contest with the magicians of Egypt, who manage, by their arts, to perform the same wonder. But the king evidently remains unmoved: the account does not give his expected reaction. The evidence seems to show that what Moses and Aaron have done is just a magic trick.

2.4.3c A PROMISE MADE AND BROKEN (EXOD. 8:4–11)

Pharaoh summoned Moses and Aaron. "Entreat Yahweh," he said, "to rid me and my subjects of the frogs, and I promise to let the people go and offer sacrifice to Yahweh." Moses answered Pharaoh, "Take this chance to get the better of me! When I pray on your account and for your courtiers, and for your subjects, what time am I to fix for the frogs to leave you and your subjects and your houses, and stay in the river?" "Tomorrow," Pharaoh said. "It shall be as you say," answered Moses. "By this you shall learn that Yahweh our God has no equal. The frogs will go from you and your palaces, your courtiers and your subjects; they will stay in the river." When Moses and Aaron had gone from Pharaoh's presence, Moses pleaded with Yahweh about the frogs with which he had afflicted Pharaoh. And Yahweh granted Moses' prayer: in house and courtyard and field the frogs died. They piled them up in heaps and the land reeked of them. But as soon as he saw that relief had been granted, Pharaoh became adamant again and, as Yahweh had foretold, he refused to listen to Moses and Aaron.

Here for the first time we have the theme of *negotiation*. The pharaoh yields to the pressure of the multitudes of frogs, and gives permission for the Hebrews' departure as demanded by Moses. Surprisingly, the king asks the Hebrews to pray to Yahweh on his behalf to rid him of the frogs—a remarkable advance over his previous attitude, when he had said, "Who is Yahweh, that I should listen to him and let Israel go? I know nothing of Yahweh, and I will not let Israel go" (Exod. 5:2).

The pharaoh hopes that the frogs will be withdrawn in exchange for the permission granted, and Moses accepts. (The text suggests that the court magicians can multiply frogs, but not eliminate them.) But when Moses manages to eliminate them, the pharaoh hardens his heart and retracts the permission he had conceded under duress. This part of the account of the frogs follows the Yahwist schema, to which the theme of negotiation belongs.

The expression "Take this chance to get the better of me!" (v. 6) translates the somewhat unusual Hebrew expression *hitpāer alaī*—literally, "Glorify yourself in me" (see Childs, *Exodus,* 128).

2.4.4 Fourth Wonder: Mosquitoes (Exod. 8:12–15)

Then Yahweh said to Moses, "Say this to Aaron, 'Stretch out your rod and strike the dust on the ground: throughout the land of Egypt it will turn into mosquitoes.' " Aaron stretched out his hand, with his staff, and struck the dust on the ground. The mosquitoes attacked men and beasts; throughout the land of Egypt the dust on the ground turned into mosquitoes. The magicians with their witchcraft tried to produce the mosquitoes and failed. The mosquitoes attacked men and beasts. So the magicians said to Pharaoh, "This is the finger of God." But Pharaoh's heart was stubborn and, as Yahweh had foretold, he refused to listen to Moses and Aaron.

This brief account follows the sacerdotal schema entirely, as does the first wonder, that of the serpents. There is no negotiation with the king—only a demonstration of Yahweh's superior might. The *kinnīm* produced when Aaron strikes the dust are insects whose exact type cannot be pinpointed. The ancient Syriac and Aramaic versions (Targum Onkelos) translates "lice." The Septuagint translates *sknips,* an insect that lives under the bark of trees.

Moses and Aaron do not meet with the king. But he understands that he is involved in a power struggle, and uses his magicians to "demystify" the power of Yahweh. But they acknowledge their defeat and confess that this wonder can be produced only by the finger of God, thus conceding the Hebrews' point that heaven is on their side—that Yahweh is more powerful than the pharaoh and his gods.

Greta Hort points out a possible connection among the disasters recounted in the text. If the water has turned putrid, the dead fish have rendered it fetid, it stands to reason that frogs would have come up to the houses in their attempt to escape. If it was a microbe that has infected the fish, then the frogs can well be carrying that. Then the mountains of frog carcasses, amassing in the space of a few days, can have infested the very dust of the earth, multiplying clouds of noisome insects. Hort's reconstruction is ingenious, but it loses probability in light of the conflation of the final text, which combines two accounts in which the sequence of plagues is not the same.

2.4.5 Fifth Wonder: Gadflies (Exod. 8:16–28)

2.4.5a YAHWEH'S MESSAGE (EXOD. 8:16–19)

Then Yahweh said to Moses, "Get up early in the morning and wait for Pharaoh as he makes his way to the water. Say to him, 'This is Yahweh's message: Let my people go to offer me worship. But if you do not let my people go, I shall send gadflies on you, on your courtiers and your palaces. The houses of the Egyptians will be infested with them, and even the very ground they stand on. But I shall set apart the land of Goshen, where my people live, on that day; there will be no gadflies there, and so you may know that I, Yahweh, am in the midst of the land. I shall make a distinction between my people and yours. This sign shall take place tomorrow.' "

The account of this wonder is Yahwist in its entirety. Up to this point, the first wonder (the serpents) and the fourth (the mosquitoes) have followed the sacerdotal form, whereas the second (the blood) and the third (the frogs) have combined the Yahwist and sacerdotal forms.

It should be noted here how the target of the plague is specified: the king, his courtiers, and his people—a tripartite division that we have already encountered in the account of the plague of frogs. This division is a synthetic description of the social organization of a tributary society such as that of Egypt or that of the city-states of Canaan. In these societies the producers are the peasants. The peasants live in villages, and have their own government, which is in the hands of the most respected of their number, the "elders." Bonds of kinship are basic to the political structure of the village, and social problems are resolved *en famille,* or at least in the extended family. These are the "people," in Egypt as in Canaan.

The state, for its part, is personalized in the king, who in Egypt is considered the offspring of God and himself a god. As titular lord of the whole land, and of all its inhabitants, he can demand for himself a part of the produce of the land and a part of the labor of the peasants. In exchange for what he receives from the peasants, he offers them protection from their enemies, distribution of grain reserves in years of scarcity, organization of labor on the canals and dykes, and maintenance of the national religion. In his person we find a concentration of the dominant class. The other group mentioned here, the courtiers, are the persons dependent on the king for their sustention. They comprise the bureaucracy of state, and include the army, the priests, the sages, and the tax collectors.

The Israelite revolution in Canaan had to have the support of the peasant population. If a king succeeded in convincing a people that it would benefit more from the stability he offered than from the liberty offered by the revolutionary alliance, Israel's strength would be undermined. Awareness of this conflict between two antagonistic class projects has left its mark on the accounts of the plagues, blurred though its traces be by the nationalistic reworking of level three and the priestly reworking of level four. In our account, Moses seeks to destroy the king's hegemony in the king-courtiers-people bloc. In particular, he seeks to gain the people, the sector that will contribute to the group that will flee from Egypt with him (Exod. 12:38). In this fifth plague there are as yet no cracks in the royal monolith. But the tripartite social analysis is evidence of redactors' awareness of the problem confronted by Moses in Egypt and the Israelite tribes in Canaan.

The type of insect (*'arob*) in this text, too, cannot be identified. They are probably a mixture of insects whose multiplication is particularly troublesome.

Here for the first time we have the theme of distinction between Israelites and Egyptians. Israel lives in the land of Goshen, and Goshen is not affected by the insects. The explicit purpose of this distinction is that the pharaoh may come to realize that "I am Yahweh." But we may also infer another motive— recovery of the support of the Israelite elders, who withdrew their support from Moses when the pharaoh made their work harder. Still another purpose would be to impress the peasant populations that did not live in Goshen.

2.4.5b NEGOTIATION (EXOD. 8:20–25)

Yahweh did this, and great swarms of gadflies found their way into Pharaoh's palace, into the houses of his courtiers, and into all the land of Egypt, and ruined the country.

Pharaoh summoned Moses and Aaron. "Go," he said, "and offer sacrifice to your God, but in this country!" "That would not be right," Moses answered. "We sacrifice to Yahweh our God animals which Egyptians count it sacrilege to slaughter. If we offer in front of the Egyptians sacrifices that outrage them, will they not stone us? We must make a three days' journey into the wilderness to offer sacrifice to Yahweh our God, as he has commanded us." Pharaoh replied, "I will let you go to offer sacrifice to Yahweh your God in the wilderness, provided you do not go far. And intercede for me." "The moment I leave you," said Moses, "I will pray to Yahweh. Tomorrow morning the gadflies will leave Pharaoh and his courtiers and his subjects. Only, Pharaoh must not play false again, and refuse to let the people go to offer sacrifice to Yahweh."

Once more Moses and the pharaoh negotiate. The repeated lesson of the accounts of the Yahwist form is that there is progress in the negotiations only when the pharaoh is under pressure. Faced with the plague of insects, he makes new concessions—a bit more precise than the ones he made in the plague of the frogs. First he says that the Hebrews may leave, but they may not go out into the wilderness. Moses' reply reveals his agility as a negotiator. It is not clear what the problem would be with Israelite sacrifices in Egypt. Perhaps this is only a pretext. In any case, the pharaoh admits its validity and grants permission for the departure, under the proviso that they not go very far into the wilderness. Recalling the pharaoh's change of heart when he was saved from the frogs, Moses is wary. He has no alternative, however, but to withdraw the insects, in the hope that this time the king will keep his word.

2.4.5c PERMISSION DENIED AGAIN (EXOD. 8:26–28)

So Moses went out of Pharaoh's presence and prayed to Yahweh. And Yahweh did as Moses asked; the gadflies left Pharaoh and his courtiers and his subjects; not one remained. But Pharaoh was adamant this time too and did not let the people go.

As happened with the plague of frogs, the king has once more hardened his position when the pressure of the plague of insects has abated. This account is calculated to strengthen the Israelites' will to perseverance in the revolution, in the face of opportunistic concessions on the part of their Canaanite lords. We may suppose that, in their struggles, the peasants have attempted to pressure these rulers into reducing their tribute of grain, and that the kings may indeed have made such a promise—only to demand great quantities when they are once again in control of the situation. The pharaoh is pictured for the Israelite rebels as a typical king, and this picture serves to teach them that they must not return to a social structure where they would be dependent upon the kings of Canaan.

2.4.6 Sixth Wonder: Livestock Killed by Pestilence (Exod. 9:1–7)

Then Yahweh said to Moses, "Go to Pharaoh and say to him, 'This is the message of Yahweh, the God of the Hebrews: Let my people go to offer me worship. If you refuse to let them go and detain them any longer, you will find that the hand of Yahweh will fall on your livestock in the fields, horse and donkey and camel, herd and flock, with a deadly plague. Yahweh will discriminate betweeen the livestock of Israel and of Egypt: nothing shall die of all that belongs to the sons of Israel. Yahweh has fixed the hour. Tomorrow, he has said, Yahweh will carry out this threat in all the land.' " Next day Yahweh kept his word; all the Egyptians' livestock died, but none owned by the sons of Israel died. Pharaoh had inquiries made, but it was true: none was dead of the livestock owned by the sons of Israel. But Pharaoh became adamant again and did not let the people go.

This plague, once more, follows the Yahwist schema, in which Moses gives the pharaoh a warning before unleashing the plague. Unlike the Yahwist accounts of the plagues of frogs and gadflies, however, there is in this case no negotiation with the king. The very nature of the plague—conceived as an overwhelming disaster, killing the livestock very quickly—leaves the pharaoh no grounds for petitioning relief. "Next day . . . all the Egyptians' livestock died. . . ."

Once more we have the theme of the distinction between Israelites and Egyptians, which appeared for the first time in the plague of the gadflies.

Some commentators have wondered how it could have happened that, in this account, the pestilence wipes out the Egyptians' livestock, and yet, later, the plague of hail still finds animals to kill. Perhaps this problem has been foreseen in the composition of our present account: it is specified that "the hand of Yahweh will fall on your livestock in the fields," and so perhaps we may suppose that livestock in stables or pens were spared.

2.4.7 Seventh Wonder: Boils (Exod. 9:8-12)

Yahweh said to Moses and Aaron, "Take handfuls of soot from the kiln, and before the eyes of Pharaoh let Moses throw it in the air. It shall spread like fine dust over the whole land of Egypt and bring out boils that break into sores on man and beast all over the land of Egypt." So they took soot from the kiln and stood in front of Pharaoh, and Moses threw it in the air. And on man and beast it brought out boils breaking into sores. And the magicians could not face Moses, because the magicians were covered with boils like all the other Egyptians. But Yahweh made Pharaoh's heart stubborn and, as Yahweh had foretold, he refused to listen to them.

The account of the boils follows the sacerdotal schema. Yahweh orders the action, and Moses executes it without warning the king and awaiting his reaction.

This is the last time that the theme of the rivalry with the magicians appears in the accounts. Their defeat at the hands of Moses is complete. With obvious humor and satisfaction, the account indicates that they could not present themselves in court because of their boils.

For the first time the hardening of the pharaoh's heart is attributed to the action of Yahweh. It has already been announced in the sacerdotal plan for liberation (§2.3: Exod. 7:3) that Yahweh would play this role, and thus have the opportunity to multiply wonders.

Hort believes that this ulcerous affliction would be anthrax or carbuncles, and that it would have followed upon the bites of the insects that have been infected by the decaying carcasses of heaps of diseased frogs.

2.4.8 Eighth Wonder: Hail (Exod. 9:13-35)

2.4.8a YAHWEH'S MESSAGE (EXOD. 9:13-21)

Then Yahweh said to Moses, "Get up early in the morning and present yourself to Pharaoh. Say to him, 'This is the message of Yahweh, the God of the Hebrews: Let my people go to offer me worship. This time I mean to send all my plagues on you and your courtiers and your subjects so that you shall learn that there is no one like me in the whole world. Had I stretched out my hand to strike you and your subjects with pestilence, you would have been swept from the earth. But I have let you live for this: to make you see my power and to have my name published throughout all the earth. Highhanded with my people still, you will not let them go. Tomorrow, therefore, at about this time, I will let fall so great a storm of hail as was never known in Egypt from the day of its foundation. So now have your livestock, and everything that is yours in the fields put under cover: on man and beast, on all that remains in the fields and is not brought indoors, the hail will fall and they will die.' " Some of Pharaoh's courtiers, terrified by Yahweh's threat, brought their slaves and livestock indoors, but those who disregarded Yahweh's threat left their slaves and livestock in the fields.

The extensive account of the hail follows neither the Yahwist nor the sacerdotal schema in their purity. But it is very similar to the Yahwist: Moses warns the monarch before unleashing the plague, thus giving him the opportunity to grant the workers' petition.

The theme of a distinction of persons takes on a new form. This time there is a distinction even among the king's courtiers—between those who fear the word of Yahweh and those who do not. Each of these two groups has its workers and livestock, so that the distinction here is not one of class, but of attitude toward the God of the Hebrews. At last we discern a crack in the solidarity of the state bureaucratic class.

Behind this account stands the experience of the Israelite revolution in Canaan, where certain sectors of state bureaucracies were allied with the peasant uprising. The most important case was the adherence of the city of Gibeon to the Israelite alliance against the royal cities of the south of Canaan (Josh. 9).

Pharaoh's courtiers, however, faced with the peril of the hail, do not go this far; they do not actually join Moses and the undertaking pursued by him and his class. They do, however, respect it, and place their personal interests, threatened by the violence predicted in Yahweh's message, ahead of their class solidarity with the pharaoh.

The phrase translated, "Had I stretched out my hand," is in the contrary-to-fact construction because of its context. It was something that Yahweh could have done, but did not do. Some interpreters think that the expression is a remnant of an account of a plague that actually did come upon human beings, the one mentioned in Psalm 78:50 (Loewenstamm, "An Observation on Source Criticism of the Plague Pericope [Ex. 7–11]"). Its morphology would admit of the meaning, "for now I shall stretch out my hand," but of course the present context precludes this translation.

2.4.8b DEVASTATION OF THE PLAGUE (EXOD. 9:22–26)

Yahweh said to Moses, "Stretch out your hand toward heaven so that hail may fall on the whole land of Egypt, on man and beast and all that grows in the fields in the land of Egypt." Moses stretched out his staff toward heaven, and Yahweh thundered and rained down hail. Lightning struck the earth. Yahweh rained down hail on the land of Egypt. The hail fell, and lightning flashing in the midst of it, a greater storm of hail than had ever been known in Egypt since it first became a nation. Throughout the land of Egypt the hail struck down everything in the fields, man and beast. It struck all the crops in the fields, and shattered every tree in the fields. Only in the land of Goshen where the Hebrews lived, was there no hail.

This second introduction to the plague of the hail appears to be more in the sacerdotal than in the Yahwist form. The order is given simply to act—not to enter into negotiations with the king. But we would expect Aaron to figure in the sacerdotal form, and he does not. The staff is in the hand of Moses. Some interpreters find this to be evidence of the hand of the Elohist in the account of this plague. To me, however, it seems merely a modification of the Yahwist form. I find no evidence of the hand of the northerners anywhere in the text on the plagues.

The theme of a distinction of persons is developed here, just as it had been in the narratives of the plagues of the frogs and the pestilence among the livestock. This time, however, the distinction is "national"—it is a distinction between the inhabitants of Goshen and the inhabitants of the rest of the country. This reflects level three of the account, in which nationality is an important factor.

2.4.8c NEGOTIATION (EXOD. 9:27–30)

Pharaoh sent for Moses and Aaron. "This time," he said, "I admit my fault. Yahweh is in the right; I and my subjects are in the wrong. Entreat Yahweh to stop the thunder and hail; I promise to let you go, and you shall stay here no longer." Moses answered him, "The moment I leave the city I will stretch out my hands to Yahweh. The thunder will stop, and there will be no more hail, so that you may know that the earth belongs to Yahweh. But as for you and your courtiers, I know very well that you have no fear yet of Yahweh our God."

The negotiation theme, which we have seen in association with the Yahwist form of these accounts, reappears here. The pharaoh makes a surprising confession of sin: Yahweh has been just (in seeking to redress the people's situation of oppression), and the pharaoh—and his subjects!—have shown themselves to be unjust (in resisting this liberation and maintaining the oppression). The pharaoh's inclusion of "my subjects" is an instance of the tactic of division. A people is divided in two, by placing on one side "one's own," joined with the sovereign in virtue of their national identity, and on the other side "the others," "foreigners." The purpose is to avoid having "one's own" people find security and identity in a class solidarity that transcends nationalistic loyalties.

Moses, prototype of the revolutionary Israelite and prophet of Yahweh, understands that the pharaoh's confession is but a manifestation of opportunism. As in the previous instances, the pharaoh is not yet ready to acknowledge the power of Yahweh and the Israelite people.

2.4.8d A PROMISE BROKEN AGAIN (EXOD. 9:31-35)

> *The flax and the barley were ruined, since the barley was in the ear and the flax budding. The wheat and the spelt, being late crops, were not destroyed. Moses left Pharaoh and went out of the city. He stretched out his hands to Yahweh and the thunder and the hail stopped and the rain no longer poured down on the earth. When Pharaoh saw that rain and hail and thunder had stopped, he sinned yet again. He became adamant, he and his courtiers. The heart of Pharaoh was stubborn and, as Yahweh had foretold through Moses, he did not let the sons of Israel go.*

The parenthetical note on the harvest destroyed by the hail is intended to explain how there can have been something left to be eaten later by locusts. For those looking for historical data, this indication would place the present plague in February or March, before the wheat had ripened.

As always, the account ends with the pharaoh's hardness of heart. He retracts what he has said under pressure of the plague of hail.

What is new in this case is the intransigence of his courtiers as well. Surely the experience was a familiar one for the Israelite revolution. The interests of bureaucracy were very closely connected with those of monarchy. The work of rereading these accounts of the plagues in Egypt shows the mark of an experience of centuries of struggle against the kings of Canaan.

2.4.9 Ninth Wonder: Locusts (Exod. 10:1-20)

This is a lengthy account, as was the previous one. And it contains new complications. Pressure is bursting the unity of the hegemonic bloc over which the pharaoh presides. Now he must negotiate not only under pressure of the plagues, but under pressure from his own bureaucracy as well.

The structure of the account is, in general terms, Yahwist, and it corresponds to the Yahwist stratum in the composition of the Pentateuch. But the form of the account has grown complex with the enfeeblement of the tyrant.

2.4.9a YAHWEH'S MESSAGE (EXOD. 10:1-6)

> *Then Yahweh said to Moses, "Go to Pharaoh, for it is I who have made his heart and his courtiers stubborn, so that I could work these signs of mine among them; so that you can tell your sons and your grandsons how I made fools of the Egyptians and what signs I performed among them, to let you know that I am Yahweh." So Moses and Aaron went to Pharaoh. They said to him, "This is the message of Yahweh, the God of the Hebrews, 'How much longer will you refuse to submit to me? Let my people go to offer me worship. If you refuse to let my people go, then tomorrow I will send locusts over your country. They shall cover the surface of the soil so thick that the soil will not be seen. They shall devour*

the remainder that is left to you, all that has survived from the hail; they shall devour all your trees growing in the fields; they shall fill your palaces, the houses of your courtiers, the houses of all the Egyptians. Your forefathers and their ancestors will never have seen the like since first they lived in the country.' " Then Moses turned away and left Pharaoh's presence.

Contrary to the pattern of the Yahwist form in earlier texts, the present structure separates the instructions to Moses for his meeting with the pharaoh from the words actually used in addressing the king. This serves to introduce the theme that God is sending the plagues as signs that the Israelites may recount to their children.

There is an evident relationship here with the sacerdotal theme of the multiplication of wonders to let it be known that "I am Yahweh"; but the specifically catechetical interest is rather the same as we find in texts of the seventh-century reform. See, for example, Deuteronomy 6:20–25 and Joshua 4:21–24, both of which are Deuteronomic texts with this catechetical interest. It is the only time in the accounts of the plagues that this interest is manifested, and may be evidence of a rereading of the account in the seventh century B.C.— a rereading that was somewhat superficial and left little evidence of its work.

Moses and Aaron place before the pharaoh the same, tireless demand: that he release the people for Yahweh's festival.

2.4.9b NEGOTIATION (EXOD. 10:7–11)

And Pharaoh's courtiers said to him, "How much longer is this man to be the cause of our trouble? Let the people go to offer worship to Yahweh their God. Do you not understand that Egypt is now on the brink of ruin?"

So Moses and Aaron were brought back to Pharaoh. "You may go," he said to them, "and offer worship to Yahweh your God. But who are to go?" "We shall take our young men and our old men," Moses answered. "We shall take our sons and daughters, our flocks and our herds, because for us it is a feast of Yahweh." "May Yahweh be with you if ever I let you and your little ones go!" Pharaoh retorted. "It is plain you are up to no good. Oh no! You men may go and offer worship to Yahweh, since that is what you wanted." And with that they were dismissed from the presence of Pharaoh.

This negotiating session before the onset of the plague is a novelty. The Yahwist form is altered, in view of a change in the concrete situation. The unity of the pharaoh's political bases is beginning to crack. The bureaucrats, some of whom took measures to protect their livestock in the face of the threat of hail, now present themselves *en bloc* before the king to try to pressure him to accede to Moses' demand. The tyrant's defeat is at hand.

For the first time, the pharaoh summons Moses and Aaron for a negotiating session before the actual onset of the plague. Any concession he may make must be implemented immediately, and so he takes care to specify his concessions exactly. Precisely who will depart? Now it is Moses' turn to take a hard line. He will not accept permission to depart without all his people and all their possessions. This hard line taken by Moses is the pharaoh's opportunity to unmask Moses' hidden intentions, and thereby (as we may suppose) appease his courtiers.

Other Egyptians do not appear in this scene, although they too are suffering Yahweh's blows. This fits the context: they cannot pressure the king. Only afterward will they indicate, by their actions, their fear of or sympathy with the Hebrews who will join Moses in the exodus—especially in terms of the things they will "lend" them.

2.4.9c DEVASTATION OF THE LOCUSTS (EXOD. 10:12-15)

Then Yahweh said to Moses, "Stretch out your hand over the land of Egypt to bring the locusts. Let them invade the land of Egypt and devour all its greenstuff, all that the hail has left." And over the land of Egypt Moses stretched his staff, and Yahweh brought up an east wind over the land and it blew all that day and night. By morning, the east wind had brought the locusts.

The locusts invaded the whole land of Egypt. On the whole territory of Egypt they fell, in numbers so great that such swarms had never been seen before, nor would be again. They covered the surface of the soil till the ground was black with them. They devoured all the greenstuff in the land and all the fruit of the trees that the hail had left. No green was left on tree or plant in the fields throughout the land of Egypt.

As with the hail, Moses invokes the plague of locusts by using his staff. In itself, a plague of locusts is not extraordinary in this part of the world, and so our text takes care to emphasize that this one is of prodigious proportions.

2.4.9d ENDING OF THE PLAGUE (EXOD. 10:16-20)

Pharaoh sent urgently for Moses and Aaron. "I have sinned against Yahweh your God," he said, "and against yourselves. Forgive my sin, I implore you, this once, and entreat Yahweh your God just to rid me of this deadly plague." So Moses left Pharaoh's presence and interceded with Yahweh. Then Yahweh made the wind veer till it blew so strongly from the west that it caught up the locusts and carried them off toward the Sea of Reeds. There was not one locust left in the whole land of Egypt. But Yahweh made Pharaoh's heart stubborn, and he did not let the sons of Israel go.

As on several previous occasions, the king sends for Moses and Aaron when he sees that he is under the scourge of Yahweh. This time he resumes the confession he has made on the occasion of the hail, adding that his sin is not only against Yahweh, but "against yourselves"—against the people, perhaps. He promises nothing specific, but his acceptance of Moses' conditions seems implicit in his confession. In any case Moses withdraws the locusts from the land of Egypt.

The hardening of the pharaoh's heart is attributed to Yahweh—the sacerdotal interpretation. In nine meetings with Moses, the pharaoh has not budged from his intention to hold the Israelites back. But his political base has commenced to break up and he will not be able to resist much longer.

2.4.10 Tenth Wonder: The Darkness; Negotiations Broken Off (Exod. 10:21–11:8)

With the plague of the darkness, the cycle of plagues and wonders against the pharaoh comes to a close. But the failure of the negotiations involving these means of forceful persuasion prepares the ground for the departure from Egypt, which will take place on a night when the king's son, and the firstborn of all other Egyptian families as well, will die. The present unit, then, serves both to close the cycle of wonders and plagues, and to prepare for the night of the exodus. This is why its form follows none of the schemata that we have recognized in the earlier accounts.

From the importance accorded the negotiations in this, their final session, it is evident that the redaction of this unit is due principally to the Yahwist redactors. They were the ones to introduce this theme of negotiation into these accounts.

The last negotiating session with the pharaoh is divided into two parts, and has two conclusions. In the first part, the pharaoh expels Moses and warns him never to seek another audience. In the second part, it is Moses who departs in annoyance at the intransigence of the king. It is as if the same scene were played twice, first from the pharaoh's viewpoint, and then from Moses'. In both viewpoints, the interview ends without the usual petition by the king that Moses withdraw the plague, and without the latter's concession to that effect. Nor does the usual formula concerning the hardening of the heart of the pharaoh appear, although the king's attitude demonstrates his continued intransigence.

Materially, the killing of the firstborn, proclaimed during the days of darkness, is a plague. But formally, we have now emerged from the series of wonders and plagues.

2.4.10a THREE DAYS OF DARKNESS (EXOD. 10:21–23)

Then Yahweh said to Moses, "Stretch out your hand toward heaven, and let darkness, darkness so thick that it can be felt, cover the land of Egypt." So Moses stretched out his hand toward heaven, and for three days there was deep darkness over the whole land of Egypt. No one could see anyone else or move about for three days, but where the sons of Israel lived there was light for them.

In Egypt, in summer, there are occasionally great windstorms that carry clouds of sand from the desert, and bring with them an insupportable heat. Our account may be indicative of one such storm, of a singular intensity.

As on several previous occasions, here again we have the theme of a distinction drawn by Yahweh between Egyptians and Israelites. The land of Goshen is not mentioned, and perhaps some other geographical divisioning is implicit in the text, which would recall levels one and two of Exodus.

2.4.10b FINAL MEETING OF MOSES AND THE PHARAOH (EXOD. 10:24-29)

Pharaoh summoned Moses. "Go and offer worship to Yahweh," he said, "but your flocks and herds must remain here. Your children may go with you too." Moses replied, "But you must let us have means of offering sacrifices and holocausts to Yahweh our God. Our livestock, too, must go with us; not one head of cattle must be left behind: it must be from our livestock that we provide for the worship of Yahweh our God; until we reach the place, we do not know ourselves what worship we shall have to offer Yahweh."

But Yahweh made Pharaoh's heart stubborn, and he refused to let them go. Pharaoh said to Moses, "Out of my sight! Take care! Never appear before me again, for on the day you do, you die!" Moses replied, "You yourself have said it: never again shall I appear before you."

As on previous occasions, the pharaoh summons Moses when he feels himself under pressure. Now he makes a new concession. The women and children may leave with the men. Only the livestock must remain, to insure the workers' return. But Moses maintains his hard line. He demands all or nothing. The animals also must leave. Moses foresees that the people will have need of them in the desert, and, besides, it is not false to say that they are leaving in order to offer sacrifice to God.

The king's displeasure is understandable. He has yielded a great deal more than he could have foreseen when the plagues began. To permit the workers to leave with their livestock would be to grant them safe conduct to withdraw from Egyptian society, where they performed useful service. And the tyrant is also thinking of the effect that such an example would have on other workers who for one reason or another do not join Moses. The Egyptian classist society would not be able to absorb a successful rebellion on the part of its oppressed class. And his response is a final no. The pharaoh is not willing to negotiate any longer. If Moses persists in his demands, he will die.

2.4.10c SPOLIATION OF THE EGYPTIANS (EXOD. 11:1–3)

> *Then Yahweh said to Moses, "One disaster more I shall bring on Pharaoh and on Egypt, just one. After this he will let you go from here. . . . Indeed, he will drive you out! Instruct the people that every man is to ask his neighbor, every woman hers, for silver ornaments and gold." And Yahweh gave the people prestige in the eyes of the Egyptians, while Moses himself was a man of great importance in the land of Egypt, and of high prestige with Pharaoh's courtiers and with the people.*

This paragraph interrupts the final negotiating session between Moses and the pharaoh. It recounts instructions given earlier by Moses to the people, and their implementation.

This spoliation of the Egyptians has already been contemplated, in the liberation strategy as first formulated (§2.1.5). The travelers will have need of these articles, as a reserve with which to engage in trade when they use up the supplies they have taken with them from their own fields. According to §2.1.5, the Israelites will also obtain clothing from their neighbors for the journey.

All this has been possible because "Yahweh gave the people prestige in the eyes of the Egyptians." According to what has been said about the attitude of some of the king's courtiers when confronted with the plagues of hail and locusts, it is understandable that the courtiers, whose class interests are contrary to those of the workers, would nevertheless agree to supply, out of respect and fear, what is necessary for their departure. Among Egyptian laborers, however, there would be genuine sympathy for the rebels. Some of them will actually join Moses in the exodus (Exod. 12:38). Indeed, on level one, the subject of the exodus will not be called "Israelites": this is an identification that presupposes reception of the account by the Israelite tribes in Canaan, and hence a term introduced on level two of the account. In addition to those who will join the exodus, there would be those who are not ready to confront the uncertainties of life in the desert, but who sympathize with the rebels' revolutionary objectives. For them the delivery of silver and gold objects and clothing will be a gesture of solidarity.

Moses, the leader of the revolution, is a person of great reputation in Egypt, as well with the king's courtiers (the state bureaucracy) as among the people. The reasons for this respect require no further explanation.

2.4.10d YAHWEH'S MESSAGE (EXOD. 11:4–8)

> *Moses said, "This is Yahweh's message, 'Toward midnight I shall pass through Egypt. All the first-born in the land of Egypt shall die: from the first-born of Pharaoh, heir to his throne, to the first-born of the maidservant at the mill, and all the first-born of the cattle. And throughout the land of Egypt there shall be such a wailing as never was heard before, nor*

will be again. But against the sons of Israel, against man or beast, never a dog shall bark, so that you may know that Yahweh discriminates between Egypt and Israel. Then all these courtiers of yours will come down to me and bow low before me and say: Go away, you and all the people who follow you! After this, I shall go.' " And, hot with anger, Moses left Pharaoh's presence.

After recounting the affair of the plunder of the Egyptians, the account returns to Moses' interview with the pharaoh. In §2.4.10b we have had the account of the breaking off of the negotiations, and now we hear what can only be understood as their continuation, ending in another version of the break off, this time on Moses' initiative alone. Moses declares that there will be no longer any need for negotiations, because, with the massacre of the firstborn, the very courtiers of the pharaoh will entreat Moses to be on his way. Without the support of his bureaucracy, the pharaoh will have no recourse but to permit the exodus of the workers.

"Go away, you and all the people who follow you!" Our attention is arrested by such a vague identification of the subject of the exodus: Moses and "all the people who follow" him. On levels three (the monarchical) and four (the sacerdotal), those who flee Egypt are "Israelites." The present form of identification is thus an echo of the fact that these "people of various sorts" (Exod. 12:38) are not yet a nation. It is, hence, an echo of levels one and two.

2.4.11 Conclusion of the Wonders and Plagues (Exod. 11:9-10)

Then Yahweh said to Moses, "Pharaoh will not listen to you; so that my wonders may be multiplied in the land of Egypt." All these wonders Moses and Aaron worked in the presence of Pharaoh. But Yahweh made Pharaoh's heart stubborn, and he did not let the sons of Israel leave his country.

This summary of the accounts of the wonders of Yahweh resumes the sacerdotal interpretation (§2.3.1) that the hardening of the pharaoh's heart was done only in order to permit Yahweh to multiply the wonders.

2.5 VICTORY OVER THE PHARAOH AND FLIGHT FROM EGYPT (EXOD. 12:1-13:16)

The account of the confrontation with the pharaoh reaches its climactic moment with his decision to permit the departure of Moses and those following him. This is the triumph of the movement that began with the request for a holiday to celebrate Yahweh's festival in the desert. Matters have never come to an armed confrontation with the king. But this does not mean that there has been no suffering in the struggle. An intensified work load had to be borne.

Then there were the moments of apparent failure, when the magicians of Egypt managed to duplicate the wonders of Moses and Aaron. Now triumph comes, suddenly, in the night, when the pharaoh's courtiers pressure him to let the workers go, knowing that they will probably not return from Yahweh's festival.

Triumph in an unequal struggle like this one is indeed the occasion for festival, and will have to be commemorated, lest the victors forget "where they have come from," and what their freedom has cost—and lest they forget Yahweh, who made the triumph of liberation possible.

Victory over the tyrant is not, of course, the definitive attainment of the objectives of the movement. But it removes the main impediment to the advance toward this objective, toward the "land where milk and honey flow"—the liberated, peaceful life of which Moses and his followers dream, animated as they are by the words of the promise of Yahweh their God. Obviously in any revolutionary movement the moment of triumph over the enemy is a basic one, marking the successful completion of the stage of struggle, and the commencement of the stage of the construction of a new society. The celebration of the triumph plays an indisputable role in keeping spirits high during this second stage, and not allowing the people to lose sight of goals during the time of deprivation accompanying revolutionary reconstruction.

And so our text pauses at the moment of triumph, to institute the yearly celebration with which Israel will call to mind its victory over the pharaoh of Egypt with the help of Yahweh its God. The celebration will take three forms: (1) the Passover, (2) the seven days of unleavened bread, and (3) the sanctification of the firstborn. The first two forms of celebration will take place annually during the first month of the year, the month in which the people escaped from Egypt. The sanctification of the firstborn is celebrated at the birth of each of them, to recall the salvation of the firstborn of the Israelites on the night of the massacre of the firstborn of the Egyptians.

An attentive examination of the regulations for these celebrations shows that they have had a history of their own. They do not always dovetail with the written account. Nor is this surprising. Take, for example, the unleavened bread, which is to be consumed for seven days, annually. The unleavened bread is explained by the flight from Egypt, but the seven days have no specific reference to the account. We see the same relative autonomy in the matter of the Passover. On the night every year when the Passover lamb is eaten, the participants are not to leave their houses. Yet according to our account, Moses and Aaron presented themselves before the pharaoh during that night, and it was precisely then that they received the urgent order to leave the country. For the sake of clarity in the following exposition, then, I shall distinguish, by the wording of subtitles in this section, the statutory texts for the celebrations, reflecting the ritual practice of Israel, from texts that are strictly narrative and continue the account of the exodus.

2.5.1 Passover Statute 1 (Exod. 12:1–13)

2.5.1a NOTHING TO BE LEFT OVER (EXOD. 12:1–6)

Yahweh said to Moses and Aaron in the land of Egypt, "This month is to be the first of all the others for you, the first month of your year. Speak to the whole community of Israel and say, 'On the tenth day of this month each man must take an animal from the flock, one for each family: one animal for each household. If the household is too small to eat the animal, a man must join with his neighbor, the nearest to his house, as the number of persons requires. You must take into account what each can eat in deciding the number for the animal. It must be an animal without blemish, a male one year old; you may take it from either sheep or goats. You must keep it till the fourteenth day of the month when the whole assembly of the community of Israel shall slaughter it between the two evenings.' "

It is characteristic of religious celebrations that they are observed on a precise day. And inasmuch as this is the celebration of the anniversary of the flight from Egypt, it is all the more important to observe it on the day it occurred, on the fourteenth day of the first month of the year. Passover is a feast of springtime, and it is the general opinion that the custom of beginning the year in the spring was an innovation dating from the time of the Babylonian exile. The present text, which presupposes a year that began in the spring, is therefore no older than the sixth century B.C. In all probability it is part of the sacerdotal version of Exodus.

The major concern of this statute is the formation of groups that will be large enough to consume the Passover victim so that nothing will remain of it.

The festival is to be celebrated *en famille*—by each family in the intimacy of its own home. The Deuteronomic reform (Deut. 16:1–8), however, establishes that it is to be celebrated "in the place Yahweh your God chooses"—Jerusalem, which makes a family celebration difficult. Our present text, although it represents the sacerdotal tradition, provides no role for priests! The celebration of national liberation is a family celebration. Yahweh has liberated each family from the servitude of Egypt.

The hour of the sacrifice, which is designated in Hebrew as "between the two evenings," has traditionally been interpreted by the rabbinical school as being between noon and sunset.

2.5.1b HASTE (EXOD. 12:7–11)

"Some of the blood must then be taken and put on the two doorposts and lintel of the houses where it is eaten. That night, the flesh is to be eaten, roasted over the fire; it must be eaten with unleavened bread and bitter herbs. Do not eat any of it raw or boiled, but roasted over the fire, head, feet and entrails. You must not leave any over till the morning: whatever

is left till morning you are to burn. You shall eat it like this: with a girdle around your waist, sandals on your feet, a staff in your hand. You shall eat it hastily: it is a passover in honor of Yahweh."

The prescription to eat the Passover lamb with "sandals on your feet, a staff in your hand" recalls the haste in which the Hebrews departed from Egypt when the pharaoh released them during the night.

2.5.1c PASSOVER AND EXODUS (EXOD. 12:12–13)

"That night, I will go through the land of Egypt and strike down all the first-born in the land of Egypt, man and beast alike, and I shall deal out punishment to all the gods of Egypt, I am Yahweh! The blood shall serve to mark the houses that you live in. When I see the blood I will pass over you and you shall escape the destroying plague when I strike the land of Egypt."

These lines link the first statute for Passover with the events of the night of the exodus. Here the explanation for the blood on the doorposts and lintels is that it is needed as evidence that these are the homes of families that are ready to flee with Moses and be integrated into the Levite-Israelite group. This explanation is at odds with the notion that we have met on level three of the account—that the people lived apart, in the land of Goshen.

2.5.2 UNLEAVENED-BREAD STATUTE 1 (EXOD. 12:14–20)

"This day is to be a day of remembrance for you, and you must celebrate it as a feast in Yahweh's honor. For all generations you are to declare it a day of festival, for ever.
"For seven days you must eat unleavened bread. On the first day you are to clean all leaven out of your houses, for anyone who eats leavened bread from the first to the seventh day shall be cut off from Israel. On the first day you are to hold a sacred gathering, and again on the seventh day. On those days no work is to be done; you are allowed only to prepare your food. The feast of Unleavened Bread must be kept because it was on that same day I brought your armies out of the land of Egypt. Keep that day from age to age: it is an irrevocable ordinance. In the first month, from the evening of the fourteenth day and until the evening of the twenty-first day, you are to eat unleavened bread. For seven days no leaven must be found in your houses, because anyone who eats leavened bread will be cut off from the community of Israel, whether he be stranger or native-born. You must eat no leavened bread; wherever you live you must eat unleavened bread.' "

In the times of the Gospels and the Talmud, Passover and unleavened bread constituted a single festival, commemorating the liberation from slavery in

Egypt. Originally, however, these were two distinct festivals. In the ancient law for the festivals of the harvests in the Book of the Covenant, the festival of the unleavened bread appears in the list containing the festival of first fruits and the festival of harvest (Exod. 23:14-17). In the "Ritual Decalogue" of Exodus 34, as well, the feast of the unleavened bread and Passover are separated. Probably each developed independently, unleavened bread in connection with agriculture, and Passover in connection with animal husbandry.

The linkage of unleavened bread with the flight from Egypt is explicit in the text. The haste with which the slaves had to depart did not allow time for the dough to rise. However, if we trace the ancient laws that place the festival of the unleavened bread among the harvest festivals, the feast of the unleavened bread acquires another rationale. Leaven was kept in perpetual supply by setting aside a small part of the dough—the "foot"—before each baking, so that it could be used to leaven the next mass of dough. When a new harvest was reaped, however, it was considered in order to start a new, pure leaven, uncontaminated by the "foot" of the dough from the flour of the old harvest. The festival of the unleavened bread was celebrated at the time of the harvest, and baking the week's bread once without leaven made it possible to start a new, pure leaven.

The statute for unleavened bread in our text, however, represents a moment in the history of the festival when it was more a memorial festival than one in celebration of a new harvest. And the concern of this statute is to underscore its obligatory nature for every Israelite. The statute has no interest in finding an explanation in the account for the seven days of celebration, but only for the unleavened bread itself.

2.5.3 Passover Statute 2 (Exod. 12:21-28)

2.5.3a THE BLOOD OF THE VICTIM (EXOD. 12:21-23)

> *Moses summoned all the elders of Israel and said to them, "Go and choose animals from the flock on behalf of your families, and kill the Passover victim. Then take a spray of hyssop, dip it in the blood that is in the basin, and with the blood from the basin touch the lintel and the two doorposts. Let none of you venture out of the house till morning. Then, when Yahweh goes through Egypt to strike it, and sees the blood on the lintel and on the two doorposts, he will pass over the door and not allow the destroyer to enter your homes and strike."*

The second Passover statute concentrates on the handling of the blood of the sacrificial victim, not with the consumption of that victim. It is a Yahwist text, but its interpretation of the need for a sign to identify the houses of the Israelites is at odds with the Yahwist notion that the Israelites lived in the land of Goshen.

2.5.3b CATECHESIS (EXOD. 12:24–27)

"You must keep these rules as an ordinance for all time for you and your children. When you enter the land that Yahweh is giving you, as he promised, you must keep to this ritual. And when your children ask you, 'What does this ritual mean?' you will tell them, 'It is the sacrifice of the Passover in honor of Yahwèh who passed over the houses of the sons of Israel in Egypt, and struck Egypt but spared our houses.' "

This catechetical passage reflects the same interest in using the accounts and rites for purposes of the transmission of the faith to new generations that we have seen in the plague of locusts (§2.4.9). It is the work of the seventh-century B.C. ideologues of the Josian reform. This passage and the foregoing are assimilated into the text of the book of Exodus as we have it today by being placed in the mouth of Moses as his instructions to the elders of Israel. The first Passover statute (§2.51) is in the form of Yahweh's words to Moses.

2.5.3c CONCLUSION (EXOD. 12:28)

And the people bowed down and worshiped. The sons of Israel then departed, and they obeyed. They carried out the orders Yahweh had given to Moses and Aaron.

This brief passage concludes the first series of ritual statutes. Now the narrative account resumes.

2.5.4 Defeat of the Pharaoh (Exod. 12:29–36)

And at midnight Yahweh struck down all the first-born in the land of Egypt: the first-born of Pharaoh, heir to his throne, the first-born of the prisoner in his dungeon, and the first-born of all the cattle. Pharaoh and all his courtiers and all the Egyptians got up in the night, and there was a great cry in Egypt, for there was not a house without its dead. And it was night when Pharaoh summoned Moses and Aaron. "Get up," he said, "you and the sons of Israel, and get away from my people. Go and offer worship to Yahweh as you have asked and, as you have asked, take your flocks and herds, and go. And also ask a blessing on me." The Egyptians urged the people to hurry up and leave the land because, they said, "Otherwise we shall all be dead." So the people carried off their dough, still unleavened, on their shoulders, their kneading bowls wrapped in their cloaks.

The sons of Israel did as Moses had told them and asked the Egyptians for silver ornaments and gold, and for clothing. Yahweh gave the people such prestige in the eyes of the Egyptians, that they gave them what they asked. So they plundered the Egyptians.

At midnight, the threat that Moses uttered against the pharaoh during the plague of the darkness comes to pass: the slaughter of the firstborn. In that interview, the pharaoh had forbidden Moses ever to attempt to see him again. But now he himself sends for him, and urgently. The pharaoh no longer feels himself to be in a position to negotiate. The Israelites may depart, and they may take their flocks with them.

By his obstinacy, the pharaoh has transformed Egypt into a land of death. It all began when he established the policy of intensifying the Hebrews' work load and killing their children to keep them from joining forces with his enemies. Thus death came first upon the "others," the Hebrew workers. But the workers' reaction was to organize. They demanded a holiday, and more reasonable work quotas. Then the king's stubbornness led the workers and their God Yahweh to turn to measures of force. Yahweh's wonders attack their oppressors' comfort (the frogs, "mosquitoes," and "gadflies"), health (contaminated water and boils), and food supplies (the livestock epidemic, hail, and locusts). Because of the king's "hardness of heart," the forceful measures have culminated in the killing of strategically selected persons in the population, and no house is without a corpse. And so the pharaoh's death-dealing policy has come to this! He has been defeated.

For their departure, the Egyptians, as already stated in §2.1.5, have provided the rebels with things they will need for their new life beyond the frontiers of Egypt. The rebels will now seek to establish, in the wilderness, living conditions that the pharaoh's class system forbade them in the fertile land of the Nile.

2.5.5 Flight from Egypt (Exod. 12:37–42)

The sons of Israel left Rameses for Succoth, about six hundred thousand on the march—all men—not counting their families. People of various sorts joined them in great numbers; there were flocks, too, and herds in immense droves. They baked cakes with the dough which they had brought from Egypt, unleavened because the dough was not leavened; they had been driven out of Egypt, with no time for dallying, and had not provided themselves with food for the journey. The time that the sons of Israel had spent in Egypt was four hundred and thirty years. And on the very day the four hundred and thirty years ended, all the array of Yahweh left the land of Egypt. The night, when Yahweh kept vigil to bring them out of the land of Egypt, must be kept as a vigil in honor of Yahweh for all their generations.

With the hasty flight from Egypt, the initial objective of the movement of which Moses had taken charge since the days of Midian has been achieved. Despite their speed, the Israelites have not departed empty-handed. They have plundered the Egyptians. And there is more. "People of various sorts" *(erev rab)* have joined them for the exodus. The word *erev* is used to refer to persons who were not originally part of the movement. The same word is used, in Nehemiah 13:3, for persons who were not Jews of pure lineage and were therefore excluded for Judah by Nehemiah. In this moment of victory, by contrast, Moses and his followers accept "others" wishing to join them in their risky venture.

According to this passage, the number of men leaving Rameses, the city of forced labor, was six hundred thousand. Even if a rebellion on the part of that many persons in Egypt were to be thinkable, it would certainly have been impossible for that large a number, plus their families, to be able to live for long in the wilderness. The more probable explanation is that the word *elef,* when used here, had not yet come to mean "thousand," but merely the number of men that a single clan of Israel could arm for battle. *Elef* was originally a military term, then, and came to mean "thousand" only later, when, in postexilic times, the basic unit of men under arms consisted of a thousand members. In premonarchical times, an *elef* would probably have averaged some six to nine men, and six hundred *elafim* would then equal some four thousand men ready for battle, plus their families (see Gottwald, *Tribes,* 270–76). If an average family numbered, say, six persons, this would mean that the group of rebels fleeing with Moses numbered about twenty-four thousand. Even that number, of course, would mean that we were dealing with an important rebellion. Nothing about the flight is recorded in the hieroglyphs, not because it would not have been a blow to the national economy, but because untoward events are not enshrined in monuments.

It is difficult to know how the figure of 430 years was calculated. Probably the tradition that the nucleus of the rebel group consisted of a group of foreigners in Egypt has a historical basis. But the text of Exodus itself gives three generations from Levi to Moses, which would exclude a calculation of 430 years. This figure, then, remains without explanation.

2.5.5a PASSOVER STATUTE 3 (EXOD. 12:43–51)

Yahweh said to Moses and Aaron, "This is what is ordained for the Passover: No alien may take part in it, but any slave bought for money may take part when you have had him circumcised. No stranger and no hired servant may take part in it. It is to be eaten in one house alone, out of which not a single morsel of the flesh is to be taken; nor must you break any bone of it. The whole community of Israel must keep the Passover. Should a stranger be staying with you and wish to celebrate the Passover in honor of Yahweh, all the males of his household must be circumcised: he may then be admitted to the celebration, for he becomes as it were a native-born. But no uncircumcised person may take part. The same law will run for the native and for the stranger resident among you." The sons of Israel all obeyed. They carried out the orders Yahweh had given to Moses and Aaron. And that same day Yahweh brought the sons of Israel in their armies out of Egypt.

This third statute for Passover seems to be a late addition to the text. Its intent is to set limits to the number of those permitted to partake of the Passover. "Everyone who lives with you" may partake, as long as males are circumcised. The stranger en route may not.

Circumcision as evidence of membership in Israel was possible only after the sixth century B.C., when the Jews were scattered among nations that did not practice it. In the land of Canaan, all peoples practiced the circumcision of males, with the exception of the Philistines and the inhabitants of Shechem, who were Hivites (Roland de Vaux, *Institutions,* 46–48). Never does the Bible refer to Canaanites as uncircumcised.

2.5.5b FIRSTBORN STATUTE (EXOD. 13:1–2)

Yahweh spoke to Moses and said, "Consecrate all the first-born to me, the first issue of every womb, among the sons of Israel. Whether man or beast, this is mine."

The safety of the firstborn of Israel in the massacre of the firstborn of Egypt serves to supply a historical reference for the practice of consecrating firstborn male children to God.

2.5.5c UNLEAVENED-BREAD STATUTE 2 (EXOD. 13:3–10)

Moses said to the people, "Keep this day in remembrance, the day you came out of Egypt, from the house of slavery, for it was by sheer power that Yahweh brought you out of it; no leavened bread must be eaten. On this day, in the month of Abib, you are leaving Egypt. And so, in this same month, when Yahweh brings you to the land of the Canaanites, the Hittites, the Amorites, the Hivites, the Jebusites, the land he swore to your fathers he would give you, a land where milk and honey flow, you are to hold this service. For seven days you will eat unleavened bread, and on the seventh day there is to be a feast in honor of Yahweh. During these seven days unleavened bread is to be eaten; no leavened bread must be seen among you, no leaven among you in all your territory. And on that day you will explain to your son, 'This is because of what Yahweh did for me when I came out of Egypt.' The rite will serve as a sign on your hand would serve, or a memento on your forehead, and in that way the law of Yahweh will be ever on your lips, for Yahweh brought you out of Egypt with a mighty hand. You will observe this ordinance each year at its appointed time."

The tone of this statute for the unleavened bread is homiletic. Its concern is to forestall the celebration of the rite in dissociation from the liberation event at its basis. Like other texts that we have seen, this one, too, reminds us of the book of Deuteronomy, and is indeed a Deuteronomist addition to the text of Exodus.

2.5.5d FIRSTBORN STATUTE CONTINUED (EXOD. 13:11–16)

"When Yahweh brings you to the land of Canaanites—as he swore to you and your fathers he would do—and he gives it to you, you are to make over to Yahweh all that first issues from the womb, and every first-born cast by your animals: these males belong to Yahweh. But every first-born donkey you will redeem with an animal from your flocks. If you do not redeem it, you must break its neck. Of your sons, every first-born of men must be redeemed. And when your son asks you in days to come, 'What does this mean?' you will tell him, 'By sheer power Yahweh brought us out of Egypt, out of the house of slavery. When Pharaoh stubbornly refused to let us go, Yahweh killed all the first-born in the land of Egypt, of man and of beast alike. For this I sacrifice to Yahweh every male that first issues from the womb, and redeem every first-born of my sons.' The rite will serve as a sign on your hand would serve, or a circlet on your forehead, for Yahweh brought us out of Egypt with a mighty hand."

The continuation of the statute for the consecration of the firstborn once again manifests the catechetical interest of Deuteronomist (or proto-Deuteronomist) additions to the text of Exodus. It was important, in this era—the sixth century B.C.—to be clear on this point, seeing that, on the very outskirts of Jerusalem, infants were sacrificed to the god Baal by fire, as we read in Jeremiah 19:4–6. Our text prescribes that the firstborn of the Israelites be ransomed by an animal surrogate—and this will recall the night of the ransom or redemption in Egypt. One of the outrages that Yahweh held against Israelites at a later time was that of "burning your children as sacrifices" (Ezek. 20:31); the present ordinance of the consecration of the firstborn is an obvious countermand.

APPENDIX 5:
THE DIVINE NAME "YAHWEH"

By Jesus' time, Jews had ceased to pronounce God's sacred name. The text of the sacred books continued to be handed down with the consonants YHWH, but the reader, seeing these letters, was to pronounce *Adonāi* instead: "my Lord." And so when the vowels began to be written in the Hebrew text of the Bible—not before the seventh century A.D.—it was the vowel points for *Adonāi* that were written with the traditional consonants YHWH. This combination resulted in the adoption, by certain European translations, of "Jehovah." Other traditions have opted to follow the Jewish custom, translating YHWH as "Lord" every time it appears. More recently, translators have begun to transliterate the divine name as "Yahweh," according to its more probable original pronunciation.

But what is the meaning of the name Yahweh? The only biblical explanation is the etymology offered in Exodus 3:14, which derives the name from the verb *HYH*. It is possible that the name does indeed derive from this verb. The most complete argument for this case is that of F. M. Cross, Jr., "Jahweh and the God of the Patriarchs." Cross finds the root *yahwi* in proper names of the Amorites of the second millennium B.C., such as Yahwi-IL and Yahwi-Haddu. In such names, Cross explains, *yahwi* is a verbal form accompanying the name of a god—in our examples, IL and Haddu—and the combination indicates the causation of being: "IL causes to be," or "Haddu causes to be." Given the frequency of occurrence of the divine name *El* in Israelite traditions—El Olam, El Shaddai, El Elyon—and the antiquity of the formula *Yahweh Sebaoth* in the Bible, Cross hypothesizes that the original form of *Yahweh* was *El du yahwi sebaoth:* "El who makes the hosts to exist." Cross's ingenious reasoning carries a degree of probability, but, for want of corroborating evidence, does not rise above the level of hypothesis.

Other researchers have taken as their point of departure the short form *Yahu.* This form is frequent in proper names: *Yirmiyāhu* (Jeremiah), *Yeshayāhu* (Isaiah), and Yehonatān (Jonathan). Bernhard Duhm, toward the end of the last century, thought that *Yahu* was originally just an ecstatic cry, *Ya! Hu!,* Martin Buber tells us (Buber, *Moses,* 50).

These two interpretations will suffice to indicate both the enormous effort that has been expended on attempts to extract a meaning from the divine name, and the little satisfaction obtained in terms of results. For our part, then, let us return to the fact that the Israelites thought the name came from the root "to be." And that is all we can say for sure.

A related matter, and one of greater importance than the meaning of the name, is its place of origin. Who introduced the use of this name of God in Israel? The testimony of the Israelite traditions on this point is rather clear that the name Yahweh was intimately associated with the exodus. According to the northern, Elohist, version of Israel's beginnings, it was to Moses that God first revealed the name Yahweh. The patriarchal traditions that came from the original tribes of Canaan give us many other names—El Shaddai, El Olam, and so on—and it is probable that when the name Yahweh appears in these traditions it is by way of retrojection of a later usage, when all Israel worshiped God as Yahweh. The Hebrews who came up from slavery in Egypt brought a religion with them, the cult of a certain Yahweh, and professed that this Yahweh had been revealed to them in the salvific act of their liberation. Thus it was Moses' group that introduced the God of liberation to the confederation of Israel and its cult of Yahweh (Gottwald, 38–40).

The group that fled Egypt in the exodus did not yet constitute "Israel." The name "Israel," curiously, contains the divine name El, and is associated in its origins with Bethel and the region round about, where the tribes of Ephraim and Manasseh lived. Thus the greater part of the demographic base of the confederation came from the groups residing in Canaan, which had risen up against the domination of the Canaanite elite; but the ideology of this revolutionary movement came from the Levite group that had fled Egypt and a life of oppression, and professed a God who was Yahweh the liberator. We cannot call the tribes in Canaan "Israel" before they gave their loyalty to Yahweh, although it would appear that they used the name "Israel." On the other hand, neither can we say that the Levites who came up from Egypt were "Israel" before they joined forces with the rebel tribes of Canaan, even though they had the Yahweh cult. For the sake of greater precision, then, it has become customary to call both groups "proto-Israelites," until the moment they joined together in a confederation under the religious banner of Yahweh.

I prescind from any attempt to trace the origins of a cult of Yahweh back beyond Moses and the exodus group. Some researchers, notably H. H. Rowley, have thought Yahwism came from the Kenites (Rowley, *From Joseph to Joshua*). The basis of this theory is Moses' kinship with Jethro, the priest of Midian (and, according to Judges 1:16, of the Kenite group), especially from the story of Exodus 18. The Kenite origin of "Yahwism" is possible, perhaps probable. But it is difficult to conceptualize what the specific character of a Yahweh cult before the exodus would have been: the God who was known by Israel as Yahweh was known as the God who had delivered Israel from the servitude of Egypt.

APPENDIX 6:
AARON AND THE AARONITE PRIESTHOOD

Aaron is mentioned 105 times in the book of Exodus. But he never attains the stature of a personage with his own identity. He appears in all three literary sources of the book, which indicates that he was part of the account at least as early as the time of Solomon, and perhaps even from the first origins of the account. In the literary strata of the tenth century B.C. (the Yahwist and Elohist), in the majority of instances Aaron is simply Moses' companion: God speaks to Moses and Aaron (Exod. 7:8, 9:8, 12:1, etc.); Moses and Aaron enter and speak to the king (5:1, 8:12, 9:27, 11:10, etc.); the Israelites murmur against Moses and Aaron, and they both respond (16:2, 6). At other times, Moses instructs Aaron as to what he is to do before the pharaoh or the people, or else Yahweh instructs Moses and Moses instructs Aaron (8:1,12, 16:8, 17:9, 19, etc.). In the battle with Amalek, Aaron and Hur support Moses' arms, which gives Israel the victory (17:8–16). In these ancient literary versions of Exodus, Aaron's greatest moment is when Moses leaves him in charge of the people while he himself ascends the mountain to receive Yahweh's revelation (24:14, 32:1–2). And here Aaron fails, unable to control the Israelites in their desire to have a tangible image of Yahweh to lead them through the desert.

In contrast with this Yahwist-Elohist picture of Aaron as Moses' companion, we have a markedly different one in the version redacted by the priests. The important texts here are Aaron's genealogy in Exodus 6:14–27, the instructions for his ordination to the priesthood in 29:1–35, and, outside the book of Exodus, the performance of the ordination rite in Leviticus 8–10. In this priestly text, Aaron is set apart by Yahweh and Moses as the sole legitimate priest and progenitor of all legitimate priests of the generations to come. In this text, this privilege implies that only the priests who are Aaron's descendants have access to the tabernacle and the altar. And only they have the right to share in the consumption of all animal sacrifices offered by any Israelite, except of course holocausts, in which the victim is entirely consumed by fire. In sacrifices other than holocausts, then, the person offering the sacrifice would slit the animal's throat and present its blood to the priest, to be spilled over the altar (Lev. 1:5, 3:2, etc.). Then the person offering the sacrifice would quarter the animal, wash the separate parts, and present the priest with the parts that belonged to him, as well as those to be burned on the altar (Lev. 1:10–13, 3:1–17, etc.). The priest had the further responsibility of caring for the sacred precincts, and seeing that their purity was preserved.

The main problem in the interpretation of the history of the Aaronite priesthood is presented by the marked contrast between the priestly tradition of the Pentateuch and what is said of priests in Ezekiel 44:9–31. According to the prophet's text, the only legitimate priests are the Zadokites, and the Levites are forbidden to perform the functions of the altar and sanctuary of the temple, being now limited to the lesser offices of the gates and porticos of the sanctuary. They may immolate sacrifices, but not present them upon the altar. Ezekiel 44 does not consider the Aaronites at all. What is curious is that both Ezekiel and the priestly tradition are very probably from the sixth century B.C.

The Zadokites were the family in charge of the Jerusalem temple from the time of Solomon to its destruction in 587 B.C. Zadok, their eponymous ancestor, was one of David's chief priests (2 Sam. 8:17), the other being Abiathar, member of the priestly family of the sanctuary of Nob and sole survivor of Saul's massacre there (1 Sam. 22:17–23). The text of Ezekiel 44 reflects the rivalry between these two houses. King Solomon exiled Abiathar to Anathoth (1 Kings 2:26), because he had supported Adonijah, David's son, in his attempt to seize the throne (1 Kings 1:7). Beginning with the reign of Solomon, then, the Zadokites were in exclusive control of worship in Jerusalem. The family of Abiathar—a Levite—continued to be influential, although they no longer held an official position in the capital. Ezekiel reflects the fact that the struggle between these families continued during the time of the exile. And in none of this do we hear of a priestly Aaronite family.

The establishment of the Aaronite monopoly over the sacrifice of the altar is an important theme of the sacerdotal revision of the Pentateuch. Leviticus 8–10 recounts the solemn ordination of Aaron. The death of Aaron's grown sons, consumed by the fire of the altar (Lev. 10:1–3), serves as a warning of the grave importance of following the priestly prescriptions in every last detail. In Numbers 17:1–8 we hear how Yahweh caused Aaron's branch to sprout, thus confirming his priestly authority in the face of a charismatic, democratic movement that sought to open the service of the altar to others. The consecration of the Aaronite priesthood is complete, according to the priestly tradition, with the story of the transfer of Aaron's authority to his son Eleazar, and Aaron's subsequent death (Num. 20:22–29).

I think that Aelred Cody has given the best interpretation of all this evidence (in *A History of the Old Testament Priesthood,* the best work on this subject, and the one I follow in most of its positions). Cody understands the Aaronite monopoly as the result of a transaction for the pacification of the conflict between the Zadokites and the Levites. The Levites had a purer Israelite record, going back all the way to Moses and Aaron, and the flight from Egypt, but they had suffered a fall from the power in consequence of a grave tactical error in the last years of David. The Zadokites, for their part, had held the monopoly of the national sanctuary for centuries, but their origin was uncertain: Zadok suddenly appears on the scene only when David has conquered the Jebusite city of Jerusalem to make it his capital. Zadok very probably was a Jebusite priest incorporated by David into his "cabinet," together with Abiathar, a Yahwist priest of impeccable credentials (see the arguments in H. H. Rowley, "Zadok and Nahushtan"). The destruction of Jerusalem cast a shadow over the Zadokites, and occasioned the rise once more of the Levite line, which had been out of power for centuries.

We do not know how the solution of the priestly tradition was reached, although it can be seen as a compromise in the conflict between the Zadokites and Levites. The Zadokites had established their credential as Levites with a lineage that passed by way of Pinchas, son of Eleazar, son of Aaron the Levite, who had been Moses' companion in the heroic enterprise of the exodus. This is how things stand as early as the book of Ezra in the fifth or fourth century B.C. (Ezra 7:1–5), and this is how they stand in the various genealogies of the book of Chronicles of the same period. The priestly tradition permits the Levites access to official worship at various levels. The descendants of Kohath (according to Exod. 6:16, one of the three sons of Levi and the grandfather of Moses and Aaron) would have charge of the ark and the implements of the sanctuary (Num. 4). Some, who could establish their credentials as descendants of Aaron, will be able to exercise the full priesthood; the others will be able to stay at a second or third level of service in the Temple that had been rebuilt in the time of Darius of Persia.

The conclusion is that no priestly family before the exile claimed legitimacy by virtue of descent from Aaron the Levite. It was the dissensions of the exile that produced an Aaronite priesthood. This is in agreement with the fact that in Exodus Aaron never functions as a priest. It might be thought that the account of his erection of the golden calf, and of an altar to Yahweh, in Exodus 32, is an exception, but it is not. The patriarchs Abraham, Isaac, and Jacob erected a number of altars (in the Yahwist and Elohist traditions—never in the priestly accounts of Genesis) without having been priests. Gideon raised an altar to Yahweh, and offered sacrifice there (Judg. 6:24). Micah of Ephraim built an altar and a carved image in his house without being a priest (Judg. 17:1-3). And Samuel, also as a member of the tribe of Ephraim, offered a great number of sacrifices without being a priest.

The first priests of whom we have any information—Jonathan, son of Gershom, son of Moses (Judg. 18:30), Eli of Shiloh (1 Sam. 1:3), and Ahimelech of Nob (1 Sam. 21:2-10)—were persons in charge of a sanctuary. The earliest priests of Yahweh also had the responsibility of relaying Yahweh's responses to petitions the faithful made, via the sacred lots—the urim and tummim or the ephod (1 Sam. 23:7-13, 30:6-10). Only in the sacerdotal material of Exodus are these functions in the hands of Aaron. Not even Aaron's connection with the golden calf is priestly. I conclude, then, that the Aaronite priesthood is postexilic, and that, in the ancient account of Exodus, Aaron is simply a Levite accompanying and supporting Moses in the liberation of Israel. In this account he is not a priest.

APPENDIX 7:
THE LEVITES

According to the book of Exodus, the leaders of the rebels in Egypt—Moses and Aaron—were Levites. It is probable, given the role played by the Levites in Israel, that a datum of historical value had been preserved here. On level one—the account as it was formed by the actual group headed by Moses in the wilderness—it is likely that the ones who actually experienced the exodus were known as Levites. It was the Levites who brought to Canaan the teaching about Yahweh and how Yahweh had delivered the oppressed from servitude in Egypt. In the atmosphere of antimonarchical rebellion that prevailed in the land of Canaan at this time, the Levites were rapidly accepted as Israel's ideologues, and Yahweh as Israel's only God. (For arguments in favor of the identification of the exodus group with the Levites, see Gottwald, *Tribes,* 35-41.)

Once in Canaan, the Levites dispersed among the rebel tribes, known collectively as Israel. In the parceling out of lands, attributed to Joshua, the Levites received forty-eight cities, scattered among the tribes of Israel (Josh. 21). This number seems excessive, but their dispersion is probably factual. The Levitical cities are somehow associated with the cities of refuge (Deut. 4:41-43, Num. 35:1-8). These were cities to which persons accused of murder could flee to receive protection from the blood avengers until the facts could be cleared up and the guilt or innocence of the refugee established. According to Deuteronomy 19:3, there were three such cities. When Israel grew, the number had to be increased to six (Deut. 19:9). The sacerdotal version of this institution (Num. 35) is that three of these cities were to the east of the Jordan and three to the west. These six cities of refuge are among the forty-eight Levitical cities listed in Joshua 21 and Chronicles 6:54-81.

We know from the narrative texts of the Bible that these cities were not inhabited solely by Levites. Rather, we find Levitical families living in the cities of Israel as *gerim,* "resident aliens."

In one unidentified village of Ephraim, a Levite lived in the house of a certain Micah (Judg. 17:7-13). He was a native of Bethlehem, in Judah, but had left there in search of a place to settle down, and had been gladly welcomed by Micah, because Levites were the privileged priestly persons, and Micah could now have a shrine in his home.

This same Levite helped the Danite troops in their excursion against Laish by consulting Yahweh on their behalf (Judg. 18:5-6), and later struck an agreement with them to serve as prefect of their new shrine in the conquered city (Judg. 18:18-31).

Judges 19-20 contains the account of another Levite, one residing in Gibeah, a city of the tribe of Benjamin. There is everything to indicate that he, too, is a *ger.* In the narrative texts sacred to Israel, then, we find the Levites scattered among the other tribes, holding privileged functions as Yahweh's representatives, at a time when the priesthood was not yet a closed function but was exercised by the fathers of the families of Israel.

Interpreters have been caused a great many problems by the inclusion of Levi among the twelve sons of Jacob (Israel), and the presence of Levi in the lists of the tribes of Israel. Levi was not a territorial tribe. And so its presence in the lists has to be explained in some other way. Levi does not appear among the ten tribes mentioned in the Song of Deborah (Judg. 5)—although this is not decisive: neither does Judah appear here. In the lists of tribes, Levi appears in the third place, after Reuben and Simeon, in Exodus 1:1-5, Genesis 29-30, 35:23-26, 46:8-27, 49, and Deuteronomy 33. On the other hand, it is not included in the ancient list in Numbers 26, where Ephraim and Manasseh are cited in the position otherwise occupied by Joseph.

Which, then, is the oldest list—the one with Levi or the one without? One response that has received considerable attention, and has been defended by authorities of the stature of Wellhausen, Rowley, and de Vaux, is that Levi was a tribe like the others when Israel was constituted in the land of Canaan, but that it lost its territory, and eventually only performed religious functions. According to this notion, the lists including Levi reflect an older historical reality than those that do not, and that subdivide Joseph.

One problem here is the lack of any evidence of a Levite territory at any time. Another is the fact that, from the earliest known history of the tribes, Ephraim and Manasseh are two powerful, clearly differentiated tribes. Joseph never appears as a tribe in the narratives, only in the lists.

Gottwald has recently proposed a solution that seems to resolve these difficulties (*Tribes,* 358-75). He suggests that the system of twelve tribes was fixed by David as the political basis of his kingdom. Until then there had been a fluctuating number of tribes, as reflected in the Song of Deborah and the tribal histories of the book of Judges. When David established his royal authority on the basis of the tribal alliance, Gottwald goes on, there were twelve tribes—the ones listed in Numbers 26 (including Manasseh and Ephraim and omitting Levi). The political and administrative importance of the tribes was that they provided the militias for a unified army, a situation referred to in the military list of 1 Chronicles 27:16–22. Levi was a group whose function was purely ideological. At this moment, the number twelve was consecrated.

With the reorganization under Solomon, Gottwald argues, the tribes would have lost their administrative importance. Solomon redistributed his kingdom into twelve administrative units, but could not use the traditional tribes for this purpose: they were too disparate in size for an equitable distribution of taxes and forced labor. His twelve administrative divisions (1 Kings 4:7–19) were more or less artificial, and were headed not by the elders of the tribes, but by officials appointed by the king. The list of the twelve tribes had now simply become the expression of the totality of Israel.

With the division of the kingdom at Solomon's death, says Gottwald, a new situation arose. The lists of the twelve tribes had lost their pertinence to politico-administrative reality, but had acquired even more importance than before for Yahweh's faithful, who held so tightly to the reality of Israel as the people of Yahweh. For these religious circles, it was important to include Levi—whose members were the ideologists of Yahwism—among the tribes. Here, according to Gottwald, is the origin of the list that eventually replaced the original one, the list in which Levi finally appears, in the third place.

Gottwald's thesis seems to be best. One of the pieces of evidence that has been used to defend the contrary thesis of the original existence of Levi as one of the tribes of Israel, is its presence in the account of the abduction of Dinah, and the subsequent conflict between Jacob's sons and the city of Shechem (Gen. 34). This account, of complex redaction in some of its parts, cites Levi and Simeon as the sons of Jacob who took the initiative in attacking the men of Shechem while the wounds of their circumcision were healing. This account has been seen as composed in memory of the event that led to the dissolution of the territorial integrity of Levi (Rowley, "Early Levite History and the Question of the Exodus").

If this were the case, however, we must wonder who maintained the tradition of Levi's conflict with the Shechemites. Rather, it has been demonstrated that the figures of Simeon and Levi were introduced into the account of Dinah after the original redaction (S. Lehming, "Zur Überlieferungsgeschichte von Gen. 34"; A. de Pury, "Genèse XXXIV et l'histoire"). Their insertion would derive from Jacob's curse ("blessing," Gen. 49:5–7), but Jacob is alluding to another event, involving the useless waste of livestock. Thus neither Levi nor Simeon appears in the conflict with Shechem, nor is there any evidence that Levi ever held any territory in the central hills of Canaan, where Shechem was situated.

Leaving aside the confusion produced by the inclusion of Levi in some of the lists of tribes, let us return to the datum that the Levites were originally *gerim* in the cities of Israel, and that, by reason of their role as vehicles of the Yahwist ideology, they were the preferred candidates for sacerdotal posts. Basic to their history during the period of the monarchy are: (1) the exile of Abiathar in the time of Solomon, and (2) the new enlistment of the Levites as ideologists and priests in the Deuteronomic reform of the seventh century B.C.

1. In David's time, there were two priests in charge of the worship in Jerusalem: Zadok and Abiathar. Zadok appears only after the conquest of Jerusalem, and was probably one of the Jebusite priests of Jerusalem (see Appendix 6). But Abiathar was the son of Ahimelek, the priest in charge of the sanctuary of Yahweh in Nob. Ahimelek had perished in Saul's massacre of the Nobites, David's sympathizers (1 Sam. 22:20). Abiathar followed David and his band of sympathizers, consulted Yahweh on his behalf with the ephod (1 Sam. 23:9–12, 30:7–8), and entered with him into Jerusalem. Abiathar was banished by Solomon, after David's death (1 Kings 2:26–27), to the Levitical city of

Anathoth, in the territory of Benjamin. The chronicler would have it that Abiathar was a Levite (1 Chron. 24:6), although there is no genealogy to link him with Levi. It is very likely that he was a Levite, given the place of his banishment, and the oracle in 1 Samuel 2:27-36. The oracle predicts the fall of the house of Eli, in Shiloh, and 1 Kings 2:27 explicitly sees the fulfillment of the oracle in Abiathar's banishment. In 1 Samuel 2:28, Eli's lineage and priestly ordination are referred to the time of Moses, which clearly identifies Eli and Abiathar as Levites. The conflict of the Levites with the Zadokites, which reaches its climax in Ezekiel 44, began, then, in the time of David and Solomon.

2. The book of Deuteronomy has often been seen by commentators as a Levitical revision of the legal tradition of Israel. It evinces a very marked preoccupation with support of the Levites, who were so deeply affected by the centralization of the worship of Yahweh in Jerusalem. (This centralization is the principal point of the legal reform.) According to Deuteronomy 18:1-8, all Levites were potentially priests, and might exercise the priesthood merely by presenting themselves in "the place chosen by Yahweh" (Jerusalem). This was a novelty, of course, inasmuch as, since Solomon's time, the Zadokites had monopolized the priesthood in the capital. Further: Deuteronomy 31:9 assigns the Levites the care of the Ark of the Covenant, and Deuteronomy 31:24-26 gives them the care of the book of the law. In sum, Deuteronomy is an attempt to effect the restoration of the Levites, who for three centuries have been excluded from the privileges of the priesthood in Jerusalem.

In Ezekiel 44:4-31 we find a violent Zadokite attack on the Levites. The latter are accused of responsibility for the apostasy of Israel and Judah, which apostasy is said to have occasioned the Babylonian exile. This attack originates with the community of that exile, which numbered few Levites, but many Zadokites (due to the fact that more persons were deported from Jerusalem, where the Zadokites lived, than from the villages, where the Levites lived). Our knowledge of the Levites through Deuteronomy and the prophets indicates that the accusations in Ezekiel are partisan, and a reflection of the passions that had aroused great rivalry between these two groups of priests.

The sacerdotal current in the Pentateuch, with the Chronicler's history, show how this priestly conflict was resolved. It was recognized that all priests ought to be Levites, and indeed descendants of Aaron. And it was recognized that the Zadokites were descendants of Aaron—by his third son Eleazar (the first two sons having been consumed by the altar fire; Lev. 10:1-3). But other Levites, as well, provided they were descendants of Aaron, could exercise the priesthood in the postexilic Jerusalem temple. The remaining Levites had the right to take their sustenance from the offerings, and performed minor tasks in the temple—that of cantor, porter, and servant.

Thus Aaron, a figure of the old account of the exodus, who on level three has no priestly characteristics, is transformed into the progenitor of all priests. And so the sacerdotal revision of the account (level four) singles out the figure of Aaron for very special consideration, and makes his ordination one of the matters imposed on Moses by Yahweh on Mount Sinai.

APPENDIX 8:
IN WHAT SENSE DID YAHWEH BRING ISRAEL OUT OF EGYPT?

In Exodus 20:2 the God of Israel says "I am Yahweh your God who brought you out of the land of Egypt, out of the house of slavery." In part 2 of my commentary (Exod. 2:23-13:16) the spelling out of this statement in narrative form—reworked by generations of Israelites—has been examined. We have seen that, if there is a single central affirmation in the faith of Israel, this is that affirmation. To the question Who is God? the Bible replies: Yahweh, who brought us out of slavery in Egypt. Martin Noth, the most lucid of the researchers of the origins of Israelite traditions, maintains that Exodus is the original nucleus of the Pentateuch (*History,* 47–51). Without the exodus event there would be no people of Israel and no Pentateuch.

But this profession of faith, constituting the kernel of the faith of Israel, poses two serious theoretical questions. The first is historical, the second philosophical.

The historical question arises from the fact that Israel was a tribal alliance formed only by the unification of various groups that were rebelling against the kings of Canaan. The Levites (or whoever were the group that followed Moses) were incorporated into this alliance only once they reached Canaan. Of course, this group that had been delivered from Egypt was of the very greatest importance in giving the tribes a sense of their historical destiny. But strictly speaking one cannot say that "Israel" was the group that Yahweh brought out of Egypt. What occurred, historically, is that the Levitical group liberated from slavery in Egypt came to be ideologically dominant in Israel, and now all the tribes could declare that they themselves had been present in the exodus—that ancient paradigm of the new liberation struggles being waged by these tribes.

The philosophical question is, in what sense is it correct to speak of God as the agent of a historical event such as the liberation of the Hebrew slaves? In the account of the plagues, God is represented as the principal agent, assaulting the pharaoh and the Egyptians in order to force them to permit the departure of the Israelites.

Let us begin by excluding two extreme interpretations of the action of God in history. First, there is the notion that God is external to the world, which constitutes a more or less closed chain of causality in which God can nevertheless intervene. We find something like this in Exodus 14:13–14:

> Have no fear! Stand firm, and you will see what Yahweh will do to save you today. . . . Yahweh will do the fighting for you: you have only to keep still.

In this first view, when God acts the ordinary chain of human events comes to a halt. The more the divine action, the less the human action. God is an exceptional cause, who takes the place of normal causes.

This interpretation enjoys the advantage of permitting a more or less direct reading of any biblical passage that speaks of God's intervention in history. But it suffers from the disadvantage of disqualifying any criteria for recognizing the divine activity other than that taking place in the absence of known causes. And it has the further, practical disadvantage of encouraging political passivity. Human organization would imply a lack of faith in divine activity. Surely we should be able to develop an interpretation of divine initiative that will not detract from the value of active human involvement.

At the other extreme is the position that Israel only *believed* that God intervened in its favor. In this interpretation, Exodus would be only the expression of the naive faith of a primitive people, and any actual divine involvement would be excluded from the objective world a priori. To be sure, Israel believed that Yahweh delivered the people from the land of Egypt. But if we deny the possibility of a genuine, objective divine participation, we postulate a humanity that will make history "by itself." No longer will our collective actions have any transcendent orientation. The poor are at the mercy of the mighty, and religion may serve to control the credulous masses, but not to instruct the elite. I resist this view of history. Indeed, I believe that the history of philosophy can be of help to us in avoiding both the extremes here presented.

Philosophical reflection in the West on the relationship between God and history begins with the Greek philosophers' critique of the official religion of their time. The received and officially countenanced religion of Athens and other Greek cities of the fifth and fourth centuries B.C. was a cult of heroic gods and goddesses, and fostered respect for the virtues of war. Socrates, Plato, and Aristotle developed a systematic critique of this religion, in the name of the more intellectual and civilized virtues. It seemed unworthy that gods would suffer the bodily passions of hunger, sexual desire, and jealousy. The philosophers held the divine to be necessarily incorporeal, and hence not subject to these passions. The human correlate of the divine was the soul, the spiritual part of human nature. The highest function of the soul was knowledge. The mind, unlike the senses, which are of the body and bound to concrete perceptions, is ignorant of concrete, tangible things, knowing only eternal, unchangeable "forms," as for example a mathematical formula. The perfection of the human soul, then, would consist in the everlasting contemplation of these unchangeable forms. But human souls, bound as they are to the body with its needs, can contemplate these perfect forms only from time to time. A divine being, not subject to these passions, would contemplate the forms without interruption.

The best expression of a spiritual theology in early Greek philosophy is probably that of Aristotle in the tenth book of his *Physics.* Here the philosopher posits the existence of God. Change is totally foreign to God: God is perfect. Were God to undergo change, God would have to become either better or worse, Aristotle held, and both alternatives were unacceptable: either alternative would postulate a less than perfect state for this divine being—either the condition before the hypothetical change, or the condition after. God cannot change, then, even in the content of divine knowledge—and so, neither can God know change, know a changing thing.

But if God cannot know change, then how can God relate to our world, where change is universal? To solve this difficulty, Aristotle's theology postulates a God who moves the world only as the object of its desire. God moves the world by attraction alone, not by impulse. God is the "unmoved mover." Imperfect, changeable beings are moved by their desire for God. In the celestial sphere of the stars (Greek astronomy had heavenly spheres for the sun, the moon, and the planets, too), with their perfectly regular movements, we have the closest approximation of a movable being to the immovable God: this sphere moves in a perfect circle, which daily repeats itself with perfect regularity. As we descend from the sphere of the stars, however, sphere by sphere we begin to discern a progressive distancing from perfection.

With the Jewish philosopher Philo, a new and important step was taken. Philo lived in Alexandria in the first century A.D., and was equally familiar with the Bible and with Greek philosophy. For Philo, God's perfection is the ability to create from nothing. God gives existence to the totally nonexistent. God guides human beings by sending prophets to orientate them. But God continues to be outside, or above, the world. Although God knows historical events (Aristotle's God did not), God is not affected by them. God influences history through the word of the prophets. Harry A. Wolfson, in a whole series of works, has demonstrated the enormous influence that this view of the relationship between God and the world exerted on Jewish and Christian thought. (The series begins with *Philo: Foundations of Religious Philosophy in Judaism, Christianity and Islam.*)

With the nineteenth-century discovery of evolution, philosophers' attitudes toward change underwent a modification. Historical change basically comports progress. Now creation was no longer seen as something that had happened once and for all. The world is being shaped over the course of millions of years by a slow but sure process of the emergence of the new and the better. For Henri Bergson, the great miracle is newness. Claude Tresmontant interprets the Bible within this theoretical framework. God is God because of the creation of what is new. God is eternally the creator. (See, for example, Tresmontant's *A Study of Hebrew Thought.*)

This history of critical reflection on God and the world provides us with the elements we need in order to answer our initial question about God's activity in the exodus. I shall synthesize these elements here in the form in which they have been developed by Alfred North Whitehead. (Whitehead's most important work in this area is *Process and Reality.*) According to Whitehead, it is essential that we assimilate the transformation that we have undergone in our evaluation of change. The real, the valid, is not the unchangeable, but precisely the emergence of what is new. The changeless forms held by the Greeks to be the most perfect reality are mere potentialities, which become real only when they take flesh. Without events, there is nothing. The ultimate reality is the emergence of newness, and if God exists, God will have to be intervening in this creative process.

We need not enter too deeply into these considerations in order to answer our question about God's activity in the exodus. I shall simply give examples of this new attitude toward change, applying it to the two areas of (1) time and (2) God's passivity.

1. If the emergence of newness is real, then the future is a series of mere potentialities—possibilities that have in no way become real as yet. In Philo's tradition, God's eternity meant that God knew everything simultaneously, whereas from the perspective of creatures time unfolded in a series of instants, unfolded little by little. For God, according to Philo, the future is as real as the present and the past. The problem with this doctrine, which does ascribe a certain importance to change (in contrast with the interpretation of the Greek philosophers), is that at least for God, there is no newness. And if there is no newness for God, then is newness only apparent. In Whitehead's philosophy, God indeed knows the future perfectly, but knows it as future, which means that God knows all the potentialities that the present contains. Which of these potentialities are actually to be realized depends on the actions of a multiplicity of agents. Only their collective actions will make this determination. This is the nature of creativity.

2. Anselm of Canterbury taught that God is that being than which no greater can be conceived. This is the logic of perfection, and the grammar of all language about God. But in speaking of passivity—of the capacity to be affected by others—correct conclusions have not always been drawn. Aristotle thought that a perfect being could not be affected by anything other than itself. But if a sensation of things, an awareness of things, is not a defect, then, quite the contrary, God's perfection will consist in "sensing," being aware of, everything. God, then, is "universally passible." Only in this way can God offer to each event as it arises an ideal of newness that will be relevant to its particular past.

Thus it is not beyond the realm of possibility that Exodus is correct when it asserts that God heard the cry of the Hebrews. For a biblical vision of reality, it is essential to assert that God hears everything—but with discernment, to be sure. It is also necessary to assert that God acts—universally. That is, there is no event of the past by which God is not affected, and no event in the present in which God is not an agent. There is no event in which God does not intervene—not as exclusive cause, but as a force that inclines created causes (and hence their effects) toward the realization of the most harmonious and comprehensive ideals possible for a particular event, given the circumstances of that event.

God, then, is the universal "instigator" of the new and better, within the spectrum of the real potentialities of each new event. In order to be this "instigator" in an appropriate way in a world of emerging newness, God must be perfectly aware of everything that is realized in this world.

In sum, God does nothing—if by "do" we mean God is the exclusive agent of anything. On the other hand, God does everything—if by "do" we mean that God is present in every event, prompting it to the realization of its fullest and best potential. God is the co-creator of everything new that emerges in this historical world.

Having made this rapid survey of the philosophical problems involved, we are now in a position to state the sense in which it is correct to say that Yahweh indeed delivered Israel from Egypt. As in every event in which a new reality arises, here too it was God who was the inspirer of the better, of the best. To a people condemned to servitude, exploitation, in Egypt, Yahweh sent Moses to sow the seed of the "good news" of a liberation that would lead to a land where milk and honey flowed.

To establish and maintain the real possibility of this totally original ideal was by no means an easy task. When Moses first arrived in Egypt and told the elders of his and God's plans for liberation, the elders joined him in these plans. But when, after the first interview with the king, the Israelites' work load was increased, the elders protested to Moses: "You have made us hated by Pharaoh and his court; you have put a sword into their hand to kill us" (Exod. 5:21)—and the vision of the possible ideal grew dim. The account solves this particular problem by having Yahweh and Moses work miracles before the pharaoh, with the people reduced to the role of spectators. It is difficult to say what this direct intervention of God could have been. God does not take action of major significance in irrational creatures—frogs, flies, and the like—because these creatures have too little margin for newness. If God effectuates the newness that consists in the actualization of the maximum potential of the real, then what God effectuates in a frog will be real, but severely limited. With Martin Buber, we may rather see in the plagues the activity of the prophet of God who interprets natural portents as God's judgment on a king who refuses to release slaves to celebrate a religious festival. It may be that the massacre of the exodus night was a terrorist action—inspired by God.

A frequent theme of the stories of the Israelites in their wanderings in the wasteland is their loss of faith in the pursuit of liberation and their wish to return to Egypt. "Were there no graves in Egypt that you must lead us out to die in the wilderness? . . . Better to work for the Egyptians than die in the wilderness!" (Exod. 14:11–12). More than once it is said that the people cursed Moses, and wanted to return to Egypt. The text reminds us of the need for continual activity on God's part to move a people toward a better destiny than that of servitude.

It is within this reflective framework that we may understand in what sense "Yahweh brought Israel out of the land of Egypt, out of the house of slavery."

Part Three

Perils of the Passage to the Promised Land: First Counterrevolutionary Threats (Exod. 13:17–18:27)

INTRODUCTION

Liberation from servitude in Egypt, and victory over the pharaoh, were only the first step—a necessary one, of course—toward the establishment of the people of Yahweh as a society of abundance and justice. The book of Exodus is not only the story of a rebellion against a class society (a tributary one, as it happens); it is also the saga of the building of a new people, Israel, which would no longer have any king but Yahweh. This—to use modern terms for a historical option made in the thirteenth century B.C.—meant the establishment of a classless society, a society of primitive communism.

The account of the book of Exodus is being faithful to the historical experience of all revolutions when it notes that the mere rejection of the old society and its oppressive structures is insufficient to consolidate a revolution. The exodus, like any revolutionary movement, was a process that developed over a certain period of time, in distinct steps, and each step had characteristics of its own.

The steps in the exodus as a revolutionary process may be identified in terms of the three respective geographical areas in which they took place: Egypt, the land of oppression and struggle for liberation; the wilderness, the place of perils, and of the maturation of a people liberated but not yet consolidated; and Canaan, the place of the construction of a new society.

Part 3 of the book of Exodus (13:17–18:27) contains stories of only the first dangers faced in the wilderness, leaving the last and most trying events for the book of Numbers. Inserted between these two narrative segments we have legislative material linked with Mount Sinai—part 4 of Exodus (19:1–40:38), the entire book of Leviticus, and the first part of the book of Numbers (1:1–10:10) (see Table 2).

Table 2

Textual Composition from Exodus 13:17 to Numbers 25:18

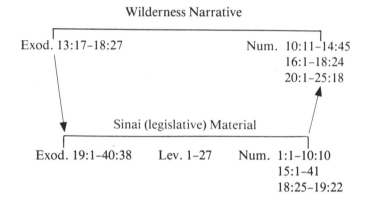

Wilderness Narrative

Exod. 13:17–18:27		Num. 10:11–14:45
		16:1–18:24
		20:1–25:18

Sinai (legislative) Material

Exod. 19:1–40:38	Lev. 1–27	Num. 1:1–10:10
		15:1–41
		18:25–19:22

Mount Sinai is the place where Yahweh reveals the norms for a new society. The theophany of Mount Sinai corresponds to the constitutional assembly in the case of modern revolutions. Here are legislated the structures that will govern the new life of the community, and provide measures to be taken to counteract the inevitable temptation to return to the old familiar structures of class societies. After all, it was a class society from which this new people emerged, and it is class societies by which it is surrounded.

The basic problem in all the wilderness accounts is counterrevolution—a movement that springs up again and again, provoked by real or imaginary dangers in the passage through the wasteland. It climaxes in an unsuccessful attempt to replace Moses with another leader, one who would lead the people back to Egypt (Num. 14:4). The most open, least disguised counterrevolution is narrated in the book of Numbers, and therefore falls outside the scope of this commentary. But even in the accounts of the wilderness journey in the book of Exodus, there are counterrevolutionary threats. Although they do not go beyond verbal protest—"murmuring," in traditional translations—they prepare the ground for the real counterrevolution that takes place after Israel's departure from Mount Sinai.

The perils of the passage through the wilderness are of three types: (1) armed attacks by enemies, (2) want and deprivation, and (3) problems of building a new social order. Each of these kinds of danger occasions the rise of movements protesting the liberation process and attempting to instigate a return to

Egypt. In Egypt, despite all the oppression that had to be suffered there, at least there was security against enemies, a dependable food supply, and a familiar social order.

It has been thought that the wilderness histories are the record of an era when Israel's ancestors were nomads, not yet a sedentary people. But there is no evidence of any nomads in the strict sense in the deserts of the Near East before the domestication of the camel. Further: the accounts of the wilderness journey are cohesive in the way they present the difficulties facing a people accustomed to living in fixed dwellings. The wanderers had to learn how to survive in the inhospitable wilderness. There is no reason why we should not think that the liberated Israelites who fled Egypt with Moses indeed had to accustom themselves to a life in regions of little rainfall and scant pasture for their animals, over a lengthy period of time, until they finally entered the land of Canaan, where they were received by other tribes engaged in securing their liberation from the kings of that land. It is probable, then, that the accounts of the perils of the wilderness, like the accounts of the struggle for liberation in Egypt, have a genuine historical basis.

To be sure, these accounts were not handed down for the sheer purpose of recalling the past. It was not a very glorious past. These accounts were handed down in order to orientate Israel in its ongoing life. The first challenge of the passage through the wilderness consisted in military attacks. And the first of them was mounted by the army of Israel's former master, the pharaoh of Egypt. The need for military defense was only too real for the revolutionary peasants once they reached the heights of Canaan, as the book of Judges eloquently testifies. To establish their revolutionary society, they had to abandon the fertile plains of Canaan and clear new fields by felling mountain forests. But the Israelites were seen by the kings of the lowland cities as "their" peasants, and so it was legitimate, in their eyes, to undertake campaigns to resubjugate them. Faced with these unremitting perils, the people of Israel had to learn the martial arts of self-defense. This is the context in which these histories have been handed down.

The privation and want of the wilderness, too, surely had its analogy here in the struggle of the peasants to clear new fields for cultivation in the mountainous regions where natural irrigation was inadequate. In the face of this hardship, what was crucial was whether Israel would be able to build cisterns to store water and dig canals to distribute it. Doubtless there were years of water shortages before these cisterns and canals could be completed, and during these years there would have been no lack of those who wished to return to their former rulers, even though it would have entailed subjecting themselves anew to unjust taxation.

Social reorganization—the construction of a classless society—was a difficult process for Israel. There was no way that it could have been an easy task. Israel had to learn to make war without an army. Untrained men had to take up arms. Israel had to learn to dispense justice without state-appointed judges. There would be councils of elders instead. And the Israelites had to learn to maintain a minimum of social harmony without a king to rule over them. They would depend on "judges" who sprang from among the people in moments of crisis. This is the context in which the histories of the problems of Moses' revolutionary administration have been transmitted.

3.0 DEPARTURE OF THE ISRAELITES (EXOD. 13:17–22)

When Pharaoh had let the people go, God did not let them take the road to the land of the Philistines, although that was the nearest way. God thought that the prospect of fighting would make the people lose heart and turn back to Egypt. Instead, God led the people by the roundabout way of the wilderness to the [Red Sea]. The sons of Israel went out from Egypt fully armed. Moses took with him the bones of Joseph who had put the sons of Israel on solemn oath. "It is sure that God will visit you," he had said, "and when that day comes you must take my bones from here with you."

From Succoth they moved on, and encamped at Etham, on the edge of the wilderness.

Yahweh went before them, by day in the form of a pillar of cloud to show them the way, and by night in the form of a pillar of fire to give them light: thus they could continue their march by day and by night. The pillar of cloud never failed to go before the people during the day, nor the pillar of fire during the night.

The road to the land of the Philistines, which ran along the coast of the Mediterranean, was the most direct route between Egypt and Canaan. It received its name from its destination, then, and was just as readily called the "road to the land of Egypt." The name is curious, however, inasmuch as the Philistines did not actually arrive on the coast to Palestine (which means, literally, "land of the Philistines") until the twelfth century B.C., or shortly after the exodus. The Philistines came from the sea and imposed themselves on the inhabitants of the coast as the dominant class. The route in question was given its name by reason of the importance of the Philistines in Israel's eyes in the time of Saul and David.

"Sea of Reeds" is the literal translation of the original Hebrew, *yam suf*. The Septuagint translates, instead, "Red Sea"—*thalassa erythra*. Now, the Red Sea, a body of salt water, has no reeds. The Septuagint reading, however, testifies to the identification of the sea of the exodus crossing—our *yam suf*— as the Red Sea by the second century B.C., an identification confirmed in 1 Kings 9:26, where we hear of Ezion-geber as being on the *yam suf,* the "sea of reeds," whereas actually it was on the Gulf of Akaba, and therefore on the Red Sea. Following the argumentation of G. I. Davies (*The Way of the Wilderness*), then, I accept the traditional interpretation, and shall refer to the Red Sea.

The Sinai peninsula is on the opposite side of the Red Sea from Egypt. It affords several possible routes from Egypt to Canaan, and it is impossible to determine which of these was the one actually taken by the group led by Moses.

Davies, in *The Way of the Wilderness,* discusses the various routes that might have been followed in the crossing of the harsh desert of the Sinai. He accepts the itinerary of Numbers 33—sacerdotal material—as the basic itinerary of the Pentateuch, and holds that details specified in the various accounts were projected from this itinerary. He devotes a great deal of effort to identifying the *yam suf,* and concludes that the expression refers to the Red Sea, as we have seen. He also identifies Mount Sinai, accepting the traditional identification with Jebel Musa, "mountain of Moses." Another study that may be consulted is that of M. Haran, "The Exodus." In any case it is clear that the fugitives made their way to the eastern shore of the Gulf of Suez, and then entered the rocky interior of the peninsula, where ancient traditions situate Mount Sinai, the mount of the revelation.

The mention of the bones of Joseph is an allusion to the oath in Genesis 50:25, and is a verbatim citation of the words of Joseph in this passage. The allusion serves to link our account, in this moment of transition to a new literary unit, to what has gone before. (For an interpretation of the literary importance of Exod. 13:17–22, see George W. Coats, "An Exposition for the Wilderness Traditions.")

The mention of Succoth has stimulated a great deal of research into the geography of the flight from Egypt. "Succoth" (Hebrew, *sukkot*) means "tents," and is perhaps not a proper name here. But it is also possible that Succoth is the hebraized form of an Egyptian locality named *TKW* (see W. Helck, "*Tkw* und die Ramsesstadt"). If this is the case, the flight will have been via Wadi Tumilat, which is approximately halfway between the Gulf of Suez and the Mediterranean. This location of the flight would tend to situate the miracle of the crossing in the region of the stagnant, shallow, reedy lakes where the Suez Canal is to be found today.

Etham seems to be the name used for the strip of land connecting Egypt with the Sinai. According to the itinerary of Numbers 33, the Israelites would have been in the wilderness of Etham twice, first before, and then after, the battle with the Egyptians.

The pillar of cloud will be important throughout the wilderness accounts. In the battle with the Egyptians it served as a protection, settling as it did between the two hostile camps (Exod. 14:19–20). According to Numbers 10:11–12, it guided the Israelites on their march. When they questioned Moses' authority, the cloud served as a visible sign that Yahweh was present and giving instructions to their leader (Num. 11:24–25). In Exodus 33:7–11, the cloud confirms the whole new social order headed by Moses: each time Moses consulted Yahweh in the tent of meeting, the cloud descended on the tent when God spoke with the prophet face to face.

It is interesting that Israel left Egypt "fully armed." It is true that the word *hamusim* does not refer specifically to arms, but it does refer to military preparations. (The word is also used in Josh. 1:14, 4:12, and Judg. 7:11.) This was not a rabble, then, but a popular army, ready to defend its triumph over the king of Egypt. It would have been foolhardy for the Israelites to seek to engage Canaanite forces without having first consolidated their own forces through the experiences of the long trek through the Sinai wilderness.

3.1 FIRST PERIL: THE EGYPTIAN ASSAULT (EXOD. 14:1–31)

Liberation is never easy. Oppressors are never resigned to the loss of fugitive servants. The first danger confronting the liberated Israelites, even before they had penetrated the wilderness, is an attack by the Egyptian army, which seeks to prevent their definitive departure.

3.1.1 Battle Strategy (Exod. 14:1–4)

Yahweh spoke to Moses and said, "Tell the sons of Israel to turn back and pitch camp in front of Pi-hahiroth, between Migdol and the sea, facing Baal-zephon. You are to pitch your camp opposite this place, beside the sea. Pharaoh will think, 'Look how these sons of Israel wander to and fro in the countryside; the wilderness has closed in on them.' Then I shall make Pharaoh's heart stubborn and he will set out in pursuit of them. But I shall win glory for myself at the expense of Pharaoh and all his army, and the Egyptians will learn that I am Yahweh." And the Israelites did this.

With the intent of manifesting the glory of Yahweh, who is still locked in a contest with Egypt, the forceful presence of the sacerdotal rereading will dominate this whole account of the battle with the pharaoh and his hosts.

Although it is not possible to establish with certitude where the battle was fought, it is clear that it is the runaway slaves who have selected the place of encounter. It is always advantageous to an army to be able to join battle on terrain that it has itself selected, where it may execute its own battle plan. In this case the enemy is enticed to a battlefield selected by the fugitives by the erratic trajectory of their flight. The Egyptians think that the Israelites have lost their way. They will be easy prey, it seems, with their backs to the sea.

The text gives the appearance of great precision. Actually, however, it is ambiguous. It admits of three possible interpretations. (1) The encounter with the Egyptian army may have taken place on a plain between the mountains and the sea, on the western bank of the Gulf of Suez, on the Red Sea. This is the traditional location, and this interpretation of our text is found as early as the first century A.D., by the historian Josephus. (See the discussion of Josephus's texts in Davies, *Wilderness*, 7–13.) (2) Or it may have taken place in the stagnant lakes midway between the Red Sea and the Mediterranean, where the Suez Canal is to be found in our own day. (3) Or, finally, it may have taken place on the banks of Lake Sirbonis, a body of water separated from the Mediterranean by a narrow strip of land. Twentieth-century research may have identified, at the western entry to this narrow isthmus, a hill that would be the

Baal-zephon of our text. (See Otto Eissfeldt, *Baal Zaphon, Zeus Kasios und der Durchzug der Israeliten durchs Meer.*)

The stagnant lakes, backwaters of the Red Sea, would constitute the natural exit from the region where work was being done on Pithom and Rameses. But this point is not decisive: our passage also states that the fugitives had to return to pitch camp where they would lay the trap for the Egyptian army.

Lake Sirvonis, in the extreme north of the Isthmus of Suez, is on the forbidden route to the land of the Philistines. But this does not mean that it could not have been the battle site. The itinerary of Numbers 33 indicates that the fugitives took no less than five days to travel from Pi-hahiroth, where they crossed the sea, to their encampment "by the Sea of Reeds" (Num. 33:7–10)— our *yam suf,* the Red Sea. This encampment, in the Numbers itinerary, is clearly on the east bank of the Gulf of Suez, above the Sinai peninsula. (Thus this itinerary actually allows any of the three sites proposed by various interpreters.)

Tradition since Josephus, Jewish and Christian alike, locates the miracle of the triumph in the Red Sea. It is probable that in its usage in the expression *yam suf,* the Hebrew *suf* does not mean rushes or reeds, but "end." This meaning of *suf* is well documented in biblical Hebrew, and would yield an expression meaning "bordering sea"—actually a very appropriate designation for the Red Sea. This was the understanding as early as the time of the Septuagint translators, and seems the most probable interpretation. (The scholarly discussion of the *yam suf* is extensive and confusing. Readers may consult Norman H. Snaith, "Yam Suf: The Sea of Reeds: The Red Sea"; Davies, *Wilderness,* 70–74. Many commentators of the nineteenth century translated *yam suf* as "Sea of Reeds" in order to facilitate a natural explanation of the miracle. The effort certainly enjoys some legitimacy, but for reasons already explained I do not follow it here.)

3.1.2 The Egyptians Tricked (Exod. 14:5–9)

When Pharaoh, king of Egypt, was told that the people had made their escape, he and his courtiers changed their minds about the people. "What have we done," they said, "allowing Israel to leave our service?" So Pharaoh had his chariot harnessed and gathered his troops about him, taking six hundred of the best chariots and all the other chariots in Egypt, each manned by a picked team. Yahweh made Pharaoh, king of Egypt, stubborn, and he gave chase to the sons of Israel as they made their triumphant escape. So the Egyptians gave chase and came up with them where they lay encamped beside the sea—all the horses, the chariots of Pharaoh, his horsemen, his army—near Pi-hahiroth, facing Baal-zephon.

The king does fall into the trap set for him by Yahweh and by Israel. The form of the narrative evinces a broad rereading of the text. First we hear that the king "was told" that the people had fled, which supposes a clandestine departure, not the permission granted by the pharaoh after the last plague as we have it in the text of Exodus today. Then at once the king is said to have regretted his decision to let the people go: "What have we done, allowing Israel to leave our service?" Here we recognize the hand of the Yahwist, who has already told us, in the narrative of the plagues, of several concessions on the pharaoh's part that were later withdrawn. Then it is said that Yahweh hardened the pharaoh's heart, in a form continuing the sacerdotal revision of the plagues.

Meanwhile the Israelites were on their way, "triumphant"—or with their "hand high" in defiance, as the original would have it—trusting in Yahweh, enthusiastic over the triumph of their recent liberation and sure of their plan for the coming encounter.

3.1.3 A People Afraid: Counterrevolutionary Sentiments (Exod. 14:10–14)

And as Pharaoh approached, the sons of Israel looked around—and there were the Egyptians in pursuit of them! The sons of Israel were terrified and cried out to Yahweh. To Moses they said, "Were there no graves in Egypt that you must lead us out to die in the wilderness? What good have you done us, bringing us out of Egypt? We spoke of this in Egypt, did we not? Leave us alone, we said, we would rather work for the Egyptians! Better to work for the Egyptians than die in the wilderness!" Moses answered the people, "Have no fear! Stand firm, and you will see what Yahweh will do to save you today: the Egyptians you see today, you will never see again. Yahweh will do the fighting for you: you have only to keep still."

It is one thing, in the tranquility of encampment, to lay plans for confronting enemies, and quite another to see them bearing down on you with their fearsome chariots. Faced with this redoubtable spectacle, some will regret ever having embarked upon this accursed revolution. And so we have the first of many times that movements will arise calling in question not only the tactics of the moment, but the entire project of leaving Egypt in search of a land where milk and honey flow. (The subject of the rebellion in the wilderness has been studied in great detail by George W. Coats in his *Rebellion in the Wilderness.* Coats holds that the origin of this tradition is the story of the spies in Num. 13–14, which he thinks was used to justify Judah's territorial pretensions. A more recent study is that of P. Buis, "Les conflits entre Moïse et Israël dans Exode et Nombres.")

The murmurers are speaking the truth: at least in their Egyptian servitude the dangers that they faced were familiar ones, and if they died they would be buried with their ancestors. What are we to make of "We spoke of this in Egypt, did we not? Leave us alone, we said, we would rather work for the Egyptians!"? The text has never cited such words until this moment. One feels that perhaps they were invented in this moment of affliction. Still, it certainly stands to reason that, during the long process of confrontation with the pharaoh, similar expressions would have been used. The account of the plagues is not interested in popular opinion during the series of confrontations.

Moses' response reasserts his confidence in the plan that has been drawn up and in Yahweh who guarantees triumph. His reply is fashioned in terms of a "holy war" (Gerhard von Rad, *Das heilige Krieg im alten Israel*). In a holy war Yahweh "fights for Israel," confounding its enemy. The number of Israel's troops is unimportant. Indeed, small numbers can have the advantage of setting Yahweh's role in relief. What is important, and this is very important, is the faith of the warriors. The timorous ought not to participate in Yahweh's war. Certain rules of conduct are to be observed, including sexual abstention (1 Sam. 21:6). No booty is to be taken, because everything the enemy has will be under a ban, consecrated to Yahweh, and hence to be destroyed (Josh. 6:17–21). These traditions have their origin in the popular wars of the Israelite tribes against their class enemies, but were systematized only in the seventh century B.C. when King Josiah revived the militia in one of his reforms (Deut. 20).

The words attributed here to Moses are probably very old, and certainly reflect the military traditions of Israel. The exhortation to the warriors not to fear, and to hope in the victory that Yahweh will give, is very important (Josh. 1:9, 10:8; Isa. 7:4; 1 Chron. 32:7). The tribes of Israel, lacking professional soldiers and the best weaponry, depended on morale. Combatants knew that Yahweh was fighting at their side against the kings who sought to subjugate them. So also was the battle with the Pharaoh and his army understood in Israel. Although the text tells us that the Israelites were armed, and although, under Yahweh's direction, they had selected the battlefield, in purely military terms the superiority of the Egyptian army was unquestionable. Only the justice of the Hebrew cause, and the presence of Yahweh the liberator God at their side, could explain their victory. Moses is here the mouthpiece of this faith, against the incipient counterrevolutionary timidity.

3.1.4 Final Battle Instructions (Exod. 14:15–18)

Yahweh said to Moses, "Why do you cry to me so? Tell the sons of Israel to march on. For yourself, raise your staff and stretch out your han ¹ over the sea and part it for the sons of Israel to walk through the sea on dry ground. I for my part will make the heart of the Egyptians so stubborn that they will follow them. So shall I win myself glory at the expense of Pharaoh, of all his army, his chariots, his horsemen. And when I have won glory for myself, at the expense of Pharaoh and his chariots and his army, the Egyptians will learn that I am Yahweh."

The strategy is to let Israel be pursued by the pharaoh's army as far as the middle of the Red Sea, whose waters Yahweh will temporarily divide to allow them to be trapped there. The sacerdotal rereading, which here speaks of a "parting" of the sea, is a clear allusion to the myth of creation by Yahweh's victory over the sea monster Leviathan (Ps. 74:12–17). The coupling of creation and the division of the sea for Israel's passage is explicit in Isaiah 51:9–11. But the mythological element is no more than an observation of secondary importance. The primary concern of the account is the destruction of the Egyptian army.

3.1.5 Yahweh Defeats the Egyptian Army (Exod. 14:19–30)

3.1.5a THE PILLAR OF CLOUD (EXOD. 14:19–20)

> *Then the angel of God, who marched at the front of the army of Israel, changed station and moved to their rear. The pillar of cloud changed station from the front to the rear of them, and remained there. It came between the camp of the Egyptians and the camp of Israel. The cloud was dark, and the night passed without the armies drawing any closer the whole night long.*

We have already been told that the cloud signaling Yahweh's presence accompanied the Israelites on their journey in order to guide them (§ 3.0). During the night of the encounter with the Egyptian army, the cloud served to separate the armies, because the battle plan did not anticipate their direct contact.

3.1.5b THE EGYPTIAN ARMY ROUTED (EXOD. 14:21–25)

> *Moses stretched out his hand over the sea. Yahweh drove back the sea with a strong easterly wind all night, and he made dry land of the sea. The waters parted and the sons of Israel went on dry ground right into the sea, walls of water to right and left of them. The Egyptians gave chase: after them they went, right into the sea, all Pharaoh's horses, his chariots, and his horsemen. In the morning watch, Yahweh looked down on the army of the Egyptians from the pillar of fire and of cloud, and threw the army into confusion. He so clogged their chariot wheels that they could scarcely make headway. "Let us flee from the Israelites," the Egyptians cried. "Yahweh is fighting for them against the Egyptians!"*

The details of the battle include minor incoherencies, due to multiple rereadings. There is the sacerdotal notion of Yahweh's dividing the sea, leaving walls of water on both sides of the Israelites' path. The tactic is to entice the pharaoh's army to a pursuit, with the cloud precluding contact, and with the water returning to its bed once the Israelites have left it, overwhelming the Egyptian army. But there is also mention of an easterly wind driving the waters, and of the chariot wheels becoming clogged, both references constituting evidence of older versions of the battle.

In any case, before the waters could return upon them, the Egyptian contingent was thrown into confusion by Yahweh's intervention from the pillar of fire and cloud. This is the classic form of Yahweh's defeat of enemies in a holy war. Thus were defeated the alliance of the kings in Gibeon (Josh. 10:10), Sisera's army on the banks of Kishon (Judg. 4:15), and the Philistines in Mizpah (1 Sam. 7:10). According to the purest traditions of Yahweh's wars, the military need only have faith, and trust Yahweh to deliver the enemy into their hands. And this Yahweh does. The enemy is thrown into confusion, and rendered incapable of defending itself. This allows Israel to pursue it and do what it wants with it.

The result of the divine intervention here is panic in the enemy army, which turns and flees, without ever having made contact with the Hebrew militias.

3.1.5c TOTAL VICTORY (EXOD. 14:26–30)

"Stretch out your hand over the sea," Yahweh said to Moses, "that the waters may flow back on the Egyptians and their chariots and their horsemen." Moses stretched out his hand over the sea and, as day broke, the sea returned to its bed. The fleeing Egyptians marched right into it, and Yahweh overthrew the Egyptians in the very middle of the sea. The returning waters overwhelmed the chariots and the horsemen of Pharaoh's whole army, which had followed the Israelites into the sea; not a single one of them was left. But the sons of Israel had marched through the sea on dry ground, walls of water to right and to left of them. That day, Yahweh rescued Israel from the Egyptians, and Israel saw the Egyptians lying dead on the shore.

In their confusion, the Egyptians flee into the rush of water as it returns to its bed. And Yahweh casts them head over heels as they ride, so that they fall into the midst of the waters.

Morning comes. The Israelites, without ever having had to use their swords, see the Egyptian corpses on the beach. All through the night the cloud has kept the two contingents (the "camps") apart. The defeat is total. There are no survivors.

3.1.5d DISSIPATION OF THE COUNTERREVOLUTIONARY THREAT (EXOD. 14:31)

Israel witnessed the great act that Yahweh had performed against the Egyptians, and the people venerated Yahweh; they put their faith in Yahweh and in Moses, his servant.

This final comment is designed to serve as a response to the counterrevolutionary sentiments of Exod. 3.1.3. Seeing the Egyptian army coming at them, some of the Israelites expressed regret at having left the security of Egypt and undergone the danger of confrontation with its army. Now we learn that this sentiment has been dissipated by victory over the attacker. No penal action is taken against those who called the project into question. It is enough that the "rug has been pulled out from under them" as they behold the great victory that Yahwch, with Moses, has achieved. (For a more detailed explanation of the threefold textual conflation of Exod. 3.1.5, see Appendix 9.)

3.2 HYMN TO YAHWEH THE WARRIOR (EXOD. 15:1-21)

The account of the victory over the Egyptian army is followed by a hymn celebrating Yahweh the warrior, Yahweh the God who has led Israel to victory in the sea, and victory over the kings of Canaan. The hymn is placed here because it opens with a celebration of Yahweh's defeat of the Egyptians in the sea. (This hymn has been much discussed by modern interpreters. I do not feel qualified to give a professional interpretation of ancient Hebrew poetry, and it is only right that readers know which authorities I have relied on. In the order of their importance for me, then, they are: Frank M. Cross, Jr., and David Noel Freedman, "The Song of Miriam"; J. D. W. Watts, "The Song of the Sea: Exodus XV"; B. S. Childs, *The Book of Exodus,* 240-53; and Martin Noth, *Exodus,* 120-26.)

The first line of the Hymn of the Sea is repeated in Exodus 15:21, but as a song of Miriam, "the prophetess, Aaron's sister." This raises a doubt as to which of the two texts would be the original. The more likely suggestion is that "Song of Miriam" ("Miriam sang"; cf. 15:1, "Moses sang") is simply another title of the same hymn, not of an independent canticle. The Hymn of the Sea, then—Exodus 15:1-18—and the Song of Miriam would be one and the same canticle, attributed to two personages of antiquity, Miriam and Moses.

A second problem to be solved before the hymn can be interpreted (or translated) is that the imperfect and perfect tenses of verbs are not in conformity with normal Hebrew usage. They seem interchangeable, as if there were no difference between them in the author's mind. Cross and Freedman point out that this is also a characteristic of fourteenth-century Ugaritic writings, and advance this as rather persuasive evidence of the antiquity of the poem. Except in the words placed in the enemy's mouth in verse 9, I prefer to translate these verbal forms in the past tense, inasmuch as Yahweh the warrior is being extolled here from the outlook of an Israel already established in its own land, despite the later attribution of the hymn to Miriam and Moses.

The mention of Yahweh's sanctuary, in verse 17, has likewise been the subject of divergent interpretations. It may refer to the temples in places like Shiloh and Gibeon, but the more natural interpretation is to take them as referring to the temple of Solomon.

One last preliminary problem is that of the date of the hymn. Because of its archaic vocabulary, certain obsolete verb forms, and preclassical spelling, Cross and Freedman argue, forcefully, that the hymn could not have been later than the tenth century B.C., the century of the construction of Solomon's temple. Its poetic form resembles that of the oldest poems in the Bible—the oracles of Balaam and the Song of Deborah. Both of these date from the eleventh century. Watts, however, is of another opinion. He claims to be able to identify accretions to the basic nucleus. In his view, only a first version of the hymn would be premonarchical. There must have been an amplification in early monarchical times. And the entire hymn would have reached its present form only in the seventh century, when it came to be attributed to Moses—an attribution requiring certain changes. For my part—because it seems to me that the hymn is not this complex, but is coherent in its present form, with the possible exception of verse 2—I hold the eleventh century as the probable time of its composition.

By reason of its subject material, the Hymn of the Sea can be divided into two parts, the first celebrating the victory in the sea over the pharaoh and his army (vv. 1–12), and the second the triumph over the rulers of Canaan (vv. 13–18). Each of these two parts seems to be likewise divisible into two parts.*

3.2.1 Yahweh, Victorious Warrior (Exod. 15:1–5)

It was then that Moses and the sons of Israel sang this song in honor of Yahweh:
> Yahweh I sing:
>> he has covered himself in glory,
> [horses and chariots]
>> he has thrown into the sea.
>>> (Yah is my strength,
>>>> my song,
>>> This is my God, I [will] praise him;
>>>> the God of my father, I [will] extol him.)
> Yahweh is a warrior;
>> Yahweh is his name.
> The chariots and the army of Pharaoh
>> he has hurled into the sea;
> the pick of his horsemen
>> lie drowned in the [Red Sea].
> The depths have closed over them;
>> they have sunk to the bottom like a stone.

3.2.2 The Egyptian Army Crushed (Exod. 15:6–12)

> Your right hand, Yahweh,
>> shows majestic in power,

---

*To conform to the author's translation, the text of the *Jerusalem Bible* has here been given distinctive indentation and punctuation. *Textual* differences are printed within square brackets.—ED.

your right hand, Yahweh,
    shatters the enemy.
So great your splendor,
you crush your foes;
    you unleash your fury,
and it devours them like stubble.
    A blast from your nostrils
and the waters piled high;
    the waves stood upright like a dike;
in the heart of the sea the deeps came together.

"I will give chase and overtake,"
    the enemy said,
"I shall share out the spoil,
    my soul will feast on it;
I shall draw my sword,
    my hand will destroy them."
One breath of yours you blew,
    and the sea closed over them;
they sank like lead
    in the terrible waters.
Who among the gods is your like, Yahweh?
    Who is your like, majestic in holiness,
terrible in deeds of prowess,
    worker of wonders?
You stretched your right hand out,
    the earth swallowed them!

3.2.3 Israel's Enemies in Dread (Exod. 15:13–16)

By your grace you led
    the people you redeemed,
by your strength you guided them
    to your holy house.
Hearing of this, the peoples tremble;
    pangs seize on the [rulers] of Philistia.
Edom's chieftains
    are now dismayed,
the princes of Moab
    fall to trembling,
Canaan's [rulers]
    are all unmanned.
On them fall
    terror and dread;

through the power of your arm
they are still as stone
as your people pass, Yahweh,
as the people pass whom you purchased.

3.2.4 Yahweh, King Forever (Exod. 15:17–18)

You [brought] them and [planted] them
on the mountain that is your own,
the place you have made
your dwelling, Yahweh,
the sanctuary [of the Lord],
prepared by your own hands.
Yahweh [is] king
for ever and ever.

3.2.5 The Song of Miriam (Exod. 15:19–21)

Pharaoh's cavalry, both his chariots and horsemen, had indeed entered the sea, but Yahweh had made the waters of the sea flow back on them, yet the sons of Israel had marched on dry ground right through the sea.

Miriam, the prophetess, Aaron's sister, took up a timbrel, and all the women followed her with timbrels, dancing. And Miriam [sang for them]:

Sing of Yahweh:
he has covered himself in glory,
[horses and chariots]
he has thrown into the sea.

3.2.1 If we omit verse 2, this first segment of the Hymn of the Sea is left with six poetic couplets. The first three celebrate Yahweh in general terms as a warrior. The other three celebrate Yahweh's victory in the Red Sea. The four lines of verse 2, which are here enclosed in parentheses, depart from the rhythmic structure of the hymn, according to Cross and Freedman, and are a later insertion—a familiar hymnic phrase that also appears in Psalm 118:14 and Isaiah 12:2.

In verse 1, many translations read: "horse and rider (he has thrown into the sea)." The Massoretic vowel points yield a phrase—*sus werkovō*—that can be so translated. But in the era from which the poem dates, horses were not yet used in Canaan for riding. They were used to pull war chariots. This is their role in the battle of the waters of Merom (Josh. 11:4, 5), and in the battle of Kishon (Judg. 5). If we discount the Massoretic vowels, which were added no earlier than the seventh century A.D., the consonants could just as well read "horses and chariots," and this is how the historical context obliges us to understand the phrase.

If this ancient hymn were the only source of our knowledge of the Red Sea event, we would not imagine that the Israelites passed through the sea. The whole emphasis of the hymn is on the defeat of the pharaoh's army. Yahweh has "thrown" the Egyptian soldiers into the sea, where they have sunk like stones. Thus Yahweh has acted as a warrior. What has taken place is a battle, and the wonder, the "miracle," is to be understood in this context.

3.2.2 The second segment of the hymn celebrates Yahweh's victory in the sea. It begins and ends with the mention of Yahweh's right hand. The last line— ". . . the earth swallowed them!"—momentarily likens the idea of drowning to a death like that of Dathan and Abiram in Numbers 16:31-33, when the earth opened its jaws and swallowed them alive. But in this context it refers to the drowning of the Egyptians in the sea.

The breath of Yahweh's nostrils heaps up the waters so that they swallow the enemy. This is what we have seen in §3.2.1, when Yahweh threw the enemy into the sea. The independent testimony of the hymn and of the prose account (Exod. 14) make it clear that the sea must indeed have played a decisive role in the Israelite victory. We may imagine that the Egyptian troops, all in turmoil, plunged over the edge of a cliff into the sea. But we can only guess at precisely how the sea intervened.

The allusion to gods or saints is an expression of the ancient Israelite notion that Yahweh was surrounded by a heavenly cortege, to carry out Yahweh's commands (see Ps. 82, 1 Kings 22, Isaiah 6, Deut. 32:8, LXX).

3.2.3 In the first half of the hymn, there is no mention either of Moses or of Israel. It is Yahweh the warrior who defeats the pharaoh. The second part of the hymn corrects this omission, focusing on the people acquired as Yahweh's own by reason of the victory over Egypt. The third segment begins and ends with the mention of "the people you redeemed," or the people Yahweh has acquired by right of purchase. Between this opening and this ending we have a poetic description of the conquest and defeat of the chiefs of Canaan, with emphasis on the terror inspired in them by Yahweh.

Redemption is a term borrowed from law, referring to the ransom of a slave with money (Exod. 21:1-11, Deut. 15:12-18). By extension, it applies to mortgaged property as well (Lev. 25). This hymn uses it metaphorically, by speaking of the rescue of the slaves from Egypt, and this usage becomes common in the Bible (Exod. 6:6, Ps. 77:16, Isa. 52:9).

Fear overcame "the rulers (*yoshve*) of Philistia," "the chieftains (*'alufe*) of Edom", "the princes (*'ele*) of Moab," and "the rulers (*yoshve*) of Canaan." (For the justification of this translation, see Gottwald, *Tribes,* 507-30.) The language is poetic, not so prosaic and transparent as a translation may suggest. But the innocuous rendition of *yoshve* as "inhabitants" in most translations fails to do justice to the poetic parallelism, the historical reference, and the semantic range of the word. Yahweh's war in Canaan was a struggle with the rulers of the societies of this land, and not with its populations. It was a class struggle, as we would call it today. In tributary societies, as we have seen, the dominant class was the state: the king and his apparatus of state. This class exploited the peasant villages through taxation in kind and forced service. It was against this dominant class that Yahweh the warrior waged combat.

Our attention is caught by the inclusion of the "rulers of Philistia" in the list of Yahweh's enemies in Canaan. The Philistines came over the sea to Palestine about the year 1175 B.C., the year in which the Egyptians managed to repulse the wave of invaders from their own shore. Some Philistines settled in the coastal plain and imposed their hegemony over the Canaanites of that region. In the initial stage of formation of Israel in Canaan, the Philistines were not yet a danger to be reckoned with, nor was the coastal territory a territory coveted by the tribes of Israel. The Philistines became the formidable enemy of Israel in the period immediately preceding the rise of the Israelite monarchy, in the second half of the eleventh century B.C. The hymn, as we have seen, dates from after this period.

The terror Yahweh inspires in the enemies of Israel is a frequently occurring theme in the histories of the wars of Israel in its first period (Exod. 23:27–28, Deut. 2:25, 11:25, Josh. 2:9, 5:1, 10:2, 1 Samuel 4:7–8). When Yahweh fills their enemies with terror, the hosts of Israel easily exterminate them, and fill their sacks with plunder.

3.2.4 The last segment of the hymn is also its climax. The tyrants of Egypt and Canaan are vanquished. Now Yahweh reigns in an earthly sanctuary! Until early in the present century it was thought that Israel had not celebrated Yahweh as king until it had organized a monarchical state of its own. But today we know that the reign of Yahweh was a basic building block in the revolutionary ideology of Israel's peasant movement, and that it was in the name of Yahweh's rule that Israel refused to install human rulers. (See Gideon's response to the elders of Israel—Judg. 8:22–23. For a brief, synthetic explanation of this matter, see my *God's Kingdom.*) Some of the oldest poems in the Bible celebrate Yahweh as a king (Exod. 15:18, Num. 23:21, Deut. 33:5, Ps. 24:9, 68:25).

The expression, "mountain that is your own"—literally, "mountain of your inheritance"—occurs in exactly the same form in Ugaritic texts of the fourteenth century B.C., where the reference is to Mount Saphon, the dwelling of El, Baal, and other gods (Cross and Freedman, *Studies in Ancient Yahwistic Poetry,* 64–65). In this hymn it probably refers to Mount Zion, although there is always the possibility that it refers to the mountainous region as a whole, where the Israelite uprising took root. The use of this old, pre-Israelitic formula indicates that Israel's Canaanite antecedents had not been forgotten. But the Hymn of the Sea is pure Yahwism in its celebration of Israel's anti-Egyptian and anti-Canaanite revolutionary roots.

3.2.5 This short passage serves to relate the hymn to the exodus account generally. Its version of how the Israelites "had marched on dry ground right through the sea" is based on the prose account, and here serves to clarify ambiguous expressions in the hymn.

3.3 SECOND PERIL: THIRST (EXOD. 15:22–27)

Moses made Israel move from their camp at the Sea of Reeds, and they made for the wilderness of Shur where they traveled for three days without finding water. They reached Marah but the water there was so bitter they could not drink it; this is why the place was named Marah. The people grumbled at Moses. "What are we to drink?" they said. So Moses appealed to Yahweh, and Yahweh pointed out some wood to him; this Moses threw into the water, and the water was sweetened.

There it was he charged them with statute and with ordinance, there that he put them to the test.

Then he said, "If you listen carefully to the voice of Yahweh your God and do what is right in his eyes, if you pay attention to his commandments and keep his statutes, I shall inflict on you none of the evils that I inflicted on the Egyptians, for it is I, Yahweh, who give you healing."

So they came to Elim where twelve water springs were, and seventy palm trees; and there they pitched their camp beside the water.

The wilderness of Shur corresponds to the desert of Etham in the itinerary of Numbers 33 (Num. 33:8). Although the names in the text are unknown to the geographers, obviously these places must have been in the extreme western part of the Sinai desert.

Delivered from the military threat of the Egyptian army, the people now confronted the perils of life in the desert. Of these, a lack of water was the most threatening. And so the people "grumbled"—*vayalīnu*—at Moses. From the use of this verb in the wilderness accounts, we know that what Moses had to deal with here were plans for a rebellion. This is the second time, then, since the triumph in Egypt, that movements against Moses have sprung up, the first being when the fugitives were caught between the Egyptian army and the sea, in Exodus 14:11–12. No wonder that there should have been this incipient counter-revolution: the Hebrews have been three days without water. The problem is a real one, and the revolutionary leadership—Yahweh and Moses—have only one choice: to find water for the people. Scolding or repressing the rebels will solve nothing. And indeed Yahweh indicates to Moses how he can make seawater potable, so that the problems of thirst and grumbling are resolved together.

"There it was he charged them with statute and with ordinance." According to prevailing tradition, it was on Mount Sinai that Yahweh laid down the norms that would govern the life of the new society. Here it is another version of the constitution of Israel that is recalled, in Marah, in the wilderness of Shur. But it is left without development, surely replaced by the Sinai tradition.

"He put them to the test." According to Exodus 17:1–6, Israel tried Yahweh, "put Yahweh to the test," in a place called Massah—a name derived from the verb *nassa,* "to test." The incident is also alluded to in Deuteronomy 6:16. But here it is Yahweh who tests Israel, by giving the people statutes and ordinances.

This again is part of the forgotten tradition of the constitution of Israel in Marah, and Yahweh's "test" is not developed.

Another undeveloped theme is that of Yahweh as physician. We find this tradition in other parts of the Old Testament, too—in Deuteronomy 32:39, Psalm 103:3, and Hosea 6:1. Yahweh, with the plagues, turned Egypt into a place of death. But here in the desert Yahweh is a physician, one who heals. In the immediate context, it is the bitter waters of Marah that Yahweh "heals," renders wholesome.

3.4 THIRD PERIL: HUNGER (EXOD. 16:1-36)

3.4.1 The Journey Continued (Exod. 16:1)

From Elim they set out again, and the whole community of the sons of Israel reached the wilderness of Sin—between Elim and Sinai—on the fifteenth day of the second month after they had left Egypt.

Israel's march follows the sacerdotal itinerary of Numbers 33, which here requires a southeasterly route, in the direction of the southernmost tip of the Sinai peninsula, the site of Jebel Musa, the traditional Mount Sinai.

3.4.2 Counterrevolutionary Accusations (Exod. 16:2-3)

And the whole community of the sons of Israel began to complain against Moses and Aaron in the wilderness and said to them, "Why did we not die at Yahweh's hand in the land of Egypt, when we were able to sit down to pans of meat and could eat bread to our heart's content! As it is, you have brought us to this wilderness to starve this whole company to death!"

A people who vanquished a tyrant, to win the right to conduct its own self-projection into the future, now lack the spirit to face the sacrifices of the transition to a new society! Life was hard in Egypt. But production structures and food-supply systems were solidly entrenched. There was no extreme want. Now Israel finds itself in a situation in which it has left the old structures behind, but has not yet been able to build new ones. The result is the threat of starvation. It is natural that, in this situation, a nostalgia for the old should have arisen. The old may not have been the best, but it was familiar.

The reaction expressed here, however, is more than nostalgia for the old order. And it is more than a criticism of defects in the process of passage to the land where milk and honey flow. Nostalgia and criticism are both altogether admissible in a revolutionary process. The want was genuine, and the demand for nourishment just. The revolutionary vanguard must have foreseen these problems of transition, and, to the extent that it was incapable of solving them (with the people's support), it deserves healthy criticism. But what we have here is not healthy criticism of defects in the revolutionary process. These are counterrevolutionary accusations: ". . . You have brought us to this wilderness to starve this whole company to death!"

The watchword of this revolution is: "Yahweh brought us out of Egypt, out of the house of slavery." In their criticism, the counterrevolutionaries allege that this project has been a death project, not a liberation project. But from the very beginning, Yahweh and Moses have looked to the wilderness as the place of passage to the "land where milk and honey flow." To accuse Moses of betrayal there, as if it were the wilderness that was the final destination, is a grave charge indeed. It is equally counterrevolutionary to make of Egypt—the "house of slavery"—a place "where we were able to sit down to pans of meat and could eat bread to our heart's content!" In the first place, it is simply not true. In no land of antiquity did peasants eat meat on days of forced labor; only on occasions considered festivals. In the second place, it is dishonest of the grumblers to recall the bread they had, and neglect the hard labor that provoked their original complaints and the very project of leaving for a land where milk and honey flowed. The "grumbling" in the wilderness of Sin thus betrays an ill will with regard to the entire liberation undertaking.

3.4.3 Bread for the Hungry (Exod. 16:4-5)

Then Yahweh said to Moses, "Now I will rain down bread for you from the heavens. Each day the people are to go out and gather the day's portion; I propose to test them in this way to see whether they will follow my law or not. On the sixth day, when they prepare what they have brought in, this will be twice as much as the daily gathering."

Yahweh takes the initiative, intervening to solve the hunger problem, and ignoring the bad will expressed in the grumbling. Moses is the one accused of bringing the Israelites out "to the wilderness," but Yahweh's responsibility for the exodus movement is reflected in this initiative to provide for a real need.

This is the earliest reference in the Bible to the Sabbath as a day of rest. It is not presented as a new commandment to be observed, but is presupposed as something normal, and recounts how Yahweh took it into consideration in the directives relating to the miraculous food. Although the account of the manna in Exodus 16 is by and large of sacerdotal origin, these directives are Yahwist (Noth, *Exodus,* 130-34).

The phrase, "to see whether they will follow my law or not," together with verses 27-28, below, express a negative attitude in Yahweh that is absent from the rest of the account, and are in all probability later additions. The idea that the perils of the wilderness were Yahweh's tests is developed in Deuteronomy 8:1-6 in a fashion that is strikingly reminiscent of these additions, and is the same idea as appears in §3.3, where it is undeveloped.

3.4.4 God's Role in the Liberation Project (Exod. 16:6–8)

Moses and Aaron said to the whole community of the sons of Israel, "In the evening you shall learn that it was Yahweh who brought you out of the land of Egypt, and in the morning you shall see the glory of Yahweh, for he has heard your complaints against him—it is not against us you complain, for what are we?" Moses said, "In the evening Yahweh will give you meat to eat, in the morning bread to your heart's content, for Yahweh has heard the complaints you made against him; your complaining is not against us—for what are we?—but against Yahweh."

Armed with confidence that the food problem will be solved, because Yahweh has spoken, Moses and Aaron turn their attention to the people—and in particular to the rebellion, which Yahweh has so serenely ignored. ". . . You shall know that it was *Yahweh* who brought you out of the land of Egypt." The exodus was not a whim of Moses, nor did it reflect any political ambition on his part. It was a project inspired by God. And it is a liberation project, this flight from the land of Egypt, that house of slavery and death.

To rebel against the exodus, therefore, is not simply rebellion against Moses. It is rebellion against God. Most modern revolutions have been atheistic. They have seen that the concept of God has been successfully manipulated by the reactionism that resists the historical progress of humankind. Marx and Engels saw atheism as an expression of the human maturity that no longer had any need to legitimate its pursuit of a better life by an appeal to heaven. They saw, correctly, that, in all objectivity, such an undertaking has no need of any legitimation other than the life it offers.

But it is easy to see why peoples hesitate to hand over to politicians the self-projections on which their future and that of their children depends. There is a popular wisdom in this insistence that liberation projects be in conformity with the will of God. If the revolution had been no more than the project of Moses (or Lenin or Castro), the people would have had reason to suspect personal ambition, which might lead to a new tyranny—or to starvation in the desert. The exodus accounts give us to understand that, behind Moses' leadership, there is a God who cherishes the life of the enslaved. This God, Yahweh, demands unconditional loyalty to the struggle against the Baals who legitimate the slavery laws of the kings of Canaan and Egypt.

Is Moses' response well stated in the account? Is there a God who liberates the poor? Is a revolution that is fought not only in the name of the people (in whose name any revolution must be fought), but also in the name of revolutionary God, politically viable? This is a question that we are asking anew in the Latin American revolutionary movement, and its answer will be decisive for the future of religion in the modern world.

Exodus answers in the affirmative. True, the answer is a bit blurred by the sacerdotal redaction of the final text. This redaction tends to oppose the human and the divine as mutually exclusive: Was it Yahweh *or* was it Moses who brought Israel out of Egypt? But this is totally unacceptable if a believing people is to be the protagonist of its own history.

3.4.5 Meat and Bread (Exod. 16:9–13)

Moses said to Aaron, "To the whole community of the sons of Israel say this, 'Present yourselves before Yahweh, for he has heard your complaints.' " As Aaron was speaking to the whole community of the sons of Israel, they turned toward the wilderness, and there was the glory of Yahweh appearing in the form of a cloud. Then Yahweh spoke to Moses and said, "I have heard the complaints of the sons of Israel. Say this to them, 'Between the two evenings you shall eat meat, and in the morning you shall have bread to your heart's content. Then you will learn that I, Yahweh, am your God.' " And so it came about: quails flew up in the evening, and they covered the camp; in the morning there was a coating of dew all around the camp.

"Present yourselves before Yahweh"—literally, "approach the face of Yahweh"—is a standard expression for going to the sanctuary to offer worship. Inasmuch as there was no tabernacle as yet, it is not clear what the redactors had in mind here. In any case, Yahweh's appearance in the cloud serves to refute the counterrevolutionary rebellion. Thus are confirmed Moses' words to the effect that this has not been a rebellion against the revolutionary leadership, but against the revolutionary liberation itself—that is, against Yahweh.

Yahweh sends meat and bread, and thus abundantly satisfies the people's hunger. There is a parallel to the quail in Numbers 11, but there the manna was a daily occurrence that satisfied hunger during this period of passage, and the desire for meat was reprehensible gluttony, which led a great number to their death in the place called Kibroth-hattaavah, or "tombs of covetousness" (Num. 11:34). A comparison of Exodus 16 with Numbers 11 reveals that the former contains the Yahwist version of the manna, and the latter contains the Yahwist version of the quail. For the Yahwist reading of the traditions, the manna was Yahweh's gift to satisfy a real need on Israel's part, whereas the quail were sent as a curse, in response to the reprehensible desire for meat at a moment when revolutionary process was not in a position to supply it. The sacerdotal reading of these traditions is to be found entirely in Exodus 16. It includes the quail as part of God's generous response to the need of the people.

There are two further readings of these traditions on the nourishment in the desert. According to Psalm 78:19–31, Yahweh gave the manna and the quail together (as in Exod. 16)—but they were both given in anger, as a reaction against the people's rebellion (as in Num. 11). And according to Psalm 105:40–41, both the bread and the meat were gifts of Yahweh's favor toward the people. The sacerdotal reading, then, is akin to this latter way of understanding the traditions.

The phenomenon of the quail has its natural basis in an event that still occurs from time to time in the Sinai peninsula. Immense flocks of birds arrive from Africa exhausted by their flight, and cover the earth.

3.4.6 Manna (Exod. 16:14–15)

When the coating of dew lifted, there on the surface of the desert was a thing delicate, powdery, as fine as hoarfrost on the ground. When they saw this, the sons of Israel said to one another, "What is that?" not knowing what it was. "That," said Moses to them, "is the bread Yahweh gives you to eat."

The text of Exodus has the Israelites feeding on this miraculous food the whole time they lived in the wilderness (§3.4.12). This tradition reflects an authentic knowledge of the Sinai desert. In the wilderness, there is a certain insect that lives on the sap of the tamarisk bush. This insect secretes a sugary substance that, in the dry, cold morning air, coagulates into edible wafers. In the heat of the sun, the wafers melt and disappear (investigated and reported by F. S. Bodenheimer, "The Manna of Sinai"—the basis of J. L. Mihelic's article "Manna" in *The Interpreter's Dictionary*). Modern observers find the substance rather scarce, and in some years it is completely absent. But when available, it could surely serve as food for a group during an emergency period.

The expression *man hu* for "What is that?" appears to be a variant of the more ordinary *mah hu*, having the same meaning. Moses answers that this delicate, powdery coating is the food Yahweh has provided the travelers, as we read in the next verses.

3.4.7 Enough to Satisfy Everyone's Needs (Exod. 16:16–26)

"This is Yahweh's command: Everyone must gather enough of it for his needs, one omer a head, according to the number of persons in your families. Each of you will gather for those who share his tent."

The sons of Israel did this. They gathered it, some more, some less. When they measured in an omer what they had gathered, the man who had gathered more had not too much, the man who had gathered less had not too little. Each found he had gathered what he needed.

Moses said to them, "No one must keep any of it for tomorrow." But some would not listen to Moses and kept part of it for the following day, and it bred maggots and smelled foul; and Moses was angry with them. Morning by morning they gathered it, each according to his needs. And when the sun grew hot, it dissolved.

Now on the sixth day they gathered twice the amount of food: two omers a head. All the leaders of the community came to tell Moses, and he said to them, "This is Yahweh's command: Tomorrow is a day of complete rest, a sabbath sacred to Yahweh. Bake what you want to bake, boil what you want to boil; put aside all that is left for tomorrow." So, as

Moses ordered, they put it aside for the following day, and its smell was not foul nor were there maggots in it. "Eat it today," Moses said, "for today is a sabbath in honor of Yahweh; you will find none in the field today. For six days you are to gather it, but on the seventh day—the sabbath—there will be none."

The miraculous food from heaven was such that, regardless of the amount of effort expended, each family had exactly the amount needed for its members for one day. If anyone ate less than that amount, in the hope of being able to put some of the manna away for the next day, it would spoil. Yahweh is teaching a revolutionary, popular ethic, everyone has needs that must be satisfied, but hoarding is intolerable.

To complete the lesson, Yahweh provides for rest on the seventh day. On the sixth day of the week, each family is to gather double the amount of each of the other days. That night, the manna will not spoil, and there will be food on the seventh day without any need to go out and gather it.

The intention of the text is obviously didactic. The lesson it teaches is one that Christians know from the words of Jesus, "Do not worry about tomorrow: tomorrow will take care of itself. Each day has enough trouble of its own" (Matt. 6:34).

3.4.8 Breaking the Sabbath (Exod. 16:27-28)

On the seventh day some of the people went from the camp to gather it, but they found none. Then Yahweh said to Moses, "How much longer will you refuse to keep my commandments and my laws?"

Here we have a fragment continuing the idea that the instructions concerning the manna were Yahweh's way of testing the people (§ 3.4.3; Exod. 16:4b). I have noted above (ibid.) that this kind of fragment seems to be a late insertion in the text. Everywhere else the manna is presented as a gift of Yahweh to satisfy a need, and the regulation that a double portion be collected the sixth day is evidence of Yahweh's concern for the people. By contrast, the insertion reflects a preoccupation with the observance of laws as the characteristic of Yahweh's authentic followers.

The people's rebellion here consists in disobedience to Yahweh's instructions, rather than in questioning the liberation project itself, as in § 3.4.2.

3.4.9 Sabbath Rest (Exod. 16:29-30)

"Listen! Yahweh has laid down the sabbath for you; for this he gives you two days' food on the sixth day; each of you is to stay where he is; on the seventh day no one is to leave his home." So on the seventh day the people abstained from all work.

Here the dominant line of the text is resumed. The Sabbath is Yahweh's generous present to the Israelites so that they may be able to take their rest on the seventh day.

3.4.10 The Taste of Manna (Exod. 16:31)

The House of Israel named it "manna." It was like coriander seed; it was white and its taste was like that of wafers made with honey.

The taste of the manna is a sign of Yahweh's favor. It tastes like honey cakes. According to Numbers 11:8, its flavor was like that of cakes made with olive oil. Today this discrepancy is explained by the different origins of the texts— sacerdotal in Exodus, Yahwist in Numbers. The classic commentators, however, saw it rather as evidence that the manna tasted different to everyone, according to each one's preference. And indeed this captures the spirit of the tradition of the manna, which understands the miraculous food as a sign of the divine care for this people on its search for a new life.

3.4.11 Grace and Law (Exod. 16:32–34)

Moses said, "This is Yahweh's command: Fill an omer with it, and let it be kept for your descendants, to let them see the food that I fed you with in the wilderness when I brought you out of the land of Egypt." Moses said to Aaron, "Take a jar and put in it a full omer of manna and place it before Yahweh, to be kept for your descendants." Accordingly, Aaron put a full omer of manna in the jar, as Yahweh had ordered Moses, and placed the manna before the Testimony, to be kept there.

The "Testimony" probably refers to the tablets of the law that Yahweh gave Moses on Sinai. Its mention here suggests that, at some moment in the history of the text, the story of the manna followed that of the Sinai revelation, instead of preceding it as it does today. We have already seen that Exodus 16:9 (§3.4.5) presupposes knowledge of the tabernacle, the place of worship at the foot of Mount Sinai.

Symbolically, the jar of manna and the tablets of the law, side by side, dramatize the two aspects of the sacerdotal religion of the Pentateuch: grace and law.

3.4.12 Recurrent Need, Recurrent Provision (Exod. 16:35–36)

The sons of Israel ate manna for forty years, up to the time they reached inhabited country: they ate manna up to the time they reached the frontier of the land of Canaan. An omer is one tenth of an ephah.

This final comment explains that the gift of the manna was continuous, that it was bestowed during the whole time of Israel's passage through the wilderness. The need that occasioned the grumbling was a permanent one in the wilderness life, and Yahweh's response was adequate to the need.

3.5 AGAIN, NO WATER (EXOD. 17:1-7)

3.5.1 Resumption of the Journey (Exod. 17:1a)

The whole community of the sons of Israel moved from their camp in the desert of Sin at Yahweh's command, to travel the further stages; and they pitched camp at Rephidim . . .

The redaction framework for these wilderness stories continues to be the itinerary of Numbers 33, except that the stops at Dophkah and Alush, between Sin and Rephidim, are omitted (Num. 33:12-13).

3.5.2 Dispute between Moses and the People (Exod. 17:1b-4)

. . . where there was no water for the people to drink. So they grumbled against Moses. "Give us water to drink," they said. Moses answered them. "Why do you grumble against me? Why do you put Yahweh to the test?" But tormented by thirst, the people complained against Moses. "Why did you bring us out of Egypt?" they said. "Was it so that I should die of thirst, my children too, and my cattle?" Moses appealed to Yahweh. "How am I to deal with this people?" he said. "A little more and they will stone me!"

There is no water at Rephidim. Once more, as when they were faced by the Egyptian army on the shore, and as when they were hungry in the wilderness of Sin, the rebels have second thoughts about having left their slavery in Egypt. They accuse Moses of being responsible for their imminent death. And as in the case of the previous counterrevolutionary grumbling, Moses refers the complaint to Yahweh.

How are we to understand this attitude on the part of Moses? Does he refuse to assume responsibility for the process he has been directing? Why does he not throw the accusation back at the complainers? After all, no one forced them to bid farewell to their slavery.

The answer is that we are dealing here with a datum of the ideological reworking of redactors whose concern it was to exalt Yahweh. They forget, or wish to forget, that this people has been the agent of its own history. Thus, to a certain extent, we may ignore the ideological interpolation.

But there is something else to consider, as well. We who affirm, with the Israelites, that Yahweh has brought this people out of Egypt, out of the house of slavery, will have to admit that God ought to address this new threat. In referring the problem to Yahweh, Moses is acknowledging that the people's search for conditions favorable to life outside Egypt was divinely inspired, and that it is therefore wrong to wish to return to Egypt or regret the flight. If Yahweh moved the people to struggle for its freedom, struggle to escape the lethal conditions of its servile existence in Egypt, it was that the people might live, not die. Hence Moses insists that the target of the challenge to the exodus is not himself, but Yahweh. Nevertheless, we as readers may be dissatisfied that the text deals with the issue of responsibility with reference only to Moses and Yahweh. After all, the *people* is responsible for its flight from Egypt—under the inspiration of Yahweh and the captaincy of Moses.

The *riv*, "dispute," is recalled in the name Meribah, derived from it. *Riv* is a legal term for a dispute between two persons that, if otherwise unresolved, is brought before a judge. The story of the dispute over the lack of water has a sacerdotal parallel in Numbers 20:1-3. According to Deuteronomy 33:8 and Psalm 81:8, it was Yahweh who initiated the dispute. But in Exodus 17 and Numbers 20, it is the people who begin the dispute with Yahweh. In reality both parties are being tried, tested. Yahweh is being tested to see whether the promise to lead this revolutionary people to a land of abundance will be kept. At the same time, Yahweh calls the people to account for its weak-spiritedness in facing the difficulties of a liberated life during the time of transition to the new society.

In our text, the complainer's dispute is with Moses, but ultimately with Yahweh. In effect, they doubt that their revolutionary action is aligned with what shapes history. If they should die in the wilderness it would mean that they had misjudged the intentions of Yahweh and his capacity to lead them to a new life, or failed to grasp, in other words, the seriousness and the direction of the progressive thrust in human history.

3.5.3 Water from the Rock (Exod. 17:5-6)

Yahweh said to Moses, "Take with you some of the elders of Israel and move on to the forefront of the people; take in your hand the staff with which you struck the river, and go. I shall be standing before you there on the rock, at Horeb. You must strike the rock, and water will flow from it for the people to drink." This is what Moses did, in the sight of the elders of Israel.

Yahweh's response to the wanderers' dispute with their leader Moses is to give them water to assuage their thirst. And Yahweh does this publicly, before the representatives of the people, the elders of Israel, thereby confirming Moses as leader of the people, and ratifying the exodus as a life-giving process supported by God. And a real need of the people is satisfied. There is not the faintest hint of disapproval of or chastisement for the "grumbling," because the protest had arisen from a vital need that the revolutionary leadership had a duty to satisfy in order to maintain the legitimacy of the exodus as source of life.

If there is a historical basis for this tradition, it is probably the sudden appearance of a spring among the rocks. This could be in Horeb (Exod. 17), or in Kadesh (Num. 20), inasmuch as the Yahwist and sacerdotal redactions of the account differ as to where the incident took place.

3.5.4 Massah/Meribah (Exod. 17:7)

The place was named Massah and Meribah because of the grumbling of the sons of Israel and because they put Yahweh to the test by saying, "Is Yahweh with us, or not?"

The double name, Massah (from *nassa,* to test) and Meribah (from *riv,* a dispute), betrays the redactor's geographical uncertainty, as well as the complexity of the history of this tradition.

3.6 THE AMALEKITES REPULSED (EXOD. 17:8–16)

The story that we are about to examine is different from the wilderness stories that we have seen up to this point. It is not a reflection on the threat of counterrevolution and ways in which Yahweh and Moses have responded to this threat. As the passage itself states, the purpose of this story is to memorialize the perpetual enmity between Israel and Yahweh on the one side, and Amalek on the other. (For more on the Amalekites, see Appendix 10.)

3.6.1 Joshua and Hur (Exod. 17:8–13)

The Amalekites came and attacked Israel at Rephidim. Moses said to Joshua, "Pick out men for yourself, and tomorrow morning march out to engage Amalek. I, meanwhile, will stand on the hilltop, the staff of God in my hand." Joshua did as Moses told him and marched out to engage Amalek, while Moses and Aaron and Hur went up to the top of the hill. As long as Moses kept his arms raised, Israel had the advantage; when he let his arms fall, the advantage went to Amalek. But Moses' arms grew heavy, so they took a stone and put it under him and on this he sat, Aaron and Hur supporting his arms, one on one side, one on the other; and his arms remained firm till sunset. With the edge of the sword Joshua cut down Amalek and his people.

Without any explanation, the text introduces a new character, Joshua. Joshua appears as military chief of Israel. In the battle with Egypt, the terrain had been so carefully prepared that it never became necessary to meet the enemy face to face. It would appear that this attack, however, is unexpected, and now Moses appoints Joshua chief of staff.

In the traditions of Israel generally, Joshua is the outstanding military leader of Israel in its struggles with the professional armies of the lords of Canaan. His hereditary lands are in a place called Timnath-serah, in the highlands of Ephraim (Josh. 24:30), so that the natural place for him to go into action would be close to the midpoint of the territory of the tribes of Israel. It is highly likely that Joshua's presence in the wilderness account was inserted at a later date; or else, just the other way around, that the tradition of the combat with the Amalekites did not have its origin in the wilderness.

After this sudden appearance in the book of Exodus, Joshua appears again as Moses' companion in the latter's ascent of the mountain to receive the tablets of the law (Exod. 24:13, 32:17), and once more in the tradition of the tent of meeting (33:11). But the only passage in Exodus where he plays a leading role is in this story of the battle with Amalek.

Amalek, too, appears in the account without introduction. The reader must suppose that the Amalekites attacked Israel because the desert was their homeland and they felt Israel's presence as a threat.

Another new character is Hur, the one who, along with Aaron, Moses' lieutenant, supports Moses' arms. Hur appears as Moses' companion, and the one in charge of the people, when Moses ascends the mountain to receive the tablets of the law (Exod. 24:14). The text does not appear to identify him with the Hur of Judah who was the grandfather of Bezalel, the craftsman who outfitted the ark and the sanctuary (Exod. 31:2, 35:30, 38:22). There are no traditions concerning Hur outside the book of Exodus that might add any further details.

The victory over Amalek is presented as the result of the strength with which the Israelite warriors were inspired by the outstretched arms of Moses on the hilltop. Nothing is said of Yahweh as yet, but a later comment serves notice that this strength came from God.

There is an ambiguity in the account—whether Yahweh's power came via the staff of God, Moses' raised arm, or both his arms. "As long as Moses kept his arms raised" is ". . . kept his hand raised" (or "arm"—in the singular in any case) in the Hebrew.

3.6.2 Unending War with Amalek (Exod. 17:14–16)

Then Yahweh said to Moses, "Write this [action] down in a book to keep the memory of it, and say in Joshua's hearing that I shall wipe out the memory of Amalek from under heaven." Moses then built an altar and named it Yahweh-nissi because he said, "[A(?) My (?)] hand on the banner of [Yah.] Yahweh is at war with Amalek from age to age!"

This short passage is replete with difficulties. It would indeed seem that it is "this action" ("this," merely, in the Hebrew) of which "the memory is to be kept." And yet there is nothing in the account to justify such deep hostility. Israel battled many peoples, and still had cordial relations with at least some of them at other moments—Moab, for instance, or Ammon. If the account in the book of Exodus is complemented by the commentary in Deuteronomy 25:17–19, we see that Amalek had attacked Israel's rear when it was exhausted. Perhaps we should also think of the Amalekite attack on David's base camp while he was on a campaign with his troops (1 Sam. 30:3). But the Exodus account itself is incomplete, in that it fails to explain the degree of hostility it records.

Moses now erects an altar, to which he gives the name "Yahweh is my standard," or "Yahweh is my banner." It was under Yahweh that the victory was won, so that Yahweh is the "banner" of the Israelite troops.

The expression "hand [as a noun] on the banner of Yah" is unclear in the Hebrew. It contains the words *kes yah,* which seem to have been transmitted incorrectly. A glance at various translations will show the lengths to which scholars have been willing to go in order to try to make sense of the language here. To me it seems best to accept a textual emendation and read *nes Yah*— "Yah's standard." This conjecture conforms to the context, and supposes the corruption of only one letter, so that it is more likely to be the original reading than are the great majority of conjectures that are without textual evidence. The *Jerusalem Bible* takes liberties with the syntax when it actually places this banner in the hand: "Lay hold of the banner. . . . " The syntax is clear: the hand is on (over, upon) the banner. It may have to do with a gesture accompanying an oath by which Moses swears to carry on Yahweh's war against Amalek.

3.7. THE EXODUS RATIFIED BY JETHRO (EXOD. 18:1–12)

3.7.1 Jethro and Zipporah (Exod. 18:1–5)

Jethro priest of Midian, father-in-law of Moses, heard of all that God had done for Moses and for Israel his people, and how Yahweh had brought Israel out of Egypt. So Jethro, father-in-law of Moses, brought Moses' wife Zipporah—after she had been dismissed—with her two sons. One of these was named Gershom because, he had said, "I am a stranger in a foreign land"; the name of the other was Eliezer because "The God of my father is my help and has delivered me from the sword of Pharaoh." So Jethro, father-in-law of Moses, came with his son-in-law's wife and children to the wilderness where his camp was, at the mountain of God.

This story does not easily fit in with the overall itinerary that has framed the wilderness accounts so far. Jethro, priest of Midian and father-in-law of Moses, comes to meet Moses at the "mountain of God," the place where Yahweh had appeared to Moses in the burning bush. According to Exodus 19:1–2, the Israelites had come to Sinai directly from Rephidim, the site of the confrontation with the Amalekites. It is unclear whether the mountain of God and Mount Sinai are the same, or whether the mountain of God is in Rephidim.

The problem is not a geographical one: we have no knowledge of the place the itinerary identifies as Rephidim. The problem is literary. On the level of the history of traditions, the problem is solved if we understand that there were originally two independent traditions, one concerning the "mountain of God," the other concerning Mount Sinai. But on the redactional level a certain ambiguity remains.

The priest of Midian is accompanied by Zipporah and "her two sons." These are Moses' sons too, obviously, as we see from their names. We have heard nothing of Zipporah and Gershom since their journey with Moses back to Egypt with the mission of liberating the Israelites (§2.1.9). Now we learn two things that the account has not mentioned before: that Moses had dismissed Zipporah, and that she had had a second son, Eliezer. There is no cause for surprise here. Moses was engaged in a dangerous confrontation with the pharaoh, and in these circumstances it would surely have been wise to send his wife and children to Jethro's house. David did the same thing during the period of his uprising, when he sent his relatives to Moab for their own safety (1 Sam. 22:1–4). From his name, we may suppose that Eliezer ("my God is help") was born when the campaign against the Egyptian tyrant was well under way. We shall hear no more about him, except for seeing his name in a late genealogy (1 Chron. 23:15,17, 26:25).

The mention of the "mountain of God" is reminiscent of the "sign" that Yahweh had promised Moses—that when he had led the Israelites out of Egypt, they would worship Yahweh in this place (§2.1.3). Now the sign is fulfilled, and the dynamics that began on this very mountain are brought to completion.

3.7.2 Yahweh Acknowledged and Worshiped (Exod. 18:6–12)

"Here is your father-in-law, Jethro, come to visit you," Moses was told, "with your wife and her two sons." So Moses went out to meet his father-in-law and bowing low before him he kissed him; and when each had inquired of the other's health, they went into the tent. Then Moses told his father-in-law all that Yahweh had done to Pharaoh and the Egyptians for the sake of Israel, and all the hardships that had overtaken them on the way, and how Yahweh had rescued them. And Jethro rejoiced at all Yahweh's goodness to Israel in rescuing them from the Egyptians' hands. "Blessed be Yahweh," said Jethro then, "who has rescued you from the Egyptians and from Pharaoh, and has rescued the people from the grasp of the Egyptians. Now I know that Yahweh is greater than all the gods. . . . "

Then Jethro, father-in-law of Moses, [accepted] a holocaust and sacrifices to God; and Aaron came with all the elders of Israel to share the meal with the father-in-law of Moses in the presence of God.

Jethro arrives at Moses' tent, announces himself, and the pair greet each other with a kiss, in the style of the Middle East. The younger does homage to the elder, and each begs the other's *shalom,* "peace." Women had no place in these formalities, although Zipporah's presence in the encampment indicates that the danger was over and life had begun to come back to normal.

Once inside Moses' tent, the two men of authority recount the events of the liberation and the vicissitudes of life in the wilderness, and we readers know the story. It is the story of "all that Yahweh had done to Pharaoh," and "how Yahweh had rescued them in the wilderness." This emphasis on God's role in the revolution, here as elsewhere, serves to confirm the historical legitimacy of the exodus. Faced with the Egyptian attack, hunger, and thirst, the people (or some of the people) had questioned whether a new, classless society was possible—and had desired to return to Egypt. Moses had always responded that the Exodus was not his own idea, and that any rebellion against the revolutionary process was a rebellion against Yahweh. Translated from theological language, this means that the exodus represents the course and direction of history. In asserting to his father-in-law that it had been Yahweh who had brought them out of Egypt and come to their aid in the wilderness, Moses is asserting that the undertaking of the Israelite people bears the mark of historical validation.

Jethro's response—"Now I know that Yahweh is greater than all the gods"—admits of two interpretations. It is possible that Jethro is hearing of Yahweh here for the first time, and that his surprise relates to his new theological knowledge—the name and personage of Yahweh. Or we may understand that Jethro, priest of Midian, has already officiated at rites of Yahweh, but that now he knows that Yahweh is a God who liberates. In the context of the whole account, it is this latter interpretation that would be the more natural.

The "mountain of God," where Yahweh once manifested himself to Moses, is familiar to Jethro. In the account of Moses' calling (§2.1.1), this mountain was referred to as if it had been a familiar place—"*the* mountain of God," precisely—and Jethro knew where to find Moses. And in the sacrifice about to be shared by Jethro, Moses, Aaron, and the elders of Israel, in thanksgiving to Yahweh, it is Jethro who invites the others.

"Now I know that Yahweh is greater than all the gods. . . . " The elliptical points indicate an incoherent expression in the Massoretic text. The untranslated expression doubtless alludes to the pride of the enemies of Yahweh, or of Israel. But it is not possible to reconstruct it. What is clear is that Jethro acknowledges Yahweh's superiority over other gods, beginning, surely, with the gods of Egypt. All oppressors seek to legitimate their supremacy by self-assured appeal to God's backing. It is understandable, then, that revolutions will naturally tend to atheism. Revolutionaries reject the gods of dominators and, if they fail to find a liberating God, they end by rejecting divinity as such. Jethro gives expression to the religious stance of the Israelite revolution. Yahweh is greater than all other gods because it is Yahweh who liberates the people from the oppression of kings who take refuge behind the shield of their religions or their gods. In secular terms, the liberative self-projection corresponds to the dynamic of history, and in the long run is more powerful than the historical self-projection of dominators.

The sacrifice offered to God in Moses' tent, with Jethro presiding, is again open to more than one interpretation. Cody ("Exodus 18:12: Jethro Accepts a Covenant with the Israelites") observes that treaties between ancient Middle Eastern peoples are frequently solemnized by sacrifices—Genesis 31:54, Exodus 24:5, Deuteronomy 27:5-8, Psalm 50:5. Further, the language used here is unusual if Jethro is the one who offers sacrifice as the priest in charge. What the Hebrew says is that he "took" or "accepted" the sacrifice—rather akin to the language of Joshua 9:14-15, where the Israelites "partook of"—"took" or "accepted," in the Hebrew—the rations offered them by the Gibeonites, and made peace with them. According to this interpretation, Jethro accepted an alliance with the people of Israel.

Other factors, however, suggest that the sacrifice was one of thanksgiving. Jethro has acknowledged Yahweh's greatness. He is a priest who has already practiced the Yahweh cult at this mountain. Now that he knows Yahweh's greatness, and identity as a liberator God, he renders Yahweh homage and worship in a spirit of thanksgiving. The fact that holocausts are mentioned is another key: the appropriate sacrifice for the solemnization of a treaty is the *zebah,* where the parties involved, along with the deity, consume the victim (Gen. 31:54, Exod. 24:5). The holocaust, on the other hand, where the victim is entirely consumed by fire, is the more natural sacrifice for an expression of thanksgiving to the deity.

It is noteworthy that it is the priest of Midian who officiates in this religious celebration of Yahweh's victory. Classic exegesis sees Jethro's "conversion" here—from his paganism to faith in Yahweh. The modern interpretation, instead, is that it was precisely Jethro who introduced the Hebrews to the religion of Yahweh, through Moses, his son-in-law. This is a reasonable hypothesis, nothing more. And even if it is correct it must still be remembered that the Midianite cult of Yahweh that antedated the exodus—Jethro's Yahwism—would be very different from the religion of the Yahweh who brought Israel out of Egypt—the only religion of Yahweh known to the Bible.

3.8 THE APPOINTMENT OF JUDGES (EXOD. 18:13-27)

3.8.1 Moses as Judge (Exod. 18:13-18)

On the following day, Moses took his seat to administer justice for the people, and from morning till evening they stood around him. Observing what labors he took on himself for the people's sake, the father-in-law of Moses said to him, "Why do you take all this on yourself for the people? Why sit here alone with the people standing around you from morning till evening?" Moses answered his father-in-law, "Because the people come to me to bring their inquiries to God. When they have some dispute they come to me, and I settle the differences between the one and the other and instruct them in God's statutes and his decisions." "It is not

*right," the father-in-law of Moses said to him, "to take this on yourself.
You will tire yourself out, you and the people with you. The work is too
heavy for you. You cannot do it alone."*

The usual manner of settling disputes in Israel was to submit them to the
elders of the people, who congregated at the entrance to a village (Ruth 4,
Amos 4:12). Justice was local, popular justice. But this is not the system
presented here. Here, plaintiffs and defendants came to their supreme leader,
the liberator, to resolve their disputes, so that they had to wait in line all day
long to present their cases. Jethro censures this procedure for its inefficiency. It
is too burdensome for Moses, and will finally exhaust both him and the people.

The system of justice condemned by Jethro, however, is not only inefficient.
It is open to criticism on political grounds, too. The Israelites had rebelled
against a society in which the tyrant pharaoh could decide the fate of the people
arbitrarily. The new society, in the land where milk and honey flowed, was to
be built on more popular political structures. And yet, lo and behold, rebels
were still looking for decisions from the supreme leader of their liberation
movement. They felt that this meant that it was God who was handing down
decisions. It is not that other expressions of popular power did not exist. The
elders had had a certain share in the movement from the start. But the elders
are not mentioned in this text on the administration of justice.

One suspects an ambiguity in the revolutionary process. One suspects that
the cloak of revolutionary legitimacy is beginning to be coopted by a system
centralized in the judiciary. There is no question of a classist system here: the
center does not live on the exploitation of a subordinate class. But neither does
power spring from the people.

Moses' explanation to his father-in-law cites three elements of the system of
justice in Israel. (1) Consultation of God when one wishes to know whether a
proposed undertaking would be pleasing to God (see 1 Sam. 28:6, 1 Kings
22:5-8, 2 Kings 3:11, etc.), or when one is faced with illness or some other
calamity and wishes to know its cause or cure (Gen. 25:22, 1 Sam. 9:9, 1 Kings
14:5, 2 Kings 1:2). (2) Consultation of elders, usually for a decision in litigation
between two Israelites—but in difficult cases from the Levites of the temple
(Deut. 17:8-13). (3) Instruction in the laws and divine norms that are to
orientate national life, a task Deuteronomy entrusts to the Levites (Deut. 31:9-
13). Moses states that, as a judge, he combines these three functions. He
concentrates, in his person, functions that were later separated in Israel. But
this is not the problem Jethro sees.

3.8.2 Bureaucratic Revolutionary Organization (Exod. 18:19-27)

*"Take my advice, and God will be with you. You ought to represent the
people before God and bring their disputes to him. Teach them the
statutes and the decisions; show them the way they must follow and what
their course must be. But choose from the people at large some capable*

and God-fearing men, trustworthy and incorruptible, and appoint them
as leaders of the people: leaders of thousands, hundreds, fifties, tens. Let
these be at the service of the people to administer justice at all times. They
can refer all difficult questions to you, but all smaller questions they will
decide for themselves, so making things easier for you and sharing the
burden with you. If you do this—and may God so command you—you
will be able to stand the strain, and all these people will go home
satisfied."

Moses took his father-in-law's advice and did as he said. Moses chose
capable men from the ranks of the Israelites and set them over the people:
leaders of thousands, hundreds, fifties, tens. They were at the service of
the people to administer justice at all times. They referred hard questions
to Moses, and decided smaller questions by themselves.

Then Moses allowed his father-in-law to go, and he made his way back
to his own country.

The solution Jethro proposes is a bureaucratic one. He has noticed problems
of inefficiency in the administration of justice, and he proposes a more
effective way of going about it. As in the typical bureaucracy, power comes
down from the top of the pyramid. It does not come up from the base, as we
would hope it would in a popular movement. Moses, as supreme authority, will
appoint persons he trusts to assist him in the administration of justice. These
will deal with the ordinary cases and refer only the difficult ones to him. Moses
will reserve to himself the functions of consulting God in order to be instructed
in God's laws, and will reserve to himself the representation of the people
before God. Ordinary decisions in minor matters will be referred to judges
named by him (and whom, therefore, he can remove from office).

We are not dealing with a class society like that of Egypt: Moses gains no
advantage from the Israelites' labor, nor does he have the power to compel
them to do forced labor. What we have here is a bureaucratic revolutionary
organization. It is revolutionary because it rejects a class society and seeks to
implement the laws of Yahweh, who is a liberator God. It is bureaucratic,
however, because, in the administration of justice, power comes from the top
down—from Moses as leader to those whom he appoints—and not from the
bottom up.

A division into thousands, hundreds, and fifties in the biblical texts is usually
a division for military purposes. Thus for example Saul appointed David
captain of a thousand men (1 Sam. 18:13). The Philistine army was divided
into platoons of a hundred men and battalions of a thousand (1 Sam. 29:2). In
the uprising led by Jehoiada against Queen Athaliah, again we read of groups
of hundreds of soldiers, under their captains (2 Kings 11:4, 9, 10, 19). This type
of division would appear natural for an army. But it is not altogether evident
that it would provide good results in the administration of justice. Even for
military purposes, this system of organization was used only in the period of
the monarchy. In more ancient texts, the word *elef*—which later meant

"thousand"—was used for the military unit, large or small, provided by a clan, and not for a specific number. (David fed an *elef* with ten loaves of bread and ten cheeses in 1 Sam. 17:17–18, and this would certainly not have been enough for a thousand men.)

The popular system of justice that prevailed in Israel imposed the task of its administration on the elders of each village. The authority of these elders derived from their being acknowledged as persons of good judgment on the part of their neighbors in a given locale. According to 2 Chronicles 19:4–10, it was Jehoshaphat, in the ninth century B.C., who instituted a system wherein judges were appointed by the king. It is anachronistic, then, for Moses to be declared the author of this bureaucratic system of justice. It is possible that the text reflects an ancient attempt, later abandoned, to establish such a system. Or it may be that the account seeks to legitimate a system that was indeed finally in force in the monarchical period.

APPENDIX 9:
THREE VERSIONS OF THE CROSSING OF THE RED SEA

It is not difficult to discern, in the account of the battle of the sea (Exod. 14:15–31), the presence of two somewhat different versions, one corresponding to the Yahwist layer of the Pentateuch, the other to the sacerdotal. In the text as we have it, these somewhat different versions are sufficiently well integrated with each other to permit the coherent reading developed in §3.1. Incoherencies are limited to minor details. But let us now subject these differences to greater systematization.

The *sacerdotal* account opens with the twofold action of Yahweh, who both leads the Israelites to the seashore, and hardens the heart of the pharaoh so that he will pursue them. This is all part of Yahweh's plan to acquire glory (exactly as with the plagues in the sacerdotal redaction). God instructs Moses to raise his staff over the sea to divide it in two, leaving a dry path for the passage of the Israelites. The Egyptian army pursues the fugitives as far as the center of the sea. Israel emerges on the farther shore. Suddenly Moses raises his staff once more, and the path is closed with the return of the waters, which become the Egyptians' tomb. The whole sequence is calculated to redound to the glory of Yahweh.

According to the *Yahwist* version of this battle, the pharaoh regrets having permitted the Israelites' departure, and sallies forth in their pursuit. But the cloud settles between the two groups, and remains there all the night long, so that they do not come in contact. The people, or part of the people, are in great fear, and accuse Moses of bringing them out of Egypt to die in the desert. But Yahweh, from out of the cloud, confuses the Egyptian army during the night, and overturns their chariots, so that they fall into the sea. Morning comes, and the Israelites see only the corpses of the Egyptians on the shore. Now they believe in Yahweh and Moses.

These two versions, each practically complete in itself, are also fairly consistent with each other. Only a few details are at odds. These include the information that the pharaoh had to "be told" of the flight of his slaves (Exod. 14:5), the mighty east wind, the angel of God between the opposing groups (14:19), and the divine action in clogging the wheels of the Egyptian chariots (14:25). It is likely, then, that these details correspond to the *Elohist* version of the battle, although they may include some minor disconnected traditions.

It is impossible to reconstruct "what really happened." The account as we have it seeks to teach something about Yahweh as savior, the perils of counterrevolution, and war waged by an Israelite militia under the conduct of a leader selected by Yahweh. Each of the two most ancient readings that can be isolated underscores certain of these elements. We have no eyewitness testimony.

Nevertheless, we can indicate certain probabilities. It is unlikely that the Egyptian king will have personally followed, all the way to the border, a group of peasants fleeing forced labor. But it is natural to think that the Egyptian border was fortified, and that the Hebrews had to contend with a border patrol. In some fashion, the Hebrews took advantage of the sea, possibly leading the pursuing chariots to a place where their wheels became enmeshed in reeds or mired in mud. Or perhaps the pursuers tumbled down a steep bank in the darkness of night. We cannot say with certainty. Our task is to read the text, rather than to reconstruct the events that gave rise to the traditions it reflects.

APPENDIX 10:
THE AMALEKITES

We have no information on the Amalekites other than that given us in the Bible itself. There the Amalekites always appear as Israel's enemies. They are not class enemies, like the Canaanites, peoples tributary to the monarchies in that same land of Canaan that Israel aspired to dominate. They were, rather, enemies who attacked from outside the country.

The oracle of Balaam in Numbers 24:20 says that the Amalekites were the most ancient of peoples. According to Israelite genealogies Amalek was the grandchild of Esau (Gen. 36:12, 1 Chron. 1:36), which would make the Amalekites a southern people related to Israel: Jacob-Israel was Esau's brother. And indeed most traditions place the Amalekites in the desert to the south of Canaan (Exod. 17:8–16; 1 Sam. 15, 27:8–9, 30:1–2). Only in the Gideon cycle do they appear from the east of the Jordan, together with the Midianites, whose homeland is also the south (Judg. 6:3,33, 7:12). What we have, then, is an incursion outside their territory.

1 Samuel 15 recounts the intent of King Saul to exterminate the Amalekites, at the instigation of and with the blessing of the prophet Samuel. Some years later, David battles the Amalekites, in order to plunder them (1 Sam. 27:8–9), and in retaliation for their treacherous attack on his rear guard (1 Sam. 30). We shall not meet the Amalekites again. Probably any of them who survived the wars with Saul and David were incorporated into other groups living to the south of Judah.

Part Four

Foundations for a New Society (Exod. 19:1–40:38)

INTRODUCTION

Exodus: A Revolutionary Memory of a Religious People

The fourth and last part of the book of Exodus presents the constitutional basis of the new society of the people of Yahweh, the liberator God. The actual account of the construction of this society in the land of Canaan is not given in Exodus (see Table 2), although some of its problems are presented in veiled form in the wilderness stories (Exod., chapters 13:17–18:27).

Furthermore, it would have been impossible for Israel to compose a cohesive account of the construction of the revolutionary society. It contented itself with the anecdotal histories collected in the books of Joshua and Judges, and for a reason. The histories of the origins of Israel took fixed, written form beginning in the tenth century B.C., in the time of Kings David and Solomon. In this era, and the one immediately following, the Yahwist and Elohist versions of these origins took shape. What the historians of the kingdom sought to create was the history of the origins of the Israelite nation. They had no interest in writing a revolutionary history—even though the materials of which they necessarily made use had arisen out of a revolutionary experience. Thus it was easier to present the account of the destruction of the old order in Egypt (which could be read as a struggle for national liberation) than to relate the experiences of an emerging people in Canaan that rejected the class societies existing in the land of Canaan. This is why, in the part of the account where we might have expected the history of the construction of a new society, we find instead the collection of laws that served as the constitution of this new society.

The constitutive laws of Israel demanded the clear authority of the experience of liberation from servitude in Egypt, both on level two—tribal Israel—and on level three—monarchical Israel. Lacking any reference to the creation of an Israelite state, these constitutive laws call for exclusive loyalty to

Yahweh—and, in their narrative frame, to Yahweh's prophet Moses.

It might appear curious, at first sight, that a revolutionary movement such as that of the rural tribes of Israel would legitimate the norms by which they thought they should live by an appeal to exclusive loyalty to God and to a hero—Moses—who had already died during the period of the construction of a classless society. But it is really not so strange. The old order against which the Hebrew peasants of Egypt, and the Israelite tribes of Canaan, had rebelled was in either case a tributary society in which the state was coextensive with the exploiting class. The state as it was known in this era lived from the tribute of its peasant villages. Israel rejected not only the pharaoh and the kings of Shechem and Hazor, but any and every form of state domination.

To this purpose, Exodus proposes an alternative legislation that would establish conditions of equality among the citizens of Israel. It does not propose means of supplying leadership. It goes without saying that there will be a "natural" leadership, springing from bonds of kinship. The head of the family will be the leader of that family, and the council of the elders will decide matters involving more than one family.

According to Exodus, it is Yahweh, with Moses the prophet, who directed the liberation movement. In the new society, Yahweh, the liberator God, will now hold the place held by kings in other nations. The first commandment of the new Israel will be the prohibition of the worship of any god but Yahweh, the God of the exodus. Any other worship would be counterrevolutionary, as it would open the door to religions that legitimate an earthly royalty.

In the construction of the new, classless society, Moses has a unique role. He will have no successors. The wilderness histories legitimate Moses' unique guiding role. On Mount Sinai, Yahweh appears in a thick cloud, and the people hear Yahweh speaking with Moses: ". . . so that the people may hear when I speak to you and may trust you always" (Exod. 19:9). Moses could say, "I have not taken so much as a donkey from them, nor have I harmed any of them" (Num. 16:15), for he always represented the interests of the revolution unswervingly. In the book of Deuteronomy, a succession of prophets of Yahweh will be contemplated, to continue the mission of Moses (Deut. 18:16–20). But in the normative account of Exodus no succession of any kind is provided for. No, Moses is the mediator of the norms that Yahweh dictates for life in the classless society, and these norms will be enough. Moses' authority is unique and untransferable.

In the absence of a recognized system of legitimation of political leadership, legislation becomes basic to the maintenance of the revolutionary character of the new society. In practice, this anti-Canaanite, antistate society was able to subsist for some two hundred years (from approximately 1200 to 1000 B.C.). Then, under relentless military pressure from the Philistines, Israel too appointed "a king as the nations have," legitimating him in the name of Yahweh, God of the exodus. The redaction of the book of Exodus dates from this period of the monarchy, and thus the omission of any mention of an institution of political leadership is not due to ignorance. It is a sign of the resistance of the Israelite legal tradition to the institution of monarchy.

In insisting on the exclusive, unique authority of Moses as the person who speaks with Yahweh as one who speaks with one's friend (Exod. 33:11), our text is "putting in their place" the kings who say they are Yahweh's designates for commanding the people. By its silence, the legislation asserts the possibility of an Israel without state institutions. In the book of Exodus, the only state to appear is the Egyptian—and this state, only too clearly, was the death of its subjects. There is no denying that this is a consistent revolutionary position in a world where there was no exploitive class but the state! And the book of Exodus, which cannot or will not report the *building* of a classless society, abundantly explains how, on Mount Sinai, Yahweh, the liberator God, revealed to Moses the laws that were to govern the life of this new society, where the stranger, the widow, and the orphan could live in security. God guarantees the revolution!

We in Latin America are accustomed to antireligious, or at least nonreligious, revolutionary theories. In Israel, the first revolutionary demand was exclusive loyalty to Yahweh, principal agent in the popular struggle for power. This has no parallel in our experience. The sometimes revolutionary language of Christian Democratic political parties has shown itself equivocal and treacherous in the hour of truth, as we saw so clearly in Chile, and now see in El Salvador. (Very instructive with regard to Christian democracy is Franz Hinkelammert's *Ideología de sometimiento: la iglesia católica chilena frente al golpe: 1973–74.*) The only consolidated Latin American revolution, the Cuban, rejects the notion that its triumphs are attributable to God. The Sandinista revolution in Nicaragua augurs a new revolutionary attitude toward religion, but a healthy skepticism will prescribe limits to any hopes that might arise in its regard.

We believers have the opposite kind of difficulty in reading this at once religious and revolutionary text. Our firmly rooted, old "liberal" tradition of the separation of religion and politics makes it very difficult for believers to perceive Exodus as the "manual of arms" of a people in a revolution. Quite the contrary of the difficulty under which revolutionary theoreticians labor, our difficulty is not a perception of God's action in the history of the people of Israel—our difficulty is reading the experience of Israel as an authentic revolution, in which a people took into its own hands the historical destiny that had been snatched from it by kings. In line with the nationalistic interpretation of the Yahwist redactors, we have been taught to read Exodus as God's rescue of the people after the temporary aberration of a time of slavery. In this reading, nationhood precedes the exodus, which serves only to restore that nationhood. If we resituate the production of Exodus in the struggles of the Israelite peasants to win and to defend their quality of life in the face of the assaults of the kings of Canaan, we give it back the revolutionary character of the struggle with the Pharaoh. It was their own struggle that the Benjaminites and other peasants of Canaan saw reflected in the earlier one of the Exodus.

Historical experiences such as the popular struggles in Central America are opening our eyes to the book of Exodus as the revolutionary manual of a deeply religious peasant people. But this reading of Exodus will not come to us without effort. In the present commentary on Exodus, I am attempting to follow this line of reading that the peoples of Latin America are opening up to us. I believe that I am being faithful to the original intention of the account. And the success of this reading will depend in part on the success of the revolutions that today are finding their inspiration in the Christian faith.

Until these revolutions are reality, it will continue to be difficult to read a revolutionary text in which God is the principal agent, both in victory over the oppressor and in the building of a new order. In Appendix 8, above, "In What Sense Did Yahweh Bring Israel out of Egypt?," I have attempted to set up some guidelines for understanding God's role in the revolutionary action of a people. For revolutionary construction, something similar must be grasped: God, as motive power of historical advance, inspires in peoples the norms by which it is possible to live in liberty and justice.

According to the text of Exodus, Yahweh imposed just laws through Moses, Yahweh's prophet, and Moses as supreme leader of the revolution has no successor. Perhaps we could understand Moses' special role by comparing it with the special role of revolutionary figures such as Lenin, Tito, Mao, Ho Chi Minh, and Castro. These revolutionaries are acknowledged as the indisputable mouthpieces of their people-in-revolution, and this function admits of no succession. How much more so, then, in the revolution of the Israelites, whose immediate goal is the elimination of the state, the elimination of the institutionalization of political leadership!

At all events, the principal theoretical text of this ancient revolution is profoundly religious. A secular revolution was not a real option for the peasants of Canaan who could no longer tolerate the taxation imposed on them by the kings. They thought that gods sent rain, they thought that gods delivered them from plagues. The alternatives they faced were not like those facing the Russian revolutionaries at the beginning of this century—between a religion that legitimated an oppressive social order, and a revolutionary doctrine that made workers the agents of their own history. The Canaanite peasants depended on gods for their survival. Their option was between the gods of the kings, Baal and his minions, and the God of the poor, Yahweh. Yahweh was a new God for them. They knew Yahweh by the testimony of the Hebrews of Egypt as a God who had once led them in their struggle against oppression. Only, they would have to tender Yahweh their exclusive loyalty, and depend on Yahweh for whatever they previously had from Baal, be it rain or anything else. By looking at it this way, we understand how an authentically revolutionary people could profess that it was God who had liberated it and imposed on it the norms of a new, classless society.

Critico-Literary Analysis of Exodus 19–40

Despite all their efforts, exegetes have been unable to achieve a very reliable analysis of the texts that have been combined to produce the text of the revelation on Mount Sinai as we have it today—a text that gives every indication of being an amalgam. It seems certain that there are three distinct elements in the Sinai material. And each of these elements is itself complex, has its own history, and lends itself only to an uncertain internal analysis, not yielding a great deal when it comes to an interpretation of the conflated text.

In my commentary, chapters 19 through 40 of Exodus are presented in three composite segments—4A, 4B, and 4C (see Table 3). A brief overview of each segment follows.

Table 3

The Continuous Text of Exodus 19–40
Divided into the Three Collections of Laws

	4B	4A	4B	4A
19:1–3a	**19**:3b–8	**19**:9–25, **20**:1–21	**20**:22–26, **21**–**23**	**24**:1–2

4B	4A	4C	4A	4C
24:3–8	**24**:9–15a	**24**:15b–18, **25**–**30**, **31**:1–17	**31**:18, **32**–**34**	**35**–**40**

(chapter numbers are in bold print)

§4A: NORMS FOR LIVING AS THE PEOPLE OF YAHWEH (EXOD. 19:9–20:21, 24:1–2, 9–15a, 31:18–34:35)

The basic account of the revelation on Sinai is a combination of the Yahwist (J) and Elohist (E) versions, which we have already met in the story of the struggle against the pharaoh's oppression. Yahweh's revelation in these old versions of the exodus has two focuses: the decalogue (Exod. 20:1–17) and the list of ten or twelve commandments presented as what Moses wrote on the stone tablets by Yahweh's command (Exod. 34:14–26). It is likely that the first pericope is the Elohist version of the revelation on Sinai, and the second is the Yahwist. They are connected in the text, as we now have it, by the breaking of the first tablets in a context of the account of the golden calf. The connection of these three moments—decalogue, golden calf, and the tablets written by Moses—is tight, and suggests the work of a redactor who made important changes in the Yahwist and Elohist traditions, a redactor referred to by literary critics as "RJE" ("Redactor of the Yahwist and the Elohist"). In its present form, then, §4A is the work of RJE, probably in the time of Hezekiah, toward the end of the eighth century B.C.

§ 4B: YAHWEH STRIKES AN ALLIANCE WITH ISRAEL (EXOD. 19:3b–8, 20:22–23:33, 24:3–8)

Wedged in among the passages of the RJE account (§4A) is an old collection of laws (Exod. 20:22–23:33), with an introduction (19:3b–8) and postscript (24:3–8). This legal code is known in modern exegesis as the Code (or Book) of the Covenant—a name bestowed on it mainly in view of its introduction and postscript, which present these laws as obligations accepted by Israel upon entering into a covenant, an alliance, with Yahweh its God. Concern with the observance of that covenant is a special characteristic of the book of Deuteronomy, and it is probable that the interpretation of the laws given on Sinai as the condition of an alliance with Yahweh comes from the same context. Thus this lengthy addition to the Sinai account would seem to come from the context of the reform in Judah in the course of the seventh century B.C. The Code of the Covenant itself, of course, is much older than its insertion in the Sinai account.

§ 4C: REVELATION OF THE INSTRUCTIONS FOR WORSHIP (EXOD. 24:15b–31:17, 35:1–40:38)

According to the sacerdotal interpretation of the revelation, its content consisted in instructions for the fabrication of the sanctuary and its furnishings, with a view to having a regularized form of approach to Yahweh. The historical context of the production of this rereading of the revelation is the sacerdotal crusade for an Israel centered around the temple as rebuilt under the protection of Persian authorities. The sacerdotal version dates from the sixth century B.C.

4.0 ARRIVAL AT MOUNT SINAI (EXOD. 19:1–3a)

Three months after they came out of the land of Egypt . . . on that day the sons of Israel came to the wilderness of Sinai. From Rephidim they set out again; and when they reached the wilderness of Sinai, there in the wilderness they pitched their camp; there facing the mountain Israel pitched camp.

Moses then went up to God. . . .

This short note mirrors the complexity of the history of the composition of the book of Exodus. The information here comes from the sacerdotal itinerary ("They left Rephidim and encamped in the wilderness of Sinai"—Num.

33:15). It connects perfectly with the geographical location of the water shortage (Exod. 17:1). But the account of the meeting with Jethro (Exod. 18) is out of order in the itinerary: this meeting is said to have taken place at the "mountain of God." The usual explanation of this doubling of the arrival at Sinai is that Exodus 18 comes from the Elohist redaction, where it was part of the Sinai cycle, whereas 19:1-2 is part of the sacerdotal redaction, and thus supposes that the events at the mountain began with Yahweh's manifestation to Moses on the mountain.

To what does "on that day" refer? The flight from Egypt, according to Exodus 12:17-18, was on the fourteenth day of the "first month." Are we to understand, then, in Exodus 19:1, that the people, arriving at the mountain after ninety days, therefore arrived in the fourth month? According to Jewish tradition, the law was given to Moses on the festival of weeks (Pentecost), seven weeks after Passover. In this case we should have to understand our text here as referring to the first day of the third month, one-and-one-half months after the flight.

4A NORMS FOR LIVING AS THE PEOPLE OF YAHWEH
(EXOD. 19:9–20:21, 24:1-2, 9–15a, 31:18–34:35)

These passages form the basic account of the Sinai material and owe their present form to the work of RJE, the redactor who joined the original Yahwist account with the Elohist. They retain certain incoherencies, owing to their double origin. There are three particularly notable incoherencies. (1) There are two very different lists of commandments delivered by Yahweh to Moses and the people as the constitution of its life as Yahweh's people—Exodus 20:1-17 and 34:14-26. (2) In some passages Yahweh comes down the mountain to meet with Moses (19:18, 20, 34:5), which is probably the interpretation of the old Yahwist account. But other passages seem to suppose that Yahweh dwells on the mountain: Moses must go up to meet with Yahweh (24:1, 9–10, 12, 34:2). (3) There are two traditions concerning who actually wrote the commandments on the tablets, Yahweh (31:18, 32:15-16), or Moses at Yahweh's direction (34:28).

RJE has resolved some of these differences with the insertion of the breaking of the first tablets because of the sin of the worship of the golden calf, thus requiring new tablets. The result is a strong, cohesive account in its general lines.

4A1 Yahweh Appears in Power (Exod. 19:9–25)

4A1.1 THE CLOUD (EXOD. 19:9)

Yahweh said to Moses, "I am coming to you in a dense cloud so that the people may hear when I speak to you and may trust you always." And Moses took the people's reply back to Yahweh.

The cloud has the twofold effect of hiding and yet effectively evidencing the presence of Yahweh. The people hear Yahweh speaking with Moses, and thus know that this revolutionary leader is to be hearkened to. The last sentence seems to have been placed here by an accident of transmission.

4A1.2 PREPARATIONS AND WARNINGS (EXOD. 19:10–15)

Yahweh said to Moses, "Go to the people and tell them to prepare themselves today and tomorrow. Let them wash their clothing and hold themselves in readiness for the third day, because on the third day Yahweh will descend on the mountain of Sinai in the sight of all the people. You will mark out the limits of the mountain and say, 'Take care not to go up the mountain or to touch the foot of it. Whoever touches the mountain will be put to death. No one must lay a hand on him: he must be stoned or shot down by arrow, whether man or beast; he must not remain alive.' When the ram's horn sounds a long blast, they are to go up the mountain."

So Moses came down from the mountain to the people and bade them prepare themselves; and they washed their clothing. Then he said to the people, "Be ready for the third day; do not go near any woman."

It is natural and understandable that the Israelites should have to purify themselves in order to meet with God. Similar preparations were undertaken by Jacob and his retinue before coming to Bethel (Gen. 35:1–5), as well as by the people of Israel before crossing the Jordan into the promised land (Josh. 3:1–13).

In the light of what happens next, it is surprising that "they" go up the mountain: only in 24:9–11 is there any mention of a group climbing the mountain—Moses, Aaron, Nadab, Abihu, and seventy elders. It is likely that our text here originally referred to this other passage. But in the present form of the text, the Israelites are afraid at the sound of Yahweh's voice, and ask Moses to go up the mountain in their place and serve as intermediary between Yahweh and themselves (20:18–21). Thus the predominant notion in the text as we have it today is that Moses went up alone to speak with Yahweh.

4A1.3 YAHWEH'S DESCENT (EXOD. 19:16–19)

Now at daybreak on the third day there were peals of thunder on the mountain and lightning flashes, a dense cloud, and a loud trumpet blast, and inside the camp all the people trembled. Then Moses led the people out of the camp to meet God; and they stood at the bottom of the mountain. The mountain of Sinai was entirely wrapped in smoke, because Yahweh had descended on it in the form of fire. Like smoke from a furnace the smoke went up, and the whole mountain shook violently. Louder and louder grew the sound of the trumpet. Moses spoke, and God answered him with peals of thunder.

It has been thought that the people recognized Yahweh's presence here in some manner of volcanic activity. In this case, we should have to find some other place than the traditional location in the Sinai peninsula, perhaps in the mountains to the east of the Gulf of Akaba. But we need not suppose volcanic activity. It may be that the basis of our text is the experience of the manifestation of God amid the incense used at worship. At all events, for purposes of understanding the text, the original experience is of little importance. What is of importance is the tremendous impression caused by Yahweh's descent upon the mountain. Amid terrible noise and great trembling of the earth, Moses addressed Yahweh and Yahweh replied. In this way Yahweh endorsed Moses as the authentic representative of the God of the exodus.

The Hebrew expression translated here "with peals of thunder" is a curious one. A literal translation would have been, "with [his] voice," although the Hebrew word *kol*, "voice," is indeed the same word as used just above for the thunderclaps in the phrase "peals of thunder . . . and lightning flashes." But the context states that the people heard the *words* addressed by Yahweh to Moses—the words of the decalogue, we may suppose. The expression is strange, then, but not incomprehensible: God was speaking, and the people heard the voice.

4A1.4 FURTHER WARNINGS (EXOD. 19:20-25)

> *Yahweh came down on the mountain of Sinai, on the mountain top, and Yahweh called Moses to the top of the mountain; and Moses went up. Yahweh said to Moses, "Go down and warn the people not to pass beyond their bounds to come and look on Yahweh, or many of them will lose their lives. The priests, the men who do approach Yahweh, even these must purify themselves, or Yahweh will break out against them." Moses answered Yahweh, "The people cannot come up the mountain of Sinai because you warned us yourself when you said, 'Mark out the limits of the mountain and declare it sacred.' " "Go down," said Yahweh to him, "and come up again bringing Aaron with you. But do not allow the priests or the people to pass beyond their bounds to come up to Yahweh, or he will break out against them." So Moses went down to the people and spoke to them. . . .*

This passage returns us to the scene of the preparations for Yahweh's manifestation. It underscores what has been said before on the importance of not transgressing the frontiers of the sacred. Its language has no close bonds with any of the strata of the Pentateuch, and so it is generally considered to be an addition. (See Childs's extended discussion of this paragraph in his *The Book of Exodus*, 361–64.)

From a formal viewpoint, it is interesting to observe how Moses uses Yahweh's own words as the basis for his rejection of Yahweh's instruction. "The people cannot come up to the mountain of Sinai," Moses tells Yahweh, "because you warned us yourself when you said, 'Mark out the limits of the mountain and declare it sacred.' " This technique of quoting one's interlocutor or adversary to refute him "out of his own mouth" is a common one with the prophets (H. W. Wolff, "Das Zitat im Prophetenspruch: Eine Studie zur prophetischen Verkündigungsweise").

The last sentence is interrupted without any indication of Moses' words to the people. The next sentence begins with God's own words.

4A2 Yahweh's Law for Israel (Exod. 20:1–17)

The decalogue is a list of commandments addressed to the adult Israelite. They are worded in the second person singular masculine. Their form is categorical, without nuances or consideration of special circumstances. They do not indicate penalties to be applied in case of violation. As a whole they constitute Yahweh's solemn declaration of the conditions for membership in Yahweh's people. Anyone not living by these norms is deprived of membership in this new people of Israel. Elsewhere, there will be laws instructing judges on the procedures to follow with criminals; here the sole concern is to set limits for the new society now being founded.

Before commenting on the ten commandments individually, it will be in order to examine the decalogue as a whole. It is not the only short collection of laws in the Old Testament, although why collections like these were made in the first place has not been clarified (see Appendix 11). In any case, there are at least three reasons for maintaining that this decalogue has a prehistory. (1) It lacks homogeneity of form. The first and second commandments are declarations by God, whereas the third is not—nor are the explanatory clauses in the fourth and fifth. The remaining five commandments are ambiguous as to the subject who is speaking. (2) Its rhythmic structure is likewise heterogeneous. Three have two accents in Hebrew, whereas the rest have three or four, not counting the explanatory clauses. (3) Finally, the insertion of the decalogue into the Sinai material shows signs of having been introduced *en bloc* into a previously existing account. Its connection with its context is unclear. (On the prehistory of the decalogue, see Appendix 13.) For all these reasons, it is clear that the decalogue represents a point of arrival in the legal tradition of Israel; it is not the beginning of that tradition. This in no way militates against its being the basic constitutional text of Israel.

In its present context, it is God who, from the summit of Mount Sinai, pronounces the words of the decalogue. Hearing the voice of God, the Israelites grow afraid, and ask that, in future, God use Moses as an intermediary in the communication of laws (Exod. 20:18–21). God reveals to Moses the legal miscellany that we know as the Code of the Covenant (20:22–23:19). Yahweh gives Moses two tablets of stone, inscribed by the finger of God (31:18). Regrettably, Moses breaks these tablets (32:19), and has to replace them with another set of tablets inscribed with the "cultic" laws of Exod. 34:14–26. Deuteronomy reinterprets this account to the effect that the content of each set of tablets was the same decalogue (see Appendix 12), but this is not the intent of the text of Exodus. In Exodus, it is the laws of worship that are on the second pair of tablets, if not indeed on the first as well.

Later tradition, recognizing the superiority of the decalogue, has generally preferred the Deuteronomic reinterpretation to the Exodus account. One need not go to this extreme, however, inasmuch as Exodus, too, singles out the decalogue as Yahweh's first revelation, and the only one to be given directly to the people, without Moses' mediation.

4A2.1 "I AM YAHWEH" (EXOD. 20:1-2)

Then God spoke these words. He said, "I am Yahweh your God who brought you out of the land of Egypt, out of the house of slavery."

The formula of self-introduction, "I am Yahweh your God," has a strict relationship with the commandments that it presents. Its function is to identify the God who is speaking as the same God who liberated the people from slavery. It is this act that gives Yahweh the authority to impose on Israel the limits of a revolutionary society. Conversely, this people of God, successful in its revolutionary struggle, is now obligated to live according to the norms of Yahweh, the God who has been its companion in the struggle.

The formula "I am Yahweh" appears numerous times in the Law of Holiness (Lev. 17-26) as the basis for the authority of its norms. It is likewise of frequent occurrence in the book of Ezekiel. By contrast, it does not appear in Amos, Micah, Isaiah, or the wisdom literature (Walther Zimmerli, *I Am Yahweh*, 1-28). The formula is used to accompany the proclamation of Yahweh's law during worship. Its social context is liturgical. Hence it is only natural to conclude that at some moment or other the decalogue was a law that was preached in a liturgical context.

In the expansion of the formula—". . . who brought you out of the land of Egypt, out of the house of slavery," we should note that the use of "brought . . . out" instead of the other verb used in similar contexts—"caused to come out"—indicates that the exodus was a redemption from the condition of slavery (J. N. M. Wijngaards, "HOSI' and "HE'ELAH: A Twofold Approach to the Exodus").

In Orthodox Judaism, "I am Yahweh your God, who brought you out of the land of Egypt, out of the house of slavery" is the first of the "Ten Words." Then, in order to keep to ten "words," the prohibitions of idolatry and images are combined. It is evident, however, that from a formal viewpoint the phrase naming Yahweh is introductory, not part of the series of laws that make up the decalogue.

4A2.2 EXCLUSIVE LOYALTY (EXOD. 20:3)

(1) "You shall have no gods except me."

This is the fundamental law for the life of Israel as a new society. Once God's nature as the "Yahweh who brought you out of the land of Egypt, out of the house of slavery" is well understood, all norms for a just social life follow. Everything is based on exclusive loyalty to Yahweh. If the God of the universe is indeed Yahweh, then no human being may dominate another in any way, by stealing, killing, or coveting. God is Yahweh, who liberates the oppressed, hearing the cries that their oppressors force from their lips.

Formally, however, the commandment is not a demand for loyalty to Yahweh, but a prohibition of other gods. It is polemical. Loyalty to Yahweh must be exclusive. This was a novelty among ancient Near Eastern peoples. Babylonians could have their first loyalty to Marduk, the god of Babylonia, but at the hour of death have recourse to Ishtar, goddess of the region of the dead, and this without any disloyalty to Marduk. By contrast, the decalogue forbids the worship of any other god alongside Yahweh.

Nor does this commandment forbid worship of other gods inasmuch as they are nonexistent. The denial of the existence and power of the gods of the gentiles will be the ironic theme of the sixth-century prophets (see Jer. 10:1–16, Isa. 44:9–20). Older texts do not deny the existence of other gods. They spurn these gods, scoffing at the impotence of Dagon, god of the Philistines (1 Sam. 5), or the inability of the Baal of Tyre to compete with Yahweh in bringing down fire from heaven to consume his sacrifice (1 Kings 18). Yahweh is seen to be mightier than the enemy god, but the text does not deny the existence and (limited) power of other gods.

What reasons might there be, then, for prohibiting the worship of other gods? First of all, we should remember that the worship of Baal, especially, was a constant temptation for the peasants of Israel. Baal was the god of rain, and rain was a vital necessity. The Baal mythology was highly developed, as can be seen in the Ugaritic tablets. (Some of these texts may be read in James B. Pritchard, *Ancient Near Eastern Texts Relating to the Old Testament,* 129–55.) Thus Hosea denounces the peasants' infidelity in giving Baal credit for the wheat and must, the wool and flax, that had actually been given to them by Yahweh (Hos. 2:4–17). The problem is not, of course, whether to call the rain god Yahweh or Baal. Behind the conflict of these gods is the social reality of a class struggle. Yahweh had given Israel a land, and sent the people rain in due season. But these facts were secondary. The primary fact about Yahweh was the support given to the Israelite uprising against those who oppressed them. Baal, on the other hand, was primarily the giver of rain, and secondarily the protector of the social order in which the king was the supreme authority, with the right to dispose of his subjects' property. The social consequences of the opposition of these two gods, Yahweh and Baal, are clearly visible in the account of King Ahab's seizure of Naboth's ancestral vineyard, in accordance with the justice of the Canaanite kings and their Baal—whereas the law of Yahweh guaranteed Naboth's right to keep his vineyard in perpetuity, notwithstanding the covetousness of kings (1 Kings 21).

The polemical formulation of the commandment to worship Yahweh, then, has its explanation in the long struggle of the peasantry to rid itself of the domination of a series of kings: first the Canaanite kings, and then the Israelite kings, who resurrected the old forms of class domination. Israel did not arise in an empty land, rooting its social order in virgin nature. Israel arose in a "civilized" society, in a struggle with real kings and bureaucracies. For a religious people, it was imperative to maintain this awareness of its God Yahweh, and to be on the alert against other gods, the gods of oppressors. It was a temptation for the peasants to abandon their inhospitable tracts in the hills and come down to the plains where they would submit to the kings of the locality and till a more fertile land. The oppression of armies like that of the Philistines tempted the people to create a professional army of its own, with an Israelite king at its head. Against these temptations, the fundamental law of Israel established that a compromise between Yahweh and other gods was impossible. An Israelite had no choice but to reject any form of loyalty to any god who had not saved the slaves of Egypt.

This first norm for the life of Israel was variously expressed in its laws: "Anyone who sacrifices to other gods shall come under the ban" (Exod. 22:19); "Do not repeat the name of other gods: let it not be heard from your lips" (Exod. 23:13); "You shall bow down to no other god, for Yahweh's name is the Jealous One; he is a jealous God" (Exod. 34:14); "Tolerate no foreign god, worship no alien god" (Ps. 81:9); "Yahweh your God you shall follow, him shall you fear" (Deut. 13:5). In all its formulations, the commandment is polemical.

Two expressions in the formulation of this law in the decalogue—which reads, literally, "You shall not have other gods before me"—call for commentary. They are: "other gods" (*elohim aherim*) and "before me" (*'al panai*).

The expression "other gods" appears to be Deuteronomic. Of the seventy-three times it occurs in the Old Testament, eighteen are in the book of Deuteronomy, eighteen are in the Deuteronomic parts of Jeremiah, twenty are in the Deuteronomic books of Joshua, Judges, Samuel, and Kings, and four are in Chronicles. The only occurrences that are earlier and independent of Deuteronomy are in Hosea 3:1, Exodus 20:3, and Exodus 23:13. The text from Hosea is in an autobiographical passage, very likely by the prophet himself in the eighth century B.C., and this leads one to suspect that the formulation of the prohibition in Exodus 20:3 and 23:13 is northern and pre-Deuteronomic. (This is in conformity with my opinion that the decalogue is Elohist material and of northern origin. The other possibility for Exodus 20:3 is that it underwent a Deuteronomic revision to adjust it to the language in use at a time when the Deuteronomists enjoyed religious hegemony. The latter is Nielsen's opinion, in his *The Ten Commandments*, 87.)

There is a problem with what the phrase "before me" actually means. The preposition *'al* frequently has an adversative denotation—"against"—including two occurrences in which it governs the noun "face" (Gen. 16:12, Deut. 21:16). Some interpreters therefore translate this first commandment: "You shall not have other gods despite me"—that is, "against me" (W. F. Albright, *From the Stone Age to Christianity*, 247, n. 29). Another possibility is to take the expression as a very realistic allusion to Yahweh's presence in the sanctuary. Several times, a pilgrimage to the sanctuary is spoken of as, literally, "being seen before the face of the Lord" (Exod. 34:24, 23:15, 17). Thus our expression would forbid the erection or positioning of idols in the sanctuary with Yahweh.

Neither of these interpretations is particularly convincing. It is better to keep the alternatives offered by the preposition *'al* open with a neutral translation such as "beside me" or "before me." What is forbidden is to pretend to be able to be loyal to Yahweh and to other gods as well. In a revolutionary society, this would be to make peace with the enemy.

4A2.3 NO IMAGES OF YAHWEH (EXOD. 20:4–6)

(2) "You shall not make yourself a carved image or any likeness of anything in heaven or on earth beneath or in the waters under the earth; you shall not bow down to them or serve them. For I, Yahweh your God, am a jealous God and I punish the father's fault in the sons, the grandsons, and the great-grandsons of those who hate me; but I show kindness [to the thousandth generation to] those who love me and keep my commandments."

The Catholic, Lutheran, and Orthodox Jewish traditions have understood the prohibition of images as part of the prohibition of worship of "other gods." The ancient interpreters Josephus and Philo, however, distinguished two commandments here, and modern critical interpreters are all but unanimous in taking the prohibition of images as a prohibition against *making images of Yahweh*, so that the prohibition of worshiping other gods would be another matter. The oldest commentary on this commandment, Deuteronomy 4:9–40, indicates that in Israel in the sixth century B.C. the prohibition of images was seen as distinct from that of the first commandment.

In the redaction of the decalogue as we have it today, this second commandment has received various amplifications, which have the effect of assimilating it to the first commandment. There is a puzzling change of grammatical object from a singular "image" to a plural "you shall not adore *them*." (See the excellent study by Walther Zimmerli, "Das zweite Gebot," in his *Gottes Offenbarung*, 234–48.)

Zimmerli has demonstrated that prohibitions of worship and service always refer, in Deuteronomic texts, to that offered to other gods, with the exception of Deuteronomy 4, which is precisely a commentary on the second commandment. He also points out that, in other cases, Yahweh is called "jealous" in contexts where worship of other gods is forbidden (Exod. 34:14, Deut. 6:14–15, Josh. 24:19). The amplification, then, is of later date than the formation of the list of commandments, and uses the phrase, "shall not bow down to them"—shall not worship them—to connect the second commandment with the first.

The prohibition against making an image of Yahweh has the finality, according to Deuteronomy 4, of safeguarding Yahweh's freedom and sovereignty. At the foot of Mount Sinai, the people heard Yahweh's voice, but saw no shape or form. The living voice with which Yahweh will continually address the people is a challenging presence, an ongoing demand for justice. Making an image of this God would serve to efface this demanding challenge. An image is mute.

This commandment, too, appears in other forms. "You shall not make gods of silver or gods of gold to stand beside me" (Exod. 20:23); "You shall make yourself no gods of molten metal" (Exod. 34:17); "Do not turn to idols, and cast no gods of metal" (Lev. 19:4); "You must make no idols; you must set up neither carved image nor standing stone, set up no sculptured stone in your land, to prostrate yourselves in front of it; for it is I, Yahweh, who am your God" (Lev. 26:1); "A curse on the man who carves or casts an idol, a thing detestable to Yahweh, the work of a craftsman's hands, and sets it up in secret" (Deut. 27:15).

None of these parallels helps us understand the motivation behind the prohibition, and we begin to appreciate the perennial difficulty of distinguishing it from the one against the worship of other gods. The most categorical formulation is that of Deuteronomy 27:15, which, together with Exodus 20:4–6, excludes any artistic representation at all. (We have an excellent commentary on the second commandment by José Porfirio Miranda in his *Marx and the Bible*, Maryknoll, N.Y.: Orbis Books, 1974, pp. 36–44.)

Unlike the religion of Canaan's dominant class, the Israelite religion worshiped Yahweh without images. The premonarchical texts speak of sacred objects—the ark, and the tent of meeting. The ark was a box containing the stone tablets which were believed to have been inscribed by the finger of God. It was a symbol of Yahweh's presence and, as such, was carried into battle (1 Sam. 46, Num. 10:33–36). In Solomon's temple it was adorned with two "cherubim"—enormous winged figures that made a throne for Yahweh. This seeming violation of the prohibition against images is never denounced as such in the texts.

The tent of meeting was a tent where Yahweh spoke with Moses and another representative of the people. Thus it was a meeting place, not a sanctuary for an image of Yahweh (Gerhard von Rad, "The Tabernacle and the Ark," in his *Old Testament Theology*, 1:234–41). Baal, on the other hand, was commonly represented as a bull, and the Canaanite goddesses were represented by female figures.

In this milieu, the prohibition against representing Yahweh in an image was for the purpose of safeguarding the Israelites' freedom and autonomy, threatened by a religion that justified class oppression. But it was very difficult to maintain this prohibition, as we see from the story of the man from Ephraim, who made himself an image and built a sanctuary, placing them in the charge of a Levite (Judg. 17). Everything indicates that this image was one of Yahweh. The same thing was done in Ophrah by Gideon, the Yahwist hero of the campaign against Midian (Judg. 8:24–27). In both cases, the text condemns the fabrication of these images, which must be understood as an application of the commandment under consideration. The arbitrary nature of its application is shown in the condemnation of Jeroboam's calves (1 Kings 12:26–33), while the cherubim in the temple were tolerated (1 Kings 6:23–30).

In other words, as late as the tenth century B.C. there was no clarity about this prohibition. The fact that its violation, by Jeroboam with his calves as by Solomon with his cherubim, was simultaneous with the establishment of class societies can be taken as the index of the prudence and correctness of the prohibition as a basic norm of the revolutionary legislation of Israel.

Yahweh's religion was an intolerant religion. Yahweh was a jealous God, then, and a warrior God (Exod. 15:3). (A great deal has been written in recent decades on Yahweh as a warrior. One brief, sensible study is that by G. Ernest Wright, "God the Warrior," chap. 5 of his *The Old Testament and Theology*.) Yahweh's jealousy demanded the exclusion from the community of any who manifested divided loyalties, along with their children, grandchildren, and great-grandchildren. Lest this severity, occasioned by the great peril of abandoning the revolutionary spirit, be misinterpreted, however, the amplification indicates that Yahweh is merciful "to the thousandth generation" (as I prefer to read), toward those who love and keep the commandments of God.

4A2.4 FALSE OATHS (EXOD. 20:7)

(3) "You shall not utter the name of Yahweh your God to misuse it, for Yahweh will not leave unpunished the man who utters his name to misuse it."

Israel considered it a great privilege to know God's name (Ps. 9:11, 91:14, Exod. 6:2–6). Solomon built the temple to the name of Yahweh (1 Kings 3:2, 5:17, 19, 8:17, 20, 29), and Yahweh "placed his name there" (Deut. 12:5, 21, 1 Kings 8:29, 2 Kings 23:27). In Yahweh's name Israel defeated its enemies (Ps. 44:6). The name of Yahweh, then, was something to be taken seriously in Israel. (On the importance of the names of persons in Israel, see Johannes Pedersen, *Israel, Its Life and Culture*, 245–59.)

As with the first two commandments, the third also is repeated in various legal collections in the Bible: "You must not make false assertions. You must not support a guilty man by giving malicious evidence" (Exod. 23:1); "You must not swear falsely by my name, profaning the name of your God. I am Yahweh" (Lev. 19:12); "It is Yahweh your God you must fear and serve; you must cling to him; in his name take your oaths" (Deut. 10:20); "You must fear Yahweh your God, you must serve him, by his name you must swear" (Deut. 6:13).

In light of these other versions of the third commandment, it becomes clear that the principal context of its reference is that of the swearing of oaths. It is not forbidden to swear by the name of Yahweh, but to use that name in false oaths. There is a very similar expression in Psalm 24:4: "He whose hands are clean, whose heart is pure, whose soul does not pay homage to worthless things and who never swears to a lie."

Still, a comparison of Exodus 20:7 with Leviticus 19:12 shows that the former is a broader formulation of the commandment than would be required by a prohibition against false oaths simply. Other "misuses" of Yahweh's name are forbidden, as well, as in sorcery and spells, which, we learn from certain papyri, was frequent at least in postbiblical times (Sigmund Mowinckel, *Psalmenstudien*, 1: 50–58).

Here it is difficult to separate religious taboo from what is simply unjust. To swear a false oath is a violation of one's relationship with Yahweh, but it is also a violation of interpersonal relationships among human beings. If God is Yahweh, naturally it will be a serious crime to use Yahweh's name to perjure oneself in order to do injury to one's neighbor.

4A2.5 SABBATH REST (EXOD. 20:8–11)

(4) "Remember the sabbath day and keep it holy. For six days you shall labor and do all your work, but the seventh day is a sabbath day for Yahweh your God. You shall do no work that day, neither you nor your son nor your daughter nor your servants, men or women, nor your animals nor the stranger who lives with you. For in six days Yahweh made the heavens and the earth and the sea and all that these hold, but on the seventh day he rested; that is why Yahweh has blessed the sabbath day and made it sacred."

There are difficulties as to the substance of this law. For all who toiled, rest was obligatory in Israel. Like the other commandments, the fourth contributes to setting the constitutional limits of the new society. The antiquity and importance of this law are attested by its inclusion with the first and second commandments in the basic list of laws in Exodus 34. Violation of the Sabbath is a capital offense (Exod. 31:15, Num. 15:32–36).

Even in its earlier forms, the fourth commandment underscored the central importance attaching to repose in the celebration of the Sabbath. "For six days you shall labor, but on the seventh day you shall rest, even at plowing time and harvest" (Exod. 34:21). "For six days you shall do your work, but stop on the seventh day, so that your ox and your donkey may rest and the son of your slave girl have a breathing space, and the stranger too" (Exod. 23:12). Unsuccessful attempts have been made to explain the origin of the Sabbath by analogy with days of ill omen among Israel's neighbors, like the monthly Babylonian *sabbatu*. But the meaning of the Israelite Sabbath is very different. In Israel's legislation it is a day of rest, and this makes a great deal of sense, for Israel was a people of laborers, in rebellion against a state that demanded forced labor. In Israel, even the stranger will be guaranteed one day of rest a week.

The expression "Remember . . ." is a strange one in the wording of a law. In the context of the book of Exodus as a whole, it recalls that Israel already practiced the Sabbath rest, as we have seen in the account of the manna (Exod. 16). Deuteronomy says "keep" instead of "remember."

It is surprising that this law is based on a creation account, a form of the creation story that is similar to the sacerdotal version of Genesis 1, thought to be of exilic origin. Deuteronomy 5:12-15 omits this basis, replacing it with an allusion to the servitude in Egypt. This and other differences between the two versions of the decalogue suggest that our present version existed independently, even after its incorporation into the account of RJE. There is no evidence of any dependence of Exodus on the written account of creation in Genesis 1. Rather it depends on an earlier oral form.

Among Israelite legal collections, the Sabbath law is presented in three forms (Nils-Erik A. Andreason, *The Old Testament Sabbath*, 154-73). (1) The earliest is the one we have already seen in Exodus 34:21 and 23:12: "For six days you shall labor, but on the seventh day you shall rest." With slight variations, this formula appears a good many times, in various legal collections (Exod. 16:26, 20:9-10, 31:15, 35:2; Lev. 23:3; Deut. 5:13-14). (2) Other laws follow the form "Keep my sabbaths," which, with slight variations, is found in Exodus 16:28, 20:8, 31:13, 14, 16, Deut. 5:12, 15, and Luke 19:3, 30. (3) The other form decrees capital punishment for a violation of the Sabbath—"Whoever profanes it shall die"—and is found in Exodus 31:14, 15, 35:2.

The form of the commandment as it appears in the decalogue makes use of two older formulas. Capital punishment, although it is not actually mentioned, may be implicit. All the laws of the decalogue are laws of limit: one cannot transgress them and continue to be called an Israelite. (None of the laws explicitly mentions a penalty for its violation here.)

Some commentators hold that the "sanctification," or keeping holy, of the Sabbath implies that its origin was a holiday celebrated in the sanctuaries. Then, with the exile, or perhaps with the reform of the seventh century, it would have become a family observance, with emphasis on rest (see Andreason, *Old Testament Sabbath*, 235-73). But the commandment gives no indication of this, nor do the historical texts attest to Sabbath gatherings. The finality of the Sabbath is rather to secure rest for all workers.

4A2.6 CARE OF THE ELDERLY (EXOD. 20:12)

(5) "Honor your father and your mother so that you may have a long life in the land that Yahweh your God has given to you."

This commandment imposes on the community the care of the elderly who are no longer productive. Proverbs 19:26 is evidence of the problem that the commandment seeks to obviate. "He who dispossesses his father and drives out his mother is a son as shameless as depraved."

This law appears in the Pentateuch only once outside the decalogue: "Each of you must respect his father and mother" (Lev. 19:3). In the wisdom literature, on the other hand, it has many parallels (Prov. 1:8, 15:5, 19:26, etc.). But in Proverbs the emphasis is on the importance of listening to the teaching of one's elders.

The most extensive biblical commentary on this commandment is in Ecclesiasticus 3:16, which says, in part:

> My son, support your father in his old age,
> > do not grieve him during his life.
> Even if his mind should fail, show him sympathy,
> > do not despise him in your health and strength
> > > [3:12–13].

In view of its affinity with the wisdom admonitions, it has been proposed that this commandment had its origin in the father's instructions given in the family (see Erhard Gerstenberger, "Covenant and Commandment," and *Wesen und Herkunft des "apodiktischen Rechts"*). In Nuzi and other Mesopotamian localities, there were contracts of adoption in exchange for care in old age, and wills sometimes threatened with disinheritance the son who neglected his parents in their old age (Rainer Albertz, "Hintergrund und Bedeutung des Elterngebots im Dekalog"). In these texts too we have the case of an elderly father who, in anticipation of his death, enjoins upon his children reverence for their mother. We also have, in these gentile texts, the case of a father who retires from active life and transmits his rights to his son, with the admonition not to despise his parents' old age.

This commandment, like the others in the decalogue listing, is addressed to the adult male. It does not exclude from its view the respect that minor children owe their parents, but this is not its principal interest. If it were addressed to minors, it would call for obedience instead of honor.

The obligation to care for one's parents is a very serious one. Exodus 21:15 prescribes capital punishment for anyone physically striking their father or mother. The same penalty is prescribed for those who curse their parents, in Exodus 21:17. And Deuteronomy 21:18–21 calls on the community to stone to death a youth who refuses to heed his parents. The promise of a "long life on the land" is a frequent motivation proposed in Deuteronomy (4:40, 5:33, 11:9, etc.). In our own text this should be understood as a proto-Deuteronomic amplification, and one more piece of evidence for the northern origin of the decalogue.

4A2.7 MURDER (EXOD. 20:13)

(6) "You shall not kill."

This is the first of the three shortest laws in the entire Israelite legal corpus. The three are all categorical demands, admitting of no excuses or exceptions. One must not take another's life.

There are many parallels, however, that flesh out the proscription. Deuteronomy 27:24 says, "A curse on him who strikes down his neighbor in secret." Exodus 21:12, "Anyone who strikes a man and so causes his death, must die." And Leviticus 24:17, "If a man strikes down any human being, he must die." For various cases of intentional homicide and involuntary manslaughter, there is special legislation in the Israelite codes.

This commandment against homicide is more stark and categorical than all the others. Like all the other commandments of the decalogue, it sets a limit that no one wishing to continue as a member of the new classless society may transgress. But what precisely is this limit? It does not exclude capital punishment by stoning at the hands of the people after a decree to this effect by competent authorities. The story of the plagues, culminating in the death of the Egyptian firstborn by Yahweh's hand, and the history of the war with the Amalekites, make it clear that Yahweh's law does not forbid killing enemies in combat.

As for the broad range of other possibilities, the only clue is the verb used in this commandment: *retzach*. This verb is used forty-six times in the Old Testament. *Harag* and *hemit*, both of which also mean "to kill," are used 75 and 201 times, respectively (J. J. Stamm and M. E. Andrew, *The Ten Commandments in Recent Research*, 98–99). It seems that *retzach* was originally used to designate violent deaths that called for vengeance, whether they had been intentional or unintentional. Beginning in the eighth century B.C., it has the meaning of a death by malicious intent (Isa. 1:21, Hos. 6:9, Job 24:14, Prov. 22:13, Ps. 94:6—see Childs, *The Book of Exodus*, 420–21). It is obvious that the law against murder in the decalogue does not seek legal precision but polemical force. Other laws will formulate attenuating circumstances.

4A2.8 ADULTERY (EXOD. 20:14)

(7) "You shall not commit adultery."

The Israelite male is to respect his neighbor's marriage. Anyone violating this norm of the common life commits a capital offense (Deut. 22:22, Lev. 20:10). The gravity of adultery is highlighted in certain ancient Israelite accounts, such as the one reporting Abimelich's horror upon learning that he is on the point of violating Abraham's marriage (Gen. 20:9), Joseph's rejections of the adulterous overtures of Potiphar's wife (Gen. 39:9), and David's condemnation for his adultery with the wife of Uriah (2 Sam. 12:7–10).

It is noteworthy that this commandment is addressed to the male although, in the laws in Leviticus 20:10 and Deuteronomy 22:22, the married woman is also held responsible. A man sins against his neighbor when he commits adultery with the latter's wife. It was not considered adultery for a man, even if he were married, to have sexual relations with a harlot (Gen. 38). Intercourse with a young unmarried woman was a crime requiring special measures, but it did not call for capital punishment, nor was it considered adultery (Exod. 22:15-16, Deut. 22:23-29). A married woman, on the other hand, sinned against her husband and committed adultery in having sexual relations with any other man, married or not.

From these different situations we may deduce that the intent of this commandment was to protect the institution of marriage, and that that institution was more exposed to injury by the free conduct of the wife than by that of the husband. Marriage was not necessarily monogamous in Israel (Deut. 21:15-17), and divorce was permitted (Deut. 24:1-4). But an existing marriage was protected to the full extent of the law.

4A2.9 THEFT (EXOD. 20:15)

(8) "You shall not steal."

The prohibition of stealing is simple and categorical, and does not detail circumstances or lay down a penalty for its violation. It has only one parallel in the Bible in this form, the "You must not steal" of Leviticus 19:11. But elsewhere there are detailed injunctions against stealing, procedures for the investigation of theft, and penalties to be applied in different cases (Exod. 21:37, 22:9-12, 22:1-3, Deut. 25:13-16).

Alone of all of the things forbidden in the decalogue, theft was not considered a capital crime in Israel. The penalty established for theft is rather restitution with interest (five oxen for each ox taken, or double what is taken from a house entered without authorization). This has led exegetes to look for a more specific, more serious meaning for "stealing" in our text than that of a simple theft. Albrecht Alt ("Das Verbot des Diebstahls im Dekalog") holds that what is referred to here is the theft of human beings. This was indeed a capital offense, as may be seen from Exodus 21:16 and Deuteronomy 24:7. It is not unlikely that, in the prehistory of this commandment, its verb governed an object. Its extremely short form suggests this. And if this was the case, that object could of course have been the human person: "You shall not steal a human being."

In the text as we have it today, however, Yahweh is simply forbidding the Israelites to take their neighbor's property—naturally, including their person—without their consent. The crime of theft is not as grave as the others listed in the decalogue, but it would be difficult for a society to maintain itself without penalizing it.

4A2.10 FALSE WITNESS (EXOD. 20:16)

(9) "You shall not bear false witness against your neighbor."

The Hebrew vocabulary betrays the concrete situation to which this commandment refers: litigation. Litigation was conducted before a group of neighbors, who had the obligation of hearing both parties and handing down their decision and sentence. These popular tribunals were never totally displaced by the judges appointed by the kings later in Israelite history. False testimony was a grave offense against the victim, the court of respected neighbors in the place where the trial was being conducted, and society as a whole. The many complaints in the Psalms against false accusers evince the frequency of this delict. And a dramatic example is furnished by the story of how Naboth was stoned to death on the testimony of persons who had been suborned to this purpose by the queen (1 Kings 21).

According to Deuteronomy 19:16-21, the penalty for false accusation was the meting out upon the accuser of the penalty that would have been applied to the accused if the court had decided against the latter. To protect the accused, tradition directed the court to sentence no one to death on the testimony of one witness only (Num. 35:30, Deut. 19:15).

The prohibition of false witness has parallels in Leviticus 19:11 and 19:16. It establishes a basic norm for justice in the new society of Yahweh's people.

4A2.11 COVETOUSNESS (EXOD. 20:17)

(10) "You shall not covet your neighbor's house. You shall not covet your neighbor's wife, or his servant, man or woman, or his ox, or his donkey, or anything that is his."

There are no exact parallels to this commandment in the other laws of Israel. It differs from the other prohibitions of the ten commandments by being directed against the impulse to violate another's rights, rather than against the actual violation. But the difference should not be exaggerated: the external act of taking what is another's is normally preceded by the internal act of covetousness (see Josh. 7:21, Mic. 2:2).

This tenth and last commandment covers approximately the same ground as the eighth. The question arises, then: How are they different? The answer can be given from two viewpoints. Either: (1) coveting denotes the internal initiation of the external act, whereas stealing denotes the external act itself. Or: (2) coveting connotes the act of a superior who has the power to take overtly what is another's, whereas stealing connotes that one feels forced to take what is another's secretly because of a lack of such power.

A thief is a person who breaks through the wall of a house in order to make off with its contents (Exod. 22:1-3). On the other hand, the rich person in Nathan's parable has no need of entering the poor man's house to make off with his ewe. He need only demand it (2 Sam. 12:1-4). Similarly with King Ahab: he coveted Naboth's vineyard, and could appropriate it through a dishonest verdict (1 Kings 21). If this interpretation is correct, this last commandment is directed especially against the powerful, who can use their privileged resources to take possession of what belongs to their weaker neighbor. Thus Yahweh is seen to be the protector of the weak.

There are two differences between the text of this commandment here and in Deuteronomy 5:21. (1) In Deuteronomy the first two terms are reserved, with the wife coming first as object of coveting and the house second. There is no doubt that the original order is that of the Exodus reading, because the "house" includes the wife, and then she ranks first among all the contents of the house. The effect of the alteration is to separate the coveting of the wife from the coveting of the rest of the neighbor's "house." This has led the Catholic and Lutheran traditions to divide this commandment into two, following Deuteronomy. (2) The verb used in Deuteronomy, *tit'aveh*, underscores the internal element in covetousness. Here too the Exodus version is the more primitive one.

4A3 Request for an Intermediary (Exod. 20:18-21)

All the people shook with fear at the peals of thunder and the lightning flashes, the sound of the trumpet, and the smoking mountain; and they kept their distance. "Speak to us yourself," they said to Moses, "and we will listen; but do not let God speak to us, or we shall die." Moses answered the people, "Do not be afraid; God has come to test you, so that your fear of him, being always in your mind, may keep you from sinning." So the people kept their distance while Moses approached the dark cloud where God was.

Beholding the spectacular manifestations surrounding the presence of Yahweh, the Israelites are frightened. Will they be able to "stand" the tremendous divine presence? Their words to Moses express both the popular disposition to obey Yahweh's laws and their fear of being close to God. If Moses will serve as intermediary of Yahweh's laws, they will be able to live in accordance with them.

This introduces a theme that will dominate the remainder of the old account of the events of Mount Sinai (4A): the theme of the leadership of the people. Yahweh is the people's revolutionary leader. Still, with a natural wisdom, the Israelites understand that it is not possible to follow God directly, and they designate Moses as their authorized mediator. This is not an attempt to reject, but an effort to follow Yahweh, with a certain political and religious prudence. The problem seems solved for the moment, but it will spring up again during a prolonged absence of Moses (Exod. 32).

The petition for a mediator is woven into the account of a theophany demanding that the Israelites prepare themselves before ascending the mountain to meet with Yahweh. "When the ram's horn sounds a long blast, they are to go up the mountain" (Exod. 19:13); and "then Moses led the people out of the camp to meet God; and they stood at the bottom of the mountain" (19:17). According to the present form of the text, Yahweh dictated the ten commandments before the Israelites ascended the mountain—but in their hearing. Deuteronomy is explicit: "On the mountain, from the heart of the fire, Yahweh spoke to you face to face" (Deut. 5:4). There seem to be two continuations of this thread: the ascent of the seventy elders who saw Yahweh (Exod. 24:9–11), and the interruption of the process with the present petition for a mediator. Surely the presence of these two alternatives reflects the prehistory of the text, which it is impossible to reconstitute from its present form.

In acceding to the request that he serve as mediator with Yahweh, Moses calms the people's fear by indicating that Yahweh only means to "try" or "test" the people. We have seen the same thing when Yahweh first handed down decrees and norms in Marah (Exod. 15:25). The notion is not perfectly clear. But it probably stresses how important it is that the people live in justice, and follow the norms that have been laid down by Yahweh the liberator God as requirements for being the people of Yahweh. A people cannot be Yahweh's people unless it lives in justice. The terrible aspects of the theophany on Sinai have the purpose of inculcating a healthy fear, one that will help the people carry out the prescriptions that have been enjoined.

4A4 Yahweh's Self-revelation to the Elders (Exod. 24:1–2, 9–11)

To Moses he had said, "Come up to Yahweh, yourself and Aaron, Nadab and Abihu, and seventy of the elders of Israel and bow down in worship at a distance. Moses alone must approach Yahweh; the others must not, nor must the people go up with him.". . .

Moses went up with Aaron, Nadab and Abihu, and seventy elders of Israel. They saw the God of Israel beneath whose feet there was, it seemed, a sapphire pavement pure as the heavens themselves. He laid no hand on these notables of the sons of Israel: they gazed on God. They ate and they drank.

This vision of God is an alternate continuation of the preceding passage, where the Israelites understandably seek to maintain a distance from God through the mediation of Moses.

Very simply, this text states that Israel's leaders "saw" the God of Israel. The word used is the ordinary Hebrew word for "seeing" anything—*ra'ah*. The verb that is translated "gazing on"—*hazah*—is the one used in the Bible for the visions of a seer or a prophet. But it is not a matter of a subjective vision here, inasmuch as it is added that the elders "ate and drank," demonstrating a normal state of awareness.

Unlike the visions described in Isaiah 6 and Ezekiel 1, this one is reported without any description of God's form, but only of the wonderful pavement beneath God's feet. This implies no intent to minimize the realism of the statement that the elders saw God, however. There are very few scenes in the Bible to compare with this one.

Another noteworthy element of the account is that it was a large group that saw God: Moses, Aaron, Nadab, Abihu, and seventy elders of Israel. Moses, then, is only first among many. Here we see a continuation of the thread drawn in the theophany of Exodus 19:13, 17. Of course there is the alternative thread as well, which makes an effort to have Moses' role stand out. During the theophany, this interest appears in 19:9,19: "I am coming to you in a dense cloud so that the people may hear when I speak to you and may trust you always"; and "Moses spoke, and God answered him ['with voice']." In later problems of political guidance in Israel, this second current was the one that prevailed, and prevails in the text of the Sinai account as we have it today. In later centuries, Yahweh's laws had to be given an authority unquestionably superior to that of elders, priests, and kings. Having Moses front and center, as intermediary of the revelation, accomplishes this.

The words from ". . . Bow down and worship" to "nor must the people go up with him," are an attempt to assimilate the first thread to the second—that it was Moses alone who spoke with Yahweh on Sinai. They are out of context, and are certainly a later addition.

E. W. Nicholson has commented on this passage at length, pointing to a great number of peculiarities which, he says, mark it as very old traditional material ("The Interpretation of Ex XXIV.9–11," "The Antiquity of the Tradition in Ex XXIV. 9–11," and "The Origin of the Tradition in Ex XXIV. 9–11"). Nicholson suggests that this tradition is reminiscent of a pilgrimage to a sanctuary in the wilderness. He interprets the meal of the elders as a solemnization of a pact between Yahweh and the people of Israel. However, the text places no emphasis on the meal. It is the vision of God that is important. Nor does it say anything about a covenant or alliance. In context, the meal serves only to underscore the naturalness of the vision, and the fact that, having seen God with their eyes, the elders did not die.

What is very special about this tradition is that it subordinates the gift of the law to the vision of Yahweh as climax of the revelation. This is a departure from the central teaching of biblical tradition.

Introduction to §§4A5, 6, 7

If a social movement does not resolve the problem of leadership, it will be dogged by conflict and uncertainty along its historical march. When the movement is a revolutionary one, an important part of the solution will be to guarantee the ideological reliability of this leadership. And when the revolutionary movement is inspired by religious convictions, the leadership will have to be such as will not clash with the will of heaven, as well as be able to interpret this will convincingly.

This is the complex problem dominating the next three units of text. Yahweh and Moses have liberated Israel from oppression in Egypt. With Yahweh's help the people of Israel has been able to face the want and the danger of life in the wilderness and, despite incipient counterrevolutionary tendencies, has held to the ideal of continuing on to the land where milk and honey flow. With the revelation of the basic law on Sinai, the limits of life in the new society have been set. The absence of Moses on the mountain, and insecurity as to whether he will return, occasion the need for Israel to reaffirm the direction of the revolutionary movement without the help of the one who was the leader in the struggle with the pharaoh.

The account approaches this theme in three units. The first tells of the attempt of the people to replace Moses with an image of Yahweh to lead it to the land where milk and honey flow. This solution is vehemently rejected in the text precisely as a rejection of Yahweh, despite the fact that the image would be of Yahweh! Then Moses appears once more, and the urgency of the question of the future leadership of the movement subsides. But now Moses understands the importance of solving the problem.

In the second unit (§4A6), Yahweh and Moses set up a tent where the people can consult Yahweh. This tent will accompany the people in its wanderings. And thus, with Moses or without him, the people will have a way to search out Yahweh's will.

In the third of these units (§4A7), Yahweh strikes an alliance with Israel, promising to expel the inhabitants of Canaan as Israel advances, and demanding in return that the Israelites make no pacts with Canaanite peoples. For the maintenance of this alliance or covenant, a series of laws is established, having to do with worship of Yahweh and centered on the rhythms of agrarian life.

Properly speaking, Moses will have no successor. He has conducted the revolutionary process. With the alliance well established and the norms for living marked out, no king will be necessary. Yahweh will lead Israel, not from behind a golden image, but by the living voice addressed to the prophets whom he will designate in the tent of meeting.

This renunciation of a successorship for Moses arises out of a revolutionary rejection of monarchy as an institution productive of slavery. The revolutionary vanguard was not to lend its authority to a new domination that would be a new form of oppression. The basic laws that have been given, together with the tent of meeting and the covenant, will have to suffice for Yahweh's people. And the historical fact is that for two centuries they did suffice until, with Saul and David, Israel fell back into a monarchical system of leadership.

The three units that we shall now take up have a complicated, unclear prehistory, especially chapters 32 and 33, which are combinations of different traditions. The familiar Yahwist and Elohist are present once more, but now they are fused together in such a fashion that they can hardly be resepa-rated.

Part of the work of rereading, in these units, was done in the time of Hezekiah, shortly after the fall of Samaria. (This redaction has been discussed by the Mexican scholar José Loza in his "Exode XXXII et la rédaction JE," following the suggestions of Julius Wellhausen.) At that moment, it was important to establish the possibility of Yahweh's pardon and a new beginning. This is the dominant thematic of Exodus 32:7–14, 30–34, 33:1–6, 12–23, and 34:1–10, and has influenced the general structure of chapters 32–34. The thematic of leadership, however, has not been effaced, and runs all through these three units.

4A5 An Unsuccessful Attempt at a Religious Leadership System
(Exod. 24:12–15a, 31:18, 32:1–35)

4A5.1 MOSES ON THE MOUNTAIN (EXOD. 24:12–15a)

Yahweh said to Moses, "Come up to me on the mountain and stay there while I give you the stone tablets—the law and the commandments—that I have written for their instruction." Accordingly Moses rose, he and his servant Joshua, and they went up the mountain of God. To the elders he had said, "Wait here for us until we come back to you. You have Aaron and Hur with you; if anyone has a difference to settle, let him go to them." And Moses went up the mountain.

The account of the golden calf unfolds in two locations: on the top of the mountain, and on the plain below. On the mountaintop we find Yahweh giving Moses instructions for the people. (Joshua accompanies Moses, but plays no significant role.) At the foot of the mountain is the people of Israel, with Aaron (accompanied by Hur) provisionally at its head. The whole action is initiated in Moses' absence. This introductory passage, separated, in the text as we have it today, by several chapters of sacerdotal material, sets the scene and assigns the roles.

All the characters have already been introduced. It only needs to be pointed out that, in the old accounts (of the Yahwist and the Elohist), Aaron has no priestly functions. Therefore we probably should not suppose that his role as Moses' temporary substitute includes priestly functions.

4A5.2 TABLETS OF THE TESTIMONY (EXOD. 31:18)

When he had finished speaking with Moses on the mountain of Sinai, he gave him the two tablets of the Testimony, tablets of stone inscribed by the finger of God.

According to Deuteronomy 5:22 and 10:1–5, what the tablets contained was the decalogue. The present passage, however, is unclear in this respect. After a long talk with Moses, Yahweh inscribes on two tablets the most important things said to Moses. Here they are called the "tablets of the Testimony," an expression reminiscent of the sacerdotal stratum. Deuteronomy calls them the "tablets of the covenant" (Deut. 9:15).

4A5.3 THE GOLDEN CALF (EXOD. 32:1–6)

When the people saw that Moses was a long time before coming down the mountain, they gathered around Aaron and said to him, "Come, make us [gods] to go at the head of us; this Moses, the man who brought us up from Egypt, we do not know what has become of him." Aaron answered

*them, "Take the gold rings out of the ears of your wives and your sons
and daughters, and bring them to me." So they all took the gold rings
from their ears and brought them to Aaron. He took them from their
hands and, in a mold, melted the metal down and cast an effigy of a calf.
"[These are your gods,] Israel," they cried, "who brought you out of the
land of Egypt!" Observing this, Aaron built an altar before the effigy.
"Tomorrow," he said, "will be a feast in honor of Yahweh."*

*And so, early the next day they offered holocausts and brought
communion sacrifices; then all the people sat down to eat and drink, and
afterward got up to amuse themselves.*

While Yahweh and Moses, on the mountaintop, secure the base of the new
society, the Israelites grow anxious at Moses' absence. They begin to wonder
what has become of the "man who brought us up from Egypt." Doubtless they
think that he will no longer return, either because he has met with some
accident or because Yahweh has taken him away somewhere. In any case, they
suddenly find themselves without the guidance of the person who, until now,
has been able to direct the liberation process so very well. This absence of
leadership is the starting point for the action of the account.

Naturally, this problem could be confronted in a number of ways. Perhaps
the most obvious would have been to appoint Aaron Moses' successor. Aaron
was Moses' brother and chief lieutenant; furthermore, he was provisionally in
charge of the people during Moses' absence. Or a council of elders could have
been named—persons who had welcomed Moses when he had come from
Midian, and who had seen Yahweh on the mountain. These, surely, could have
joined together to lead the people to the land where milk and honey flowed.
But Israel conceives a political novelty. It will appoint God its leader, to lead it
forward.

To do justice to this initiative, it is important to note that it does not
constitute the abandonment of Moses' undertaking. And it certainly is not a
counterrevolutionary effort to return to Egypt. Caught between the Egyptian
troops and the sea, some of the Israelites had expressed their repudiation of the
liberation project, and had given voice to their wish that they had never been a
part of it. Later, when scouts report on the defenses that have been thrown up
in the land of Canaan, there will be a movement to name another leader and
return to Egypt (Num. 14:4). But this is not the case at the foot of Mount Sinai.
The Israelites want gods "to go at the head of us," to lead them on their journey
toward the land where milk and honey flow. And so the present experience is
not to be confused with the various "grumblings" in the wilderness: this is a
rebellion neither against the liberation project nor against Moses.

Aaron makes the golden calf, and says, "Tomorrow will be a feast in honor
of Yahweh." The calf, then, is an image of Yahweh, or at least this is how Aaron
understands it. This agrees with the people's refrain before the image, as well:
"Here is your God [or, "These are your gods"], Israel, who brought you out of
the land of Egypt!" Only Yahweh could have brought Israel out of Egypt. The

case at hand, then, is not the forerunner of the numerous times when, in Canaan, the people "went after other gods." The calf is not an image of Baal, the Canaanite god who so often became the object of the people's attention.

In the Hebrew (as also in the RSV and NEB) the word "god" is here used in the plural: "Make us gods to go at the head of us," and "these are your gods, Israel." Some translations (JB, NAB) opt for the singular: "god" or "God." There is no way of understanding this plural except in reference to the calves set up in Bethel and Dan by Jeroboam, with the refrain: "Here are your gods, Israel; these brought you up out of the land of Egypt!" (1 Kings 12:28). It is probably to these that Hosea refers when he speaks of the calf of Samaria (Hos. 8:4–7). Bethel was an ancient sanctuary of Yahweh, consecrated by the manifestation of God to the patriarch Jacob (Gen. 28). When Jeroboam placed himself at the head of a movement of protest against David's abusive dynasty, he did so under the inspiration of Yahweh, the god of the exodus, and at the instigation and authorization of Yahweh's prophet Ahijah (1 Kings 11:26–40). Jeroboam made Bethel a national shrine, and acknowledged his calf to be the image of Yahweh. But he also recognized the authenticity of the image in the sanctuary of Dan, in the extreme north of the kingdom. And this caused the Deuteronomist redactors of the books of Kings to consider his religion a worship of "gods," in the plural.

Thus the account of the golden calf at the foot of Sinai has been corrupted with material from the history of Jeroboam. Besides what we have already seen, it is curious that Jeroboam had sons named Nadab and Abijah, the former murdered in a coup after two years on the throne (1 Kings 15:25–31), and the latter dying of an illness considered to be a punishment from Yahweh (1 Kings 14:1–18). Aaron, who made the golden calf at the foot of Mount Sinai, had four sons. The elder were called Nadab and Abihu, and they died by the hand of Yahweh while they were offering service at the altar (Lev. 10:1–3). Thus tradition has joined the figures of Jeroboam and Aaron. We may suppose that the original names of the sons were Nadab and Abijah, and that they were sons of Jeroboam, seeing that Nadab was a well-known figure as king, whereas the sons of Aaron left no descendancy among the priestly houses of Israel.

It is likely that the connection between Aaron and the golden calf is an ancient one, and that it served to legitimate the Yahwist cult of Bethel. Indeed, according to Judges 20:27–28, Phinehas, Aaron's grandson, served in the sanctuary at Bethel. Probably in the origins of the account of the golden calf at the foot of Sinai, the appearance of Aaron was intended to legitimate the Bethel cult, which was served by Aaron's descendants. When the polemics with the Bethel cult began—perhaps when, in David's time, Jerusalem became the place where Yahweh's ark was kept—the Bethel calf came to be interpreted as a violation of the commandment not to make images of Yahweh, and this was also the way the account of the calf of Sinai was read. The present state of Exodus 32 reflects a later polemic—the Deuteronomic notion that Jeroboam worshiped more than one god.

For the interpretation of §4A5.3, it is important not to allow ourselves to be distracted by the original Hebrew plural, "gods." The Israelites were not attempting to erect gods other than Yahweh, and Aaron did not intend to create another god with the image he made. The problem in this passage is a different one—that of who is to guide the people after Moses is gone.

Aaron made Yahweh's image of gold, given voluntarily for this purpose. Because it was intended to lead the people, probably it was not a large sculpture, but a small one, mounted on a shaft (Otto Eissfeldt, "Lade und Stierbild," in his *Kliene Schriften,* 2:282–305). Thus it would not be unlike the serpent that Moses made, that was later to be found in the temple of Jerusalem (Num. 21:4–9, 2 Kings 18:4), or Yahweh's standard in the battle with the Amalekites (Exod. 17:8–16).

4A5.4 MOSES' INTERCESSION FOR ISRAEL (EXOD. 32:7–14)

Then Yahweh spoke to Moses, "Go down now, because your people whom you brought out of Egypt have apostatized. They have been quick to leave the way I marked out for them; they have made themselves a calf of molten metal and have worshiped it and offered it sacrifice. 'Here is your God, Israel,' they have cried, 'who brought you up from the land of Egypt!' " Yahweh said to Moses, "I can see how headstrong these people are! Leave me, now, my wrath shall blaze out against them and devour them; of you, however, I will make a great nation."

But Moses pleaded with Yahweh his God. "Yahweh," he said, "why should your wrath blaze out against this people of yours who whom you brought out of the land of Egypt with arm outstretched and mighty hand? Why let the Egyptians say, 'Ah, it was in treachery that he brought them out, to do them to death in the mountains and wipe them off the face of the earth?' Leave your burning wrath; relent and do not bring this disaster on your people. Remember Abraham, Isaac and Jacob, your servants to whom by your own self you swore and made this promise: I will make your offspring as many as the stars of heaven, and all this land which I promised I will give to your descendants, and it shall be their heritage for ever." So Yahweh relented and did not bring on his people the disaster he had threatened.

Once more the action is on the mountaintop, where Yahweh has now finished giving Moses the tablets of the law. Not without a certain craftiness, Yahweh begins giving Moses all the credit for the escape from the land of Egypt, and acknowledges the people to be Moses' people. Moses refuses to accept this interpretation of the facts, and insists that it was Yahweh who brought the people out of Egypt, so that it is Yahweh's people. It is precisely this duality of leadership that the account seeks to preserve, and Yahweh, like Moses, is telling only part of the truth.

"They have been quick to leave the way I marked out for them. . . ." This is an allusion to the second commandment, according to which Israel is not allowed to make images (of Yahweh). With the intent of making their revolution a purely religious movement, under the exclusive direction of Yahweh, the Israelites have strayed from Yahweh's path. The Yahweh cult of an image on a standard can be manipulated, and utilized to legitimate a great number of things that cannot be tolerated by Yahweh, the living one, who speaks through prophets. This is unacceptable.

". . . How headstrong these people are!" They have failed to understand that the true God has need of historical vehicles for the work of salvation-liberation. But here Yahweh too shows a revolutionary weakness, and Moses calls him to account. Here is a people ill-suited to salvation, Yahweh reasons. Let it be cast aside, then, another people be found, one more tractable. This is the temptation to elitism. The vanguard—here, Yahweh—is well established, theoretically and practically, and possesses a high degree of revolutionary commitment. Failures are due to the weakness and lack of popular commitment. Moses' response is clear: the problem is not with the people, but with Yahweh. Yahweh has allowed the salvific will to flag. Moses does not refute Yahweh's affirmation about the Israelites; but abandoning the project will scarcely solve anything. Leave your burning wrath! Relent! Remember! The solidarity of Yahweh and Moses must transcend the weakness of the people. Otherwise Yahweh will not be a saving God, and Moses will not be Yahweh's prophet.

A theological reflection on this text is important because of the notion here of God's "relenting"—an idea also strikingly expressed in Jeremiah 18:1–12 and Jonah 3:10, as well as, in less direct forms, in other parts of the Bible. Under the influence of the teaching that any change in the divinity would be an imperfection, traditional theology refused to take these passages at their face value. But in the Bible God's greatest perfection is love. Now, when has a lover ever been unaffected by the beloved? God's repentance is motivated here by loyalty to the patriarchs and by love for Israel. Moses calls Yahweh's attention to what is most characteristic of Yahweh's very nature—commitment to humankind. The gospels will go so far as to state that God's solidarity with the poor leads God to suffer the repression that they suffer. In sum, then: in the Bible, change is not an imperfection when it occurs for love of others.

4A5.5 THE TABLETS AND GOLDEN CALF DESTROYED (EXOD. 32:15–20)

Moses made his way back down the mountain with the two tablets of the Testimony in his hands, tablets inscribed on both sides, inscribed on the front and on the back. These tablets were the work of God, and the writing on them was God's writing engraved on the tablets.

Joshua heard the noise of the people shouting. "There is the sound of battle in the camp," he told Moses. Moses answered him:

"No song of victory in this sound,
no wailing for defeat this sound;
it is the sound of chanting that I hear."

> *As he approached the camp and saw the calf and the groups dancing,*
> *Moses' anger blazed. He threw down the tablets he was holding and*
> *broke them at the foot of the mountain. He seized the calf they had made*
> *and burned it, grinding it into powder which he scattered on the water;*
> *and he made the sons of Israel drink it.*

Joshua does not play an independent role in this account. He has been
introduced as Moses' companion on the journey to the mountaintop. In its
present form, leaving its prehistory out of account, our text supposes that
Moses already knows what the others have done, and knows too Yahweh's
negative reaction to the image-making project. Joshua, on the other hand,
shows by his remark that he has not been privy to the earlier dialogue.

The gesture of casting the tablets to the earth is Moses' dramatic way of
denouncing this "feast in honor of Yahweh" that was being celebrated before
the golden calf. It is likely that, in an earlier stage, he was represented as doing
so spontaneously, in violent reaction before an astonishing discovery. But in the
text as we now have it, it is a premeditated gesture, calculated to indicate to the
people that the feast is a grave offense against Yahweh. It violates the second
commandment (in both lists of fundamental laws, Exodus 20 and 34).

Now Moses turns to the calf. He "burns" it (melts it down), pulverizes the
remains, casts the pieces into water, and makes the people drink the water. This
last detail recalls the juridical test prescribed for a woman accused of adultery
in the absence of any witnesses (Num. 5:11–31). She must drink the "water of
bitterness." If she is guilty, the water will produce an inflammation. In spite of
similarities of form, however, the cases are different. The Israelites are guilty,
beyond any doubt of "leaving the way" Yahweh has "marked out for them."
To distinguish between the two cases, the parallel account in Deuteronomy has
Moses cast the pieces of the calf into the river and the water carries them away
(Deut. 9:21). The Exodus text is more dramatic. Moses makes the Israelites
consume their fetish. It was gold, nothing more, and the aura of sanctity with
which it was surrounded did not correspond to reality.

The Israelites had obtained the gold from the Egyptians, "plundering" their
neighbors of their jewelry on the night they fled Egypt (Exod. 12:35–36). Its
first use was adornment. Then, in hard times, it served as exchangeable tender,
and provisions were purchased with it (Gen. 47:13–14). But in itself it has no
nutritive value. As an image of Yahweh, it is a lie, a fetish. It cannot lead the
Israelites to the land where milk and honey flow, and it cannot feed them in the
desert.

4A5.6 AARON'S EXCUSE (EXOD. 32:21–24)

> *To Aaron Moses said, "What has this people done to you, for you to*
> *bring such a great sin on them?" "Let not my lord's anger blaze like this,"*
> *Aaron answered. "You know yourself how prone this people is to evil.*
> *They said to me, 'Make us a god to go at our head; this Moses, the man*

who brought us up from Egypt, we do not know what has become of him.' So I said to them, 'Who has gold?', and they took it off and brought it to me. I threw it into the fire and out came this calf."

Having demonstrated the uselessness of the fetish as a guide for Israel in its pursuit of liberation, Moses looks for the ones responsible, and first of all for the person he has left in charge. Aaron immediately takes the defensive, throwing all the blame on the people. His reaction is like Yahweh's, when Yahweh called the people "headstrong."

What is at stake in both these conversations, however, is not the popular level of consciousness. What is at stake is the salvation project itself. A responsible vanguard does not look for scapegoats. It is consumed with a zeal for attaining the goal of the revolution. Self-criticism is valid when it leads to more correct ways of attaining the goal. But if it is granted that the people as such is responsible for these failures by reason of their inherent intrinsic shortcomings, then it is granted that sooner or later the whole project will fail. Aaron was willing to defend his good name at the cost of the project. Moses, in his dialogue with Yahweh, has demonstrated his zeal for the project.

Nothing is said about Moses' reaction to Aaron's apologia. It has already been stated that it was Aaron who made the image, and it is unnecessary to comment on the weak excuse offered by the person left in charge.

4A5.7 INVESTITURE OF THE LEVITES (EXOD. 32:25–29)

When Moses saw the people so out of hand—for Aaron had allowed them to lapse into idolatry with enemies all around them—he stood at the gate of the camp and shouted, "Who is for Yahweh? To me!" And all the sons of Levi rallied to him. And he said to them, "This is the message of Yahweh, the God of Israel, 'Gird on your sword, every man of you, and quarter the camp from gate to gate, killing one his brother, another his friend, another his neighbor.' " The sons of Levi carried out the command of Moses, and of the people about three thousand men perished that day. "Today," Moses said, "you have won yourselves investiture as priests of Yahweh at the cost, one of his son, another of his brother, and so he grants you a blessing today."

The price of keeping to the correct path is very high. Three thousand persons fall for their share in the events surrounding the image. And they were not counterrevolutionaries. They were simply persons who believed that the revolution called for purely religious leadership. They were idealists, lacking in a sense of political reality. Moses views their error as a grave one. The salvation of the people as a whole demands that the idealists be sacrificed.

It is recorded that the agents of the purge were the Levites. Deuteronomy 33:8–11, too, acknowledges that the Levites' authority in the teaching of

Yahweh's law arose from their fidelity to the covenant even at the sacrifice of their "brothers" and "children." In the later history of Israel, matters became more complex. But in the premonarchical period the Levites were held to be the authentic representatives of faith in Yahweh.

4A5.8 MOSES' INTERCESSION REPEATED (EXOD. 32:30–35)

On the following day Moses said to the people, "You have committed a grave sin. But now I shall go up to Yahweh: perhaps I can make atonement for your sin." And Moses returned to Yahweh. "I am grieved," he cried, "this people has committed a grave sin, making themselves a god of gold. And yet, if it pleased you to forgive this sin of theirs . . . ! But if not, then blot me out from the book that you have written." Yahweh answered Moses, "It is the man who has sinned against me that I shall blot out from my book. Go now, lead the people to the place of which I told you. My angel shall go before you but, on the day of my visitation, I shall punish them for their sin." And Yahweh punished the people for molding the calf that Aaron had made.

The new confrontation between Yahweh and Moses on the mountain resumes the subject of the previous one, but with a new focus and outcome. Now Moses acknowledges that the construction of the image was a grave sin, and he asks Yahweh to forgive it. In the previous discussion, Moses resisted Yahweh's intention to abandon the liberation project. Moses refused to admit the innate unfitness of the Israelites—literally, the "stiffness of their necks"—and he accused Yahweh of inconstancy. Now he admits that their deed was a serious crime. And he intercedes for the people. The first discussion concluded with Yahweh's abandonment of the intention to destroy the people. But now we see that this does not mean that God does not condemn what the people did.

Moses offers his life on behalf of the people. The "book of life" is also mentioned in Psalms 69:28–29 and 139:16. It contains the names of the living, from the very womb, and to erase a name from the book is tantamount to its bearer's destruction. This is not the book that, in later, apocalyptic, literature, is the record of each person's faults, the indictment to which everyone must answer at the last judgment.

Moses' offer is a dramatic one, but Yahweh refuses to yield. When the right time comes, an accounting will be demanded of sinners. The punishment seems severe, considering that three thousand of those responsible have already died for their crime. History teaches that revolutions do not forgive mistakes.

Still, Yahweh's vexation does not mean the end of the liberation project. Moses must continue to lead the people, and Yahweh will send an angel to go before Moses. This promise creates a problem for Moses, and will be the subject of the following unit of passages on the revolutionary, religious leadership of the Israelite undertaking.

4A6 Yahweh to Be Present on the Journey (Exod. 33:1-23)

The result of the people's action at the foot of the mountain is that doubt has been cast on Yahweh's presence on the journey to the land where milk and honey flow. The Israelites have gone about assuring themselves of Yahweh's presence in the wrong way—with an image of Yahweh, failing to understand that Yahweh is not a God to be "imaged" but to be obeyed. Now not even Moses is sure of Yahweh's presence on the remainder of the march. The varied traditions composing this unit all take up this matter.

4A6.1 A HEADSTRONG PEOPLE (EXOD. 33:1-6)

Yahweh said to Moses, "Leave this place, with the people you brought out of the land of Egypt, and go to the land that I swore to Abraham, Isaac and Jacob I would give their descendants. I will send an angel in front of you; I will drive out the Canaanites, the Amorites, the Hittites, the Perizzites, the Hivites, the Jebusites. Go on to the land where milk and honey flow. I shall not go with you myself—you are a headstrong people—or I might exterminate you on the way." On hearing these stern words the people went into mourning, and no one wore his ornaments.

Then Yahweh said to Moses, "Say to the sons of Israel, 'You are a headstrong people. If I were to go with you, even for a moment only, I should exterminate you. Take off your ornaments, then, that I may know how to deal with you!' " So, from Mount Horeb onward, the sons of Israel stripped themselves of their ornaments.

Despite the stumbling block of Sinai, Yahweh orders the liberation pursuit to continue. Release from the land of Egypt must be completed by entry into the land of Canaan. Yielding to Moses' arguments, Yahweh has not withdrawn support from the project to found a new society in a land where milk and honey flow. Still, a certain distancing from this project is implicit in the reference to "*your* people whom *you* brought out of Egypt" in speaking to Moses. Yahweh has relented in the decision to destroy Israel, but still insists that Israel is a headstrong people. For the Israelites' own good, Yahweh should not accompany them: in a fit of rage Yahweh might destroy them. Instead, a representative—an "angel"—will accompany Moses. (This messenger is never mentioned again.) The Israelites take this as disturbing news. In order to persuade Yahweh to reconsider, they take off all their showy finery and prepare to leave it at Mount Horeb. Now Yahweh wonders what to do.

4A6.2 THE TENT OF MEETING (EXOD. 33:7-11)

Moses used to take the Tent and pitch it outside the camp, at some distance from the camp. He called it the Tent of Meeting. Anyone who had to consult Yahweh would go out to the Tent of Meeting, outside the camp. Whenever Moses went out to the Tent, all the people would rise. Every man would stand at the door of his tent and watch Moses until he reached the Tent; the pillar of cloud would come down and station itself at the entrance to the Tent, and Yahweh would speak with Moses. When they saw the pillar of cloud stationed at the entrance to the Tent, all the people would rise and bow low, each at the door of his tent. Yahweh would speak with Moses face to face, as a man speaks with his friend. Then Moses would turn back to the camp, but the young man who was his servant, Joshua son of Nun, would not leave the Tent.

Ignoring the promise of a representative, Moses takes the initiative in setting up a permanent, portable meeting place for consulting Yahweh. What he needs is a kind of portable Mount Sinai. Until now, Moses has climbed the mountain to meet with Yahweh and receive instructions. Now he pitches a tent to meet with Yahweh along the road, whenever he has need of divine assistance. He pitches his tent outside the camp, to assuage Yahweh's uneasiness about suddenly consuming the people in rage were Yahweh to be always with them.

The descent of the cloud at the entrance of the tent when Moses enters it indicates that Yahweh has accepted the institution that Moses has established to stay in contact with Yahweh. Any Israelite may go to the tent to consult Yahweh. But when Moses enters, the cloud dramatically symbolizes Yahweh's presence. Moses is the unquestioned leader of Israel.

In terms of the history of traditions, it is evident that two distinct traditions existed with respect to the tent in the wilderness. According to the sacerdotal writings, the tent was in the middle of the camp (Num. 2), with the twelve tribes encamped all around. The cloud hovered over the tent continuously, and at night had the look of fire (Num. 9:15–23). Within the tent was the ark of witness, covered by the cherubim (Exod. 25:10–22). The tent was a portable temple, the place of God's permanent presence in the midst of the people.

By contrast, according to the tradition cited in our text, the ark was outside the encampment, and was the place where, from time to time, Yahweh came to meet the leadership of the people. Nothing is said here of what was in the tent, which was not a sanctuary or place of worship. The person in permanent charge of the tent was Joshua, who was neither a priest nor a Levite.

The tent of meeting is a way of renouncing the institutionalization of Yahweh's presence in the new society. It is a way of acknowledging that this revolution needs God, but does not control God. Simply, there is a certain vacant space on the outskirts of the encampment where Yahweh appears to the appointed leader of the people, when Yahweh wishes so to appear.

4A6.3 YAHWEH'S PRESENCE (EXOD. 33:12–17)

Moses said to Yahweh, "See, you yourself say to me, 'Make the people go on,' but you do not let me know who it is you will send with me. Yet you yourself have said, 'I know you by name and you have won my favor.' If indeed I have won your favor, please show me your ways, so that I can understand you and win your favor. Remember, too, that this nation is your own people." Yahweh replied, "I myself will go with you, and I will give you rest." Moses said, "If you are not going with us yourself, do not make us leave this place. By what means can it be known that I, I and [your] people, have won your favor, if not by your going with us? By this we shall be marked out, I and [your] people, from all the peoples on the face of the earth." Yahweh said to Moses, "Again I will do what you have asked, because you have won my favor and because I know you by name."

In context, this dialogue in the tent of meeting must be understood as an attempt by Moses to ensure the visible presence of Yahweh in the tent. Yahweh continues to refer to Israel as "your people" in speaking to Moses, and Moses speaks with equal insistence on the importance of Yahweh's presence along the journey with "us," and refers to his group as "I and your people."

The Jerusalem Bible makes the conjectural emendation, "I and my people," but this reveals a failure to understand the subtleties of the interchange between Yahweh and Moses.

Moses has been told that he has found grace in Yahweh's eyes, but this is not enough for Moses. At stake is the whole historical movement, and the movement requires the presence of Yahweh, not just that of Moses. At no time does Moses accept Yahweh's proposal to send an "angel" with the people. This is a people doing something new—constructing a kingless revolutionary society— and it must be marked off from all the other peoples on the face of the earth by the visible presence of Yahweh the liberator God.

In reply, Yahweh promises that the divine presence—literally, "my face"— will accompany Moses, and "give him rest." In the language of the Pentateuch, to "give rest" means to give a land to live in (Deut. 3:20, 12:10, etc.). Yahweh has yielded, then, to a degree, but does not unambiguously attest Israel to be the people of Yahweh. The doubt will continue, and will be dissipated only later, with the alliance, covenant, to be offered to the people.

4A6.4 MOSES GIVEN A VISION OF GOD (EXOD. 33:18-23)

Moses said, "Show me your glory, I beg you." And he said, "I will let all my splendor pass in front of you, and I will pronounce before you the name Yahweh. I have compassion on whom I will, and I show pity to whom I please. You cannot see my face," he said, "for man cannot see me and live." And Yahweh said, "Here is a place beside me. You must stand on the rock, and when my glory passes by, I will put you in a cleft of the rock and shield you with my hand while I pass by. Then I will take my hand away and you shall see the back of me; but my face is not to be seen."

Moses has one more request. He is not yet quite sure that Yahweh can accompany the Israelites on the journey to Canaan without destroying them on the way. Moses and Yahweh are alone, and Moses asks Yahweh to grant him a vision to confirm his confidence.

This is a passage in tension with the other traditions assembled in this unit. In the other traditions, there is no doubt of the relationship between Yahweh and Moses. The whole problem has been the relationship between Yahweh and the people. This difference reflects the distinct origins of the traditions. In this context, Moses' request comes as the climax of his conversation with Yahweh on their joint leadership of the people.

"I have compassion on whom I will, and I show pity to whom I please," Yahweh replies, maintaining a reserve. Yahweh is a merciful God, but will not be compromised in making decisions or commitments. Yahweh will not be manipulated, and is even less inclined to make a commitment to the Israelites after seeing them attempt to replace Moses with a molten image.

". . . Man cannot see me and live." This notion is a familiar one in the Bible. When Isaiah saw Yahweh seated on his throne, his reaction was: "What a wretched state I am in! I am lost . . ." (Isa. 6:5). Gideon, too, cries out, "Alas, my Lord Yahweh! I have seen the angel of Yahweh face to face!" (Judg. 6:22). On the other hand, an old tradition places on Jacob's lips: ". . . I have seen God face to face, and I have survived" (Gen. 32:31). And, with reference to Yahweh's manifestation on Sinai, Deuteronomy quotes the people as saying: "Today we have seen that God can speak with man and man still live" (Deut. 5:24). Finally, in this same chapter it has been stated that Yahweh was accustomed to speak with Moses face to face. Evidently, it was considered dangerous to meet up with God directly. And yet God could make exceptions, and be seen by a human being if God so chose.

On the manifestation itself, there is little left to say. Yahweh makes a self-manifestation to Moses with a reserve that underscores the reserve of Yahweh's words. Not even Moses can impose his will on Yahweh.

4A7 Yahweh Proposes a Covenant for Life in Canaan (Exod. 34:1–35)

Yahweh's reaction to the Israelites' attempt to make an image of God to guide them, and thus—supposedly—to escape human leadership, has been surprisingly violent. Thanks to Moses' initiative, the crisis has been resolved, and a means of consultation has been created for the journey through the wilderness—the tent of meeting. This has preserved the revolutionary rejection of a state with a king at its head. But it has not legislated an alternative form of leadership.

This indefinition reflects the de facto situation in premonarchical Israel. Moses' high status in speaking with Yahweh face to face suggests that prophets will be the key figures in the governance of the people. But at the same time it is recognized that Moses will not have successors. Thus the leadership problem is left without positive solution, although two possible paths have been rejected:

monarchy (abandoned with the flight from Egypt, without its being replaced with another monarchy), and the fetishism of a people that sought to become a theocracy.

The incident of the golden calf has ended with another serious problem, and it too is still pending: Yahweh's reserve with respect to future involvement with this "headstrong" people. The last chapter of the ancient Sinai account (Exod. 34) solves the problem in one fell swoop with the divine proposal of a covenant in which both parties, Yahweh and Israel, would accept certain commitments. After the trouble Moses has had in pressuring Yahweh not to abandon the project and to come with the people, suddenly Yahweh demonstrates mercy with this proposal, which Moses accepts on the mountaintop in the name of the people.

The stipulations of the pact have to do with life in the land of Canaan. This is the only chapter in the book of Exodus where this land is the focus of attention. And thus it is an appropriate way of closing the Sinai account, with all eyes on the goal of the movement whose basis is here being established.

4A7.1 THE COVENANT RENEWED (EXOD. 34:1–5)

Yahweh said to Moses, "Cut two tablets of stone like the first ones and come up to me on the mountain, and I will inscribe on them the words that were on the first tablets, which you broke. Be ready by morning, and come up to the mountain of Sinai at dawn; await my orders there at the top of the mountain. No one must come up with you, no one be seen anywhere on the mountain; even the flocks and herds may not graze in front of this mountain." And so Moses cut two tablets of stone like the first and, with the two tablets of stone in his hands, he went up the mountain of Sinai in the early morning as Yahweh had commanded him. And Yahweh descended in the form of a cloud, and Moses stood with him there. He called on the name of Yahweh.

The preparations for this ascent of Moses are like those made on the occasion of the theophany (§4A1). In its present form our text distinguishes between these stone tablets and the former ones, in that the others were inscribed by the finger of God (Exod. 32:16). This time Moses has to prepare them himself and bear them to the mountaintop. Perhaps he is being disciplined for having broken the ones made by Yahweh. Yahweh will write on these tablets what was written on the others. We the readers still do not know what was written on the first pair, because Moses broke them before reading them to the people.

4A7.2 COMPASSION AND COVENANT (EXOD. 34:6–13)

Yahweh passed before him and proclaimed, "Yahweh, Yahweh, a God of tenderness and compassion, slow to anger, rich in kindness and faithful-

ness; for thousands he maintains his kindness, forgives faults, transgression, sin; yet he lets nothing go unchecked, punishing the father's fault in the sons and in the grandsons to the third and fourth generation." And Moses bowed down to the ground at once and worshiped. "If I have indeed won your favor, Lord," he said, "let my Lord come with us, I beg. True, they are a headstrong people, but forgive us our faults and our sins, and adopt us as your heritage."

Yahweh said, "I am about to make a covenant with you. In the presence of all your people I shall work such wonders as have never been worked in any land or in any nation. All the people around you will see what Yahweh can do, for what I shall do through you will be awe-inspiring. Mark, then, what I command you today. I mean to drive out the Amorites before you, the Canaanites, the Hittites, the Perizzites, the Hivites, the Jebusites. Take care you make no pact with the [rulers] of the land you are about to enter, or this will prove a pitfall at your very feet. You are to tear down their altars, smash their standing stones, cut down their sacred poles."

Yahweh opens the dialogue with Moses with a cry of self-affirmation, a proclamation of mercy and compassion. It may surprise the reader to hear of this boundless mercy and compassion after the severity of Yahweh's reaction to the molten image the Israelites had made. This reaction must be understood as an expression of the lesser affirmation that "he lets nothing go unchecked, punishing the father's fault in the sons. . . ." Yahweh, then, first is merciful; but then is vengeful.

Roles have been reversed. Now it is Moses who reminds Yahweh that Israel is a headstrong people. Moses' sudden switch—saying what he would not admit before—is obviously to take advantage of Yahweh's new declarations of great mercy. Previously, when it was Yahweh who was accusing the people of being headstrong, Moses cited the project that Yahweh had initiated and that the nations would say Yahweh could not conclude. There was simply no way to conclude the good work that had been begun except by having Yahweh continue to maintain a presence in the midst of the people. Now that Yahweh has declared in favor of forgiveness, by reason of superabundant mercy, Moses seizes upon the people's headstrong nature as the occasion for obtaining Yahweh's continued presence. Yahweh must be there, Moses says in effect, to forgive the people. Moses' tireless objective is to maintain Yahweh's presence. This revolution will be meaningless without the God who has inspired it.

This whole discussion of forgiveness probably derives from the RJE redaction, in the time of Hezekiah. The formula, "Yahweh, Yahweh a God of tenderness and compassion, slow to anger . . ." appears in nearly identical form in Numbers 14:18, which is also an RJE text. The refrain is a much used one from the seventh century onward in Judah (Ps. 86:15, 103:8, 111:4, 112:4, 116:5, 145:8, Joel 2:13, Jon. 4:2, Nah. 1:3, 2 Chron. 30:9, Neh. 9:17). In difficult times, it was a source of encouragement to know of Yahweh's mercy, and of Yahweh's severity in passing judgment on the unjust.

In response to Moses' request for the divine presence on the people's journey, Yahweh proposes an alliance. This will be a pact binding on both parties, and will bear very particularly on life in Canaan. Yahweh will work wonders to expel the Amorites, the Canaanites, the Hittites, and so on. In return, Israel will guard against entering into pacts with the rulers of that country, and will take care to destroy objects of worship discovered there. (The word for rulers, frequently translated "inhabitants" [RSV, JB, NAB; "natives," NEB] is the same word used in the Hymn of the Sea—*yoshvei* (§3.2.3)—and the justification for my preferred translation is found in Gottwald's *Tribes of Yahweh*, 507–30.) To enter into pacts with the rulers of Canaan would be to renounce the whole movement that began in Egypt with the exodus and the victory over the pharaoh.

Never is as radical an opposition between Israel and Egypt posited in the biblical texts as the opposition here between Israel and the rulers of Canaan, even though Exodus treats of the oppression of the Egyptians, not that of the Canaanites. To be an Israelite is not only not to be Canaanite, but to be aggressively anti-Canaanite: to destroy, uproot, cut down the Canaanite symbols, and to refuse to marry one's sons to their daughters. This aggressive attitude toward the Canaanites has its rationale in the constant struggles of the tribes of the "Israel" alliance to maintain its identity and freedom in the presence of the classist societies from which they have emerged. The hostility distilled in this text comes from the existence of the class struggle between the Canaanites, an urban class, and the oppressed Israelite peasants. To enter into pacts with these rulers would be to prefer the tranquility of submission to the combativeness of freedom. This, Yahweh will not tolerate. Yahweh is ready to give the Israelites victory over these rulers and their hosts, provided Israel, for its part, commits itself not to enter into relations with them afterward.

There follow the conditions that Yahweh imposes on Israel, in more detailed form: twelve norms, inscribed on tablets of stone. This list, attributed by literary critics to the Yahwist tradition, is devoted most particularly to the establishment of conditions for life in Canaan. It in no way replaces the decalogue of §4A2, which contains the basic norms of a common life in a just society. The Sinai account would have it that, in his first manifestation to the people of Sinai, Yahweh dictated the Decalogue orally. At the moment of the inscription of the tablets which, according to the present context, will contain the conditions of the alliance, the general conditions for being Yahweh's revolutionary people are supposed as known. The intent of the new tablet is to guide life in Canaan, where the people will have to live with the constant temptation to submit to the "rulers of the land."

4A7.3 NO OTHER GOD (EXOD. 34:14–16)

(1) "You shall bow down to no other god, for Yahweh's name is the Jealous One; he is a jealous God. Make no pact with the inhabitants of

the land or, when they prostitute themselves to their own gods and sacrifice to them, they may invite you and you may consent to eat from their victim; or else you may choose wives for your sons from among their daughters and these, prostituting themselves to their own gods, may induce your sons to do the same."

The commandment, "You shall bow down to no other god," is the same first commandment that we have in Exodus 20, and the reader may refer to the commentary in §4A2.2, above. Here, the commandment clearly constitutes a polemic against the gods of the Canaanites specifically. The worship of these gods would mean assimilation into the materially superior Canaanite culture, and sooner or later into its class society. It would mean abandoning the liberation project that began with the exodus.

Yahweh is a jealous God. Theologically, this expresses the irreconcilability of the Canaanite and Israelite societies. As Elijah, in the ninth century B.C., put it, one had to choose between Yahweh and Baal. Freedom and oppression cannot be reconciled. On the occasion of the apostasy to the Baal of Peor, the priest Phinehas felt such zeal for Yahweh that he ran the apostates through with his lance (Num. 25:1–8). According to Deuteronomy 6:15 and Joshua 24:19, Yahweh's jealousy is in the same line: if Israel follows after other gods, Yahweh will wipe it out, notwithstanding all the favors done for it. There is no neutral ground in a class struggle such as the one the Israelite peasants experience during their centuries in Canaan. Yahweh's jealousy is the theological expression of this economic and political reality.

4A7.4 NO MOLTEN IMAGES (EXOD. 34:17)

(2) "You shall make yourself no gods of molten metal."

The second commandment in this list is the same as that of the decalogue in Exodus 20 (see the commentary in §4A2.3). The story of the golden calf reveals the extreme gravity with which this matter was regarded. Yahweh could not be represented by a mute image. Yahweh was the God who challenged the people with a living voice.

4A7.5 FESTIVAL OF UNLEAVENED BREAD (EXOD. 34:18)

(3) "You shall celebrate the feast of Unleavened Bread: you shall eat unleavened bread, as I have commanded you, at the appointed time in the month of Abib, for in the month of Abib you came out of Egypt."

Abib comes in the spring, toward the end of the rainy season in Canaan. This is the month the barley was harvested, the first grain to ripen. Israel was composed mostly of peasantry, and the eating of the unleavened bread was surely part of an ancient celebration. The new harvest was inaugurated with a week of celebration of its purity, without the "foot" of leavened dough taken from the dough of the year before. Very likely this practice was native to Canaan itself. The Israelite tribes surely did not invent it when they rose up against the rulers of Canaan, nor had Moses and his group brought it with them from Egypt.

Among the commandments of the alliance with Yahweh there is included, then, a feast to be baptized, as it were, so that it will no longer be a festival of Baal, the Canaanite rain god. Israel fled Egypt in the month of Abib, however, and thus the festival of unleavened bread was no longer merely a festival of harvest time—as it was for Canaanites—but a festival of Yahweh, who had brought Israel out of its slavery in Egypt.

4A7.6 CONSECRATION OF THE FIRST BORN (EXOD. 34:19-20)

(4) "All that first issues from the womb is mine: every male, every first-born of flock or herd. But the first-born donkey you must redeem with an animal from your flocks. If you do not redeem it, you must break its neck. You must redeem all the first-born of your sons. And no one is to come before me empty-handed."

The fourth and fifth laws interrupt a collection of instructions for the harvest festivals—commandments 3, 6, 7, and 8 in our list here. The same collection, without the interruption, appears in Exodus 23:14-19.

There is a relationship between the feast of unleavened bread and the redemption of the firstborn, which lends a rationale to the insertion of this fourth law here. In Exodus 13:1-2, the firstborn are consecrated to Yahweh to commemorate the salvation experience of the night of slaughter in Egypt. Clearly, the sacrifice of firstborn animals originated with shepherds. Because spring was the breeding time, there is a calendric connection with the harvest celebration (unleavened bread).

4A7.7 SABBATH REST (EXOD. 34:21)

(5) "For six days you shall labor, but on the seventh day you shall rest, even at plowing time and harvest."

This is the third and last law to appear both in the decalogue of Exodus 20 and among these laws of the alliance. It is a very old law. What is distinctive about its formulation here is the mention of the times when farm work was more demanding. Nothing is said of sanctifications or assemblies. Yahweh is establishing a weekly day of rest for workers for the whole year, and this requires neither religious justification nor public celebration.

4A7.8 FESTIVALS OF WEEKS AND INGATHERING (EXOD. 34:22)

(6) "You shall celebrate the feast of Weeks, of the first-fruits of wheat harvest . . .

(7) ". . . and the feast of Ingathering at the close of the year."

With these two commandments, Yahweh personally enjoins the celebration of two additional agrarian festivals, thereby "baptizing" practices that were not originally Yahwist. The feast of weeks (*shavuōth*) was celebrated, according to the late sacerdotal calendar (Lev. 25:15–20), seven weeks after the laying of the scythe to the grain. The harvest was over by then. This is the feast that is later called Pentecost (the festival of the "fiftieth day"). In one ancient liturgical calendar, it is called, very accurately, the harvest festival (Exod. 23:16).

The festival of the ingathering was celebrated "at the close of the year." In preexilic times the year ended in the fall. This was the time of the harvest of the summer fruits, the most important being olives and grapes. This festival is mentioned in an ancient narrative text (Judg. 21:15–23) as a time of dancing among the vines. It was also the custom to set up tents in the vineyards, so that the festival also came to be called the feast of tents (*sukkoth*). Before the exile it was the principal feast of the year.

4A7.9 PILGRIMAGE TO YAHWEH'S SANCTUARY (EXOD. 34:23–24)

(8) "Three times a year all your menfolk must present themselves before the Lord Yahweh, the God of Israel. When I have dispossessed the nations for you and extended your frontiers, no one will covet your land, if you present yourselves three times in the year before Yahweh your God."

This law provides that the three festivals already recorded (commandments 3, 6, and 7) are to be feasts of pilgrimage to a sanctuary of Yahweh. This is part of the "baptism" of these feasts. In premonarchical times, several shrines of Yahweh were recognized as legitimate—at Gilgal, Shiloh, Bethel, Gibeon, and elsewhere—and this law decrees that every male Israelite is to present himself before Yahweh in one of these places. In the seventh century B.C., with the reform of Josiah, these shrines were done away with, and Jerusalem alone remained as Yahweh's sanctuary.

This commandment links the obligation to "stand before Yahweh" with Yahweh's promise to extend Israel's frontiers so that it will be feasible to leave one's family and fields on the occasion of this celebration. Possibly the need for this security increased with the Israelite uprising: there were now fewer shrines to the honor of Yahweh than there had previously been to Baal, so that the distances to travel would be greater.

This commandment is a corollary of the bilateral commitment involved in the pact or alliance that Yahweh was establishing with Israel.

4A7.10 OFFERING OF BLOOD AND BREAD (EXOD. 34:25a)

(9) "You must not offer the blood of the victim sacrificed to me at the same time as you offer unleavened bread . . ."

According to Leviticus 7:13 and 23:17, on the contrary, a presentation of cakes or bread made with leaven must be made along with the communion sacrifice and the first fruits of the harvest. And according to Amos 4:5, leavened items were burned in thanksgiving in Gilgal. Amos condemns this practice, but it is more likely that he does so because of the injustice of the persons making the offering than because of the leaven of their sacrifices. According to the medieval Jewish commentator Rashi, this prohibition specifically applied to the Passover lamb. This would solve the contradiction, but the law itself does not make this limitation.

Possibly in an earlier era the use of unleavened bakery in sacrifices was peculiar to the Israelites among the inhabitants of Canaan. But this can only be inferred from the spirit and tenor of the list, which seeks to establish a Yahwist agrarian cult for Israel.

The prohibition had sufficient importance to warrant its inclusion in this basic list, as well as in Exodus 23:18.

4A7.11 PASSOVER VICTIM (EXOD. 34:25b)

(10) ". . . nor is the victim offered at the feast of Passover to be put aside for the following day."

This commandment repeats the instruction in Exodus 12:10. The parallel to this law in Exodus 23:18 mentions not Passover, but the fat of the victim. This treatment of the fat is confirmed in late sacerdotal regulations requiring the fat to be burned on the altar. But the law in Exodus 34:25b speaks only of Passover, and it is unclear how this would differ from Canaanite practices, among which, to be sure, Passover did not figure.

4A7.12 FIRST FRUITS (EXOD. 34:26a)

(11) "You must bring the best of the first-fruits of your soil to the house of Yahweh your God."

In the agrarian culture of Canaan, first fruits were offered to God. What this law is emphasizing, then, is the presentation of this offering in Yahweh's temple. The first fruits are to be borne to a sanctuary of Yahweh, not to a temple of Baal. This law has a parallel in Exodus 23:19. It takes on special meaning when, under Josiah, temples to Yahweh outside Jerusalem were prohibited.

4A7.13 MILK AND MEAT (EXOD. 34:26b)

(12) "You must not boil a kid in its mother's milk."

This law occurs three times in Israelite legislation (Exod. 23:19, 34:26, Deut. 14:21)—evidence of its importance for drawing a distinction between Israel and Canaan. Probably what is being forbidden here is a Canaanite practice of some importance. There is a Ugaritic text that, if the modern reconstruction is correct, speaks of "boiling a kid in milk, a lamb in butter" (see Childs, *Exodus*, 485–86). This commandment has important consequences for Jewish cuisine, which maintains a strict separation between milk products and meat products.

4A7.14 COMMANDMENTS AND COVENANT (EXOD. 34:27–28)

Yahweh said to Moses, "Put these words in writing, for they are the terms of the covenant I am making with you and with Israel."

He stayed there with Yahweh for forty days and forty nights, eating and drinking nothing. He inscribed on the tablets the words of the Covenant—the Ten Words.

The tablets contain the stipulations that Israel will accept in order to strike an alliance with Yahweh. Generally, they set up a Yahwist cult for agrarian life, a cult manifesting a special interest in tracing the lines of differentiation between this worship of Yahweh and the cult of the rulers of Canaan, lest the Israelites "prostitute themselves" to the Canaanite gods. Yahweh takes responsibility for the Israelites' being able to vanquish the Canaanites and take possession of the land. Yahweh will provide sufficient security for the men to leave their houses and go to an authorized sanctuary three times a year.

The incidents surrounding the fabrication of the golden calf have served to confirm Moses' authority to the extent that he can leave the people for forty days without anxiety. Further: Yahweh acknowledges Moses as the people's authorized representative, in such wise that Moses can strike the alliance on his own authority, on the mountaintop, in the name of the people. Here no ratification ceremonies take place. The alliance is in force from the moment Moses accepts it.

It was probably revolutionary Israel's experiences in Canaan that led it to take steps to avoid precedents for one or more persons to arrogate power to themselves in this egalitarian society. Moses is a unique figure, and may not be utilized for the legitimation of the person or projects of any later leader, whether king, judge, priest, or whoever. To a certain extent, a prophet may be considered a follower in Moses' footsteps (except that no prophet ever spoke face to face with God, as Moses did).

In view of the fact that this list seems to contain twelve commandments, a difficulty arises in speaking of "the Ten Words" inscribed on the stone tablets. There are three possible solutions to this problem: (1) Originally this list may have consisted of ten commandments, with two others added later. (2) The Deuteronomic interpretation that tablets contained the familiar decalogue of Exodus 20 (see Deut. 4:13, 5:22, 10:1-5) is correct, and the present list (Exod. 34:14-26) does not claim to be the content of the tablets, but additional laws instead. (3) The phrase "the Ten Words"—the ten commandments—in Exodus 34:28 is an insertion carried back from Deuteronomy 10:4. This third interpretation is the most probable. The text of Exodus does not use the phrase in connection with the laws of Exodus 20. Deuteronomy is clearer, and scribes familiar with Deuteronomy could well have made this little insertion in order to "clarify" the Exodus text.

4A7.15 MOSES, NULLI SECUNDUS (EXOD. 34:29-35)

When Moses came down from the mountain of Sinai—as he came down from the mountain, Moses had the two tablets of the Testimony in his hands—he did not know that the skin on his face was radiant after speaking with Yahweh. And when Aaron and all the sons of Israel saw Moses, the skin on his face shone so much that they would not venture near him. But Moses called to them, and Aaron with all the leaders of the community came back to him; and he spoke to them. Then all the sons of Israel came closer, and he passed on to them all the orders that Yahweh had given him on the mountain of Sinai. And when Moses had finished speaking to them, he put a veil over his face. Whenever he went into Yahweh's presence to speak with him, Moses would remove the veil until he came out again. And when he came out, he would tell the sons of Israel what he had been ordered to pass on to them, and the sons of Israel would see the face of Moses radiant. Then Moses would put the veil back over his face until he returned to speak with Yahweh.

Special masks for worship are familiar to many cultures. This particular mask, however, is different: Moses takes it off when he enters into negotiations with Yahweh, and dons it to go about his daily affairs! Thus this cannot be the origin of a ceremonial practice in Israel.

In its present context, the radiance of Moses' face serves to call attention to the unique nature of the bond between him and Yahweh. Moses is not the prototype of any later leader. We might compare his role to that of Lenin in the Soviet Union or Mao in China.

A token of the ongoing relationship between Yahweh and Moses is the tent of meeting. It was erected by Moses for regular consultation with Yahweh during the march through the wilderness.

The Hebrew root for the "radiance" of Moses' face—*ORN*—also has the meaning of "horn," and was so translated in the Vulgate, so that Moses would have had horns appear on his head after he had spoken with Yahweh. Hence the custom in medieval art of painting Moses with horns.

4B YAHWEH STRIKES AN ALLIANCE WITH ISRAEL
(EXOD. 19:3b–8, 20:22–23:33, 24:3–8)

The passages that we are about to treat form an insertion in the combined Yahwist and Elohist account (RJE), the account upon which I have just commented. The kernel of this insertion is the old Book of the Covenant (Exod. 20:22–23:19). It is obvious from its content that this legal collection envisages a society of small farmers in a classless village society. Neither kings nor priests appear here. All of this indicates that these laws were compiled in the first tribal era, before Israel had set up a monarchy. Gerhard von Rad (*Studies in Deuteronomy*) has demonstrated that Deuteronomy represents a later stage in these same legal traditions—a reformulation of the old laws, to give the king and the Levites a position that would seem appropriate, and to make sure that there would be only one legitimate place of worship.

This ancient Book of the Covenant is marked off by two passages (Exod. 19:3b–8 and 24:3–8) situating it at the center of a formal ceremony of ratification of the alliance between Yahweh and Israel. This ceremony is a solemn one, in blood, in the presence of the people. Thus the alliance becomes more solemn than it has appeared in the previous reading of the treaty on Sinai, which was an arrangement strictly between Yahweh and Moses, on the mountaintop (Exod. 34). The notion that the alliance with Yahweh was a solemn event in which the whole people took on serious commitments is the basic supposition of the book of Deuteronomy, and everything suggests that the present insertion, whose purpose is to correct Yahweh's revelation on Sinai and bring it into conformity with this view, proceeds from circles close to Deuteronomy. It is very likely an insertion was made in the seventh century B.C., although the legal collection that it contains is much older.

4B1 An Alliance Proposed by Yahweh and Accepted by the People
(Exod. 19:3b–8)*

. . . *and Yahweh called to him from the mountain, saying, "Say this to the House of Jacob, declare this to the sons of Israel,*
> *'You yourselves have seen what I did with the Egyptians,*
> *how I carried you on eagles' wings*
> *and brought you to myself.*
> *[Now, if you obey my voice,]*
> *and hold fast to my covenant,*
> *you of all the nations shall be my very own,*

---

* To conform to the author's translation, the text of the *Jerusalem Bible* has here been given distinctive indentation. One *textual* difference is printed within square brackets.—ED.

for all the earth is mine.
I will count you a kingdom of priests,
a consecrated nation.'
These are the words you are to speak to the sons of Israel."
So Moses went and summoned the elders of the people, putting before
them all that Yahweh had bidden him. Then all the people answered as
one, "All that Yahweh has said, we will do." And Moses took the people's
reply back to Yahweh.

Yahweh's words are a succinct expression, in free poetic language, of the theology of the covenant. Israel has been marked off from the other nations of the earth by the grace of Yahweh, who brought it out of slavery in Egypt and led it through the wilderness. Yahweh having thus demonstrated a favorable disposition toward Israel, the other side of this mutual commitment is that Israel show Yahweh obedience, listening to the voice and keeping the commandments of Yahweh. Fulfilling its side of the commitment, Israel will be Yahweh's *segula*, Yahweh's "my very own," in the JB translation.

The historical context in which this theology arose was that of the national renewal of Judah in the seventh century B.C., which spurred hopes of liberation from Assyrian domination and a return to the glories of David. Two elements are worthy of special note. (1) The exodus is interpreted as a divine favor proceeding from a mysterious love, and bestowing on Israel a certain privileged position in human history. In the old forms of the exodus account, this benefit to the Hebrews is due to their position as an oppressed class in Egypt, so that there is nothing at all mysterious about the divine decision in their favor. (2) On Israel's side, this theology demands obedience. Yahweh has laid down a law, and Israel must obey it without further ado. In practice, this implies that persons must submit to the authorized interpreters of the law.

Despite the arbitrary note introduced by this pact into the constitution of Israel by explaining everything purely by Yahweh's sovereign will, this theology did have the virtue of redeeming old laws for the protection of the poor. Its impact on the history of humanity has been great, for good and ill. St. Paul comments on this theme extensively, because he recognizes that although God's law is good, it leads to prejudicial consequences—so that instead of being an occasion of justice it becomes an occasion of sin.

The image of "eagles' wings" is rare in the Bible, but it does recur in Deuteronomy 32:11—again in a context of Yahweh's leading the people through the wilderness. The expression "very own" is widely used in Deuteronomic circles (Deut. 7:6, 14:2, 26:18, Mal. 3:17, Ps. 135:4). On the other hand, the expressions "kingdom of priests" and "consecrated nation" are not Deuteronomic. Their meaning has been a matter of discussion, but perhaps 1 Peter 2:9-10 is correct in interpreting them as the qualities of a people chosen for a mission from God to the nations of the earth.

The people's response to Yahweh's proposal is positive. As at other moments, the people is represented by its elders. The acceptance is still provisional, however, inasmuch as Yahweh has not yet revealed the laws that Moses will later write in the Book of the Covenant.

4B2 The Book of the Covenant (Exod. 20:22–23:19)

This important old legal collection reveals its origin in the popular justice of a classless society. There are no police, judges, or jails. Although the narrative framework presents this "book" as law revealed by God, the laws it contains show it to be more a matter of traditional and popular measures. But lest we confuse it with legal systems prevailing today, it is important that we form an idea of what a legal tradition is where there is no authority to decree and enforce it.

The function of any legal system is to provide for the orderly resolution of conflicts arising in social life. A state has the task of establishing limits governing the common life, and levying suitable penalties for their transgression. To be sure, the state may not do this without taking into consideration the people's customs, moral standards, and judgment as to suitable penalties. Now, all this is very different where there is no state to lay down laws or to enforce them, and no apparatus of "law enforcement." Here, although laws are of course intended to settle conflicts in an orderly fashion, they are not legislated by an authority external to the people itself. Here the laws are merely the traditional norms received by the people from earlier generations, modified to fit new circumstances, and handed on to the next generation. Thus when we speak of a code or "book" of laws in this context, the word does not imply the decrees or edicts of an authority, but the compilation of the legal wisdom of the people. This is what we are dealing with in the Book of the Covenant.

The power of decision in this system of justice lies with the "elders," who sit at the village gates to hear litigants and hand down decisions. This is what Amos is referring to when he denounces injustice committed "at the city gate" (Amos 5:10). We have an example of this kind of judicial process in Ruth 4:1–8, where the elders of the city hear an estate case and preside over its solution.

In the absence of a state, with its police and jails, the imposition of penalties is in the hands of the people itself. Capital punishment is carried out by stoning: the whole people shares in the execution, with the offended party at its head. If the case has been one of theft, the elders see to it that the guilty party restores what has been taken and pays punitive damages.

The laws of this "book" or code are uneven with respect to their social origins. Based on their form, the laws of this collection may be divided into three main types, each coming out of a different social context:

1. Most numerous are the casuistic laws. They begin with a conditional "when" or "if": "If a man sells his daughter as a slave, she shall not regain her liberty like male slaves" (Exod. 21:7). A subdivision of this casuistic type of law in the Book of the Covenant is found in another series of hypothetical situations introduced by a different Hebrew word for the conditional "if": "If she does not please her master who intended her for himself, he must let her be

bought back: he has not the right to sell her to foreigners, thus treating her unfairly" (Exod. 21:8). These laws have extensive parallels with Mesopotamian laws, not only in form but in content as well. They are in the classic form of the popular legal tradition of "the gate."

2. Other laws of this collection are characterized by (a) an introductory (Hebrew) participle serving as both subject and verb, and (b) a demand for the death penalty: "Anyone who has intercourse with an animal must die" (Exod. 22:18). The categorical form of these laws marks them as edicts by some authority, perhaps that of the most venerable of the elders.

3. There are also laws in this collection that are formulated in the prohibitive form. They too are categorical, and are worded in the second person singular: "You must not molest the stranger or oppress him . . ." (Exod. 22:20). The thematic of these laws is generally religious, and they are addressed to the individual Israelite. They have no true parallels in the legal codes of Mesopotamia. It is likely that these are laws of Yahweh's sanctuaries, Yahweh's categorical instructions to the faithful.

Besides these three types of laws, distinguishable by their grammatical form, there are a number of others consisting of instructions for the celebration of worship: "Three times a year you are to celebrate a feast in my honor" (Exod. 23:14).

As a whole, this compilation of Israelite laws is the oldest in the Bible. These laws show us what popular justice meant in revolutionary Israel.

4B2.1 NORMS CONCERNING YAHWEH (EXOD. 20:22-26)

Yahweh said to Moses, "Tell the sons of Israel this, 'You have seen for yourselves that I have spoken to you from heaven. You shall not make gods of silver or gods of gold to stand beside me; you shall not make things like this for yourselves.

'You are to make me an altar of earth, and sacrifice on this the holocausts and communion sacrifices from your flocks or herds. In every place in which I have my name remembered I shall come to you and bless you. If you make me an altar of stone, do not build it of dressed stones; for if you use a tool on it, you profane it. You shall not go up to my altar by steps for fear you expose your nakedness.' "

The verses that immediately precede this passage (Exod. 20:18-21; §4A3) can be seen as a redactional adaption for the purpose of inserting the Code of the Covenant in the book of Exodus. They recall that Moses, named in the first verse of the code (20:22), was asked by the Israelites to serve as intermediary between Yahweh and themselves. The laws that follow are in the form of direct address—Yahweh to Israel—but twice the text indicates that they are what Moses is to say to Israel (20:22 and 22:1).

The first law in the Book of the Covenant is the basic law of Israel: "You shall not make gods of silver or gods of gold to stand beside me." This is a prohibition of images, but this time what is prohibited are images of other gods. This commandment combines the first two commandments of the decalogue of Exodus 20. But, as is evident from the additions to the second commandment of that decalogue, the two prohibitions are easily confused (see §4A2).

Yahweh's altars are to be made of earth and untrimmed stone—wherever "I have my name remembered." We are reminded of the monument erected by Jacob after his dream at Bethel (Gen. 28:18), or of the altar erected by Gideon after Yahweh had appeared to him (Judg. 6:24). This law concerning altars is older than the limitation imposed by the law of Deuteronomy 12:1–28, which permits the offering of sacrifice "only in the place [Yahweh] himself will choose . . . to set his name there and give it a home" (Deut. 12:5)—Jerusalem.

The law of a single place of worship was an innovation, sprung from the Levite circle that produced Deuteronomy in the seventh century B.C. The books of Kings were written under this influence, and condemn places of worship outside Jerusalem. But the Yahwist and Elohist patriarchal accounts are in line with the flexibility of the Book of the Covenant. Noah, Abraham, Isaac, and Jacob offer sacrifices in several places, all consecrated by different divine manifestations. The sacerdotal accounts in Genesis, on the other hand, which presuppose the Deuteronomic legal reform, nowhere indicate that the patriarchs offered any sacrifices or knew any altars. Here, then, we have a very old law.

4B2.2 LAWS CONCERNING SLAVES (EXOD. 21:1–11)

"This is the ruling you are to lay before them: 'When you buy a Hebrew slave, his service shall be for six years. In the seventh year he may leave; he shall be free, with no compensation to pay. If he came single, he shall leave single; if he came married, his wife shall leave with him. If his master gives him a wife and she bears him sons and daughters, wife and children shall belong to her master, and the man must leave alone. But if the slave declares, "I love my master and my wife and children; I renounce my freedom," then his master shall take him to God, leading him to the door or the doorpost. His master shall pierce his ear with an awl, and he shall be in his service for all time. If a man sells his daughter as a slave, she shall not regain her liberty like male slaves. If she does not please her master who intended her for himself, he must let her be bought back: he has not the right to sell her to foreigners, thus treating her unfairly. If he intends her for his son, he shall deal with her according to the ruling for daughters. If he takes another wife, he must not reduce the food of the first or her clothing or her conjugal rights. Should he cheat her of these three things she may leave, freely, without having to pay any money.' "

We are surprised to discover that there were slaves in the new revolutionary society. But this law is irrefutable proof that slavery was indeed practiced in

Israel despite the Israelites' own painful experience of slavery in Egypt. This law, which likewise appears (with variations) in Deuteronomy 15:12-18 and Leviticus 25:39-43, is for the purpose of controlling and moderating the practice.

As far as we know, slavery in Israel was always for reason of indebtedness. According to 2 Kings 4:1, a prophet's widow faced the imminent abduction of her children by her late husband's creditors to cover his debts. Leviticus 25:39 implies that slavery is the result of poverty. And Amos 2:6 condemns the process of enslaving small debtors.

This is not the same type of slavery that existed in Egypt, the slavery from which the Israelites fled. In Egypt slavery was general (Gen. 47:18-19)—that is, the whole population was subject to any forced labor the king might demand. They had control of their own land (not its formal title, however), and for practical reasons the king could not separate them from their land for a long time. But, besides cultivating their land, they were obliged to work on the king's construction projects) Solomon later introduced this same system for his own construction projects (1 Kings 5:27-32). But it was unknown in the premonarchical revolutionary period, and no law of Israel ever legitimated it.

Our attention is arrested by the use of the word "Hebrew" in the sense of nationality, as a synonym for "Israelite." Originally "Hebrew" referred to outlaw groups of any nationality (see §1.2.2). But because their forebears were rebels, or "hebrews," in Egypt, the new nation later sometimes called itself the Hebrews. The law concerning slaves in the Law of Holiness (Lev. 17-26) lays down a clear difference between slaves taken from "the nations," who could be property in perpetuity, and slaves from among "your brothers," concerning whom limits were set (Lev. 25:35-54). This same national distinction appears to be implicit in the law under consideration here.

The basic limitation on slavery is that it is not to extend beyond six years. In the seventh year the slave will go free, regardless of the size of the debt occasioning the enslavement. Surprisingly, the Code of Hammurabi (eighteenth century B.C.), no. 117, is less severe, establishing a limit of three years of slavery for a Babylonian citizen. In its Deuteronomic version (Deut. 15:12-18), this law concerning slaves, besides freeing them at the appointed time, requires slave owners to provide them with what they will need to begin their new life, "from your flock, your threshing floor, your winepress." Both Deuteronomy and the Law of Holiness treat slavery in a context of laws controlling money-lending, which was to be without interest, with all loans canceled in the sabbatical year.

In view of what we have observed on the causes of slavery in Israel, this connection would seem quite natural. The Law of Holiness takes a further step, and connects the freeing of slaves with the cycle of sabbatical years. This poses practical problems that would lead one to think that this last law was an ideal that was never applied. There are two cases of general liberation of Israelite slaves in the Bible: in Jeremiah 34:8-20 and Nehemiah 5:1-13. In both cases, authorities provided for liberation as an extraordinary measure. No actual law concerning slaves was applied. There is no reason to doubt, however, that the simple form in which slavery is regulated in the Book of the Covenant was put into effect in social life in Israel. To be sure, with the establishment of the monarchy, with its peculiar interests, application became more problematic, and this would be what led to instances of legal idealism such as we find in some of the applications of the sabbatical legislation.

4B2.3 PHYSICAL VIOLENCE (EXOD. 21:12–27)

4B2.3a Murder (Exod. 21:12–15)

> *"Anyone who strikes a man and so causes his death, must die. If he has not lain in wait for him but God has delivered him into his hands, then I will appoint you a place where he may seek refuge. But should a man dare to kill his fellow by treacherous intent, you must take him even from my altar to be put to death.*
> *"Anyone who strikes his father or mother must die."*

The law on murder, with its initial participle ("anyone who . . .") and the solemn terminal formula "must die," is addressed to community leaders. In the absence of a state in this revolutionary society, they have charge of public order. There being no police or prisons, the execution of a murderer will normally fall to the victim's relatives. These laws imply that it is the responsibility and right of the nearest relative (the *goēl*, or "redeemer") to take the murderer's life, and they seek to limit and control this responsibility and right.

The basic limitation is the establishment of a place of refuge, where the murderer can flee to safety while those responsible for the community investigate the case. The investigation will be conducted for the purpose of determining whether or not the alleged murderer is indeed guilty as charged by the *goēl*, and whether the misdeed has been committed with the intent of causing death, or was without premeditation or treachery. If the determination is that the homicide was involuntary or without premeditation, the accused will not be handed over to the *goēl*.

In other biblical laws, six cities, carefully selected for their location throughout the land of Canaan, are designated as cities of refuge (Num. 35:10–34, Deut. 19:1–13, Josh. 20:1–9). Arriving in one of these cities, the accused has the right to have an investigation conducted, and if the act in question is found to have been involuntary or without premeditation, the right of domicile in this city is guaranteed. The *goēl* is helpless to interfere. But if the determination of the investigation is intentional homicide, not even the altar of Yahweh will protect the perpetrator from being carried off to execution. The law says all this very clearly.

The law singles out the case of the murder of a father or mother. In these cases there may very well be no *goēl* at hand, as the victim's brothers may be elderly or deceased. In such cases the community itself will have to take charge of executing any sentence. The usual penalty will be death by stoning.

4B2.3b Abduction; Contempt of Parents (Exod. 21:16–17)

"Anyone who abducts a man—whether he has sold him or is found in possession of him—must die. Anyone who curses father or mother must die."

The list of laws with the initial participle continues. The law against abduction for profit is also found in Deuteronomy 24:7. The Code of Hammurabi (no. 14) likewise prescribes capital punishment for this crime.

The protection of parents was of prime interest to the ancient Israelites and their neighbors alike. Both the Law of Holiness (Lev. 20:9) and Deuteronomy 27:16 also prescribe the death penalty for open contempt for one's parents.

4B2.3c Assault (Exod. 21:18–21)

"If men quarrel and one strikes the other a blow with stone or fist so that the man, though he does not die, must keep his bed, the one who struck the blow shall not be liable provided the other gets up and can go about, even with a stick. He must compensate him, however, for his enforced inactivity, and care for him until he is completely cured.

"If a man beats his slave, male or female, and the slave dies at his hands, he must pay the penalty. But should the slave survive for one or two days he shall pay no penalty because the slave is his by right of purchase."

Once more we meet with laws of casuistry. The law concerning nonfatal injuries is clear enough: the perpetrator will be responsible for the time lost in convalescence as well as for the expenses of treatment. No damages are imposed for permanent effects, perhaps because the victim is presumed to have been fighting as well, and thus to share in the guilt.

The murder of a proprietary slave is a special case of homicide, not considered to be covered by the law prescribing capital punishment (Exod. 21:12). Despite revolutionary Israel's concern for persons, a slave continued to be treated as inferior to a free person. If we compare this law to the one prescribing capital punishment for the murder of a free person, we are struck by the lack of precision about the penalty in this latter case: ". . . he must pay the penalty." The logic of this ambiguity is clear from the law concerning the wounding of a slave, which prescribes no penalty "because the slave is [his owner's] by right or purchase." One suffers damage oneself if one kills one's slave, but the relatives of a free person have the right of vengeance.

The Code of Hammurabi (no. 199) concerns itself with wounds suffered by the slave of another citizen, and imposes compensatory damages in money, just as for any crime against the property of another. But the Code of Hammurabi does not penalize the murder of one's own slave.

4B2.3 d Miscarriage; *Lex Talionis* (Exod. 21:22–25)

> *"If, when men come to blows, they hurt a woman who is pregnant and she suffers a miscarriage, though she does not die of it, the man responsible must pay the compensation demanded of him by the woman's master; he shall hand it over, after arbitration. But should she die, you shall give life for life, eye for eye, tooth for tooth, hand for hand, foot for foot, burn for burn, wound for wound, stroke for stroke."*

It seems strange to find provision in this legal tradition for a case that one would think would be unusual—that of a miscarriage occasioned by the blows of a struggle between two men. We are reminded of a situation in Deuteronomy 25:11–22, where a woman interferes to stop a quarrel.

The case of a voluntary abortion procured by blows, however, is the object of a great deal of attention in the legal codes of antiquity. Several laws of the Code of Hammurabi (nos. 209–214) bear on the subject, foreseeing various circumstances, and imposing varying fines according to the woman's social class. In the Assyrian Laws (no. 21) not only a fine, but a scourging is prescribed for the culprit. The Hittite Code addresses itself to the matter (nos. 17 and 18), distinguishing, like the Code of Hammurabi, women's social classes in order to determine the amount of the fine. All of this special attention to abortion is owing to the great importance attached to having an heir, and the consequent temptation to injure one's enemy through his pregnant wife.

The mention of arbitration, which conflicts with the rule that the compensation be determined by the woman's husband, seems to be a later addition, motivated by the impracticality of leaving the amount of damages to the sole determination of the man affected.

A subordinate clause introduces the famous *lex talionis*, the law of retaliation. Its vocabulary, with "hand," "foot," and "burn," makes it clear that the phrase is not applicable to quarrels and abortion alone. Leviticus 24:18–19 applies it to wounds generally, including wounds to other persons' animals. Deuteronomy 19:15–19 applies the *lex talionis* to cases of false accusation, so that those making a false accusation will pay whatever penalty the accused would have had to pay if they had been found guilty. Thus the law of retaliation is a viable, self-adjusting principle of justice. It is an ancient one, as well, and is found in the Code of Hammurabi (nos. 3–4).

It is instructive that the Code of Hammurabi applies the law of retaliation in cases of wounds inflicted by one member of nobility on another, but is satisfied with a fine when a member of the nobility wounds a private citizen (nos. 196–201). The Book of the Covenant recognizes no such class distinctions (other than that between slaves and free persons). The prescription of corporal punishment for the wounding of another has the virtue of making it impossible for a wealthy person to escape responsibility merely by paying a fine. Recent research has suggested that this legal principle is not a primitive one, but has been developed over generations of experience (B. S. Jackson, "The Problem of Exodus XXI. 22-5 (*Jus talionis*)"; Tikva Frymer-Kensky, "Tit for Tat: The Principle of Equal Retribution in Near Eastern and Biblical Law").

4B2.3e Assaulting a Slave (Exod. 21:26–27)

"When a man strikes at the eye of his slave, male or female, and destroys the use of it, he must give him his freedom to compensate for the eye. If he knocks out the tooth of his slave, male or female, he must give him his freedom to compensate for the tooth."

The legal tradition of the ancient Near East, as we know it from the Code of Hammurabi and the Hittite Code, does not enter into the matter of injuries inflicted on one's own slaves. It only sets up a scale of damages to be paid in cases of wounds inflicted on the slaves of others, which of course are reducible to property damage. The Book of the Covenant, however, recognizes the human value of slaves and protects them against their owners' abuse.

4B2.4 ANIMALS, PROPERTY DAMAGE, AND THEFT (EXOD. 21:28–22:5)

4B2.4a Damage Caused by Animals (Exod. 21:28–32)

"When an ox gores a man or woman to death, the ox must be stoned. Its flesh shall not be eaten, and the owner of the ox shall not be liable. But if the ox has been in the habit of goring before, and if its owner was warned but has not kept it under control, then should this ox kill a man or woman, the ox must be stoned and its owner put to death. If [compensation] is imposed on him, he must pay whatever is imposed, to redeem his life. If the ox gores a boy or a girl, he must be treated in accordance with this same rule. If the ox gores a slave, male or female, the owner must pay over to their master a sum of money—thirty shekels—and the ox must be stoned."

The word "ox" does not correspond exactly to the Hebrew *shor*, which simply denotes any draft animal (René Péter, "*PR* and *ShOR*: Note de lexicographie hébraïque"). The prohibition against eating its flesh reflects a concern to extirpate the homicidal spirit from the community.

The penalty to be levied on the negligent owner is very severe compared with that prescribed in the Code of Hammurabi (no. 251), which imposes compensation on a scale proportioned to the victim's social class. Here the amount of compensation is not specified, and the only case where the death penalty is specifically excluded is that of a slave who is gored to death. Once more we note

Israel's tolerance of the institution of slavery, despite this people's radical revolutionary commitment.

4B2.4b Animals Killed (Exod. 21:33-36)

"When a man leaves a pit uncovered, or when he digs one but does not cover it, should an ox, or donkey, fall into it, then the owner of the pit shall make up for the loss: he must pay its owner money, and the dead animal shall be his own. If one man's ox harms another's so that it dies, the owners must sell the live ox and share the price of it; they shall also share the dead animal. But if it is common knowledge that the ox has been in the habit of goring before, and its owner has not kept it under control, he must repay ox for ox; the dead animal shall be his own."

The series of casuistic laws concerning animals in village life continues. Israel's other legal codes omit these laws, perhaps because the measures established here were deemed sufficient, as well as because the other collections were compiled in a more urbanized culture.

4B2.4c Theft (Exod. 21:37-22:3)

"If a man steals an ox or a sheep and then slaughters or sells it, he must pay five oxen for the ox, four sheep for the sheep.
"If a thief is caught breaking in and is struck a mortal blow, there is to be no blood vengeance for him, but there shall be blood vengeance for him if it was after dawn. Full restitution must be made; if he has not the means he must be sold to pay for what he has stolen. If the stolen animal is found alive in his possession, ox or donkey or sheep, he must pay double."

Here the basic law handles cases of the theft of animals, and the penalty is clear. If the thief has already disposed of the animals, he is to restore them fivefold, or fourfold. If they are still in his possession and still alive, he is to restore them twofold. If he lacks the means to comply, he is to be sold into slavery, in order thus to make restitution to the victim of what has been taken, plus the applicable damages.

Another law, concerning a thief caught in the act of housebreaking, is inserted here, in the law on the theft of animals. In all the extant legal codes of antiquity, this is the solitary instance of legislation to protect the thief's life. The killing of the thief by day, even on the intended victim's premises, is murder, and a capital offense. The thief's relatives have the right of vengeance, and may take the murderer's own life, as prescribed in the general laws on murder. If the thief is killed by night, blood vengeance is not applicable, because the killing is not a murder. The Code of Hammurabi, on the other hand (nos. 21 and 25), prescribes the death penalty simply for entering another person's house for the purpose of theft. The comparison shows that Israel ascribed more value to the right to life than to the right to property.

4B2.4d Damage to Fields (Exod. 22:4–5)

> *"When a man puts his animals out to graze in a field or vineyard and lets his beasts graze in another's field, he must take restitution for the part of the field that has been grazed in proportion to its yield. But if he has let the whole field be grazed, he must make restitution in proportion to the best crop recorded in the injured party's field or vineyard.*
>
> *"When a fire spreads, setting light to thorn bushes and destroying stacked or standing corn or the field itself, the man responsible for the fire must make full restitution."*

This casuistic series concludes with two more cases, which would be common ones in a pastoral society. The ambiguity of the word *biēr* admits of two interpretations of the first of these laws. It may refer to a fire raging out of control—but then the two laws would be indistinguishable. Or it may refer to a herd of animals, as the JB translation has it.

4B2.5 DAMAGE TO ARTICLES ENTRUSTED FOR SAFEKEEPING OR ON LOAN (EXOD. 22:6–15)

> *"When a man has entrusted money or goods to another's keeping and these are stolen from his house, the thief, if he can be caught, must repay double. Should the thief not be caught, the owner of the house must swear before God that he has not laid hands on the other man's property.*
>
> *"Whenever there is breach of trust in the matter of ox, donkey, sheep, clothing, or any lost property for which it is claimed 'Yes, this is it,' the dispute shall be brought before God. The person whom God pronounces guilty must pay double to the other.*
>
> *"When a man has entrusted to another's keeping a donkey, ox, sheep, or any beast whatever, and this dies or is injured or carried off, without a witness, an oath by Yahweh shall decide between the two parties whether one man has laid hands on the other's property or not. The owner shall take what remains, the other shall not have to make good the loss. But if the animal has been stolen from him, he must make restitution to the owner. If it has been savaged by wild beasts, he must bring the savaged remains of the animal as evidence, and he shall not be obliged to give compensation.*
>
> *"When a man borrows an animal from another, and it is injured or dies in the owner's absence, the borrower must make full restitution. But if the owner has been present, the borrower will not have to make good the loss. If the owner has hired it out, he shall settle for the price of its hire."*

These laws cover two types of situations—the entrusting of animals or other property to the care of a neighbor, and the loan or lease of animals to a neighbor. In either case, a problem arises only when the property in question is stolen or permanently damaged.

If the thief is apprehended the case is solved on the general principles of theft: the thief is obliged to make restitution. If the trustee alleges theft without being able to produce a thief, it will be difficult to know whether he is telling the truth, and the case will have to be solved by having recourse to God. This is exactly what is provided for in the Code of Hammurabi (nos. 120–126). There was probably a procedure to be followed for such cases at the Yahwist shrines, in order to have a decision in God's name. A solemn oath in the presence of God was surely not a casual matter, and the owner had to accept it as sufficient evidence of truthfulness. If the robbery has taken place in the presence of the trustee, then the trustee is obliged to restitution, because he should have defended his neighbor's property.

The last law in the series covers the case of loans, which differs from the previous case in that the initiative here is from the side of the person desiring to make use of a neighbor's beast. The animal in question would be a work animal, borrowed by a neighbor for a particular task. If the animal is injured or killed, responsibility lies with the borrower, unless the owner was present at the moment of the injury. If the owner was present, he must assume responsibility himself. If someone pays for the use of another's beast, however, there would seem to be no obligation of restitution.

4B2.6 VIOLATION OF A VIRGIN (EXOD. 22:16–17)

"If a man seduces a virgin who is not betrothed and sleeps with her, he must pay her price and make her his wife. If her father absolutely refuses to let him have her, the seducer must pay a sum of money equal to the price fixed for a virgin."

This case must be clearly distinguished from that of adultery, for which the death penalty is prescribed for both parties (Lev. 20:10, Deut. 22:22). The purpose of this law is to protect an unmarried woman. If she has been seduced, her seducer will be responsible for her. He will be required to marry her, and to pay the *mohar*, the bridal price that he would have had to pay for her in normal circumstances. The *mohar* is not a dowry, the more usual marriage offering among people of the land. The dowry is the sum a virgin brings with her to the matrimonial contract. The *mohar*, quite the other way about, is the price paid by the groom to the bride's father. It is mentioned only in very old biblical texts (Gen. 34:12, Isa. 18:25), and probably fell into disuse in Israel.

The virgin's father's right to refuse this marriage is protected, but without releasing the culprit from the obligation to pay the bridal price. Deuteronomy 22:28–29 legislates on cases of violation in the same manner, but adds that the seducer may never divorce his bride. Otherwise, of course, divorce is the husband's prerogative (see Deut. 24:1-4).

4B2.7 NORMS FROM THE SANCTUARY (EXOD. 22:18-31)

4B2.7a Capital Crimes (Exod. 22:18-20)

> *"You shall not allow a sorceress to live.*
> *"Anyone who has intercourse with an animal must die.*
> *"Anyone who sacrifices to other gods shall come under the ban."*

Here is another list of commandments with the initial participle. They cite capital crimes, and are worded as absolute commands of God. This is not simply popular legal tradition, then, but divine law, handed down at the sanctuary.

Every society fears persons who are deemed to be possessed of unknown powers, and who consider themselves exempt from the ordinary norms of community life. The Code of Hammurabi (no. 2) likewise prescribes the death penalty for the practitioner of sorcery, as does the Middle Assyrian Code (A47). In the Hittite Code (no. 70) capital punishment is levied on anyone killing a serpent while pronouncing someone's name, obviously referring to a magic rite.

In Israel, these practices were thought of as things that foreigners, strangers, did. By definition, sorcery is the use of practices that are "strange" and a threat to society. According to Exodus 7:11, the Egyptians practiced sorcery. According to Deuteronomy 18:10, so did the Canaanites, and Deuteronomic law contains the promise that Yahweh will raise up prophets instead, so that Israel will not have to have sorcerers (Deut. 18:15). According to 2 Kings 9:22, Jezebel, Princess of Tyre and Queen of Israel, practiced sorcery. According to Nahum 3:4, the Assyrians practiced sorcery. According to Isaiah 47:9, 12, so did the Babylonians, and according to Daniel 2:2, the Chaldeans. Sorcery is always cited as a practice foreign to Israel.

According to the Law of Holiness (Lev. 20:6, 27), sorcerers are to be stoned to death.

Copulation with animals is also condemned in Leviticus 18:23 and Deuteronomy 27:21, but it is not referred to as a capital crime. According to the Code of Hammurabi (nos. 187-88 and 199-200) coitus with cows, lambs, or hogs is a capital offense—not, however, with horses and mules, perhaps because these are not destined for human consumption.

The prohibition of sacrifices to gods other than Yahweh is implicit in the first commandment of both the decalogue and the Book of the Covenant.

4B2.7b Oppression of the Defenseless (Exod. 22:21-24)

> *"You must not molest the stranger or oppress him, for you lived as strangers in the land of Egypt. You must not be harsh with the widow, or*

with the orphan; if you are harsh with them, they will surely cry out to
me, and be sure I shall hear their cry; my anger will flare and I shall kill
you with the sword, your own wives will be widows, your own children
orphans."

These prohibitions against the exploitation of the defenseless are uniquely
Israelitic; they have no parallels in the legal traditions of the ancient Near East.
Their formulation is apodictical. They are not addressed to the elders seated at
the village gates, as are the casuistic laws. They are addressed to every free
Israelite. Their stated motivation, which recalls the oppression in Egypt, has a
tone more homiletic than legal. The *gerim*—"resident aliens"—are those
permanently domiciled in the country without right of full membership in
Israel.

For parallels on the privileged place of foreigners, widows, and orphans in
Yahweh's eyes, see Leviticus 19:33-34, Deuteronomy 10:18-19, 24:17-18,
27:19; Isaiah 1:17.

4B2.7c Taking Advantage of the Poor (Exod. 22:25-27)

"If you lend money to any of my people, to any poor man among you,
you must not play the usurer with him: you must not demand interest
from him.
   "If you take another's cloak as a pledge, you must give it back to him
before sunset. It is all the covering he has; it is the cloak he wraps his body
in; what else would he sleep in? If he cries to me, I will listen, for I am full
of pity."

Despite a certain appearance of casuistry, it is Yahweh who is speaking in this
set of instructions—Yahweh the God who brought the Hebrews out of slavery,
the God of the poor. Yahweh speaks in the second person singular, personally
and directly to every Israelite, proclaiming a fundamental human right. Like
the foregoing instructions on the rights of foreigners, orphans, and widows,
these too protect basic human rights. They deserve our most careful attention.

For Latin America, these laws against selfishness are supremely instructive.
Here, with limpid clarity, we are told that basic human rights arise from basic
human needs. Misery is not to be trafficked in. The right to life takes prece-
dence over the right to property. It is not that property is not protected. The
same code—the Book of the Covenant—condemns theft and establishes procedures for penalizing various cases of theft. But ownership is for the sake of life,
and it is restricted by the necessities of life. When persons fall into misfortune, they are to be provided the necessities of life. And there will be nothing
to pay for what is necessary in order to live. Nor will anything be borrowed
that is necessary to protect its possessor's life. In Hebrew, the word used here
for "interest" is *neshēk*, and literally means "biting." Its connotation is very
negative. Among the people of Yahweh, there must simply and absolutely be
no "biting" of anyone in need.

The importance of this law is evident from its appearance in the Law of Holiness (Lev. 25:35–37) and in Deuteronomy (23:20–21). In an urban society this law would be impracticable. In a city, where mutual strangers live elbow to elbow, no one would lend anything without hope of gaining something in return, and thus the whole intent of the law would go by the board. But the law was viable in the rural, egalitarian society envisaged by the Book of the Covenant.

In Israel, the poor were, first, the orphans and widows, and then peasants who by reason of bad weather, fire, or illness, had lost their harvest. These accident victims must be assisted in their vital needs. To this end, laws were established permitting the poor to take from the fields of others what they required for their own sustenance (Deut. 23:25–26, 24:19–22). And so Yahweh insists here that Israelites lend, without demanding interest, whatever these peasants need to stay alive until the next harvest. On the other hand, generosity is not the whole story: the debtor in default will be enslaved.

It is true that Deuteronomy 23:21 permits the taking of interest on loans to foreigners (loans to *nokrim*, foreigners domiciled abroad, not *gerim*, resident aliens). Relations with them were commercial, not societal. This exception made it possible for Jews in medieval Europe to engage in moneylending, where they played an important role in the dawn of capitalism. Contact with foreigners abroad, or from abroad, is scarcely contemplated in the Book of the Covenant. The law of Deuteronomy will make explicit what the law of the Covenant permits implicitly.

The philosophy behind §4B2.7c is of great importance for an understanding of the social implications of the exodus and the religion of the God of the exodus. Human rights arise from the right to life. The touchstone of human rights in a society is how well this society meets the vital needs of the poor. Property rights have a place when they are needed to guarantee the maintenance of resources a person must have in order to live. But they cannot be preferred to the fundamental right of all human beings to have access to the goods necessary to sustain life.

4B2.7d First fruits and First born (Exod. 22:28–31)

> *"You shall not revile God nor curse a ruler of your people.*
> *"Do not be slow to make offering from the abundance of your threshing-floor and your winepress. You must give me the first-born of your sons; you must do the same with your flocks and herds. The first-born must remain with its mother for seven days; on the eighth day you must give it to me.*
> *"You [shall] be [holy] to me. You must not eat the flesh of an animal that has been savaged by wild beasts; you must throw it to the dogs."*

The best commentary on the prohibition against blaspheming God is to be found in Leviticus 24:10–16. The son of Shelomith, of the tribe of Dan, had cursed God. And so the whole community, after consulting Yahweh, stoned him to death. It is unclear who the "ruler (*nasi*) of your people" is here. In any case it is not a king, because there is a specific word for king (*melek*).

It is likewise unclear what "abundance of your threshing floor and your winepress" means. In Numbers 18:27, the context of the word here translated "winepress" indicates that it refers to grapes, but perhaps also indicates that it refers to olives.

The law of the firstborn has been commented on in §2.5.2.

The instruction "You shall be holy to me" recalls the watchword of the Law of Holiness, "You have become holy because I am holy." The context of this edict in Leviticus 11:44 and Deuteronomy 14:21 is that of dietary laws.

The prohibition against consuming the flesh of an animal torn to death by other beasts was not a grave matter, judging it in the light of Leviticus 17:15–16, where its consumption renders one unclean merely for a day and may be removed by bathing oneself. Further, this instruction conflicts with Exodus 21:35, which permits the use of an ox gored to death by another ox. But perhaps the use envisaged in Exodus 21:35 is not that of human consumption.

4B2.8 JUDICIAL PROCESSES (EXOD. 23:1–9)

This short collection warns against the dangers involved in the correct administration of justice. The laws here are formulated by and large as apodictical prohibitions, are placed in the mouth of God, and are addressed to the adult Israelite in the second person singular. The laws dealing with an enemy's animals (23:4–5) interrupt the series.

4B2.8a Favoritism (Exod. 23:1–3)

> *"You must not make false assertions. You must not support a guilty man by giving malicious evidence. You must not take the side of the greater number in the cause of wrongdoing nor side with the majority and give evidence in a lawsuit in defiance of justice; nor in a lawsuit must you show partiality to the poor."*

There are various textual problems here that render precision of interpretation difficult. Nevertheless the general sense, except in verse 2b, is clear.

"Supporting a guilty man by giving malicious evidence" may mean conspiring with an unjust person to bear malicious testimony—literally, to have a "violent witness," in the sense that the testimony of such a witness will result in violence to the accused.

The risk of following the "greater number" is evident. Or instead, the word *rabbīm* here may refer to the powerful rather than to the majority, which would also make good sense.

The last instruction comes as a surprise, inasmuch as judges and witnesses would more likely be tempted to side with the wealthy. But persons of good will might unduly favor someone who is poor, as Leviticus 19:15 anticipates: "You must not be guilty of unjust verdicts. You must neither be partial to the little man nor overawed by the great; you must pass judgment on your neighbor according to justice."

4B2.8b Animals of One's Enemy (Exod. 23:4-5)

"If you come on your enemy's ox or donkey going astray, you must lead it back to him. If you see the donkey of a man who hates you fallen under its load, instead of keeping out of his way, go to him to help him."

Despite their casuistic exordium, these instructions are intended as guidelines for the behavior of any Israelite. This is confirmed by their formulation in the second person singular. Originally this was casuistic law, as we can see from the parallel in the Hittite Code (no. 45): "When anyone finds tools, he is to return them to their owner, who will reward him. If he does not return them, he is a thief." The Hittite law is for use in a court; it specifies when a defendant is to be treated as a thief. But the law of the Book of the Covenant is addressed to the Israelite, to guide him in his behavior.

The second law, dealing with the overburdened beast, has no obvious casuistic antecedent. Both laws are repeated in Deuteronomy (22:1-4), where instead of "enemy" we read "brother." Probably the enemy here is one's personal enemy. The last phrase of the second law, "go to him to help him," is a free reconstruction: in the original it reads ". . . most certainly abandon it," and thus contradicts the phrase immediately preceding.

4B2.8c Doing Justice (Exod. 23:6-9)

"You must not cheat any poor man of yours of his rights at law. Keep out of trumped-up cases. See that the man who is innocent and just is not done to death, and do not acquit the guilty. You must not accept a bribe, for a bribe blinds clear-sighted men and is the ruin of the just man's cause.

"You must not oppress the stranger; you know how a stranger feels, for you lived as strangers in the land of Egypt."

The list of trial laws concludes with instructions requiring no commentary.

4B2.9 RITUAL OBLIGATIONS (EXOD. 23:10-19)

4B2.9a The Sabbatical Year (Exod. 23:10-11)

"For six years you may sow your land and gather its produce, but in the seventh year you must let it lie fallow and forgo all produce from it.

Those of your people who are poor may take food from it, and let the wild animals feed on what they leave. You shall do the same with your vineyard and your olive grove."

The law of the sabbatical year is also to be found in Leviticus 25:2-7 and Deuteronomy 15:1-11, but its most ancient form is the present one. Here the sabbatical year is strictly limited to allowing the land to lie fallow for a year, and it may be that the origin of the sabbatical year is to be found in the knowledge and practice of good farming. But the emphasis here is on social advantages: a fallow field will be accessible to the poor, and to grazing animals.

The Law of Holiness amplifies this law, without changing it substantially. Deuteronomy, which is legal reform and not just a compilation from tradition, seeks closer control of the practice, by establishing a uniform sabbatical year for the whole population. A uniform sabbatical cycle would not be practical for farming, and Deuteronomy 15:1-11 is more concerned with the condoning of debts in this year.

The law prescribing that fields be left fallow every seventh year would be viable if the cycle of fields were staggered, and so it is probable that this law was in effect in premonarchical times.

4B2.9b Sabbath Rest (Exod. 23:12)

"For six days you shall do your work, but stop on the seventh day, so that your ox and your donkey may rest and the son of your slave girl have a breathing space, and the stranger too."

This very important law of revolutionary Israel makes its appearance once more. It is significant that "the son of your slave girl" and the stranger are included among its beneficiaries.

4B2.9c No God but Yahweh (Exod. 23:13)

"Take notice of all I have told you and do not repeat the name of other gods: let it not be heard from your lips."

This law, homiletic in form, echoes Israel's first and basic commandment.

4B2.9d The Three Harvest Festivals (Exod. 23:14-17)

"Three times a year you are to celebrate a feast in my honor. You must celebrate the feast of Unleavened Bread: you must eat unleavened bread, as I have commanded you, at the appointed time in the month of Abib, for in that month you came out of Egypt. And no one must come before me empty-handed. The feast of Harvest, too, you must celebrate, the feast of the first-fruits of the produce of your sown fields; the feast of

Ingathering also, at the end of the year when you gather in the fruit of your labors from the fields. Three times a year all your menfolk must present themselves before the Lord Yahweh."

This list of three festivals is the same that we find in Exodus 34:18, 22–23, the only difference being that here its formulation is more compact and orderly. These three harvest festivals clearly have their roots in ancient Canaanite rural life. Their connection with the exodus is not much stressed, and Passover is left unmentioned. Just where the males are to be presented to the Lord is not specified—probably at the nearest sanctuary.

4B2.9e Final Laws (Exod. 23:18–19)

"You must not offer unleavened bread with the blood of the victim sacrificed to me, nor put by the fat of my festal victim for the following day.
"You must bring the best of the first-fruits of your soil to the house of Yahweh your God.
"You must not boil a kid in its mother's milk."

These laws are very similar to their parallel in Exodus 34:25–26, and the reader is referred to §4A7.

4B3 Exhortation for Entry into the Land of Canaan (Exod. 23:20–33)

The Book of the Covenant ends with a homily promising Yahweh's help in taking possession of the land of Canaan. It contains injunctions concerning behavior to be maintained when that land is reached, including advice for maintaining good relations with Yahweh.

In the homily at the close of a legal collection we expect to find an exhortation to obedience to the laws just listed. Here instead we have an exhortation to maintain strict separation from the inhabitants of the land. The focus is on the land of promise, then, and the themes are themes that have not appeared since the flight from Egypt (Exod. 13:11)—although the text has always looked to Canaan as the goal of the movement (Exod. 3:8). This theme will be mentioned again in Exodus 34:10–13, in the last instructions to Moses on the mountain. The reader is not to forget that the end of the book of Exodus is not the end of the story! Exodus ends with instructions for life in the wilderness, but the real goal is Canaan.

"I myself will send [a messenger] before you to guard you as you go and to bring you to the place that I have prepared. Give him reverence and listen to all that he says. Offer him no defiance; he would not pardon such a fault, for my name is in him. If you listen carefully to his voice and do all that I say, I shall be enemy to your enemies, foe to your foes. My angel

will go before you and lead you to where the Amorites are and the
Hittites, the Perizzites, the Canaanites, the Hivites, the Jebusites; I shall
exterminate these. You must not bow down to their gods or worship
them; you must not do as they do: you must destroy their gods utterly and
smash their standing stones. You are to worship Yahweh your God, and I
shall bless your bread and water, and remove sickness from among you.
In your land no woman will miscarry, none be barren. I shall give you
your full term of life.

"I shall spread panic ahead of you; I shall throw into confusion all the
people you encounter; I shall make all your enemies turn and run from
you. I shall send hornets in front of you to drive Hivite and Canaanite
and Hittite from your presence. I shall not drive them out before you in a
single year, or the land would become a desert where, to your cost, the
wild beasts would multiply. Little by little I will drive them out before you
until your numbers grow and you come into possession of the land. For
your frontiers I shall fix the [Red Sea] and the Philistine sea, the desert
and the river; yes, I shall deliver the inhabitants of the country into your
hands, and you will drive them out before you. You must make no pact
with them or with their gods. They must not live in your country or they
will make you sin against me; you would come to worship their gods, and
that would be a snare for you indeed!"

This homily has great similarity with the one appearing in Deuteronomy 7:1–26. Of the themes of the present text, the only ones not appearing in Deuteronomy 7 are Yahweh's messenger and the boundaries of the land. No literary dependency, however, is evident. Both texts belong to a single literary tradition—the Deuteronomic, which arose in Judah beginning with the destruction of Samaria (722 B.C.), and which laid the groundwork for the reform of Josiah (622 B.C.). In the Deuteronomic tradition, the collapse of Israel is attributed to excessive contact with the Canaanites. And so total separation is demanded. There was no longer a class distinction between Israel and Canaan, and the religious separation between the cult of Yahweh and those of the Baals was now independent of its origins in the class struggle of the thirteenth to the eleventh centuries.

Yahweh's "messenger" or "angel" would indeed appear to be a celestial personage of some sort. It could seem that the messenger was Moses, but the parallels (Exod. 14:19, 32:34, 33:2) exclude this possibility. The functions of a messenger are those of a prophet. This homily does not assign the angel military functions, but a comparison with Exodus 14:19 and Joshua 5:13–15, as well as the mention of the conquest of the land in the homily itself, incline one to think that, besides prophetical functions, this angel of Yahweh will have military ones, too. Our homily seems ignorant of the whole debate over the revolutionary leadership, as we have observed it in Exodus 32–33.

The destruction of the monuments of the Canaanites and other inhabitants of the country is one of the favorite Deuteronomic themes. The Yahwists of the seventh century B.C. held that it was these Canaanite cults that had occasioned the fall of the kingdom of Israel, and they viewed the idolatries of King Manasseh of Judah with concern. Shortly afterward King Josiah would carry out the utter destruction of the monuments and "standing stones" demanded by this homily and others in the same tradition.

Yahweh's blessing is an extensively developed concern of Deuteronomy 7 and 28. The Deuteronomic homiletic tradition was very much interested in the material welfare of the nation and held it to be directly dependent on fidelity to Yahweh, especially to purity of ritual in worship. This theory is not, however, a creation of this era. We also read of Yahweh as Israel's physician in Exodus 15:26.

The "hornets" that Yahweh intends to send before the advancing Israelites is a strange notion, appearing as well in other texts of the Deuteronomic milieu (Deut. 7:20, Josh. 24:12). This translation of the word *tsir'ah* originates with the Greek Septuagint. *Tsir'ah* appears only three times in the Old Testament, and it is impossible to determine its actual meaning from these occurrences. Lexicographers Ludwig Koehler and Walter Baumgartner prefer to translate it "depression" or "discouragement" (Koehler and Baumgartner, *Lexicon in Veteris Testamenti Libros*, 817).

The notion that the Canaanites must be expelled only gradually, to keep the territory from falling prey to wild beasts, appears to be an attempt to explain how Yahweh could have permitted the coexistence of Israelites and Canaanites if the latter were the cause of the fall of Israel. Israel's rise in Canaan as a revolutionary movement internal to the country is forgotten here. Nor is the omission an innocent one. Beginning with the establishment of the monarchy, the dominant class had an obvious interest in finding other than class reasons for the conflict with Canaan.

The territory marked off here—from the Gulf of Akaba (the *Suf* Sea) to the Mediterranean (the "Philistine sea"), and from the "desert" (of the Sinai) to "the river" (the Euphrates)— represents the maximal extent of the Israelite empire, during the reigns of David and Solomon. The homily looks on all this territory as intended for Israel by Yahweh. And indeed King Josiah will strive, in vain, to recover it.

4B4 The Ceremony of the Alliance (Exod. 24:3–8)

Moses went and told the people all the commands of Yahweh and all the ordinances. In answer, all the people said with one voice, "We will observe all the commands that Yahweh has decreed." Moses put all the commands of Yahweh into writing, and early next morning he built an altar at the foot of the mountain, with twelve standing stones for the twelve tribes of Israel. Then he directed certain young Israelites to offer holocausts and to immolate bullocks to Yahweh as communion sacrifices. Half of the blood Moses took up and put into basins, the other half he cast on the altar. And taking the Book of the Covenant he read it to the listening people, and they said, "We will observe all that Yahweh has decreed; we will obey." Then Moses took the blood and cast it toward the people. "This," he said, "is the blood of the Covenant that Yahweh has made with you, containing all these rules."

Despite all that theologians have written about the covenant of Sinai, this is the only text in Exodus that clearly and indisputably presents a ceremony of ratification of an alliance between Yahweh and the people of Israel. The reciprocal act by which Yahweh offers an alliance and the people accepts it we have already encountered in Exodus 19:3–8. Our present text finishes what that passage began. Between the two pericopes we have the collection of laws laid down by Yahweh as the conditions for the alliance—the laws referred to here as the Book of the Covenant.

The ceremony of ratification of the alliance—with the erection of twelve standing stones, the reading from the Book of the Covenant, and the blood splashed on the altar and people—very probably reflects a ceremony repeated in Israel on various solemn occasions. The ratification of the alliance with Yahweh was celebrated under Josiah (2 Kings 23:1–3), but the text does not describe the ceremony. In view of the strong evidence that the text of §4B dates from the seventh century, it is likely that the alliance of Yahweh with Judah in that century was confirmed from time to time by a ceremony such as that described in §4B4.

The theology of the covenant does not appear in the older strata of the Sinai account, but only in §4B, which exegetes acknowledge to be an insertion in the ancient account. It is true that the Yahwist account speaks of an alliance, *brith*, granted by Yahweh to Moses on the mountain (Exod. 34:27). But *brith* does not imply the reciprocity so dear to the later theology of the covenant. It does not suppose any formal acceptance on the part of the people. And the ancient Elohist stratum never mentions the alliance. The meal taken before God on the mountain (Exod. 24:9–11) could be interpreted as an alliance ceremony, but this does not seem to be its original intent. The Elohist seems to have been speaking of laws given by God on the mountain, but not of a formal pact between Yahweh and Israel—not of an alliance.

The theology of the alliance was developed from elements of these ancient accounts under the impact of the fall of Samaria, and of the theological reevaluation that this event demanded: Yahweh had chosen Israel as "Yahweh's own people" (for mysterious reasons, of which we human beings are ignorant), and, along with giving them laws, had entered into a formal pact with Israel. The violation of this pact, and especially of the commandment not to render worship to other gods, had invalidated the alliance. And so Yahweh had abandoned Israel into the hands of its enemies. With this theology was introduced a regrettable arbitrariness into the basis of God's relationship with the people of Israel, with consequences to be felt down through the centuries.

4C THE SANCTUARY AND ITS MINISTERS
(EXOD. 24:15b–31:17, 35:1–40:38)

Scarcely had the reign of Joachim begun in Judah (598 B.C.), when the Babylonian army carried off into exile most of Israel's educated persons and skilled workers. According to 2 Kings 24:14, the deportees numbered ten thousand. Among them were nearly all the priests, including the priest and prophet Ezekiel. It is not elitist to say that Israel's future depended on this exile community, as was admitted even by someone as closely bound to the people as Jeremiah (Jer. 24). Little more than a decade later, another Babylonian invasion destroyed Jerusalem (587 B.C.), and led its whole population to Babylon. Only the peasants in their villages were left.

It was in this situation of exile that the restoration project of Ezekiel 40–48 was forged. Here everything turned on the new temple that would have to be built. It was thought that the reason for the exile and the destruction of Jerusalem was the impurity of a people that did not know how to distinguish the sacred from the profane. To avoid a repetition of this calamity, Ezekiel prepared a stronger priestly caste for Israel and laid down precise instructions for preserving the holiness of the temple, the geographic and cultural center of the country.

It was in this context that the revisionist interpretation of the Sinai revelation was composed. It occupies a goodly part of the second half of the book of Exodus. According to earlier traditions, Yahweh, on the mountain in the wilderness, revealed, to the heterogeneous people just released from Egypt, norms for a just communitarian life in the promised land. This is what is preserved in the text of §4A. The §4B additions, which are from the seventh century B.C., set down as the central experience in the Sinai the celebration of an alliance between Yahweh and Israel. This alliance established the norms for the life of liberation and formalized them ceremonially. In both cases the preexilic texts stress the importance of Sinai: it was there that the basis for public life in Israel was cemented. It was at Sinai that the political constitution of Israel as the people of Yahweh was established.

The sacerdotal version of these traditions—§4C—is revisionistic, giving a very different meaning to the Sinai revelation. According to this revision, what God revealed was the blueprint for the place where the divine presence would dwell—the tabernacle—and what God ordained was the institution of a sacrificial system. To the sacerdotal mind, civil affairs had no special importance for an Israel of the restoration, and had not entered into what Yahweh revealed on Sinai. And indeed, when the new Israel was constructed, civil laws were imposed by Persian authorities, being taken out of Israelite hands. What was important for the community of the exile, the community that revised the Sinai account, was that God had enjoined the structures and norms for divine worship. The sacerdotal revision was not just a revision of the Sinai account. It was a revision of all sacred history, commencing with the creation. Unlike the older Israelite traditions, the priests' version would have it that, before the revelation on Sinai, humanity did not know how to render worship to God. In the ancient traditions, the patriarchs offered sacrifice to God wherever God appeared to them. In the sacerdotal revision they knew nothing of sacrifice, for God had not yet revealed it to them.

But the central focus of the Sinai revelation, in the priestly tradition, was the abode, the dwelling place, where in the presence of Yahweh would remain in the midst of the people. The dwelling place, or "tabernacle," was designed as a visual lesson in the sacerdotal concept of holiness. Everything was in simple, clearly symmetrical lines, as if to underscore the divine perfection with straight lines and round numbers. The materials followed a sequence: from the commonest, on the exterior, to the finest, as one approached the holy of holies, where the ark was kept. First there was bronze, then silver, then gold plate, and finally, for the implements within the "tent," solid gold. It was the same with the fabrics of the curtains. Thus the increasing sacred value of the divinity was represented by the increasing value of the materials. Finally, the absolute darkness of the interior of the tent or tabernacle, pierced only by the light of the lamps of the golden candelabrum, symbolized, with a division between the natural light outside and the artificial light within, the absolute separation of the sacred and the profane.

In addition to the dwelling place, God also revealed, according to this text, the setting apart of Aaron and his sons for the service of worship, and the sacrifice of animals and incense as the correct form of that worship. Up to this point in the account, Aaron has been presented only as Moses' brother, his lieutenant and mouthpiece in interviews with the king of Egypt. The genealogy of Exodus 6:14–27, as we have already indicated, is part of the sacerdotal revision. It emphasizes the figure of Aaron, but without yet saying why. Now we see the reason. Aaron has been set aside by God as the only person authorized to render worship in the name of the people in the place of God's dwelling.

To make this separation crystal clear, special vestments are specified, which Aaron is to don when entering the sacred precincts, and a special ordination ceremony is prescribed, to set him apart for his special tasks. His sons after him will continue his service, once they have been duly ordained and have donned the correct vestments. In these norms, the privilege of the priests, a matter of the utmost importance in the sacerdotal program of the exile, is retrojected all the way back to Sinai.

Where did the priests obtain their model for God's dwelling? We know at least part of the answer. The division of the sacred precincts into two parts, one of them cubic and the other rectangular, with the long side twice the length of the short side, was traditional in Canaanite temples. The idea that the sacred precincts constituted the dwelling place of God, and not a meeting place, is likewise of Canaanite origin. The bronze basin for the ablutions is borrowed from the temple of Solomon, whose interior design was very similar to that of the tabernacle, except that it was of larger dimensions. The ark of the testimony may very well have had its origin in the wilderness: it is mentioned as a symbol of Yahweh's presence on the people's journeys (Num. 10:33–36). The ark also appears in traditions of premonarchical origin (1 Sam. 4–6). The idea of a tent as a place of meeting God is already present in the ancient traditions of Exodus 33, although the tent there differs significantly from the tabernacle of the priestly texts.

We may conclude, then, that the tabernacle of the sacerdotal traditions was an eclectic construction, bringing together various traditions of the past, some of which (the ark, or the tent, for example) dated from the pre-Israelite wilderness history. It was furthermore intended to prepare for the construction of a new temple, which would be more suitable for maintaining the separation of the sacred and the profane, under the supervision and control of the legitimately ordained priests.

The identification of the sacerdotal materials which are in this commentary, presented as §4C, has the substantial consensus of exegetes. It is not difficult to distinguish the sacerdotal material from the older parts of the Sinai history because of the radical revision it supposes.

The sacerdotal material of the Sinai history is divisible into three parts: (1) God's instructions to Moses on the mountain for forty days and nights (Exod. 24:15b–31:17); (2) Moses' instructions to the people at the foot of the mountain concerning the fabrication of the apparatus of worship, and the implementation of these instructions by the people (Exod. 35:1–39:43); and (3) the consecration of the sanctuary and its occupation by God (Exod. 40:1–38).

Each of these parts has a number of subdivisions, to which I have applied the decimal system used throughout this book. My treatment does not attempt to distinguish in these subdivisions the stages of accretion undergone by the sacerdotal text. I examine them only in their present state. The internal evolution of the sacerdotal traditions of the Sinai history is still the subject of controversy among exegetes, and I shall not propose a theory in this regard.

4C1 How Yahweh Is to Be Worshiped (Exod. 24:15b–31:17)

Yahweh's discourse to Moses is divided, by the formula "Yahweh spoke to Moses and said," into seven points, of varying length. In the first part (Exod. 25:1–30:10), Yahweh's future dwelling place is described to Moses and he is told how it is to be constructed. In the second part (30:11–16) Moses is instructed on the acquisition of materials. In the third (30:17–21) he is given instructions for the bronze basin. In the fourth (30:22–33) he is instructed on the composition of the sacred oil. In the fifth (30:34–38) he is told how to prepare the incense. In the sixth (31:1–11) Yahweh identifies the master craftsmen who are to direct the work. And in the seventh (31:12–17) Yahweh demands the Sabbath rest.

There is an obvious parallel between Yahweh's seven-part discourse to Moses on the mountain and the sacerdotal account of the seven days of creation (Gen. 1:1–2:4a). Indeed the actual content of some of the parts of the discourse, especially the third, sixth, and seventh, manifests a correspondence with its respective day of creation account. This correspondence serves to underscore the solemn importance of the instructions contained in the discourse (Peter J. Kearney, "Creation and Liturgy: The P Redaction of Ex. 25–40").

4C1.1 YAHWEH MEETS MOSES ON MOUNT SINAI (EXOD. 24:15b–18)

The cloud covered the mountain, and the glory of Yahweh settled on the mountain of Sinai; for six days the cloud covered it, and on the seventh day Yahweh called to Moses from inside the cloud. To the eyes of the sons of Israel the glory of Yahweh seemed like a devouring fire on the mountain top. Moses went right into the cloud. He went up the mountain, and stayed there for forty days and forty nights.

The cloud, at once the manifestation of Yahweh's presence and the instrument of concealing Yahweh's glory, is part of the ancient tradition that we have already seen in Exodus 19 and 33. The Hebrew word that is here translated "glory," *kabod,* comes from a root meaning "heavy," "weighty." A person with glory is a person with "weight," a person of honor. The cloud proclaims Yahweh as someone worthy of honor and recognition, while at the same time hiding Yahweh's form. Ezekiel's vision is the most daring attempt in the Bible to describe the appearance of God, and the effect is impressive, if not very enlightening. Our text is more modest. Through the cloud, one descried the devouring fire that was the glory of Yahweh.

For six days the people beheld the phenomenon on the mountaintop, and on the seventh, Yahweh spoke, calling Moses.

4C1.2 CONTRIBUTIONS FOR THE SANCTUARY (EXOD. 25:1–9)

Yahweh spoke to Moses and said, "Tell the sons of Israel to set aside a contribution for me: you shall accept this contribution from every man whose heart prompts him to give it. You shall accept from them the following contributions: gold, silver and bronze, purple stuffs, of violet shade and red, crimson stuffs, fine linen, goats' hair; rams' skins dyed red, fine leather, acacia wood; oil for the lamps, spices for the chrism and for the fragrant incense; onyx stones and gems to be set in ephod and pectoral. Build me a sanctuary so that I may dwell among them. In making the tabernacle and its furnishings you must follow exactly the pattern I shall show you."

Before going into detail, Yahweh indicates the purpose of all that is about to be revealed. The Israelites are to build a sanctuary *(mīkdash)* or abode *(mīshkan),* so that Yahweh may dwell among them. For the moment, Yahweh has descended to the mountain to speak with Moses. But when the abode is ready, Yahweh will dwell permanently with the people.

The idea is very priestly. God is too holy to live just anywhere. God can live only in a place reserved for the divine presence, protected from the contamination of the profane. The priestly attitude toward the presence of God contrasts with that of Isaiah 57:15, where God dwells among the downtrodden, and of Matthew 25:31, 40, where the "Son of Man" is present in the very neediest of one's brothers and sisters. But for the priests, the apparatus of religion is needed in order to encounter God.

The notion of a heavenly "pattern" for the dwelling place is no different from that found in many other religions. Sacred realities on earth are copies of models kept in Heaven. It is on the basis of this text that the author of the New Testament letter to the Hebrews sweeps aside a Levitical worship carried out in earthly gloom, not in the heavenly sanctuary itself (Heb. 8:1–5, 9:1–10).

The list of materials for the construction of the sanctuary is impossible to translate with precision. It is especially difficult to specify the dyed stuffs and leathers listed here. Where our translation reads "fine leather," the Hebrew seems to name the hide of an aquatic mammal of the Red Sea, a kind of porpoise.

4C1.3 THE DWELLING AND ITS FURNISHINGS (EXOD. 25:10–27:21)

4C1.3a The Ark (Exod. 25:10–16)

> *"You are to make me an ark of acacia wood, two and a half cubits long, one and a half cubits wide, one and a half cubits high. You are to plate it, inside and out, with pure gold, and decorate it all around with a gold molding. You will cast four gold rings for the ark and fix them to its four supports: two rings on one side and two rings on the other. You will also make shafts of acacia wood plated with gold and pass the shafts through the rings on the sides of the ark, to carry the ark by these. The shafts must remain in the rings of the ark and not be withdrawn. Inside the ark you will place the Testimony that I shall give you."*

The Ark will be a box just over one meter long, and half a meter wide, covered with gold. Its sole purpose is to be the receptacle of the "Testimony"— surely the stone tablets inscribed by the finger of Yahweh. There are no sacerdotal instructions concerning the tablets themselves, and this is an indication that the priests knew, and were supplementing, the ancient texts (the Yahwist and the Elohist) that mention these tablets.

Given the volume of the ark—half a cubic meter—the "Testimony" tablets would be of considerable dimensions. Portability of the ark is assured by means of lateral poles, fixed to the box with large gold rings.

4C1.3b The Throne of Mercy (Exod. 25:17–22)

> *"Further, you are to make a throne of mercy, of pure gold, two and a half cubits long, and one and a half cubits wide. For the two ends of this throne of mercy you are to make two golden cherubs; you are to make*

them of beaten gold. Make the first cherub for one end and the second for the other, and fasten them to the two ends of the throne of mercy so that they make one piece with it. The cherubs are to have their wings spread upward so that they overshadow the throne of mercy. They must face one another, their faces toward the throne of mercy. You must place the throne of mercy on the top of the ark. Inside the ark you must place the Testimony that I shall give you. There I shall come to meet you; there, from above the throne of mercy, from between the two cherubs that are on the ark of the Testimony, I shall give you all my commands for the sons of Israel."

Above the ark is to be placed a slab of solid gold adorned with two winged animals: the cherubim. From here, between the fantastic animals, God will dictate to Moses the instructions that will be given the Israelites from time to time.

It has sometimes been thought that the cherubim were *guardians* of the ark and its precious contents. In this case, however, they would not have been facing inward, toward where Yahweh will be speaking. According to Psalm 18:11, Yahweh rides to battle astride a cherub, and this may be the function envisaged for these animals here. They are to be represented as reposing upon the *kappōreth*—here translated "throne of mercy"—within Yahweh's abode.

The word *kappōreth* was translated *hilasterion* in the Septuagint and, hence, *propitiatorium* in the Vulgate: a means or place by which sin is forgiven. But there is nothing in the text to indicate that this gold tile or plaque had any function in rites of propitiation for sins. The root *KPR* means "to cover," and late texts do speak of "covering" sins. I shall not attempt to solve the etymological problem of *kappōreth*. I observe only that its function is to serve as a lodging for God from which to instruct Moses.

4C1.3c The Offertory Table (Exod. 25:23–30)

"You are to make a table of acacia wood, two cubits long, one cubit wide, and one and a half cubits high. You are to plate it with pure gold, and decorate it all around with a gold molding. You are to fit it with struts, one hand's breadth wide, and decorate these with a golden molding. You are to make for it four gold rings and fix these at the four corners where the four legs are. The rings must lie close to the struts to hold the shafts for carrying the table. You are to make the shafts of acacia wood and plate them with gold. The table is to be carried by these. You are to make dishes, cups, jars and libation bowls for it; you are to make these of pure gold. On the table, before me, you must place the bread of continual offering."

The ancients often offered the gods food and drink for their sustenance. Indeed, according to Enuma Elish, the Babylonian creation myth, this was why human beings had been created. From remotest antiquity, this practice continued in the sanctuaries of Yahweh's cult as well, as evidenced in the account of David's flight to Nob, where he ate the bread that had been consecrated to Yahweh (1 Sam. 21:2–7). By the time of the Babylonian exile, the priests had developed instructions for the regularization of this practice (Lev. 24:5–9): on the table here described, twelve loaves of bread are deposited each Sabbath, and when the priests are rotated they eat the loaves that have been deposited there.

It is impossible to determine the precise identity of each and every utensil prescribed in this text for use in worship. There were the vessels to hold the bread and wine offered to Yahweh, and there was incense to be burned on the table. For the table itself, we have a depiction of the bas relief on the Arch of Titus in Rome, which represents the table taken from the temple in the destruction of Jerusalem.

4C1.3d The Lampstand (Exod. 25:31–40)

"You are to make a lampstand of pure gold; the lampstand must be of beaten gold, base and stem. Its cups—calyx and petals—must be of one piece with it. Six branches must extend from the sides of it, three from one side, three from the other. The first branch is to carry three cups shaped like almond blossoms, each with its calyx and petals; the second branch, too, is to carry three cups shaped like almond blossoms, each with its calyx and petals, and similarly for all six branches extending from the lampstand. The lampstand itself is to carry four cups shaped like almond blossoms, each with its calyx and petals, thus: one calyx under the first two branches extending from the lampstand, one under the next pair, one under the last pair: corresponding to the six branches extending from the lampstand. The calyxes and the branches must be of one piece with the lampstand, and the whole made from a single piece of pure gold, beaten out. Then you are to make lamps for it, seven of them, and set them so that they throw their light toward the front of it. The snuffers and trays must be of pure gold. You are to use a talent of pure gold for making the lampstand and all its accessories. See that you make them according to the pattern shown you on the mountain."

The lampstand was a heavy thing, of solid gold. It supported seven olive-oil lamps. Its trunk and arms afforded a spacious surface for the execution of art work in the form of a great number of almond blossoms.

We do not know whether the lamps on the lampstand were always lighted, or if they burned only during the night. The text that gives the pertinent instructions (Lev. 24:1–4) is ambiguous on this point. The importance of the lampstand is clear, however, inasmuch as the tabernacle had no windows or doors through which daylight could enter, so that its interior would have been totally dark without the illumination of the lampstand.

4C1.3e The Dwelling and the Tent (Exod. 26:1-14)

"The [dwelling] itself you are to make with ten sheets of fine twined linen, of purple stuffs, violet shade and red, and of crimson stuffs; you are to have these sheets finely brocaded with cherubs. The length of a single sheet is to be twenty-eight cubits, its width four cubits, all the sheets to be of the same size. Five of the sheets must be joined to each other, and the other five similarly. You must attach loops of violet stuff to the border of the last sheet in one set, and do the same for the border of the last sheet in the other set. You are to put fifty loops on the first sheet and, matching them one by one, fifty loops on the border of the last sheet in the second set. And you are to make fifty gold clasps to draw the sheets together. In this way the [dwelling] will be a unified whole.

"You are to make sheets of goats' hair to form a tent over the [dwelling]; you will make eleven of these. The length of a single sheet is to be thirty cubits, its width four cubits, the eleven sheets to be all of the same size. You must join five of these sheets together into one set, the remaining six into another; the sixth you will fold double over the front of the tent. You must attach fifty loops to the border of the last sheet in one set, and do the same for the border of the last sheet in the second set. You must make fifty bronze clasps and put them into the loops, so as to draw the tent together and make it a unified whole.

"As one sheet of the tent will be left over, half of this extra sheet is to hang over the back of the [dwelling]. The extra cubit on either side along the length of the tent sheets is to hang over the sides of the [dwelling] as a covering for it.

"For the tent you will further make a covering of rams' skins dyed red, and a covering of fine leather to spread over that."

This text describes two huge curtains, the one covering the other. The first, the more important, bore the name *mīshkan,* "dwelling" (RSV, NEB, JB "tabernacle"; NAB, "dwelling"). Its name corresponds to the purport of Moses' instructions to prepare an abode for Yahweh. Exodus 25:8 also calls it *mīkdash,* "sanctuary." Over the dwelling, completely covering it, was an *ōhel,* a "tent." This was larger than the dwelling, and hung down over it on all sides, so that the dwelling could not be seen from the outside. Over the ten, in turn, hung a covering of rams' skins, and another of porpoise (?) skins, "fine leather."

In accordance with the principle that the finest materials are to be reserved for the interior of the new place of worship, the dwelling itself is to be fashioned of twined linen, brocaded with cherubs. The walls of the tent are to be of goat's hair cloth, and the covering will be of skins. The dwelling and the tent are each to be fashioned in two large pieces, and joined by fifty clasps holding loops of material. The clasps of the dwelling will be of gold, and those of the tent of bronze.

We have no detailed description of the covering. We do not even know how the dwelling is to be mounted, but we do know that it is to consist of a linen curtain, and that the wooden frame to be inserted into it is solely for the purpose of holding it in place. (For the dwelling, I am following the careful study of A. R. S. Kennedy, "Tabernacle," in the *Hastings Dictionary.*) The overall dimensions of this double curtain will be 28 by 40 cubits, or about 14 by 20 meters, in the form of a rectangle.

The dimensions of the tent are a little larger, 30 by 44 cubits in all. The excess length is in front, while the excess breadth is distributed equally so as to cover the linen curtain on both sides. The dimensions of the covering of skins are not specified.

4C1.3f Frames and Curtains (Exod. 26:15–30)

> "You are to make frames of acacia wood for the tabernacle, these to stand upright. Each frame is to be ten cubits long and one and a half cubits wide. Each frame must be fitted with twin tenons; for all the frames of the [dwelling] you must do this. You are to make the frames for the [dwelling]: twenty frames for the southern side, facing the south country. You are to make forty silver sockets for putting under the twenty frames thus: two sockets under the first frame to receive its two tenons, and so on for the other frames. The other side of the [dwelling], on the north, is to have twenty frames supported by forty silver sockets, two sockets under each frame. For the back of the [dwelling], on the west, you must make six frames. You are to make two frames for the corners at the back of the [dwelling]. These frames must be coupled at their lower end and so to the top, up to the level of the first ring; this for the two frames that are to form the two corners. Thus there will be eight frames with their sixteen silver sockets: two sockets under the first frame and so on.
>
> "You are to make crossbars of acacia wood: five to hold together the frames for one side of the [dwelling], five to hold the frames for the other side of the [dwelling], and five to hold the frames that form the west end of the [dwelling]. The middle bar, fixed halfway up, is to run from one end to the other. The frames are to be plated with gold, and with gold rings on them to take the crossbars which you are to plate with gold. This is how you are to erect the [dwelling] according to the model shown to you on the mountain."

Kerashim, frames, has also been translated "boards," "planks," or "panels." I prefer "frames," because I hold (with Kennedy) that they were not solid panels. There are two reasons for this belief. (1) The dimensions of the *kerashim,* ten by one-and-one-half cubits (5m. by 75cm.), even allowing for round numbers, are too large for a portable sanctuary. (2) The dwelling is made of linen curtains brocaded with cherubim: it would make no sense to cover these over with the tent from the outside and with solid panels from the inside.

But if the *kerashim* are frames, this rich embroidery would be visible from within the dwelling.

Together the frames form the north and south sides, thirty cubits long and ten cubits high. The eastern side has no wooden frame, the western has eight. The two corner ones on the west are special. It is likely that, once mounted, they had the internal dimensions of the curtains, and hence of the dwelling— thirty cubits long and ten wide. The six frames at the bottom will be nine cubits wide, and the two corner ones will each be one-half cubit wide, plus unspecified dimensions of depth calculated to stabilize the corners.

Because no posts are mentioned inside the dwelling, we must suppose that the curtains hung from the lateral frames alone, giving the whole the form of a closed box. The curtains of the dwelling, measuring twenty-eight cubits in length, will be one cubit short on each side, and will not reach the ground. The tent of goatskins, whose curtains measure thirty cubits in length, will reach the ground, covering the silver supports from the outside. The tenons will emerge from the lower part of the frames to fit into these supports, and thus hold up the frames, which must bear the weight of four layers of curtain. Inasmuch as the curtains of the dwelling measure forty cubits from east to west, and the wooden structure only thirty, the curtain will reach the ground at the western base of the dwelling. The tent of goatskins is to cover the front of the dwelling, on the east, and so it has one more curtain than the dwelling itself.

4C1.3g The Veil and the Screen (Exod. 26:31–37)

> *"You are to make a veil of purple stuffs, violet shade and red, of crimson stuffs, and of fine twined linen; you are to have it finely embroidered with cherubs. You are to hang it on four posts of acacia wood plated with gold and furnished with golden hooks and set in four silver sockets. You must hang the veil from the clasps and there behind the veil you must place the ark of the Testimony, and the veil will serve you to separate the Holy Place from the Holy of Holies. The throne of mercy you must place on top of the ark inside the Holy of Holies. The table you must set outside the veil, and the lampstand on the south side of the [dwelling], opposite the table. You must put the table on the north side. For the entrance to the tent you are to make a screen of purple stuffs, violet shade and red, and of crimson stuffs and fine twined linen, the work of a skilled embroiderer. For this screen you are to make five posts of acacia wood plated with gold, with golden hooks; for these you are to cast five bronze sockets."*

Once suspended from the acacia frames, the dwelling measures thirty cubits by ten, with a height of ten cubits. The dwelling itself, of twined linen brocaded with cherubs, is closed on the west, but open in the front, on the east. The opening in front is partly covered by the goatskin tent, which falls four cubits down from the top.

The veil and curtain of the entryway serve several purposes. At one end, the four interior columns of acacia, plated with gold, support the dwelling, and hold up the veil that divides its interior into two unequal parts. The smaller part, a cubical area of ten cubits, contains both the ark of the Testimony and the *kappōreth* with its cherubim. The larger part, measuring twenty cubits by ten, and ten high, opens out on the entryway to the east, and contains the lampstand and bread table. The entryway is completely closed off by a curtain held up by five columns of acacia, also plated with gold. This curtain has the purpose of shutting out daylight, as well as the human gaze. The dwelling, then, is totally shut off. Evidently the eastern curtain was not considered an integral part of the dwelling: the bases of its columns are of bronze whereas the sockets of the frames and columns holding up the veil are of silver.

4C1.3h The Altar of Sacrifice (Exod. 27:1–8)

> *"You are to make the altar out of acacia wood, a square five cubits long and five cubits wide, its height to be three cubits. At its four corners you are to put horns, the horns to be of one piece with it, plating it with bronze. For the altar you are to make pans for the ashes from the fat, shovels, sprinkling basins, hooks, fire pans; you must make all the vessels for the altar out of bronze. You are also to make a grating for it of bronze network, and on the four corners of this fix four bronze rings. This grating you must set under the altar's ledge, below, so that it reaches halfway up the altar. And for the altar you are to make shafts of acacia wood and plate them with bronze. These are to be passed through the rings, so that they are on either side of the altar when it is carried. You are to make the altar hollow, of boards; you will make it in the way that was shown to you on the mountain."*

The principal object in front of the dwelling is the altar on which Yahweh's offerings will be burned. The basic problem facing redactors was how to visualize it as suitable for burning sacrificial victims, and yet portable. The solution was to design it of bronze-plated acacia panels and have it hollow. Its utensils too are of bronze, because they must of course be fireproof, and yet must be inferior to the utensils of the dwelling itself.

4C1.3i The Court (Exod. 27:9–19)

> *"You are to make the court of the [dwelling]. Facing the south country, on the southern side, the hangings of the court are to be of fine twined linen, one hundred cubits long for one side. Their twenty bronze posts are to be set in twenty bronze sockets and to have their hooks and rods of silver. So too for the northern side there are to be hangings one hundred cubits long, and twenty posts set in twenty bronze sockets, with their hooks and rods of silver. Across the width of the court, on the western side, there are to be fifty cubits of hangings, carried on ten posts set in ten sockets. The width of the court on the eastern side facing the sunrise*

is to be fifty cubits. On one side of the gateway there are to be fifteen cubits of hangings, carried on three posts set in three sockets. On the other side of the gateway there are also to be fifteen cubits of hangings, carried on three posts set in three sockets. The gateway to the court is to consist of a screen twenty cubits wide made of purple stuffs, violet shade and red, of crimson stuffs and fine twined linen, the work of a skilled embroiderer, carried on four posts set in their four sockets. All the posts enclosing the court are to be connected by silver rods; their hooks are to be of silver, their sockets of bronze. The length of the court is to be one hundred cubits, its width fifty cubits, its height five cubits. All the hangings are to be made of fine twined linen, and their sockets of bronze. All the furnishings for whatever use in the tabernacle, all the pegs of it and of the court, must be of bronze."

The dwelling will be surrounded by a curtain five cubits high, with columns every five cubits to hold it up. The dimensions will be one hundred cubits by fifty (50 m. by 25 m.), and its only opening will be on the east, where the fine curtain measuring twenty cubits will close off the entryway. In all these measurements we see a concern for perfect symmetry.

4C1.3j Olive Oil for the Lamps (Exod. 27:20-21)

"You are to order the sons of Israel to bring you pure olive oil for the light, and to keep a flame burning there perpetually. Aaron and his sons are to set this flame in the Tent of Meeting, outside the veil that is before the Testimony. It must burn there before Yahweh from evening to morning perpetually. This is an irrevocable ordinance for their descendants, to be kept by the sons of Israel."

This brief instruction on the olive oil for the lamps appears as a parenthesis in the description of the dwelling, and will be followed by instructions for the priests' vesture.

The whole sacred structure is suddenly called the "Tent of Meeting" instead of the "dwelling" (the only term used in these sacerdotal chapters up to this point). Doubtless there has been some internal evolution here, but we are unable to determine its precise nature.

In the present form of the text, light plays an important role. Yahweh's first discourse (§4C1.1) mentions the lampstand at the beginning, the oil in the middle, and the aromatic incense at the end. All this is reminiscent of the first day of creation: Let there be light.

4C1.4 PRIESTLY VESTMENTS (EXOD. 28:1-43)

4C1.4a Aaron and his Sons (Exod. 28:1-5)

"From among the sons of Israel summon your brother Aaron and his sons to be priests in my service: Aaron, Nadab and Abihu, Eleazar and

Ithamar, sons of Aaron. For Aaron your brother you are to make sacred vestments to give dignity and magnificence. You are to instruct all the ablest craftsmen, whose ability I have given them, to make Aaron's vestments for his consecration to my priesthood. These are the vestments they must make: pectoral, ephod, robe, embroidered tunic, turban and girdle. They are to make sacred vestments for your brother Aaron and his sons to be priests in my service. They must use gold, purple stuffs, violet shade and red, crimson stuffs, and fine twined linen."

In the sacerdotal revision of these traditions, Aaron has the privilege of being the person to oversee the worship established by the Sinai revelation. Thus he replaces Moses, who, from the moment of the dedication of the dwelling, will now no longer have access to direct conversation with Yahweh. One of the signs of this privilege of Aaron and his sons is the priestly vesture.

In the oldest traditions of the plagues, Aaron has been no more than Moses' companion in the latter's meetings with the pharaoh. In the account of the golden calf, Aaron bore a large part of the blame for the people's sin. By the sixth century, however, the Aaronite priests had acquired hegemony over the worship of Yahweh, and religion had acquired a hegemonic function among the people of Israel. This is reflected in the exalted figure of Aaron in the sacerdotal revision of the book of Exodus.

4C1.4b The Ephod and Onyx Stones (Exod. 28:6–14)

"They are to make the ephod of gold, purple stuffs, violet shade and red, crimson stuffs, and fine twined linen, the work of a skilled embroiderer. It must have two shoulder straps fitted to it to join its two ends together. The woven band on it to hold it is to be of similar workmanship and form one piece with it: this must be of gold, purple stuffs, violet shade and red, crimson stuffs, and fine twined linen. You will then take two onyx stones and engrave them with the names of the sons of Israel, six of their names on one stone, the remaining six on the other, in the order of their birth. With the art of a jeweler, of an engraver of seals, you are to engrave the two stones with the names of the sons of Israel, and mount them in settings of gold mesh. You are to fasten the two stones commemorating the sons of Israel to the shoulder straps of the ephod. In this way Aaron will bear their names on his shoulders in the presence of Yahweh, so as to commemorate them. You must also make golden rosettes, and two chains of pure gold twisted like cord; you are to attach these cord-like chains to the rosettes."

Here the ephod is a sacred garment of some sort, something like an apron. In Judges 8:27 and 18:14, 18 it refers to an image whose worship is censured. In 1 Samuel 2:18 and 2 Samuel 6:14, just as in our present text, it is a special garment used in the worship of Yahweh.

The onyx stones, bearing the names of the twelve sons of Israel, on Aaron's ephod are an indication of the representative function of the priest at worship.

4C1.4c The Pectoral of Judgment and the Robe of the Ephod
(Exod. 28:15–35)

"You are to make the pectoral of judgment, finely brocaded, of the same workmanship as the ephod. You are to make it of gold, purple stuffs, violet shade and red, crimson stuffs, and fine twined linen. It is to be square and doubled over, a span in length and a span in width. In this you are to set four rows of stones. Sard, topaz, carbuncle, for the first row; emerald, sapphire, diamond the second row; the third row, hyacinth, ruby, amethyst; the fourth row, beryl, onyx, jasper. These are to be mounted in gold settings. They are to bear the names of the sons of Israel and, like the names on them, are to be twelve in number. They are to be engraved like seals, each with the name of one of the twelve tribes. For the pectoral you will make chains of pure gold twisted like cords. For the pectoral you must make two gold rings and fix them to its two upper corners. You must fasten the two gold cords to the two rings fixed on the corners of the pectoral. The other two ends of the cords you must fasten to the two rosettes, so that they will be attached to the shoulder straps of the ephod, on the front. You are to make two gold rings and fix them to the two lower corners of the pectoral, on the inner hem, next to the ephod. You are to make two more gold rings and fix them low down on the front of the two shoulder pieces of the ephod, close to the join, above the woven band of the ephod. You must secure the pectoral by passing a ribbon of violet-purple through its rings and those of the ephod, so that the pectoral will sit above the woven band and not come apart from the ephod. Thus by means of the pectoral of judgment, when Aaron enters the sanctuary, he will bear the names of the sons of Israel on his breast to call them to mind continually in the presence of Yahweh. To the pectoral of judgment you will add the Urim and the Thummim so that Aaron may have them on his breast when he goes into Yahweh's presence. Thus in the presence of Yahweh Aaron will continually bear on his breast the oracle of the sons of Israel.

"You are to make the robe of the ephod entirely of violet-purple. In the center it must have an opening for the head, the opening to have around it a border woven like the neck of a coat of mail to keep the robe from being torn. The lower hem you are to decorate with pomegranates of purple stuffs, violet shade and red, crimson stuffs, and fine twined linen, with golden bells between: gold bells and pomegranates alternately all around the lower hem of the robe. Aaron is to wear it when he officiates, so that the tinkling of the bells will be heard whenever he enters the sanctuary into Yahweh's presence, or leaves it; thus he will not die."

The pectoral over the ephod, attached to it by chains of gold twisted like cords, was called the "pectoral of judgment," because the Urim and Thummim were pocketed in it. The exact nature of these latter artifacts is unknown, but their function was to indicate, in a manner similar to that of casting lots, the divine will in response to a question proposed to Yahweh (see Num. 27:21, Deut. 33:8, 1 Sam. 28:6, and Ezra 2:63). Like the ephod, the pectoral was set with stones bearing the names of the tribes of Israel.

4C1.4d The Diadem (Exod. 28:36–39)

> *"You are to make a [diadem] of pure gold and engrave on it 'Consecrated to Yahweh' as a man engraves a seal. You will secure this to the turban with a ribbon of violet-purple; it is to be placed on the front of the turban. Aaron is to wear it on his brow, and so take on himself any shortcomings there may be in what the sons of Israel consecrate in any of their sacred offerings. Aaron must always wear it on his brow, to draw down on them the goodwill of Yahweh. The tunic you must weave of fine linen, and make a turban of fine linen, and a girdle, the work of a skilled embroiderer."*

As with the names of the tribes on the stones of the ephod and pectoral, the golden diadem on Aaron's forehead too, has a representative character. It will cleanse Israel's ritual sins, although how or why is not explained in this passage.

4C1.4e An Everlasting Decree (Exod. 28:40–43)

> *"For the sons of Aaron you are to make tunic and girdle and headdress to give dignity and magnificence. You will put these on your brother Aaron and his sons. You will then anoint and invest and consecrate them to serve me in the priesthood. You are to make them linen breeches to cover their nakedness from loin to thigh. Aaron and his sons must wear these when they go into the Tent of Meeting and when they approach the altar to serve in the sanctuary, as a precaution against incurring some fault that would mean death. This is an irrevocable ordinance for Aaron and for his descendants after him."*

This passage states explicitly that the instructions being given for making the vestments of Aaron and his sons are everlasting decrees for all priests, all of whom will be Aaron's descendants. The reference to the dwelling as the tent of meeting is yet another indication of the complexity of the traditions embraced in the sacerdotal revision of the Sinai texts. In the earlier sources, the tent was a place where God met with Moses (Exod. 33:7–11). But to the priestly mind, this concept has been superseded by the idea of the tent as God's dwelling place, where one may encounter God in worship but not hear God's voice. With the approaching inauguration of the place of worship, the prophet Moses will be replaced by the priest Aaron. Yahweh will have said everything necessary. The people will simply have to comply with Yahweh's dispositions. And to this purpose Yahweh has established the priesthood of Aaron and the apparatus of worship.

4C1.5 ORDINATION OF AARON AND HIS SONS (EXOD. 29:1-37)

In the whole complexus of the sacerdotal reading of Exodus, the institution of the official worship, effectuated at the foot of Mount Sinai, represents a crucial historical transition, both for Israel and for humanity at large. From the priestly viewpoint, the history of Israel begins with the alliance with Abraham, as represented by the circumcision of Abraham and his male descendants. Leadership in Israel is thence handed over to a succession of regal figures: Abraham, Jacob, Joseph, and especially Moses. Yahweh's authority over the people is exercised through human beings who govern after the fashion of leaders of nations. But with the divine institution of the official worship, the relationship of the people with Yahweh changes. The Israelites have now been told of the only form in which Yahweh desires to be approached by them. The national leader is replaced by the priest, whose main task is to see to it that the prescribed form of worship is faithfully observed.

The exodus itself takes on a new meaning. Instead of a revolution clearing that way for the human organization of society, the exodus becomes the necessary condition for the implementation of the cultus, the worship, desired by Yahweh. This religious view of God is a response to the social realities of exilic and postexilic Israel. From the priestly viewpoint, a good king—national or Persian—will be the one who will permit the worship God prescribes. A bad one will be the one who prevents it or places obstacles in its way.

This change appears in the sacerdotal Sinai account in Moses' replacement by Aaron. From the peak of Mount Sinai, from out of the cloud, Yahweh instructs Moses how to ordain Aaron for the priestly service. Once the tabernacle is erected and Aaron ordained, the cloud will descend from the mountain to the dwelling, where Aaron will be able to go in and offer worship—and Moses will now be excluded!

The instructions for Aaron's ordination, logically enough, are accompanied by instructions for his vestments. The implementation of these instructions is narrated in Leviticus 8–9. The implementation does not match the instructions in every detail—an indication of the existence of slightly different traditions concerning the priestly ordination. I shall not discuss these variants in my commentary, and indeed their significance has yet to be explained.

4C1.5a Preparations (Exod. 29:1-3)

"This is the ritual you must use for them when you consecrate them to serve me in priesthood. Take one young bull and two rams without

blemish, unleavened bread, unleavened cakes mixed with oil, and unleavened wafers spread with oil, made from fine wheat flour. You must put these into a basket and present them in the basket, at the same time as the young bull and the two rams."

Before giving instructions for the ceremony, Yahweh lists for Moses the items that are to be prepared.

4C1.5b The Anointing (Exod. 29:4–9)

"You are to bring Aaron and his sons to the entrance of the Tent of Meeting and they are to be bathed. Take the vestments and dress Aaron in the tunic, the robe of the ephod, the ephod, and the pectoral, and gird him with the woven band of the ephod. Put the turban on his head, and on the turban fix the sacred diadem. Then take the chrism and pour it on his head, and so anoint him.

"Next, bring his sons and clothe them with tunics. Pass the girdles around their waists and put the headdresses on their heads. And by irrevocable ordinance the priesthood will be theirs. This is how you are to invest Aaron and his sons."

Three elements common to priestly ordinations in numerous religious traditions are prescribed here as preliminaries to the ordination of Aaron and his sons: ablutions, vesting, and an anointing. The text underscores the exclusion from the priesthood for all time of any but the sons of Aaron.

4C1.5c Animal Offerings (Exod. 29:10–14)

"You are to bring the bull in front of the Tent of Meeting. Aaron and his sons are to lay their hands on its head. Immolate the bull there before Yahweh at the entrance to the Tent of Meeting. Then take some of its blood and with your finger put it on the horns of the altar. Next, pour out the rest of the blood at the foot of the altar. And then take all the fat that covers the entrails, the fatty mass which is over the liver, the two kidneys with their covering fat, and burn them on the altar. As for the bull's flesh, its skin and its dung, you must burn them outside the camp, for it is a sin offering."

The ordination includes the sacrifice of three animals—one young bull and two rams—in three separate sacrifices. The bull is a sacrifice for sin. The form of its implementation here coincides with the instructions for the sin offering as prescribed in Leviticus 4:3–12. According to these directions, it is Moses who will offer the sacrifice for Aaron's sins, and Leviticus 8:14–17 reports the implementation of this directive. This is in conflict with Leviticus 9:5–11, however, where Aaron himself offers the sacrifice.

In the sacrifice for sin, the flesh of the animal is not burned on the altar, but outside the encampment, in token of the expulsion of evil.

4C1.5d Holocaust (Exod. 29:15-18)

"Next you are to take one of the rams. Aaron and his sons are to lay their hands on its head. You are to immolate the ram, take up its blood and pour it out on the surrounds of the altar. Next, divide the ram in pieces and wash the entrails and legs and put them on top of the pieces and the head. Then burn the whole ram on the altar. This will be a burnt offering whose fragrance will appease Yahweh; it will be a holocaust in honor of Yahweh."

The distinguishing characteristic of the holocaust is that the victim is completely burned up on the altar. The dispositions of our text coincide with the general instructions for holocausts given in Leviticus 1:3-9. The purpose of the entire procedure is to cause a pleasing aroma to ascend to Yahweh.

4C1.5e The Investiture Ram (Exod. 29:19-22)

"Next you are to take the other ram. Aaron and his sons are to lay their hands on its head. You are to immolate the ram, take some of its blood and put it on the lobe of Aaron's right ear, on the lobes of his sons' right ears, the thumbs of their right hands, and the big toes of their right feet, and pour out the rest of the blood on the surrounds of the altar. Then take some of the blood that remains on the altar, together with the chrism, and sprinkle it on Aaron and his vestments and on his sons and their vestments: so that he and his vestments will be consecrated and his sons too, and their vestments.

"You are to take the fatty parts of the ram: the tail, the fat that covers the entrails, the fatty mass which is over the liver, the two kidneys with their covering fat and also the right thigh, for this is a ram of investiture."

Of the three animals immolated, this last one is the special victim for the ordination of a priest. The most distinctive thing about this particular sacrifice is what is done with the blood. It is used to anoint Aaron and his sons on the specified parts of their bodies, as well as to sprinkle on their vestments.

4C1.5f Other Offerings (Exod. 29:23-25)

"You are to take a loaf of bread, a cake of bread made with oil, and a wafer, from the basket of unleavened bread placed before Yahweh, and put it all into Aaron's hands and those of his sons and make the gesture of offering before Yahweh. Then you are to take them back and burn them

on the altar, on top of the holocaust, an appeasing fragrance before Yahweh. This will be a holocaust in honor of Yahweh."

This does not seem to be a distinct sacrifice. Rather it is part of the other offerings in this ceremony.

4C1.5g The Portion Set Aside for the Priests (Exod. 29:26–28)

"You are to take the breast of the ram of Aaron's investiture and make the gesture of offering before Yahweh; this is to be your portion. You are to consecrate the breast that has been thus offered, as also the thigh that is set aside—the breast, that is, which has been offered and the thigh that has been set aside from the ram of investiture of Aaron and his sons. This, by perpetual law, will be the portion that Aaron and his sons are to receive from the sons of Israel, since it is the portion set aside, a portion the sons of Israel are to set aside from their communion sacrifices, the portion they owe to Yahweh."

This is not a communion offering, for which instructions will be given in Leviticus 3. The disposition of the breast and thigh of the ordination victim is a legitimation of the customary practice of designating these parts of the animal for consumption by the priest.

4C1.5h Seven Days (Exod. 29:29–35)

"Aaron's sacred vestments are to pass to his sons after him, and they will wear them for their anointing and investiture. The son of Aaron who succeeds him in the priesthood and enters the Tent of Meeting to serve in the sanctuary must wear them for seven days.
"You are to take the ram of investiture and cook its meat in a holy place. Aaron and his sons will eat the meat of the ram, and also the bread that is in the basket, at the entrance to the Tent of Meeting. They are to eat what was used in making atonement for them at their investiture, their consecration. No layman may eat these; they are holy things. If any of the meat from the investiture sacrifice, or the bread, should be left till morning, you must put what is left in the fire. It is not to be eaten; it is a holy thing. For Aaron and his sons you are to do exactly as I have commanded you: you are to take seven days over their investiture."

The best parts of the animal are set aside for consumption by the priests. The same ceremony is to be used for all those who succeed Aaron in the priesthood.

4C1.5i Atonement for the Altar (Exod. 29:36–37)

"On each of the days you are also to offer a bull as a sacrifice for sin, in atonement; by offering an atonement sacrifice for sin you will take away

sin from the altar; then you must anoint it, and so consecrate it. For seven days you are to repeat the atonement sacrifice for the altar and consecrate it. So it will excel in holiness, and whatever touches it will be holy."

The dedication of the altar parallels the seven days of Aaron's ordination. The notion of expiation for an altar sounds strange to our ears. Sin is not conceived here as a voluntary act, but as a profaneness attaching to whatever is not close to God. In order to be drawn within the ambit of the sacred, even the altar must be purified of its profaneness.

4C1.6 THE EXODUS LINKED WITH AARON (EXOD. 29:38-46)

"This is what you are to offer on the altar: two yearling lambs each day in perpetuity. The first lamb you must offer in the morning, the second between the two evenings. With the first lamb you must offer one tenth of a measure of fine flour mixed with one quarter of a hin of purest oil and, for a libation, one quarter of a hin of wine. The second lamb you must offer between the two evenings; do this with the same oblation and the same libation as in the morning, as an appeasing fragrance, an offering burned in honor of Yahweh. This is to be a perpetual holocaust from generation to generation, at the entrance to the Tent of Meeting in the presence of Yahweh; that is where I shall meet you and speak [with] you.

"I will meet the sons of Israel in the place consecrated by my glory. I will consecrate the Tent of Meeting and the altar. I will consecrate Aaron too, and his sons, to be priests in my service. I will remain with the sons of Israel, and I will be their God. And so they will know that it is I, Yahweh their God, who brought them out of the land of Egypt to live among them: I, Yahweh their God."

This text establishes rules for the daily sacrifices. Two lambs, burned as holocausts, are to be offered, together with an oblation of flour, olive oil, and wine.

This text is especially interesting because it combines the concepts of dwelling and tent of meeting, despite the different origins of the two concepts. We also have the priestly theology of exodus: Yahweh brought Israel out of Egypt in order to dwell in their midst. Thus the exodus event is used to legitimate the worship presided over by Aaron and his lineage.

4C1.7 THE ALTAR OF INCENSE (EXOD. 30:1-10)

You must make an altar on which to burn incense; you are to make it out of acacia wood. It is to be one cubit long, and one cubit wide—that is to say, square—and to stand two cubits high; its horns are to be of one piece with it. The top of it, its surrounding sides, and its horns, are to be plated with pure gold, and decorated with a gold moulding all around. You are to fix two gold rings to it below the moulding on its two opposite sides: these are to take the shafts used for carrying it. These shafts you must make of acacia wood and plate with gold. You are to set up the altar before the veil that is in front of the ark of Testimony, opposite the throne of mercy that covers the Testimony, the place appointed for my meeting with you. There Aaron must burn fragrant incense each morning when he trims the lamps, and between the two evenings, when Aaron puts the lamps back, he must burn it again. You must make these offerings of incense before Yahweh unfailingly from generation to generation. You must not offer profane incense on it—no holocaust, no oblation; and you must pour no libation on it. Once a year Aaron is to perform the rite of atonement on the horns of the altar; with the blood of the sacrifice offered for sin he is to perform the rite of atonement once a year. And you shall do the same in the generations to come. This altar of supreme holiness is to be consecrated to Yahweh."

Somewhat *hors série* here are the instructions for the fabrication of the altar of incense, which, along with the bread table and the lampstand, constitute the furniture of the holy place. The offering of the incense is very closely tied to the lamps of the lampstand. The fire of both is to illuminate and perfume the sacred area, cut off from daylight.

4C1.8 THE CENSUS TAX (EXOD. 30:11–16)

Yahweh spoke to Moses and said, "When you take a census and make a register of the sons of Israel, each is to pay Yahweh a ransom for his life, so that no plague comes on them when the census is being made. Everyone subject to the census must pay half a shekel, reckoning by the sanctuary shekel which is twenty gerahs, and this half shekel shall be set aside for Yahweh. Everyone subject to the census, that is to say of twenty years and over, must pay the sum set aside for Yahweh. The rich man is not to give more, nor the poor man less, than half a shekel as payment of the sum set aside for Yahweh, the ransom for your lives. You will devote this ransom money given to you by the sons of Israel to the service of the Tent of Meeting. It will remind Yahweh of the sons of Israel and will be the ransom for your lives."

Later this half-shekel tax was collected every year. In Jesus' time it was one of the main sources of income for the temple of Jerusalem (Matt. 17:24–27). In other Old Testament texts mentioning censuses, the purpose is military recruitment (2 Sam. 24, Num. 1, 26). Inasmuch as the present text dates from the time when Israel had no army—being under the domination of foreign powers—it is probable that the sole function of this tax was maintenance of the worship of Yahweh.

The shekel was a basic unit of weight. There was no minted tender at this time. The usual material for payments of this kind was silver. Complete precision is impossible, but the shekel fluctuated between eight and sixteen grams (O. R. Sellers, "Weights and Measures"). Some prices or measures will give an indication of its value. According to Numbers 18:16, a firstborn male child was to be "redeemed"—inasmuch as the firstborn of animals were to be offered in sacrifice to Yahweh, then given to the priests—for five shekels. According to 2 Samuel 14:26, when the great Absalom would cut his hair, as he did every year, it would weigh 200 royal shekels (as distinguished from the shekel of the sanctuary). The field purchased by Jeremiah in Anathoth cost him seventeen silver shekels (Jer. 32:9). In normal times, a measure of wheat flour, or two measures of barley, cost one shekel (2 Kings 7:1). In the time of the Assyrian domination, the king of Israel was forced to levy a tax of fifty shekels each on the leading men of Israel (2 Kings 25:20). In short, a shekel was a not inconsequential amount—being equal to twenty gerahs, the smallest measure—but neither was it out of the reach of the people. This text imposes on each Israelite a half-shekel tax for the construction of Yahweh's place of worship.

4C1.9 THE BRONZE BASIN (EXOD. 30:17–21)

> *Yahweh spoke to Moses and said, "You must also make a bronze basin on a stand, for washing. You must place it between the Tent of Meeting and the altar and put water in it. In this Aaron and his sons must wash their hands and feet. When they are to enter the Tent of Meeting they must wash in water for fear they die, and when they have to approach the altar for their service, to burn the offering burned in honor of Yahweh. They must wash their hands and feet for fear they die. This is a lasting ordinance for them, for Aaron and his descendants from generation to generation."*

As with the text on the altar of incense, the placement of this passage suggests that it is a later addition to the basic text of instructions for the furnishings of the dwelling. As with the other texts dealing with instructions for the court or atrium (§4C1.1i; Exod. 27:9–19), the preferred name for the dwelling is "tent of meeting."

The bronze basin probably had its origin with the bronze "sea" of Solomon's temple (1 Kings 7:23–28). The latter was of imposing dimensions—five cubits high and thirty in circumference—and rested on twelve bronze bulls. Evidently it could not have been portable. In the Sinai text the dimensions of the bronze basin are not specified, but it is obvious that what was intended was something smaller and less ornate. Its function was a necessary one where animals were slaughtered, and where fires were maintained for burning the victims, leaving ashes and other remains.

4C1.10 THE CHRISM OF ANOINTING (EXOD. 30:22-33)

Yahweh spoke to Moses and said, "Take the choicest spices: of liquid myrrh five hundred shekels, half this weight of fragrant cinnamon—that is, two hundred and fifty shekels—and of scented cane two hundred and fifty shekels; of cassia five hundred shekels (reckoning by the sanctuary shekel) and one hin of olive oil. These you are to compound into a holy chrism, such a blend as the perfumer might make; it is to be a holy chrism. With it you are to anoint the Tent of Meeting and the ark of the Testimony, the table and all its furnishings, the lampstand and all its accessories, the altar of incense, the altar of holocaust with all its furnishings, and the basin with its stand. These you are to consecrate. Thus they will excel in holiness, and whatever touches them will be holy. You must also anoint Aaron and his sons and consecrate them, so that they may be priests in my service. Then you are to say this to the sons of Israel, 'You must hold this chrism holy from generation to generation. It is not to be poured on the bodies of common men, nor are you to make any other of the same mixture. It is a holy thing; you must consider it holy. Whoever copies the composition of it or uses it on a layman shall be outlawed from his people.' "

The olive oil for the chrism is to be mixed according to the formula that Yahweh here gives Moses. The ceremony of consecration of the tent and its furnishings includes an anointing. The utterance, "Whatever touches them will be holy," is a threat, not a promise, as can be seen from the death of Uzzah for having touched the ark of Yahweh (2 Sam. 6:6-7). The mixing of this perfume for any other use is punishable by expulsion from the community.

4C1.11 THE INCENSE (EXOD. 30:34-37)

Yahweh said to Moses, "Take sweet spices: storax, onycha, galbanum, sweet spices and pure frankincense in equal parts, and compound an incense, such a blend as the perfumer might make, salted, pure, and holy. Crush a part of it into a fine powder, and put some of this in front of the Testimony in the Tent of Meeting, the place appointed for my meetings with you. You must regard it as most holy. You are not to make any incense of similar composition for your own use. You must hold it to be a holy thing, reserved for Yahweh. Whoever copies it for use as perfume shall be outlawed from his people."

The translation of the list of ingredients for the incense is mostly guesswork. The terminology used here is little used elsewhere in the language of the Old Testament. As in the case of the chrism, severe restrictions are imposed on the use of the incense.

4C1.12 THE ARTISANS (EXOD. 31:1–11)

> *Yahweh spoke to Moses and said, "See, I have singled out Bezalel son of Uri, son of Hur, of the tribe of Judah. I have filled him with the spirit of God and endowed him with skill and perception and knowledge for every kind of craft: for the art of designing and working in gold and silver bronze; for cutting stones to be set, for carving in wood, for every kind of craft. Here and now I give him a partner, Oholiab son of Ahisamach, of the tribe of Dan; and to all the men that have skill I have given more, for them to carry out all that I have commanded you: the Tent of Meeting; the ark of the Testimony; the throne of mercy that covers it, and all the furniture of the tent; the table and all its furnishings; the pure lampstand and all its accessories; the altar of incense; the altar of holocaust with all its furnishings; the basin with its stand; the sumptuous vestments— sacred vestments for Aaron the priest, and vestments for his sons—for the priestly functions; the chrism and the fragrant incense for the sanctuary. In this they are to do exactly as I have directed you."*

In order for the artisans to be able to conform their work to Yahweh's commands, they must be persons inspired by God. Thus all will be carried out in accordance with Yahweh's instructions.

4C1.13 THE SABBATH COMMANDMENT (EXOD. 31:12–17)

> *Yahweh said this to Moses, "Speak to the sons of Israel and say, 'You must keep my sabbaths carefully, because the sabbath is a sign between myself and you from generation to generation to show that it is I, Yahweh, who sanctify you. You must keep the sabbath, then; it is to be held sacred by you. The man who profanes it must be put to death; whoever does any work on that day shall be outlawed from his people. Work is to be done for six days, but the seventh day must be a day of complete rest, consecrated to Yahweh. Whoever does any work on the sabbath day must be put to death. The sons of Israel are to keep the sabbath, observing it from generation to generation: this is a lasting covenant. Between myself and the sons of Israel the sabbath is a sign for ever, since in six days Yahweh made the heavens and the earth, but on the seventh day he rested and drew breath.' "*

In the present order of the text of Exodus, Israel has repeatedly been commanded to keep the Sabbath. In the Book of the Covenant the reason given for the Sabbath observance is so that workers may have their rest (Exod. 23:12). The presence of the Sabbath precept in §4C1.11 reflects its "religious" importance in the postexilic period and in the priestly teaching. The reason given for it is the same as for circumcision in Genesis 17:10: it will be a sign of Yahweh's alliance with the people.

Its place in Yahweh's seventh discourse atop Mount Sinai is parallel with the sacerdotal account of creation. With the institution of the worship of Yahweh, at Mount Sinai, God was now creating the possibility of a consecrated life for the people, paralleling the earlier creation of the physical context of this life.

4C2 Construction of the Dwelling (Exod. 35:1–39:43)

The record of Yahweh's instructions to Moses is followed by a narrative of the execution of those instructions, composed in great detail and with a great deal of verbatim repetition. It is not exciting reading. Its purpose is to underscore the importance of a literal execution of whatever God commands, and to recount that the Israelites acted accordingly.

In this section of the book of Exodus there are notable differences between the Hebrew Massoretic text and the Septuagint. The most remarkable of these differences is in the ordering of the description of the work. Exegetes have been unable to produce a satisfactory explanation for the divergency. My commentary will follow the order given in the Hebrew, and I shall not comment on the Greek variants.

4C2.1 THE SABBATH (EXOD. 35:1–3)

Moses assembled the whole community of the sons of Israel and said to them, "These are the things Yahweh has ordered to be done: Work is to be done for six days, but the seventh is to be a holy day for you, a day of complete rest, consecrated to Yahweh. Whoever does any work on that day shall be put to death. You must not light a fire on the sabbath day in any of your homes."

Yahweh concluded the instructions to Moses with the Sabbath commandment. Moses begins his instructions to the people with the same commandment. The reason is clear.

The whole construction of the dwelling will be executed in conformity with the divine commandment to rest on the Sabbath. Even household tasks will cease on the Sabbath, and no cooking will be done that day.

4C2.2 READYING MATERIALS AND WORKERS (EXOD. 35:4–36:7)

4C2.2a The Contributions Needed (Exod. 35:4–19)

Moses spoke to the whole community of the sons of Israel. "This," he said, "is what Yahweh has commanded: Set aside a contribution for Yahweh out of your possessions. Let all give willingly and bring this contribution for Yahweh: gold, silver and bronze; purple stuffs, of violet shade and red, crimson stuffs, fine linen, goats' hair, rams' skins dyed red and fine leather, acacia wood, oil for the light, spices for the chrism and for the fragrant incense; onyx stones and gems to be set in ephod and pectoral. Let all the most skilled craftsmen among you come and make all that Yahweh has commanded: the tabernacle, its tent and its covering, its hooks and its frames, its crossbars, its posts, and its sockets; the ark with its shafts, the throne of mercy and the veil that screens it; the table with its shafts and all the furnishings for it, and the loaves of offering; the lampstand for the light, with its accessories, its lamps, and the oil for the light; the altar of incense with its shafts, the chrism, the fragrant incense, and the screen for the entrance to the tent; the altar of holocaust with its bronze grating, its shafts, and all the furnishings for it, the basin and its stand; the hangings of the court, its posts, its sockets, and the screen for the gateway to the court; the pegs of the tabernacle and of the court, together with their cords; the sumptuous vestments for service in the sanctuary—sacred vestments for Aaron the priest, and his sons' vestments—for the priestly functions."

The call for offerings for the construction of the dwelling must be compared with Yahweh's first instructions to Moses in §4C1.2 (Exod. 25:1-9). Moses' instructions to the people are far more detailed than Yahweh's to Moses, because now both Moses and the reader know precisely for what these materials are to be used.

In addition, a new theme is introduced here that will be a constant in the instructions that Moses gives the people. Moses orders the people to follow exactly what Yahweh has ordered. Yahweh has told Moses to do everything in accordance with the pattern shown him on the mountain. Such emphasis on obedience to God's word is a hallmark of the Deuteronomic teaching, the dominant current in the writings of Israel. This suggests that the instructions for the execution of the construction project have been reworked to bring them into conformity with Israel's dominant theology.

4C2.2b Enthusiastic Response (Exod. 35:20-29)

Then the whole community of Israel's sons withdrew from Moses' presence. And all those whose heart prompted them to give came, bringing their contribution for Yahweh for making the Tent of Meeting, for all its functions and for the sacred vestments. They came, men and women, all giving willingly, bringing brooches, rings, bracelets, necklaces, gold things of every kind, all those who had vowed to Yahweh some article of gold. All those who happened to own purple stuffs, of violet shade or red, crimson stuffs, fine linen, goats' hair, rams' skins dyed red, or fine leather, brought them. All who could contribute to the collection of silver and bronze brought their contribution for Yahweh. And all who happened to own acacia wood, suitable for any of the work to be done, brought it. All the skilled women set their hands to spinning, and brought purple stuffs, of violet shade and red, crimson stuffs and fine linen, from what they had spun. All the women willingly used their special skill and spun the goats' hair. The leaders brought onyx stones and gems to be set in ephod and pectoral, and the spices and oil for the light, for the chrism and for the fragrant incense. All the men and women whose heart prompted them to contribute to all the work that Yahweh had ordered through Moses to be done—the sons of Israel brought their free offering to Yahweh.

The Israelites set about their task with great willingness, and collect the materials for the work that Yahweh has commanded.

4C2.2c Bezalel and Oholiab (Exod. 35:30–35)

Moses said to the sons of Israel, "See, Yahweh has singled out Bezalel son of Uri, son of Hur, of the tribe of Judah. He has filled him with the spirit of God and endowed him with skill and perception and knowledge for every kind of craft: for the art of designing and working in gold and silver and bronze; for cutting stones to be set, for carving in wood, for every kind of craft. And on him and Oholiab son of Ahisamach, of the tribe of Dan, he has bestowed the gift of teaching. He has filled them with skill to carry out all the crafts of engraver, damask weaver, embroiderer in purple stuffs, of violet shade and red, in crimson stuffs and fine linen, or of the common weaver; they are able to do work of all kinds, and to do it with originality."

The selection of artisans comes toward the end of the instructions on the mountain (cf. Exod. 31:1–11), but must of course be done before the execution of any of the other instructions.

4C2.2d Other Workers (Exod. 36:1)

Bezalel and Oholiab and all the skilled craftsmen whom Yahweh had endowed with the skill and perception to carry out all that was required for the building of the sanctuary, did their work exactly as Yahweh had directed.

The instructions on the mountain have given the impression that Bezalel and Oholiab would do all the work themselves. Here it is clear that they are only the master builders, and that a good many Israelites have been filled with the spirit of wisdom in order to be able to share their task.

4C2.2e No Further Contributions Needed (Exod. 36:2–7)

Moses then summoned Bezalel and Oholiab and all the skilled craftsmen whose hearts Yahweh had endowed with skill, all whose heart prompted them to offer to do the work. From Moses they received all that the sons of Israel had brought as contributions for the work of building the sanctuary. As these continued each morning to bring their offerings, the skilled craftsmen, busy with the various works on the sanctuary, all left their work and went to tell Moses, "The people are bringing more than is needed for the work Yahweh has directed us to do." At Moses' command, therefore, this proclamation was made throughout the camp: "Let no one, man or woman, do anything more toward the collection for the sanctuary." So the people were stopped from bringing any more; the material they had was enough, and more than enough, to complete all the work.

According to the older accounts of the exodus and the events on the mountain, the Israelites despoiled their Egyptian neighbors of their gold, jewelry, and raiment. It was of this plunder that they fashioned the golden calf that was condemned by Yahweh and Moses. The sacerdotal account seems to propound the notion that the booty taken from the Egyptians was used to fashion the implements of official worship. The offering was voluntary, and the intent of narrating it in such detail is to provide the Israelites of a later age with motivation for generosity of their own, by means of an account of how their forebears had willingly given of what they had for the worship of Yahweh.

4C2.3 CONSTRUCTION WORK (EXOD. 36:8–38:31)

4C2.3a Sheets of Linen, and Goats' Hair (Exod. 36:8–19)

All the most skilled craftsmen among the workers made the tabernacle. He made it with ten sheets of fine twined linen, of purple stuffs, violet shade and red, and of crimson stuffs, finely brocaded with cherubs. The length of a single sheet was twenty-eight cubits, its width four cubits, all the sheets being of the same size. He joined five of the sheets together, and the other five similarly. He attached loops of violet stuff to the border of the last sheet in one set, and did the same for the border of the last sheet in the other set. He put fifty loops on the first sheet and, matching them one by one, fifty loops on the border of the last sheet in the second set. He made fifty gold clasps and with them drew the sheets together. In this way the tabernacle was a unified whole.

Next he made sheets of goats' hair to form a tent over the tabernacle; he made eleven of these. The length of a single sheet was thirty cubits, its width four cubits, the eleven sheets were all of the same size. He joined five of these sheets together into one set, the remaining six into another. He attached fifty loops to the border of the last sheet in one set, and fifty loops to the border of the last sheet in the second set. And he made fifty bronze clasps, so as to draw the tent together and make it a unified whole.

For the tent he made a covering of rams' skins dyed red, and a covering of fine leather to spread over it.

This is an almost exact repetition of §4C1.3e (Exod. 26:1–4): what is commanded there is carried out here. The singular subject ("he") seems to be the artisan Bezalel (see §4C2.3j; Exod. 38:22–23).

4C2.3b Frames and Sockets (Exod. 36:20–34)

For the tabernacle he made frames of acacia wood, these to stand upright. Each frame was ten cubits long and one and a half cubits wide. Each frame was fitted with twin tenons; this he did for all the frames of the tabernacle. He made the frames for the tabernacle: twenty frames for the southern side, facing the south country. He made forty silver sockets for putting under the twenty frames: two sockets under the first frame to receive its two tenons, and so on for the other frames. For the other side of the tabernacle, on the north, he made twenty frames and forty silver sockets, two sockets under each frame. For the back of the tabernacle, on the west, he made six frames. And he made two frames for the corners at the back of the tabernacle. These frames were coupled at their lower end and so to the top, up to the level of the first ring; this he did with the two frames that were to form the two corners. Thus there were eight frames with their sixteen silver sockets; two sockets under each frame. He made crossbars of acacia wood: five to hold the frames together that were to form one side of the tabernacle, five on the other side to hold the frames that were to form the end of the tabernacle on the west. He made the middle bar, fixed halfway up, to run from one end to the other. He plated the frames with gold, and put gold rings on them to take the crossbars which he plated with gold.

The instructions of §4C1.3f (Exod. 26:15–30) are followed to the letter.

4C2.3c The Veil and the Screen (Exod. 36:35–38)

He made the veil of purple stuffs, violet shade and red, of crimson stuffs, and of fine twined linen skillfully embroidered with cherubs. For hanging this veil he made four posts of acacia wood and plated them with gold, with golden hooks, and he cast four silver sockets for them. For the entrance to the tent he made a screen of purple stuffs, violet shade and red, and of crimson stuffs and fine twined linen, the work of a skilled embroiderer. For the hanging of this he made five posts, and their hooks; their capitals and rods he plated with gold; their five sockets were of bronze.

The work on the veil for the holy of holies and the curtain or screen to cover the entrance of the tent conforms to the instructions of §4C1.3g (Exod. 26:31–37), except that here there is no mention of the furnishings of the dwelling, prescribed in the other text.

4C2.3d The Ark and the *Kappōreth* (Exod. 37:1–9)

> *Bezalel made the ark of acacia wood, two and a half cubits long, one and a half cubits wide, one and a half cubits high. He plated it, inside and out, with pure gold, and decorated it all around with a gold molding. He cast four gold rings for the ark, attaching them to its four feet: two rings on one side and two rings on the other. He also made shafts of acacia wood plating them with gold; and he passed the shafts through the rings on the sides of the ark, for carrying it. Also he made of pure gold a throne of mercy, two and a half cubits long, and one and a half cubits wide. For the two ends of this throne of mercy he made two golden cherubs; he made them of beaten gold, the first cherub for one end and the second for the other, and fastened them to the two ends of the throne of mercy so that they made one piece with it. The cherubs had their wings spread upward so that they overshadowed the throne of mercy. They faced one another, their faces toward the throne of mercy.*

The description of the work on the ark and *Kappōreth* follows the instructions of §§4C1.3a/b (Exod. 25:10–22). Here we note a difference between the order of instructions and the order of execution. In general terms, the instructions proceed from the more important to the less important, beginning with the ark, the table, and the lampstand, then showing the pattern for the dwelling itself, then describing the altar, the atrium or court, and the priestly vestments. The actual fashioning of the sacred furnishings follows rather a natural order of execution: first the dwelling, then its furnishings, and then the altar, the basin, the atrium, and finally the vestments.

4C2.3e The Table and the Lampstand (Exod. 37:10–24)

> *He made the table of acacia wood, two cubits long, one cubit wide, and one and a half cubits high. He plated it with pure gold, and decorated it all around with a gold molding. He fitted it with struts, one hand's breadth wide, and decorated these with a golden molding. He cast four gold rings for it and fixed these at the four corners where the four legs were. The rings lay close to the struts to hold the shafts for carrying the table. He made the shafts of acacia wood and plated them with gold; these were for carrying the table. He made the furnishings of pure gold for the table: dishes, cups, jars and libation bowls.*
> *He made the lampstand of pure gold, and made the lampstand, base*

and stem, of beaten gold. Its cups—calyx and petals—were of one piece with it. Six branches extended from the sides of it, three from one side, three from the other. The first branch carried three cups shaped like almond blossoms, each with its calyx and petals; the second branch, too, carried three cups shaped like almond blossoms, each with its calyx and petals, and similarly all six branches extending from the lampstand. The lampstand itself carried four cups shaped like almond blossoms, each with its calyx and petals, thus: one calyx under the first two branches extending from the lampstand, one under the next pair, one under the last pair: corresponding to the six branches extending from the lampstand. The calyxes and the branches were of one piece with the lampstand, and the whole was made from a single piece of pure gold, beaten out. Then he made the lamps for it, seven of them, and its snuffers and trays of pure gold. He used a talent of pure gold for making the lampstand and all its accessories.

The discrepancies with respect to the instructions in §§4C1.3d/e (Exod. 25:23–40) include the omission of the actual placement of these articles, and any mention of the heavenly model or pattern shown to Moses. We must suppose, then, that Moses exercised a meticulous supervision over the work, so that it could be done in conformity with Yahweh's instructions on the mountain and with the model that Moses saw there.

4C2.3f The Altar of Incense (Exod. 37:25–29)

He made the altar of incense out of acacia wood. It was one cubit long, and one cubit wide—that is to say, square—and two cubits high; its horns were of one piece with it. The top of it, its surrounding sides, and its horns, he plated with pure gold, and decorated it all around with a gold molding. He fixed two gold rings to it below the molding on its two opposite sides, to take the shafts used for carrying it. These shafts he made of acacia wood and plated with gold. He also made the sacred chrism and the pure, fragrant incense, blending it as perfumers do.

The altar of incense occupies a more natural place here than in the instructions to Moses (§4C1.7; Exod. 30:1–10), where it follows the description of the priests' vestments and the commandment concerning the daily holocaust. Here its fabrication is related along with that of the ark, the table, and the lampstand—the other articles to be placed within the dwelling. We also encounter here the first attempt to abbreviate the text of the instructions. §4C2.3f combines the instructions concerning the altar of incense (§4C1.7; Exod. 30:1–10), the chrism (§4C1.10; Exod. 30:22–3), and the incense (§4C1.11; Exod. 30:34–37).

4C2.3g The Altar of Holocaust (Exod. 38:1–7)

He made the altar of holocaust out of acacia wood, a square five cubits
long and five cubits wide, its height three cubits. At its four corners he put
horns, the horns being of one piece with it, and plated it with bronze. He
made all the altar vessels: pans for the ashes, shovels, sprinkling basins,
hooks, fire pans; he made all the vessels for the altar out of bronze. He
made a grating for it of bronze network which he set under the ledge,
below, so that it reached halfway up the altar. He cast four rings and fixed
them on the four corners of the bronze grating to take the shafts. He
made the shafts of acacia wood and plated them with bronze. He placed
these through the rings fixed to the sides of the altar for carrying it, and
he made the altar hollow, of boards.

The fashioning of the altar of holocaust strictly follows the instructions
given in §4C1.3h (Exod. 27:1–8).

4C2.3h The Bronze Basin (Exod. 38:8)

He made the bronze basin and its bronze support from the mirrors of the
women who served at the entrance to the Tent of Meeting.

A mysterious passage! The description of the fashioning of the basin departs
dramatically from the directions given in §4C1.9 (Exod. 30:17–21), where
Aaron's ablutions are prescribed. It does not seem plausible that Bezalel melted
mirrors to make the basin. True, mirrors were made of polished bronze in those
days. But here the mirrors belong to women who serve at the entrance to the
tent, and the tent is only just now being built. And so it is some future service
that is being referred to. What might that service be?

According to 2 Kings 23:7, there were women in the temple of Jerusalem
who wove gifts for Asherah, a Canaanite god. But it is inconceivable that this
practice, reprobated by the priests, would have been accepted in this foundational text of Yahweh's official worship. In foundational texts women are not
permitted to participate in worship in any way. This makes the present passage
very difficult to explain.

The Septuagint translation (Exod. 38:26 LXX) speaks of women who
worked at the door of the tent the day it was disassembled for transport. This
Septuagint translation is probably an attempt to find an acceptable interpretation for the mysterious Hebrew text of Exodus 38:8.

4C2.3i The Court (Exod. 38:9–20)

He made the court. For the southern side of the court, facing the south
country, there were one hundred cubits of hangings of fine twined linen.
Their twenty posts with their twenty sockets were of bronze, their hooks

and rods of silver. For the northern side there were one hundred cubits of hangings; their twenty posts and their twenty sockets were of bronze, their hooks and rods of silver. For the western side, fifty cubits of hangings, carried on ten posts set in ten sockets, with their hooks and rods of silver. Fifty cubits, too, for the eastern side facing the sunrise. On one side of the gateway there were fifteen cubits of hangings, carried on three posts set in three sockets. On the other side—either side of the entrance to the court—there were fifteen cubits of hangings with their three posts and three sockets. All the hangings enclosing the court were of fine twined linen. The sockets for the posts were of bronze and their hooks of silver, like the plating on their capitals. The posts for the court all had their rods of silver. The screen for the gateway of the court, the work of a skilled embroiderer, was made of purple stuffs, violet shade and red, of crimson stuffs, and fine twined linen. It was twenty cubits long and, along the width of it, five cubits high, like the hangings of the court. Its four posts with their four sockets were of bronze. The hooks for the posts were of silver, like the plating on their capitals and like their rods. The pegs for the tabernacle and for the court enclosure were all of bronze.

The fashioning of the curtains and columns for the atrium or court follows the instructions of §4C1.3i (Exod. 27:9–19). The curtain was rectangular, 100 by 50 cubits, and was held up by five-cubit columns, and silver "sockets," or hinges, which could have been some type of hook or rib.

4C2.3j The Amounts of Metal Used (Exod. 38:21–31)

Here is the account of metals used for the tabernacle—the tabernacle of the Testimony—the account drawn up by order of Moses, the work of the Levites under the direction of Ihtamar son of Aaron, the priest.

Bezalel son of Uri, son of Hur, of the tribe of Judah, made all that Yahweh had directed Moses to have made. His partner was Oholiab son of Ahisamach, of the tribe of Dan, engraver, damask weaver, embroiderer in purple stuffs, of violet shade and red, in crimson stuffs and fine linen.

The amount of gold used in the work—the entire work for the sanctuary—(this was gold consecrated by offering) was twenty-nine talents and seven hundred and thirty shekels (reckoning by the sanctuary shekel). The silver collected when the census of the community was taken weighed one hundred talents and one thousand seven hundred and seventy-five shekels (reckoning by the sanctuary shekel), one beqa per head, or half a shekel (reckoning by the sanctuary shekel) for everyone of twenty years and over included in the census. These numbered six hundred and three thousand five hundred and fifty. The hundred talents of silver were used for casting the sockets for the sanctuary and for the veil: one hundred sockets out of the hundred talents, or one talent per socket.

With the one thousand seven hundred and seventy-five shekels he made the hooks for the posts, the plating for their capitals, and their rods. The bronze consecrated by offering amounted to seventy talents and two thousand four hundred shekels, and with this he made the sockets for the entrance of the Tent of Meeting, the bronze altar with its grating of bronze and all the furnishings for it, the sockets for the enclosure of the court, those for the gateway to the court, all the pegs for the tabernacle, and all the pegs for the court enclosure.

A talent was a fairly heavy unit of weight, not less than 65 or 70 pounds. The inventory here of course supposes the contribution of half a shekel per person, as ordered by Moses (§4C1.8; Exod. 30:11–16). Then too, before beginning work, Moses had asked a voluntary offering. It would appear that the text supposes both contributions—the tax and the freewill offering.

4C2.4 THE PRIESTLY VESTMENTS (EXOD. 39:1–32)

4C2.4a The Ephod (Exod. 39:1–7)

From the purple stuffs, violet shade and red, the crimson stuffs, and the fine linen he made sumptuous vestments for service in the sanctuary. They made the sacred vestments for Aaron, as Yahweh had directed Moses.

They made the ephod of gold, purple stuffs, violet shade and red, crimson stuffs, and fine twined linen. They beat gold into thin plates, and cut these into fine strips to weave into the purple stuffs, violet shade and red, into the crimson stuffs and the fine linen, as does the weaver of damask. For the ephod they made two shoulder straps, joined to it at its two ends. The woven band on it to hold it formed one piece with it and was of similar workmanship: this was of gold, purple stuffs, violet shade and red, crimson stuffs, and fine twined linen, as Yahweh had directed Moses. They fashioned the onyx stones, mounted in settings of gold mesh and engraved, as a seal is engraved, with the names of the sons of Israel. They fastened the stones to the shoulder straps of the ephod, stones commemorating the sons of Israel, as Yahweh had directed Moses.

Without any reference to the introductory passage in §4C1.4a (Exod. 28:1–5), the account of the execution of Yahweh's instructions passes directly to the fashioning of Aaron's ephod, in accordance with the prescriptions of §4C1.4a (Exod. 28:6–14). Twice it is emphasized that everything was done as Yahweh had commanded Moses.

4C2.4b The Pectoral (Exod. 39:8–21)

They made the pectoral, finely brocaded, of the same workmanship as the ephod, of gold, purple stuffs, violet shade and red, and fine twined linen. It was square and they doubled it over, a span in length and a span in width. In this they set four rows of stones. Sard, topaz, carbuncle, for the first row; emerald, sapphire, diamond, the second row; the third row, hyacinth, ruby, and amethyst; the fourth row, beryl, onyx, jasper. These were mounted in settings of gold mesh. They bore the names of the sons of Israel and, like their names, were twelve in number. They were engraved as seals are, each with the name of one of the twelve tribes. For the pectoral they made chains of pure gold twisted like cords. They made two gold rosettes and two gold rings, and they fastened the two gold cords to the two rings fixed on the corners of the pectoral. The other two ends of the cords they fastened to the two rosettes; they were thus attached to the shoulder straps of the ephod, on the front. They made two gold rings and fixed them to the two lower corners of the pectoral, on the inner hem, next to the ephod. And they made two more gold rings and fixed them low down on the front of the two shoulder straps of the ephod, close to the join, above the woven band of the ephod. They secured the pectoral by passing a ribbon of violet-purple through its rings and those of the ephod, so that the pectoral would sit above the woven band and not come apart from the ephod, as Yahweh had directed Moses.

The pectoral is made with brocade, precious and semiprecious stones, and gold work, following the instructions of §4C1.4c (Exod. 28:15–30). Only the Urim and Thummim are left unmentioned. Possibly these mysterious elements of discernment are taken to have been given by God, so that they did not have to be fashioned by artisans.

4C2.4c The Robe of the Ephod (Exod. 39:22–26)

Then they made the robe of the ephod woven entirely of violet-purple. The opening in the center of it was like the neck of a coat of mail; around the opening was a border to keep the robe from tearing. The lower hem of the robe they decorated with pomegranates of purple stuffs, violet shade and red, crimson stuffs, and fine twined linen. They also made bells of pure gold and placed them all around the lower hem of the robe between the pomegranates, bells and pomegranates alternately all around the lower hem of the robe of office, as Yahweh had directed Moses.

The directions given in §4C1.4c (Exodus 28:31–35) are followed.

4C2.4d Other Vestments (Exod. 39:27–29)

Then they made the tunics of finely woven linen for Aaron and his sons, the turban of fine linen, the headdresses of fine linen, the breeches of fine twined linen, the girdles of fine twined linen, of purple stuffs, violet shade and red, and of crimson stuffs, finely embroidered, as Yahweh had directed Moses.

In comparison with the instructions given in §4C1.4e (Exod. 28:40–43), the account of the making of these articles is summarized and condensed.

4C2.4e The Diadem (Exod. 39:30–32)

They also made the plate, the holy diadem, of pure gold, and engraved on it "Consecrated to Yahweh," as a man engraves a seal. They attached to this a ribbon of violet-purple to secure it to the top of the turban, as Yahweh had directed Moses.

So all the work of the tabernacle, the Tent of Meeting, was completed. In carrying it out the sons of Israel had done exactly as Yahweh had directed Moses.

4C2.5 CONCLUSION OF THE TASK (EXOD. 39:33–43)

They brought to Moses the tabernacle, the Tent and all its furnishings: its hooks, frames, crossbars, posts, sockets; the covering of rams' skins dyed red, the covering of fine leather, and the screening veil; the ark of the testimony with its shafts and the throne of mercy; the table with all its furnishings, and the loaves of offering; the lampstand of pure gold with its lamps—the lamps that were to be set on it—and all its accessories; the oil, too, for the light; the golden altar, the chrism, the fragrant incense, the screen for the entrance to the tent; the bronze altar with its grating of bronze, its shafts and all its furnishings; the basin and its stand; the hangings of the court, its posts, its sockets, and the screen for the gateway to the court, its cords, its pegs, and all the furniture for the service in the tabernacle, the Tent of Meeting; the sumptuous vestments for service in the sanctuary—sacred vestments for Aaron and the priest, and vestments for his sons—for the priestly functions. The sons of Israel had done all the work exactly as Yahweh had directed Moses.

Moses examined the whole work, and he could see they had done it as Yahweh had directed him. And Moses blessed them.

A recapitulation of the account of the work of fashioning the implements of worship drives home once more the insistent theme of this account—that everything was done in conformity with what God had commanded. The tireless repetition of details serves the redactors as a literary method to the same end.

4C3 The Dwelling and Its Furnishings Put into Service (Exod. 40:1–38)

As far as the sacerdotal version is concerned, the exodus is over when everything necessary for Yahweh's official worship has begun to function, in accordance with what Yahweh has commanded Moses on Mount Sinai. This is described in three steps: (1) Yahweh commands Moses to erect and consecrate the dwelling and all its furnishings built by Bezalel and the other inspired artisans. (2) Moses carries out Yahweh's orders. (3) Yahweh takes possession of the dwelling.

4C3.1 YAHWEH'S FINAL ORDERS TO MOSES (EXOD. 40:1-15)

Yahweh spoke to Moses and said, "On the first day of the first month you are to erect the tabernacle, the Tent of Meeting, and place the ark of the Testimony in it, screening it with the veil. Bring in the table, arranging what is to be set in order on it. Bring in the lampstand, too, and set up its lamps. Place the golden altar of incense in front of the ark of the Testimony, and set up the screen at the entrance to the tabernacle. Place the altar of holocaust in front of the entrance to the tabernacle, the Tent of Meeting. Place the basin between the Tent of Meeting and the altar, and fill it with water. Set up the enclosure of the court and hang the screen at the gateway of the court. Then, taking the chrism, anoint the tabernacle and everything in it, consecrating it with its furniture, to make it a holy place. Anoint the altar of holocaust with all its furnishings; and consecrate the altar which henceforth will be a most holy thing. Anoint the basin with its stand, and consecrate it. Bring Aaron and his sons to the entrance of the Tent of Meeting and see that they bathe. Then clothe Aaron with the sacred vestments, and anoint and consecrate him, to serve me in the priesthood. Next, bring his sons and clothe them with tunics. Anoint them as you have anointed their father, to serve me in the priesthood. This anointing of them is to confer the priesthood on them in perpetuity from generation to generation."

It is somewhat puzzling where and how Yahweh speaks with Moses this last time. Yahweh tells him nothing new—only that now, a little less than one year from the flight from Egypt, the moment has arrived to inaugurate the official worship. The main intent seems to be to underscore that, from now on, in virtue of these ritual forms, Aaron and his lineage will replace Moses in approaching God in worship. For a year now, for emergency reasons, Moses has served as the people's leader, and as intermediary between Yahweh and Israel. Now the normative institutional structure is in place: the perpetual priesthood of Aaron. Moses will have one last indispensable function to perform—the anointing and consecrating of the sanctuary and of Aaron and his lineage. Thereafter, the Aaronic priesthood will function without him.

4C3.2 MOSES EXECUTES YAHWEH'S ORDERS (EXOD. 40:16-33)

Moses did this; he did exactly as Yahweh had directed him. The tabernacle was set up on the first day of the first month in the second year. Moses erected the tabernacle. He fixed the sockets for it, put up its frames, put its crossbars in position, set up its posts. He spread the tent over the tabernacle and on top of this the covering for the tent, as Yahweh had directed Moses. He took the Testimony and placed it inside the ark. He set the shafts to the ark and placed the throne of mercy on it. He brought the ark into the tabernacle and put the screening veil in place; thus he screened the ark of Yahweh, as Yahweh had directed Moses. He placed the table in the Tent of Meeting, on the north side of the tabernacle, outside the veil, and on it arranged the loaves before Yahweh, as Yahweh had directed Moses. He put the lampstand in the Tent of Meeting, opposite the table, on the south side of the tabernacle; and he set up the lamps before Yahweh, as Yahweh had directed Moses. He put the golden altar in the Tent of Meeting in front of the veil, and on it burned fragrant incense, as Yahweh had directed Moses. Then he put the screen at the entrance to the Dwelling. He put the altar of holocaust at the entrance to the Dwelling, the Tent of Meeting, and on it offered the holocaust and the oblation, as Yahweh had directed Moses. He put the basin between the Tent of Meeting and the altar, and filled it with water for the ablutions; this was for Aaron and his sons to wash their hands and feet: whenever they entered the Tent of Meeting or approached the altar they washed, as Yahweh had directed Moses. Moses then set up the court around the tabernacle and the altar and placed the screen at the gateway to the court. Thus Moses completed the work.

The most emphatic thing in this paragraph is the refrain "as Yahweh had directed Moses." Everything has been done to the letter, we see, and now all is in readiness for the transfer of the mediating authority from Moses to Aaron, in accordance with Yahweh's own instructions. The expression, "the Dwelling, the Tent of Meeting," looks artificial, and may be an attempt to join the two traditions—the one that refers to the "tabernacle" or "Dwelling" and the one that refers to the "Tent of Meeting"—the two currents that we have seen running all through the sacerdotal text.

4C3.3 YAHWEH TAKES POSSESSION OF THE DWELLING (EXOD. 40:34–38)

The cloud covered the Tent of Meeting and the glory of Yahweh filled the Dwelling. Moses could not enter the Tent of Meeting because of the cloud that rested on it and because of the glory of Yahweh that filled the Dwelling.

At every stage of their journey, whenever the cloud rose from the Dwelling the sons of Israel would resume their march. If the cloud did not rise, they waited and would not march until it did. For the cloud of Yahweh rested on the Dwelling by day, and a fire shone within the cloud by night, for all the House of Israel to see. And so it was for every stage of their journey.

Just as Yahweh has proclaimed from the beginning when ordering that this dwelling be built, the divine glory now enters the tent, visibly, in the cloud, to dwell there. Herewith Moses is removed from his role as daily intermediary between God and the people. Moses can no longer enter the dwelling, for the glory of Yahweh fills it. Until now, he has ascended the mountain to receive Yahweh's instructions for the people, and has entered the cloud that covered the mountain. But now Yahweh is present in the tent that has been pitched in the midst in the encampment of Israel, and Moses, not having been sacralized as a priest, has no access to this place of Yahweh's presence. Such access is to be the ever-abiding prerogative of Aaron and his descendants.

In virtue of this state of affairs, the social order that, according to the priestly reading of the Sinai account, has been divinely legitimated, is to remain in force. The time of transition, a period when a political leader had direct access to Yahweh, has ended. Things are now "normal," where priests are the exclusive intermediaries between heaven and the people.

One is struck by the contrast between this interpretation of the organization of Yahweh's people and the one presented in the story of the golden calf. In the incident of the golden calf, Yahweh rebuffed Aaron's attempt to establish direct divine leadership, as symbolized by this new image in the midst of the people, and at the same time confirmed Moses' leadership. By contrast, the priests, in their version of the constitutive episode of the revelation on the mountain, assert the validity of the religious leadership that the old traditions reject. In the final redaction, Aaron's condemnation in the incident of the golden calf is limited in its causality to his having made an image without the direct mandate of Yahweh. Meanwhile, the ark with its cherubim is legitimate, in virtue of having been made in express obedience to Yahweh's command to Moses. Aaron can meet with Yahweh there because he has been consecrated for this purpose. Thus is legitimated the society of the Persian empire, where all internal power is held by the Aaronite priests, whereas secular power is in the hands of the Persians. The period of the kings, represented in the story of the exodus by Moses' leadership, has not only been left behind in the past, but has been supplanted—"as Yahweh directed."

APPENDIX 11:
DECALOGUES IN THE BIBLE

Among the laws of Israel, there are a number of brief lists manifesting either a thematic or a formal unity. Among these lists, exegetes have claimed to find a number of lists of ten, and this arouses our curiosity, because the number ten has no symbolic meaning in the Bible as do the numbers seven and twelve. Ten is simply a "practical" number, easy to count.

Exodus 34:28 refers to the "words of the Covenant—the Ten Words." Deuteronomy takes up this expression, "the Ten Words," and uses it for the more familiar decalogue (Deut. 4:13, 10:4).

In Deuteronomy 27:15-26, there is a series of twelve curses, whose function is more liturgical than legal. Some interpreters suggest that the first (27:15) and the last (27:26) are glosses. Thus the original series would consist of ten curses.

In Leviticus 18:6-17, there is a list of twelve prohibitions, all beginning, "You must not uncover the nakedness of . . ." and establishing the limits of sexual relations by defining what is to be considered incest. The list is very old. Like the familiar decalogue, it is formulated as a series of prohibitions in the second person masculine. Like the decalogue too, it opens with the self-introductory formula "I am Yahweh."

Leviticus 20:2-21 contains a series of laws mostly concerning prohibited sexual relations, and typically prescribing that the transgressor "must die." This expression indicates that their original context must have been one of instructions for those who were to administer justice in cases of accusation against members of the community. Thus they are laws in the strictest sense of the legal tradition of the ancient Near East, and in this they differ from all the other series mentioned so far. This series contains thirteen laws, some of which could be considered to be additions, so that the original series could have been in the form of a decalogue.

Sigmund Mowinckel thought that two decalogues are to be distinguished in Leviticus 19:2-18: one earmarked by a construction in (second person) plural, and the other phrased in the singular ("Zur Geschichte der Dekaloge"—summarized by Edward Nielsen, *The Ten Commandments in New Perspective,* 44-51). The series using the plural is in Leviticus 19:3-12, but it does not make up a formally homogeneous list. Furthermore, it depends on the decalogue of Exodus 20. The other decalogue, the one in the singular, in Leviticus 19:13-18, is difficult to distinguish. No conclusions can be drawn from these scrambled lists.

Finally, Psalm 15 contains a list of rules for admittance to worship, numbering perhaps more or less ten. It was Mowinckel, again, who pointed out the importance of this analogy to the decalogue (in his 1927 book, *Le Décalogue*—cited by Nielsen, *Commandments,* 22-23). In this psalm, the function of the list is clear—to establish the conditions for participation in the worship of Yahweh. It may be that the familiar decalogue itself had this function at some moment in its prehistory.

APPENDIX 12:
THE DEUTERONOMY DECALOGUE

The book of Deuteronomy accords the familar decalogue (whose text, in Deut. 5:6-21, is very similar to the text of Exod. 20:1-17), a much more prominent place than it has in the book of Exodus.

The account itself is very similar. Yahweh reveals the ten commandments to the people face to face (Deut. 5:4). Frightened, the Israelites ask Moses to serve as intermediary in future, by listening to Yahweh's words himself and then transmitting those words to them (5:22-31). Moses then ascends the mountain and receives from Yahweh, as he says, "the two stone tablets inscribed by the finger of God, and all the words on them that Yahweh had spoken to you on the mountain from the midst of the fire on the day of the Assembly" (Deut. 9:10). Coming down from the mountain and learning of the worship of the golden calf, Moses casts the tablets to the earth and shatters them.

Besides the words cited from Deuteronomy 9:10 (just above), the key to the Deuteronomic rereading is in 10:1-5, which states that the second set of tablets was inscribed by Yahweh so that there would be tablets to be kept in the ark of the covenant.

Here there can be no doubt that the words on the second set of tablets were the same as those on the first: both sets were written by the finger of God. Having quoted the words on the first tablets, Deuteronomy does not repeat them for the second. The latter tablets are designated "the two tablets of the covenant" (Deut. 9:15).

A comparison of Exodus 19-24 and 32-34 with Deuteronomy 5-10 shows that the Deuteronomy text is a revision of the Exodus account. The revision has the effect of eliminating the Code of the Covenant and the cultic list of laws (Exod. 34), and leaving, as the only law revealed on Mount Sinai, the familiar "ethical" decalogue. Thereby it makes this decalogue the basis of the covenant or alliance between Yahweh and Israel. Later generations found this interpretation very attractive, and it became ingrained in the popular consciousness. We must keep in mind, however, that although this decalogue is clearly the basis of the alliance in Deuteronomy, in Exodus this is not so clear.

The decalogue, in the form in which it appears in Deuteronomy, shows evidence of a transmission that is very similar to, but independent of, that of Exodus. This may be because the Deuteronomists had knowledge of it in the context of a covenant ceremony in the north of the country, the locale generally accepted as the origin of Deuteronomy. Deuteronomy would thus present a rectification of the Yahwist/Elohist version of Exodus along the lines of the northern tradition.

APPENDIX 13:
FORMAL ANALYSIS AND PREHISTORY OF THE DECALOGUE

The decalogue in Exodus 20 manifests considerable formal heterogeneity, especially in comparison with other series of laws—for example, Deuteronomy 27:15-26 and Leviticus 18:6-17. Two of the present laws—those concerning the Sabbath and honor to be paid to one's parents—are positive commands, whereas eight are prohibitions. Three of the prohibitions—those of murder, adultery, and theft—are extremely brief: two Hebrew words. Four of the norms—those having to do with images, the Sabbath, honor to one's parents, and coveting—have explanations or reasons attached, thus interrupting the rhythm of the series. This heterogeneity betrays a complicated prehistory, and calls on the interpreter to find a hypothetical original uniformity that must have undergone later alterations and expansions.

The first step in the search for this uniformity is an easy one. It consists in a comparison of the text of the decalogue in Exodus 20:1-17 with that in Deuteronomy 5:6-21. This comparison yields three significant differences. (1) The clause proposing a motive for observing the Sabbath rest in Exodus appeals to the divine rest after the creation was finished, whereas in Deuteronomy what is recalled is the time of slavery in Egypt (when there was no rest). It is not evident that one of these explanations derives from the other; rather, each motivation is an independent amplification of the original commandment. (2) The commandment concerning covetousness shows changes in Deuteronomy: the neighbor's wife is detached from the rest of the objects of this coveting. Only with regard to the neighbor's wife is "coveting" spoken of. The verb governing the remaining objects in the commandment is "desire." The version of this commandment in Deuteronomy is thus a modification of the version in Exodus. (3) Deuteronomy assimilates the language of the commandment against false witness to that forbidding the taking of Yahweh's name abusively. As in the former case, the Exodus version of the decalogue is the older of the two.

The above comparison affords certain insights into the process of the evolution of the decalogue, and allows us to see that, as late as the sixth century B.C. (when this part of

Deuteronomy was written), there were still variants in the form, not only of the commentaries on the laws of the decalogue, but of the laws themselves.

If we now go a step further in our formal analysis, and attempt to reconstruct the ten commandments in their nucleus as apodictical sentences without commentary, we find that we have pared the text down to the following:

1. You shall not have foreign gods [beside me].
2. You shall not make yourself images.
3. You shall not take the name of Yahweh [your God] to misuse it.
4. Remember the Sabbath day, and keep it holy.
5. Honor your father and your mother.
6. You shall not kill.
7. You shall not commit adultery.
8. You shall not steal.
9. You shall not bear false witness against your neighbor.
10. You shall not covet your neighbor's house.

We can be sure that, at one time, the decalogue had approximately this form, and that anything else is added commentary.

And yet this list of sentences, purified of their explanatory and motivational amplifications, is still not uniform. Now, there are two possible ways to proceed in the face of this fact. (1) We might continue with our formal analysis until we arrive at a hypothetical primitive stage in which there was uniformity. We should have to put commandments 4 and 5 in negative form, and find objects for the verbs of numbers 6, 7, and 8. The result would be a hypothetical decalogue with a poetic uniformity. (This is the procedure followed by Nielsen, *Commandments,* 94–131.) But this procedure supposes that the number ten is important here, and this is uncertain. Furthermore, even supposing that this were the case, our reconstruction of the original decalogue would call for too much speculation to inspire confidence. (2) The other possibility is to suppose that the decalogue was formed by the combination of various minor series, each with its own internal uniformity. (Here I am following the line proposed by Georg Fohrer in "Das sogennante apodiktisch formulierte Recht und der Dekalog," in his *Studien zur alttestamentlichen Theologie und Geschichte.*) The result will be three series of apodictical sentences: (a) sentences with four accents in Hebrew—commandments 1, 2, 3, 9, and 10; (b) sentences with two accents—commandments 6, 7, and 8; and (c) sentences with three accents and a positive formulation—commandments 4 and 5. The prehistory of the decalogue will of course continue to be a matter for speculation, but this latter course is the one that would seem to be the better one.

If I am correct in this, then the decalogue must have been the result of a rather lengthy process of synthesis of the laws of Israel, finally resulting in a single basic series. This would seem to be confirmed by the presence of laws 1 and 2 in the list given in Exodus 34, and the presence of 6, 7, 8, and 9 in the prophetic denunciation of Hosea 4:2. By contrast, Jeremiah 7:8–9 and Leviticus 19:2–19 reveal a knowledge of the decalogue in its combined form.

The content of the decalogue shows us that the motivation leading to the joining together of these series of laws was not a strictly legal one. It is not addressed to judges deciding cases at the gates of the towns. Rather it enjoins on the male Israelite the limits of what is permitted him as a member of the people of Yahweh.

It is likely that the process of the formation of the decalogue took place in the north of

Israel. It would not have carried the authority of the king but of the Levites or other masters of the tradition of Israel's national origins. The Elohist, in the tenth or ninth century B.C., then took this as the basic summary of the obligations enjoined by Yahweh on the people at the foot of Mount Sinai. Here we would have a plausible picture of the intention leading to the compilation of this marvelous list of basic norms for social conduct.

Annotated Bibliography

Aberbach, Moses, and Smolar, Leivy. "Aaron, Jeroboam and the Golden Calves," *Journal of Biblical Literature* 86 (1967) 129–40. The authors point out the many parallels between the account of Aaron's golden calf at Mount Sinai and Jeroboam's in Bethel.

Albertz, Rainer. "Hintergrund und Bedeutung des Elterngebots im Dekalog," *Zeitschrift für die alttestamentlichen Wissenschaft* 90 (1978) 348–73.

Albright, W. F. *From the Stone Age to Christianity.* Garden City, N.Y., Doubleday, 1957.

———. "Jethro, Hobab, and Reuel in Early Hebrew Tradition," *Catholic Biblical Quarterly* 25 (1963) 1–11.

Alonso Schökel, Luis. *Exodo.* Los Libros Sagrados, Madrid, Cristiandad, 1969. This commentary, with a very good, new Spanish translation, is short, but enjoys the advantage of its author's fine literary intuition.

Alt, Albrecht. "Das Verbot des Diebstahls im Dekalog," in *Kleine Schriften zur Geschichte des Volkes Israel.* Vol. I. Tübingen, Mohr, 1953.

Andreason, Nils-Erik. *The Old Testament Sabbath.* Missoula, Mont. Society of Biblical Literature, 1972.

Asensio, Felix. *El éxodo: Dios en medio de los suyos.* Santander, Sal Terrae, 1963. A medium-length commentary for dedicated Christians. It does not pay much attention to the work of exegetes, and has a tendency to psychologize history and wander a bit from the text of Exodus.

Auzou, Georges. *De la servidumbre al servicio: Estudio del libro del Exodo.* Madrid, FAX, 1969. Thanks to the FAX edition, this commentary, by a French biblical scholar, is the most readily available one in Spanish. As its title indicates, the emphasis is on "level four" of the text of Exodus, the priestly version of the account, in which the Israelites are brought out of slavery so that they may render God the service of worship.

Bartina, Sebastián. "Exodo," in *La Sagrada Escritura: Texto y comentario por profesores de la Compañia de Jesús*, 1:293–526. Madrid, BAC, 1967. A scholarly commentary, with special attention paid to philological problems and geographical discussion of places cited in the accouut.

Beyerlin, Walter. *Origins and History of the Oldest Sinaitic Traditions.* Oxford, Blackwell, 1965. The author's thesis is that the traditions concerning Sinai were formed in a context of the liturgical celebrations of the Israelite tribal confederation. To support this thesis, he makes a meticulous analysis of the texts concerning Sinai. The general lines of his argumentation appear correct, although the confidence with which he proposes his conclusions seems at times exaggerated.

Bodenheimer, F. S. "The Manna of Sinai," *Biblical Archaeologist* 10 (1947) 1–6.

Buber, Martin. *Moses: The Revelation and the Covenant.* New York, Harper Torchbooks, 1958 (original, 1946). The stimulating work of a great Jewish theologian and biblical literary critic.

Buis, P. "Les conflits entre Moïse et Israël dans Exode et Nombres," *Vetus Testamentum* 28 (1978) 257–70. An excellent analysis of the different structures present in the accounts of rebellion in the wilderness.

Carroll, B. H. *An Interpretation of the English Bible.* Nashville, Broadman, 1948 (originally published 1916). Hostile to a critical study of the Bible. On many points, reflects a problematic foreign to the Hispanic world.

Childs, Brevard S. "A Traditio-Historical Study of the Reed Sea Tradition," *Vetus Testamentum* 20 (1970) 406–18. An analysis of the sea traditions in the Yahwist, Elohist, and sacerdotal versions, of the canticle of Exodus 15, and of Psalm 78 leads Childs to think that the account of the crossing of the Re(e)d Sea originated with the exodus itself rather than with the passage through the desert. (Contrast this with G. W. Coat's position in "An Exposition" [below].

———. *The Book of Exodus: A Critical Theological Commentary.* Philadelphia, Westminster, 1974. The most thoroughgoing recent commentary on the Book of Exodus. Includes a consideration of the whole history of the Jewish and Christian use of the book, and discusses the main critico-literary positions with respect to it. I have turned to this book many, many times.

Coats, George W. "The Traditio-Historical Character of the Reed Sea Motif," *Vetus Testamentum* 17 (1967) 253–65.

———. *Rebellion in the Wilderness: The Murmuring Motif in the Wilderness Traditions of the Old Testament.* Nashville, Abingdon, 1968. The most exhaustive analysis that we have of the traditions of the "grumbling" in the wilderness.

———. "A Structural Transition in Exodus," *Vetus Testamentum* 22 (1972) 129–42.

———. "An Exposition for the Wilderness Traditions," *Vetus Testamentum* 22 (1972) 288–95.—The three *Vetus Testamentum* articles by Coats, a gifted biblical literary critic, constitute an important contribution to the analysis of the structure of the exodus and wilderness traditions. The first ("The Tradition-Historical Character") argues that the crossing of the sea belongs originally to the wilderness traditions. "A Structural Transition" points to Exodus 1:1–14 as a transitional text between the theme of the patriarchs and that of the exodus. "An Exposition" argues that Exodus 13:17–22 is an introduction to and synthesis of the theme of the passage through the wilderness.

Cody, Aelred. "Exodus 18.22: Jethro Accepts a Covenant with the Israelites," *Biblica* 49 (1968) 153–66.

———. *A History of Old Testament Priesthood.* Rome, Pontificio Istituto Biblico, 1969.

Colunga, Alberto, and García Cordero, Maximiliano. "Introducción y comentario al Exodo," in *Biblia Comentada por profesores de Salamanca,* 1:378–618. Madrid, BAC, 1962. Similar to Bartina's commentary (above), but with less attention to technical questions.

Croatto, José Serverino. *Liberación y libertad: Pautas hermeneuticas.* Lima, Centro de Estudios y Publicaciones, 2nd ed., 1980. (English translation, *Exodus: A Hermeneutics of Freedom.* Maryknoll, N.Y., Orbis, 1981.) A very important work, written with a hermeneutical awareness as yet unsurpassed in Latin America. Croatto offers us a critical reading of the principal "moments" in the Bible—creation, the prophets, Jesus, and Paul—using the key furnished by the book of Exodus, liberation.

———. "Yavé, el Dios de la 'presencia' salvífica: Ex 3, 14 en su contexto literario y querigmático," *Revista Bíblica* 43 (1981) 153–63. In this excellent study, Croatto concludes that the apparent theophoric names in Mari, Ugarit, and Ebla, seemingly variants of the divine name *YHWH*, are not actually such, but are variants of the verb "to be," *HWH*. Exodus 3:13–14, at any rate, offers only a popular etymology, which tells us nothing about the actual origin of the divine name "Yahweh." In its context, however, it conveys the meaning "I am [the one] who will be [with you]"— the sense of Genesis 3:12.

Cross, Frank Moore, Jr. "Yahweh and the God of the Patriarchs," *Harvard Theological Review* 55 (1962) 225–59. The renowned study in which Cross proposes his theory on the origin of the divine name Yahweh as an attribute of the God El: "he who creates."

———. "The Priestly Houses of Early Israel," in *Canaanite Myth and Hebrew Epic* (chap. 8, pp. 195–215). Cambridge, Harvard University Press, 1973. The author suggests a solution to the enigmas of the conflicts among priestly groups in Israel by postulating the existence of two priestly houses, the one Mushite, claiming descendancy from Moses, with its original seat in Shiloh and Dan, and the other Aaronite, with seats in Hebron and Bethel. According to this schema, Exodus 32 would be a Mushite tradition.

Cross, Frank M., Jr., and Freedman, David Noel. "The Song of Miriam," *Journal of Near Eastern Studies* 14 (1955) 237–50.

———. *Studies in Ancient Yahwistic Poetry.* Missoula, Mont. Scholars Press, 1975.

Davies, G. I. *The Way of the Wilderness: A Geographical Study of the Wilderness Itineraries of the Old Testament.* Cambridge, Cambridge University Press, 1979. This little book shows the improbability of the route proposed by the Pentateuch texts as the one actually used to cross the Sinai wilderness.

de Pury, A. "Genèse XXXIV et l'histoire," *Revue Biblique* 76 (1969) 5–49.

de Vaux, Roland. *Ancient Israel: Its Life and Institutions.* New York, McGraw Hill, 1961.

———. "The Settlement of the Israelites in Southern Palestine and the Origins of the Tribe of Judah," in *Translating and Understanding the Old Testament,* Harry Thomas Frank and William Reed, eds., pp. 108–34. Nashville, Abingdon, 1970.

———. *The Early History of Israel.* Philadelphia, Westminster, 1978.

Dubarle, M. "La signification du nom de Iahwéh," *Revue de Sciences Philosophiques et Théologiques* 34 (1951) 1–21.

Eissfeldt, Otto. *Baal Zaphon, Zeus Kasios und der Durchzug der Israeliten durchs Meer.* Halle, Niemeyer, 1932.

———. "Lade und Stierbild," in *Kleine Schriften,* 2:282–305. Tübingen, Mohr, 1963. Eissfeldt studies the ark and the golden calf, interpreting both as *Führersymbole* of the pre-Canaanite Hebrews in the wilderness.

———. "Protektorat der Midianiter über ihre Nachbarn im letzten Viertel des 2. Jahrtausends v. Chr.," *Journal of Biblical Literature* 87 (1968) 383–93.

Ellis, Peter F. *The Yahwist, the Bible's First Theologian.* Notre Dame, Ind., Fides, 1968.

Fensham, F. C. "Did a Treaty Between the Israelites and the Kenites Exist?" *Bulletin of the American Society of Oriental Research* 175 (1964) 51–54.

Fohrer, Georg. *Überlieferung und Geschichte des Exodus.* Berlin, Töpelmann, 1964. A minute critico-literary analysis of the first fifteen chapters of Exodus. The author holds for a convergence of four narrative currents here: two Yahwist (J and N), the Elohist, and the sacerdotal. Although, in my opinion, this goes beyond the evidence, the author's commentaries on the text are most incisive.

———. "Das sogenannte apodiktisch formulierte Recht und der Dekalog," in *Studien zur alttestamentlichen Theologie und Geschichte* (pp. 120–48). Berlin, de Gruyter, 1969.

Frymer-Kensky, Tikva. "Tit for Tat: The Principle of Equal Retribution in Near Eastern and Biblical Law," *Biblical Archaeologist* 43 (1980) 230–34.

Gerstenberger, Erhard. "Covenant and Commandment," *Journal of Biblical Literature* 84 (1965) 38–51.

———. *Wesen und Herkunft des "apodiktischen Rechts."* Neukirchen-Vluyn, Neukirchener, 1965.

Gottwald, Norman K. *The Tribes of Yahweh: A Sociology of the Religion of Liberated Israel, 1250–1050* B.C. Maryknoll, N.Y., Orbis, 1979. Recent, but already a classic. Furnishes the socio-political context of what I have designated "level two" of the production of the text of Exodus.

Habel, N. "The Form and Significance of the Call Narratives," *Zeitschrift für die alttestamentliche Wissenschaft* 77 (1965) 297–323.

Haran, M. "The Exodus," in *Interpreter's Dictionary of the Bible, Supplement*, pp. 304–10. Nashville, Abingdon, 1976.

Helck, W. "*Tkw* und die Ramsesstadt," *Vetus Testamentum* 15 (1965) 35ff.

Hinkelammert, Franz J. *Ideología de sometimiento: La Iglesia Católica Chilena frente al golpe: 1973–1974.* San José, Costa Rica, Editorial Universitaria Centroamericana, 1977.

Hort, Greta. "The Plagues of Egypt," *Zeitschrift für die alttestamentliche Wissenschaft* 69 (1957) 84–103; 70 (1958) 48–59.

Huesman, John E. "Exodo," in *Comentario bíblico "San Jerónimo,"* 1:157–205, Madrid, Cristiandad, 1971. A commentary bearing strictly on critical questions in the book of Exodus. Too short to be very useful.

Jackson, B. S. "The Problem of Exodus XXI.22–5 (*Jus talionis*)," *Vetus Testamentum* 23 (1973) 273–304.

Jenks, Alan W. *The Elohist and North Israelite Traditions.* Missoula, Mont., Scholars Press, 1977. The most complete study to date of the Elohist source. The author relies mainly on the patriarchal accounts to identify this source, but he believes he finds Elohist material in the Sinai section as well, the most important of it coming in Exodus 32. The Elohist, we read, wrote (or composed orally) in antimonarchical prophetical circles having a connection with the tenth-century schism of Jeroboam. The difficulty here, for purposes of my commentary, is the uncertainty in the identification of the Elohist in Exodus.

Jones, Hywel R. "Exodus," in *The New Bible Commentary, Revised*, Donald Guthrie and J. A. Motyer, eds. Grand Rapids, Eerdmans, 1970. A very short commentary, addressing critical questions with the greatest caution, as one would expect of a work originally published by Intervarsity Press.

Kearney, Peter J. "Creation and Liturgy: The P Redaction of Ex. 25–40," *Zeitschrift für die alttestamentliche Wissenschaft* 89 (1977) 376–87. Kearney shows that the final redaction of Exodus 25–31 follows an outline derived from the seven days of creation in the sacerdotal account of Genesis 1.

Kennedy, A. R. S. "Tabernacle," in *Hastings Dictionary of the Bible*, 4:653–68. New York, Scribner's, 1902. An excellent study and interpretation of the technical expressions used to describe the dwelling in the last chapters of the Book of Exodus.

Koehler, Ludwig, and Baumgartner, W. *Lexicon in Veteris Testamenti Libros.* Leiden, Brill, 1948–53.

Kosmala, Hans. "The Bloody Bridegroom," *Vetus Testamentum* 12 (1962) 14–28.

Lehming, S. "Zur Überlieferungsgeschichte von Gen. 34," *Zeitschrift für die alttestamentliche Wissenschaft* 70 (1958) 228–50.

Loewenstamm, S. E. "An Observation on Source Criticism of the Plague Pericope (Ex. 7–11)," *Vetus Testamentum* 24 (1974) 374–78.

Long, Burke O. "*The Problem of Etiological Narrative in the Old Testament*," Beiträge zur alttestamentlichen Wissenschaft, 108. Berlin, Töpelmann, 1968.

Loza, José. "Exode XXXII et la rédaction JE," *Vetus Testamentum* 23 (1973) 31–55. This Mexican biblical scholar points out the importance of the redaction combining the Yahwist and Elohist sources in the account of the golden calf as we have it today. He holds that this redaction was done in the time of Hezekiah, shortly after the destruction of the kingdom of Israel (Samaria).

McKenzie, John L. *The World of Judges.* London, Chapman, 1967.

Mejía, Jorge. "La liberación: Aspectos bíblicos," in *Liberación: Diálogos en el CELAM*, pp. 271–307. Bogotá, Secretariado General del CELAM, 1974.

Mendenhall, George E. "The Hebrew Conquest of Palestine," *Biblical Archaeologist* 25 (1962) 66–87.

———. *The Tenth Generation.* Baltimore, Johns Hopkins University Press, 1973.

Mihelic, J. L. "Manna," in *The Interpreter's Dictionary of the Bible*, 3:259–60. New York, Abingdon, 1962.

Mowinckel, Sigmund. *Psalmenstudien*, 1:50–58. Kristiania, Norway, Jacob Dybwad, 1921.

———. *Le Décalogue.* Paris, Alcan, 1927.

———. "Zur Geschichte der Dekaloge," *Zeitschrift für die alttestamentliche Wissenschaft* 55 (1937) 215–35.

Nicholson, E. W. *Exodus and Sinai in History and Tradition.* Oxford, Blackwell, 1973. Written to refute Martin Noth's conclusion that the traditions of the exodus and those of Mount Sinai were formed independently. On this point I hold that Nicholson is right. I do not, however, agree with all his opinions on the socio-political context of these traditions.

———. "The Interpretation of Ex. XXIV.9–11," *Vetus Testamentum* 24 (1974) 77–97.

———. "The Antiquity of the Tradition in Ex. XXIV.9–11," *Vetus Testamentum* 25 (1975) 69–79.

———"The Origin of the Tradition in Ex. XXIV.9–11," *Vetus Testamentum* 26 (1976) 148–60.

Nielsen, Eduard. *The Ten Commandments in New Perspective.* London, SCMP, 1968.

Noth, Martin. *Exodus: A Commentary.* Philadelphia, Westminster, 1962. Focuses mainly on a critico-literary analysis of the book, and on the formation of its traditions in the oral stage.

———. *A History of Pentateuchal Traditions.* Englewood Cliffs, N.Y., Prentice-Hall, 1972. The best analysis to date of the oral and written traditions entering into the redaction of the Pentateuch.

Otto, Eckart. "Erwägungen zum überlieferungsgeschichtlichen Ursprung und 'Sitz im Leben' des Jahwistischen Plagenzyklus," *Vetus Testamentum* 26 (1976) 3–27. Through a careful analysis of Exodus 11–13, Otto concludes that the Yahwist plague cycle was formed in a context of the celebration of the unleavened bread, which included the sacrifice for the firstborn. The Yahwist basis for Passover in Exodus 12:21–27 will be a later addition, then, because it does not agree very well with the account of the night of the massacre. Otto's arguments are persuasive.

Pedersen, Johannes. "Passahfest und Passahlegende," *Zeitschrift für die alttestamentliche Wissenschaft* 52 (1934) 161–75.

———. *Israel, Its Life and Culture*, vols. 1 and 2. London, Cumerlege, Oxford University Press, 1953–54.

Péter, Rcné. "PR et ShOR. Note de lexicographie hébraïque," *Vetus Testamentum* 25 (1975) 486–96.

Pixley, George V. *God's Kingdom: A Guide for Biblical Study.* Maryknoll, N.Y., Orbis, 1981.

Pritchard, James Bennett. *Ancient Near Eastern Texts Relating to the Old Testament.* Princeton, Princeton University Press, 1950.

Rowley, H. H. "Zadok and Nahushtan," *Journal of Biblical Literature* 58 (1939) 113–41.

———. "Early Levite History and the Question of the Exodus," *Journal of Near Eastern Studies* 3 (1944) 73–78.

———. *From Joseph to Joshua.* London, Oxford University Press, 1950.

Ruppert, Lothar. "El yahvista: pregonero de la historia de la salvación," in *Palabra y mensaje del Antiguo Testamento*, Josef Schreiner, ed., pp. 133–57. Barcelona, Herder, 1972.

Schild, E. "On Exodus iii.14—'I Am That I Am,' " *Vetus Testamentum* 4 (1959) 296–302.

Sellers, O. R. "Weights and Measures," in *The Interpreter's Dictionary of the Bible*, 4:828–39. New York, Abingdon, 1963.

Snaith, Norman H. "Yam Suf: The Sea of Reeds: The Red Sea," *Vetus Testamentum* 15 (1965) 395–98.

Stamm, J. J., and Andrew, M. E. *The Ten Commandments in Recent Research.* London, SCMP, 1967.

Tresmontant, Claude. *A Study of Hebrew Thought.* New York, Desclée, 1960.

Uphill, P. "Pithom and Rameses: Their Location and Significance," *Journal of Near Eastern Studies* 27 (1968) 291–316; 28 (1969) 15–39.

von Rad, Gerhard. *Das heilige Krieg im alten Israel.* Zurich, Zwingli, 1951.

———. *Studies in Deuteronomy.* London, SCMP, 1953 (German original, 1948).

———. *Old Testament Theology*, 2 vols. New York, Harper, 1962.

Watts, J. D. W. "The Song of the Sea, Ex. XV," *Vetus Testamentum* 7 (1957) 371–80.

Whitehead, Alfred North. *Process and Reality: Corrected Edition.* New York, Free Press, 1978.

Wijngaards, J. N. M. "*HOSI'* and *HE'ELAH*: A Twofold Approach to the Exodus," *Vetus Testamentum* 15 (1965) 91–102. A comparison of the formulae, "I brought you out of Egypt," and "I brought you up from Egypt"—the first coming from a legal formula in which "bringing out" means "setting free," whereas the seoond is common in the eighth-century prophets and often occurs in association with "entry" into the land.

Wolff, H. W. "Das Zitat im Prophetenspruch: Eine Studie zur prophetischen Verkündigungsweise," in *Gesammelte Studien zum Alten Testament*, pp. 36–129. Munich, Kaiser, 1964.

———. "The Kerygma of the Yahwist," *Interpretation* 20 (1966) 131–58.

Wolfson, Harry A. *Philo: Foundations of Religious Philosophy in Judaism, Christianity and Islam,* 2 vols. Cambridge, Harvard University Press, 1947.

Wright, G. Ernest. *The Old Testament and Theology.* New York, Harper, 1969.

Zimmerli, Walther. *Gottes Offenbarung: Gesammelte Aufsätze zum Alten Testament.* Munich, Kaiser, 1963.

———. *I Am Yahweh.* Atlanta, John Knox, 1982.